MW00770163

EDGEFIELD COUNTY, S.C. RECORDS

Compiled by
JANIE REVILL

SOUTHERN HISTORICAL PRESS, INC.
% The Rev. Silas Emmett Lucas, Jr.
P.O. Box 738
Easley, South Carolina 29641-0738

ISBN 0-89308-531-6

ABBERNATHY, SALLY--Dau. of James Carson, Sen'r. Will 1822. Edgefield

ABNEY, DENNET--Petit Juror 1788-List 12. Edgefield

ABNEY, DOROTHY--Dau. of James Rutherford--Will 1797. Edgefield

ABNEY, GEORGE--Petit Juror 1789 List 15 and 18. Edgefield

ABNEY, GILLY--Dau. of Hezekiah Gentry--Will 1820. Edgefield

ABNEY, HIRAM -w- MILLY--Heirs of Amey Hazel, dec'd. and heirs of Charity
     Johnson. See Johnson card. Edgefield Receipt Bk. B-161 1849

ABNEY, JOHN R.--Dec'd. Real Estate sold 1835-6. Distributees: Lewis
     Sample and wife--½. James M. Abney, minor--½. Lewis Sample, Gdn.
     Edgefield Receipt Bk. A-233

ABNEY, M. W. -w- CAROLINE S.--Distributees of Estate of John Blocker,
     dec'd. See Blocker card. Edgefield Receipt Bk. A-158 1833

ABNEY, MARTIN -w- HARRIET--Heirs of Ebenezer Hill. See Hill card.
     Edgefield Receipt Bk. A-256 1839.

ABNEY, NATHAN--Grand Juror 1786. List 5, 6, 16. Also Nathaniel.
     Edgefield

ABNEY, PAUL--Petit Juror Edgefield 1788. List 11
     -Paul Abney applied for permission to keep tavern. Granted. S:
     Duane and John Cadle.
     -On same card: John Abney, Adm. Wm. Brown, Dec'd.
                     Dan'l or Dennett Abney, Appr. Est. Peter Buffington.
                     Dennett Abney S. Est. Pleasant Barnett. See
                     Buffington card.
     Edgefield Ct. Minutes.   March Ct. 1795

ABNEY, SAMUEL--Petit Juror Edgefield 1794. List 20

ABNEY, WILLIAM--Grand Juror Edgefield 1786. List 4, 10, 18

ACKRIDGE, JOHN--Petit Juror Edgefield 1789. List 14

ADAMS, BENJAMIN--Excused as overseer of road from New Market to Horns
     Creek on the Hatcher's Pond Road and Fielding Runnels appointed
     in his place. Edgefield Ct. Min. Jan. Ct. 1795

ADAMS, CATHERINE--Sister of Pressly G. Sullivan-Will 1836. Edgefield

ADAMS, CHARLES--Dec'd. Real Estate sold. Edgefield Sale and Division
     Real Est. Bk. A-58. Distributees:
     John Still and wife 1/6-78.61½ acres. Rec't. 2 Nov. 1832
     Fanny Bartlett   "   "   "   Mrs. Deen Apt. Gdn. 15 Oct. 1832
     William Adams   "   "   "
     Willey Adams   "   "   "
     Mary Ann Adams   "   "   "
     Sarah Adams   "   "   "
     Pur. by Mrs. Sarah Deen at $491.00. Receipt by Wm. Deen for share
     of his wife, Mary Ann, dated 30 June 1836. Fr. Sarah Deen, Gdn.
     Receipt by Frances Bartlett 25 July 1836 rec'd from Sarah Deen.

ADAMS, DRURY--Grand Juror Edgefield 1786. List 1 and 21
        Petit Juror   "   "   "   20

ADDAMS, ELIZABETH--Dau. of Jacob Fudge, Sen'r.-Will 1789 Edgefield

ADAMS, ELIZABETH--Dau. of Wright Nicholson-Will 1807 Edgefield

ADAMS, ELIZABETH--Sister of William Lindsey--Will 1827 Edgefield

ADAMS, JAMES--Will Pleading and Judgements-Mar. term 1801 Edgefield P. 7
    Drury Adams and Thos. Adams-Exor's. Devised part of estate to his
    daughter, Elizabeth, to wit; negro girl-Patt, etc. upon the death
    of wife of Testator, Sarah Adams who died in April 1801, and said
    Elizabeth -m- William Flin, the Plaintiff.

ADAMS, JAMES--Son in law of Thomas Youngblood-Will 1816 Edgefield

ADAMS, JAMES--Dec'd intestate 1842. Edgefield Ordinary
    Widow: Nancy Adams
    Dau: Elizabeth
    Sons: Robert, Abner, Micajah
    Dau: Hicksey -w- John Day
    Son: James Quincey Adams)
           John Landon Adams) Minors in 1845
    Dau: Caroline   )

ADAMS, JAMES--Will 28 May 1850 Edgefield
    Bro: Charles
        Ch. of Charles: Wm. Wiley   Elizabeth
                    Frances   Mary Ann
                    Nancy   Sarah
    Bro: Henry
    Bro: Amos
        Son of Amos: James
    Bro: John
        Ch. of John: James C., John, Asa
    Bro: William
        Ch. of William: James   Levi
                     Charles   Patsy
                     Aaron   Elizabeth
                     Daniel   Milly
                     William   Polly
    To: Elizabeth, wife of John Quattlebaum

ADAMS, JOHN--Petit Juror Edgefield 1787. List 8 and 18

ADAMS, JOHN--Permission to keep Tavern. S: Samuel Carter and John
    Hill. Edgefield Ct. Min. March 1795
    Same card: Jan. Ct. 1795--Drury Adams Appr. estate of Samuel
    Edmonds. See Edmonds card.
    March Ct. 1795--Thomas Adams-Gdn. John Herndon. See Herndon card.

ADAMS, JOHN -w- CATHERINE--Heirs of Pressley Sullivan. See Sullivan
    card. Edgefield Receipt Bk. A-213 1835

ADAMS, JOHN M. -w- SARAH S.--Heirs of Keziah P. McMurphey. See Murphey
    card. Edgefield Receipt Bk. A-246 1836

ADAMS, JUDITH--Dau. of Ann Conner-Will 1824. Edgefield

ADAMS, KHADIJAH--Legatee of Asa Holloway-Will 1823 (seems a dau.)
Mary A. Adams, a dau. of Testator.

ADAMS, LETITIA--Dau. of Mary Nicholson-Will 1821. Edgefield

ADAMS, LEVI--Distributee of estate of Catherine Butler-1838. Relation
not shown. June 4, 1838, William Adams gave receipt for part of
his wife, Rachel, a dau. of Catherine Butler. Edgefield Receipt
Bk. A-298

ADAMS, LITTLEBERRY--Petit Juror Edgefield List 11 1788

ADAMS, MARIAM--Dec'd. R. E. sold 1842. Edgefield Receipt Bk. B-61
Distributees: Jeremiah Burnet and wife 1/6 - $125.27
              Sarah E. Adams   "   "
              Mary N. Adams   "   "
              Frances Adams   "   "
              B. F. Boyd -w- Elizabeth   "   "
              Thos. E. Coleman and wife "   "
Mary N. Adams married Andrew J. Sleigh
Frances Adams married John Piaster (?)

ADAMS, MARTHA, SUSAN, JOHN, DRURY S.--Half Bros and sisters of Benjamin
Roper-Will 1841

ADAMS, M. G.--Heir to estate of Cad Evans. See Evans card. Seems she
was formerly widow Mary Evans. John Key her agent. Edgefield
Receipt Bk. A-100 1832

ADAMS, MRS. REBECCA--Will of Thomas Adams. Dower favor of Edmond
Whatley. Edgefield October Ct. Minute Bk. 1787

ADAMS, SARAH--Dau. of Samuel Dolittle-Will 1799. Edgefield

ADAMS, SARAH -m- William Deen, Sen'r. Marriage agreement 12 Sept.
1828. See also card William Dean, Sen'r. Edgefield Misc. F.
Page 359 1828

ADAMS, SUSANNA--Dau. Robert Moseley--Will 1796 Edgefield

ADAMS, THOMAS--Petit Juror Edgefield 1787 List 8
-Thomas Adams -w- Mary wit. deed Oct. 30. 1805 from Collier to Harris
Bk. 26 Pg. 341.

ADAMS, WILEY T.--Heir of J. J. Still. See Still card. Edgefield Equity
Roll 1849

ADAMS, WILLIAM--His children legatees of Benjamin Lindsey-Will 1841

ADAMS, WILLIAM, SEN'R.--Will 5 Feb. 1842 Edgefield

ADDISON, ALLEN of Saxagotha--Will Edgefield File.
Wife: Lucretia--Plt'n. on Stephen's Creek
My 3 ch: Joseph, John, and Elizabeth-all minors-property in Va.
Exor: Benjamin Bell
Wit: Wm. Bell, John Conrad Gallman, Thomas Lennon 28 Nov. 1790

ADDISON, AMY--Dec'd. and her heir, Joseph Addison et al--Heirs of John
    Cogburn. See Cogburn card. Edgefield Receipt Bk. A-225 1824

ADDISON, JOHN--Apt'd. Overseer of Road from Edgefield Court House to
    Horn's Creek in the room of Casper Gallman, excused. Edgefield
    Ct. Min. Jan. 1795

ADDISON, JOHN -w- SARAH--Heirs of Josiah Cartledge. See Cartledge
    card. Edgefield Receipt Bk. A-3 About 1827

ADDISON, JOSEPH--Letters of Adm. gra nted Elizabeth Addison, widow.
    Bond 500 lbs. S: Wm. Brown, Seth Howard, Bartlett Brown, James
    Brown. Edgefield Ct. Met 14 July 1789. Min. Bk. Pg. 252

ADDISON, JOSEPH--Dec'd. Edgefield Min. Bk. Pg. 270 Oct. Ct. 1789
    Apprs: George Miller, Fred Tilman, Stephan Tilman, James Cobbs

ADDISON, JOSEPH -w- and Benjamin -w-: Children of Henry Waldren and
    heirs of James Butler. See Butler card. Edgefield Bk. A-124 1833

ADDISON, PATIENCE--Step dau. of Henry W. Lowe-Will 1828. Edgefield

ADKERSON, TABITHA--Gr. dau. of Nathaniel Abney-Will 1800 Edgefield

AGERSBY, CONSTANT--Petit Juror Edgefield 1794 List 23

ALAWINE, JOSEPH -w- REBECCA--Heirs of George Litesey. See Litesey
    card. Edgefield Receipt Bk. B-167 1843

ALLAWINE, THOMAS -w- MARGARET--Heirs of Wm. H. Cannon. See Cannon
    card. Edgefield Receipt. Bk. B-215 1851

ALINBAKER, NANCY--See Will of John Clackler 1790 Edgefield

ALLEN, CARY W. -w- MARY ANN--Heirs of Keziah P. McMurphey. See card
    McMurphey. Edgefield Receipt Bk. A-246

ALLEN, DRURY--Son in law of Handley Webb-Will 1826. Edgefield

ALLEN, ELIZABETH and JESSE --Gr. dau. and gr. son wo Wm. West. Will
    1779 Edgefield

ALLEN, GEORGE--Son of Elizabeth Mackquarter -w- Moses Mackquarter-Will
    1797 Edgefield

ALLEN, JAMES--Petit Juror Edgefield 1786 List #4

ALLEN, JOHN--Of Turkey Creek, Edgefield Co. to John Lewis Gervais, Esq.
    In consideration of the loss he sustained by reason of being paid
    off in the year 1777, with depreciation money, and 10 shillings
    paid by John Lewis Gervais, the younger, 17 Feb. 1789. Pres. of:
    John Ewing Calhoun, Abraham Mackley. Prov. by Abraham Mackley on
    13 March 1789 before D. Mazyek. Edgefield File. Archives XX 626

ALLEN, CAPT. JOHN--Mentioned in Will of Wilson Woodroof-Will 1809
    Mentioned as father of Caroline Walker. Edgefield

ALLEN, JOHN--Petit Juror Edgefield 1789 List 13

ALLEN, JOSIAH--Dec'd. Edgefield Probate Bk. 1-20
    Cit: 5 July 1782   Bond 20 Aug. 1782
    Adm'r: James Allen   S: Enoch Grigsby, Jered Sison
    Slaves: Frank, Cloe and child, Duke-a boy, Isaac-a boy, Easter-
        a girl, Fillis-a girl.

ALLEN, JOSIAH--Of 96 "Collington Co." Will 7 Oct. 1796
    Wife: Jennet Allen--1/3 qualified
    Son: William Winn Allen--1/3
        Benjamin Allen--1/3
    Exors: Thomas Van Marjenhoff, William Hoff, Young Allen
    Dated 7 Oct. 1796. Proven: 26 Oct. 1796
    Arch. Dept. C. T. Wills 1793-1800 Pg. 338

ALLEN, JOSIAH--Former husband of _____? whe -m- 2nd. Aaron Etheredge
    Etheredge Will 1811. Ch. of Josiah Allen: Nancy Mathis, Milbury
    Clark, Drury Allen. Edgefield

ALLEN, ROBERT--Petit Juror Edgefield 1789 List 15 and 20

ALLEN, ROBERT--No dower 17 Dec. 1810 To: John Pope 225 Acres on
    Beaver Dam of Cloud's Creek of Little Saluda. Pt. of Gr of 500 A.
    to Robert Allen 1 April 1799. Edgefield Deed Bk. 34-262

ALLEN, SUSANNAH--Dau. of Amos Richardson-Will 1809. Wife of Young
    Allen. Gr. son: Aaron Allen. Gr. dau: Rebecca Allen Edgefield

ALLEN, YOUNG--Apt'd. Overseer of road from Cambridge to Charleston,
    that part from Burton's old place to Amos Richardson's. In the
    room of John Pool, Excused. Edgefield Ct. Min. Oct. 1794

ALLEN, YOUNG--Dec'd. 26 June 1834. Edgefield Equity Roll 745
    Wife: Susannah--sister of David Richardson. died 1833 Sur-
    vived by husband, Young Allen
    3 dau. of dec'd: Rebecca -w- Benj. Frazier
    dau.   1.Eleanor -w- Henry Spa___?) Children of Young
                2.Elizabeth   ) Allen's dec'd. dau.
                3.Clifton Frazier   ) Rebecca Frazier.

ALLISON, RICHARD--Grand Juror Edgefield 1786 List 1 and 2

ALLISON, RICHARD--Dec'd. Will proved by oath of William Anderson, Esq.
    and Abney Mays. Mrs. Sarah Allison, Ex'x.-qualified. Edgefield
    Ct. Min. Bk. Pg. 231. 12 Jan. 1789

ALMON, HEZEKIAH--Dec'd. Edgefield Sale and Div. R. E. Bk. A-62
    Distributees: Widow (seems Mary) 1/3
                Solomon Alman 1/10
                Holsten Alman 1/10 Rec. 18 Dec. 1830
                Hezekiah, Jr. 1/10
                Thomas Claxton -w- Rebecca 1/10 Rec. 18 Dec. 1830
                Charles Sutton -w- Mary 1/10
                Derrick Holsonback -w- Elender 1/10
                Lewellyn Alman
                William, Aaron, Moses Alman-minorso Derrick Hol-
                sonback, Gdn. Pur. by Hezekiah Alman at $ 860.00

ANDERSON, ALLEN, SEN'R.--Will 6 Jan. 1828 Edgefield

ANDERSON, CHARITY--Dec'd. Edgefield (Stray) Sale 22 April 1783
   Purs: Sela Williams   Jacob Smith
         John Watson   Robert Melton
         Arthur Watson   William Sciggon
         Martha Watson   William Clark
         James Harrison   Archibald Browning
         Lewis Watson   Roland Williams
         John Watson, Jr.   Samuel Williams
   Pet'rs. Cash paid:
         Ezakiah Watson   Hannah McKinna
         Arden Watson   Jacob Odom
         Celia Williams   Daniel Lesly
         Roland Williams   John Watson, Adm'r.
                          Abner Watson, Wit.
   -Charity Anderson--Dau. of John Watson-Will 1788
   -Charity Anderson--Dec'd. Edgefield Min. Bk. 233 12 Jan. 1789
      "Ordered on motion of James Harrison that John Watson, Adm'r.
      of Charity Anderson, produce his vouchers on the first day
      of next term and make a final settlement of the said estate."
   -Charity Anderson--Dec'd. Edgefield Min. Bk. 324 April 1790
      "The papers relating to the estate of Charity Anderson were
      produced to this Court by John Watson, Adm'r. Which papers
      contained an account of receipts and payments made by the
      said Administrator--Ordered that they be received and filed
      in Clerk's Office."

ANDERSON, GEORGE--Gr. son of Elizabeth Barrott (Bassott?)-Will 1827

ANDERSON, JAMES--Grand Juror Edgefield 1786 List 4, 12, and 18

ANDERSON, JOHN--Petit Juror Edgefield 1788 List 12 and 15

ANDERSON, MARY--Dau. of John Hardy-Will 1799 Edgefield

ANDERSON, MARY--Dau. of Abraham Taylor-Will 1805 Edgefield

ANDERSON, MARY--Mother in law of David Langley-Will 1822 Edgefield

ANDERSON, MARY--Sister of John Lyon-Will 1841 Edgefield

ANDERSON, PATIENCE--Dau. of Martha Odom-Will 1817 Edgefield

ANDERSON, ROBERT--Petit Juror Edgefield 1786 List 1, 2, 11, 12, 15

ANDERSON, THOMAS--Grand Juror Edgefield 1787 List 6, 14, 18

ANDERSON, WILLIAM, OSWELL EAVE, THOMAS WILSON, JAMES ROBERT MAYSON,
   WILLIAM WHITE--Apt'd. Comm'rs. to build a bridge over Wilson's
   Creek at Eve's Ford or near there. Jan. Ct. 1795. John Anderson
   Qualified as Constable.

ANDERSON, WILLIAM--Of Edgefield. Will Edgefield Probate Bk. A-15
   Wife: Eliza Ann
   Son: Thomas--Land adj. John Anderson
   Dau: Rachel Anderson
        Elizabeth Anderson
   Wife's dau: Mary Sarah Purvis

ANDERSON, G. A. -w- MARY A.--Heirs of Joseph P. Jones. See Jones
   Card. Edgefield Receipt Bk. A-105 1846

ARDIS, ABRAM, GEORGE RINGLAND, CRADOCK BARNELL, PHILLIP LEMER, ROBERT
COCHRAN--Comm'rs. to build a bridge over Horse Creek at Bevan's
Bridge. Edgefield Ct. Min. Oct. 1794
-Same card: Isaac Ardis, Gdn. for Mary Bowers. See Bowers card.
-March Ct. 1795--Isaac Ardis, surety for Joseph Dick--He's to keep
Tavern.

ARDIS, ABRAM -m- set 24 April 1809 Sarah Bender-widow of George Bender,
both of Edgefield. Both had children by former marriage.
Edgefield Dist. Misc. B-594 1809
-Abram Ardis--To dau: Mary -w- Arthur Simkins Deed gift 15 Jan.
1815. Wit: Matthias Ardis. Edgefield Misc. C-186

ARDIS, DAVID--Legacy in trust for Grand children of Casper Neil. Will
1833. Edgefield

ARDIS, HENRY--Legacy in trust for Louisa-dau. of Casper Neil. Will 1833

ARDIS, ISAC and Wm. Shinholster--Prov. Will of Sophia Hiler. See card
Sophia Hiler. Edgefield Min. Bk. 1788

ARDIS, ISAAC--Petit Juror Edgefield 1789 list 15, Grand Juror 1789
List 22

ARDIS, ISAAC--Son of Mathias Ardis died intestate May or June 1795
Widow: Mary -m- James Richardson. David Ardis, Adm'r.
Only child: John Ardis. Edgefield Equity Roll #1

ARDIS, MATHIAS--Will Dec'd. 1781/2 Edgefield Equity Roll #1
Wife: Christian died 6 May 1785
8 Youngest Children: John, Elizabeth, and Jacob--all died before
their mother. David afterward.
Son: Isaac
Dau: Sarah -m- Benj. Bowers, father of oratrix. Dau. Mary -m-
Jacob Zinn
Son: Jacob--died about 1784
Dau: Elizabeth -w- Francis Carlisle. 1 dau. died in infancy.

ARMSTRONG, JAMES and wife--Ch. of Henry Waldran and heirs of James
Butler. See Butler card. Edgefield Receipt Bk. A-124 1833

ARMSTRONG, MARTIN--Revolution Rec. Archives Dept. A A 152
1. Duty Col. Roebuck's Reg't.
2. Under Wm. Wood--as Lieut. assigned to John Bynem
3. Capt. Moses Wood--Col. Roebuck's Reg't.

ARNOLD, ELIJAH B.--Cobb Georgia Reports Vol. 10-506
Married prior to 1849 Susannah Ware-dau. of James Ware from
Morgan Co. Susannah was niece of Mrs. Susannah Stamper who made
deed gift to her 1815. (Not sure Stamper is correct. FC)
Wit: Lucy Ware, Bonvill M. Ware, James Ware, Sr.

ARNOLD, ISAAC--Of. S. C. from Richard Marchant -w- Elizabeth Deed
27 Sept. 1810. Edgefield Deed 31-462
-Pg. 463--Jacob Arnold of Newberry from John Marchant 3 Sept. 1808
-w- Rachel

ARNOLD, ISAAC--Dec'd. Cit: 28 Jan. 1814 Edgefield Box 5-154
   Adm'r.: Jacob Arnold and Daniel Arnold
   Bond: 18 Feb. 1814
   S: James Arnold, John Marchant
   Widow: Mary Arnold--renounced right to adm'r. 16 Feb. 1814
   Pet. Mar. 14, 1814 "To six years maintenance for John, Ezekial,
   and Virtinda Arnold which _____? is final as appears from the
   small estate that the widow had received nothing."
   May 1816--Pd. James Arnold on acc't.
           Pd. Margaret Dunkin on note
           Pd. Tax.
           Pd. John Arnold on acc't.

ARNOLD, ISAAC --Dec'd. Edgefield Deed 43-482 1820
   Heirs: In Newberry
   Wife: (?) Polly Arnold   Ezekiel Arnold
          John Arnold   Lenny Arnold

ARNOLD, RUTH--Dau. of James Summers-Will 1826 Edgefield

ARRINGTON, WILLIAM--Petit Juror Edgefield 1788 List 9

ATCHERSON, EDMOND and wife--Heirs of Peter Robertson. See Robertson
   card. Edgefield Receipt Bk. B-33 1841

ATKINSON, CHARLOTTE--Dec'd. dau. of John Hatcher-Will 1825 Edgefield

ATTAWAY, NANCY--Dau. of Daniel Rogers-Will 1843. Wife of Thubal
   Attaway. Edgefield

ATTAWAY, SIMEON -w- Frances--Heirs of Amy Hazen and of Charity Johnson.
   See Johnson card. Edgefield Receipt Bk. B-161 1849

ASBELL, MARY--Dau. of Samuel Satcher-Will 1813 Edgefield

BACON, LUCY--Gr-dau. of Robert Ware. Will 1817. Edgefield
   -Lucy Ware--Gr-dau. of Margaret Ware-Will 1829. Edgefield

BACON, NATHANIEL--Petit Juror 1788 List 9 and 17. Grand Juror-List 21

BACON, NATHANIEL--Edgefield Wills. Univ. A-2-428 10 July 1805
   Wife: Mary-All for life
   Son: Lyddell-Home plt'n. at mouth Wateree Br.
   Dau: Elizabeth-To raise the Wood children
          Sally Wood-Dec'd.
          Fanny Derby
   Gr-son: Nathaniel Bacon-son of dau. Elizabeth
   Legatees: Jeremiah Wood, son in law; His oldest son, Joseph Wood;
          His dau. Mariah Wood. Edmond Wood.
   Step Dau: Mrs. Ketty Spikes
   Son in Law: Jeremiah Derby and wife. Son apt'd. Ex.
   (Evident--dau. Elizabeth had illigitiment son, Nathaniel.

BACON, THOMAS, ESQ.--Sd certificate for James Harrison as J. P. See
   Harrison card. Edgefield Ct. Min. March 1795
   -Same card: Also apt'd. James Moore, dec'd. See Moore card.
   Nathaniel Bacon one of Appr's.

BAILEY, ELIZABETH--"Nee Lewis"-sister of Leroy Hammond-Will 1790

BAILEY, ELIZABETH--Dau. of Moses Robertson-Will 1795. Rec'd. 1800
    Also dau: Susannah Bailey and her dau. Fanny. Edgefield

BAILEY, FRANCES -w- Jesse Bailey. Dau. of James Lesuer-Will 1799

BAILEY, JOHN--Will 1 July 1842. Edgefield

BAILEY, MILLEY--Dau. of William Howle, Sen'r.-Will 1830. Edgefield

BAKER, CALPHARNA--Dau. of William Jeter-Will 1793. Edgefield

BAKER, JAMES--Son in Law of James Youngblood-Will 1791. Edgefield

BAKER, JAMES and ELIZABETH--Legatees of Mary Fagna-Will 1794. Edgefield

BAKER, MARY--Dau. of Paul Abney-Will 1819. Edgefield

BAKER, THOMAS--Petit Juror 1786 List 1 and 2. Edgefield

BAKER, WILLIAM--Petit Juror 1787. List 8. Edgefield

BALLENTINE, REBECCAH--Dau. of James Butler-Will 1811 Edgefield

BALLENTINE, REBECCA and her heirs-Heirs of James Butler. See Butler
    Card. Edgefield Rec't. Bk. A-124 1833

BANKS, AMOS--Will 12 April 1842. Edgefield

BANKS, CATERENE--Dau. of George Long-Will 1815 Edgefield

BANKS, SUSANNAH--Wife of Charles Banks. Dower favor of Abraham Richard-
    son. Jan. Ct. 1789. Edgefield Min. Bk.

BANKS, THOMAS--Petit Juror Edgefield 1788. List 11
    -Thomas Banks-Lic. to keep Tavern. S: John Cadle and Ogden
    Cockeroff. Edgefield Ct. Min. March 1795

BANTHALL, A. G. -w- ELIZABETH--Heirs of Stephen Terry, Dec'd. See
    Terry card. Edgefield Rec. Bk. A-314 1839

BARDEN, ELLEN--and her 2 children, Thos. S. and _____?--Heirs of
    Reuben Carpenter. See Carpenter card. Edgefield Rec. Bk-77 1843

BARFIELD, JAMES and wife--Heirs of Aaron Moore. See Moore card. 1812
    Edgefield Deed 31-77. Typed on back: Pendleton Messenger 21 Feb.
                                                   1840

BARKER, ELISHA -w- Susan--Heirs of William Scott. See Scott card.
    Edgefield Rec. Bk. B-53 1841

BARKSDALE, DANIEL--Grand Juror Edgefield 1794. List 21
    -Daniel Barksdale--App'r. Est. Featherstone Cross. See Cross card.
    Edgefield Ct. Min. 1795

BARKSDALE, SUSANNAH--Dec'd. Dau. of Robert Ware⌐Will 1817. Her Ch:
Patsy Key, Peggy Merriweather, Lucinda Crafton. Edgefield

BARLOW, MARTHA--Dau. of Drury Hearn-Will 1840. Edgefield (Martha of Ga.)

BARNES, BENEDICT--Legatee of William Robertson-Will 1840. Edgefield
Also: Benedict Barnes and Macey Barnes now -w-. "one Tally" (?)

BARNES, CATHERINE--Dau. of David Bowers-Will 1833. Edgefield

BARNES, JANE--Dau. of Paul Abney-Will 1819 Edgefield

BARNES, MARTHA M.--Dau. of Alexander Stewart-Will 1821. Wife of Henry
W. Barnes. Edgefield

BARNETT, ELIZABETH--Dau. of Michael Vessalls-Will 1805. Edgefield

BARROTT, MATHEW--Petit Juror Edgefield 1790. List 8 and 18 (or Barrett)

BARRANTON, ANN--Dau. of Sarah Wise-Will 1837. Edgefield

BARRINTON, ELISHA--Overseer of Road from Lee's Bridge to the Pine
House--excused and Bibby Bush apt'd. See Bush card. James Barrin-
ton's house on road to be overseed by Wm. Bush. (Same card).
Edgefield Ct. Min. March 1795

BARRONTON, SARAH--Sister of Henry W. Lowe-Will 1828. Edgefield

BARRONTON, WADE -w- MARY--Heirs of Sarah Lott. See Lott card.
Edgefield Rec. Bk. A-138. 1833

BARTEE, JESSE and his 5 children: Seaborn, Lewis W., Thos. P., Eliza A.
Charles Q.--Heirs of William Pond-See Pond card. Edgefield Rec.
Bk. A-235. 1835

BARTLETT, FANNEY--Dau. of Charles Adams-Will 1824. Edgefield
-Fanny Bartlett--Distributee Est. of Charles Adams. See card 1832.
Mrs. Sarah Deen her Gdn. Edgefield Rec. Bk. A-58

BARTON, JOSEPH--Dec'd. R. E. sold 1833. Edgefield Rec. Bk. A-296
Distributees: John P. Cullum purchased 2 shares of Isaac Barton
William Williams--$78.28
Bailey Chaney -w- Sarah   1/7 $39.14
Enoch Barton, minor-Wm. Williams Gdn. "   "
Bethany Barton,   " "   "   "   "   "
Mahala Barton   " "   "   "   "   "
Joshua Barton   " -Solomon Davis,Gdn. "   "
Isaac Barton   "   "

BARTON, JOSHUA -w- MARY--Heirs of John Lowe. See Lowe card. Edgefield
Rec. Bk. B-214 1852

BARTON, ROBERT--Petit Juror Edgefield 1786. List 5

BASKENS, JOHN--Will 25 Oct. 1767. Of Granville. Edgefield File.
    Wife: Elizabeth)
    "my little son": ?) All
    Bro: James Baskin.
    Wit: Robert Garat, Joseph Carson, John Ramsay. C. T. Wills

BASKERVILLE, ROBERT E. -m- Permelia Broadwater. See card Scarborough
    Broadwater, Dec'd. Edgefield Rec. Bk. A-221 1835

BATES, MARGARET and her children--Heirs of John Cogburn. See Cogburn
    card. Edgefield Rec. Bk. A-225 1834

BATY, SARAH--Sister of Wilson Lee--Will 1813 Edgefield

BAUGH, MARY--Gr. dau. of Elias Blackburn-Will 1827. Also Sarah Ann
    Baugh and Charlotte Baugh. Edgefield

BAY, ELIZABETH M.--Mother in law of William Burton-Will 1815. Edgefield

BEALLE, CATHERINE--Wife of Charles T. Bealle of Columbia Co. Ga. and
    niece of John Fox▼Will 1837

BEAL, JAMES--Petit Juror 1787 Edgefield List 7

BEALL, JOSHUA--Dec'd. R. E. Sold. Edgefield Sale and Div. R. E. Bk-A-80
    Distributees: James Robertson -w- Mary 1/3   1830
                 Sarah Ann Beall   1/4 of 2/3
                 Joseph   "   "   "   "
                 Pleasant   "   "   "   "
                 Martha   "   "   "   "
                 Mary   "   "   "   "
                 Joshua   "   "   "   "

BEALL, JOSHUA--Dec'd. Edgefield Sale and Div. R. E. Bk. A-106
    James Robertson et al -vs- Jno. W. Munday-Guardian ad litem.
    "Commenced thru mistake. Entered at page 80"

BEAN, MARSHAL J. -w- Rhoda--Heirs of Hezekiah Nobles. See Nobles card.
    Edgefield Rec. Bk. A-274 1837
    -Marshal J. Bean -m- Rhoda Nobles, dau. of Hezekiah Nobles and -w-
    of Alcey or Elcy. Marshal J. Bean sd Rec't. 7 Jan. 1839.
    -Rec't. Bk. A-274

BEAN, ALEXANDER--Dec'd. Edgefield Deed Bk. 31-200/1 16 May 1812
    Wife: Christiana Bean
    Children: James Bean
              Joseph Still
              James I. Still
              John Lee
              Thomas Youngblood--son of Jacob Youngblood
              John Bean
              William Bean.

BEAN, ALLIN--Petit Juror Edgefield 1786. List 3

BEAN, JAMES, SEN'R.--Box 49-2088
    BARTLETT------- " 49-2089
    JAMES---------- " 82-3302

BEAN, JAMES, et al -vs- Moses Sanders. Equity Bill 2524. Edgefield

BEAN, JAMES--Mental case. His wife, Rebecca, a dau. and Legatee of
Samuel Walker 1810. Edgefield

BEANS, JAMES--et al -vs- Harriet W. Beans, et al. Equity Bill 85

BEANS, JONES, et al -adv- Benjamin Harrison. Equity Bill 271.

BEARNS, REBECCA -w- _____? Bearns. Dau. of Samuel Walker of Edgefield.
See card of Chaney Farrow. McCords Report Vol. 1-313. For
Edgefield File. 1818

BEATY--See Betty or Bettis. Edgefield

BECKHAM, MARY--of Georgia--dau. of Mary Daly-Will 1832. Wife of
Sherwood Beckham

BECKUM, NANCY--Dau. of Michael Buckhalter-Will 1804. Jesse Beckum-Wit.

BECKHAM, RUSSELL--Petit Juror Edgefield 1788 List 10 and 23

BEDDINGFIELD, JOHN--Dec'd. Edgefield Ct. Min. Oct. 1794.
Cradock Barnhill, Adm'r. Inv. and Ret. made.
Per. property to be sold at house of Alexander Donner on 1st. Mon.
in Nov. next.
-March Ct. 1795--Cradock Barnell, Adm'r. with the Will annexed, of
John Beddingfield ret'd. amt. sale sd. estate.

BEDENBOUGH, MATHIAS H.--Dec'd. R. E. Sold 1851. Children not shown
if any. Edgefield Rec. Bk. B-204

BETCHER, EDWARD -w- Mary-dau. of Robert Anderson-Will 1808. Edgefield

BELCHER, ROBERT--Grand Juror Edgefield 1787. List 6 and 12
-Oct. Ct. 1789 Edgefield Bk. Pg. 263 (Minute Book)
Will proved by oath of Alexander McKay. Susannah Belcher, Ex'x.
S: John Win and James Harrison
-Ct. met 12 Jan. 1789. Minute Bk. Pg. 231. Robert Belcher, Dec'd.
Will proved by oath of James Harrison, which was ordered to be
recorded.

BELCHER, W.--Adv't. estate of Dinwiddie Evans. See card Cad Evans, Dec'd.
Edgefield Rec. Bk. A-100 1832

BELL, BENJAMIN--100 Acres on Gills Creek. 14 Feb. 1764. Archives Dept.
200 " " Coffee Town 2 April 1764
300 " " Little Mine Cr. 15 Nov. 1768
200 " " Rocky Creek 1 Mar. 1770
200 " " Between Saluda and Sab. 13 Dec. 1771

BELL, BENJAMIN--Dec'd. Edgefield Deed Bk. 1-255 16 Feb. 1798
Samuel Walker, Ex. conveyed to Wm. Daniel of Fairfield various
tracts 1769 on. (Grants)

BELL, BLENFORD, JAMES, WILLIAM, CHARLES N.,--Nephews
PEGGY**sister of James Holladay-Will 1827 Edgefield

BELL, CLARECY--Dec'd. Dau. of David Richardson-Will 1842. Her ch:
Frances Hill (may be middle name)
Susan Minter ("   "   "   ")
David R. Bell.

BELL, DAVID--200 Acres both sides Stephens Creek. 10 Nov. 1772.
Wm. Goode, D. S. Archives Dept. Prev. Rev. Plats.

BELL, ELIZABETH--100 Acres Fork Congaree and Watereee on Cedar Creek.
13 April 1768. 100 Acres on Cedar Creek 30 Jan. 1768. Bd. Henry
Touchstone and Mark Davy's. Archives Dept. Prev. Rev. Plats.
-Elizabeth Bell--Edgefield Ct. Min 1785-90. "Deeds of L. and R. E.
from Elizabeth Bell to John Child for 100 Acres land was proved
by the oath of Robert Higgins and James Haskins which was ordered
to be recorded.
-Elizabeth Bell--Edgefield Deed Bk. 8-391. To Anne Bell 2 May 1792
100 Acres on Reedy Creek. 12 Hogs, etc. Wit: Wm. Pool Kennett
Mary Bell.

BEALL, JACOB--Archives Dept. Prev. Rev. Plats. 200 Acres Granville
on Sav. River below the falls. Bd. S-Robert Vaughn. Prec. 3 Feb.
1756. Cert. 7 Aug. 1756-Joseph Chatwin, D. S.
Jeremiah Beall--200 A. Beaver Dam Creek of Turkey Creek. Prec.
3 Feb. 1756. Cert 14 Mar. 1756. Joseph Chatwin, D. S.
John Bea 11--100 A. 96 Creek 17 Nov. 1770. Bd. Wm. Beall and Benj.
Edwin, etc.
Thomas Beall--Prec. 3 Feb. 1756 400 A. Granville on Stephen's Cr.
Bd. Thos. Lamar and vac. Cert. 11 Mar. 1756. Joseph Chatwin, D.S.

BELL, JAMES--Legatee of Jacob Smith-Will 1805. Edgefield

BELL, JOHN- Old Index of Misc. Volumns. H-376 Edgefield
Martha Bell--Adm'x. Letters of Adm. 20 March 1741

BELL, JOHN--Apt'd. Ensign in Militia 10 Oct. 1757. Archives Dept.
KK 506/7
LL 306--Thos. Bell apt'd. Lieut. in Militia 18 Sept. 1760
LL 307--John Bell apt'd. Lieut. 7 Nov. 1760.

BELL, JOHN, ENSIGN--Of Keowa Town. Edgefield File Indian Bk 222
A Journal of Happenings 16 Feb. 1760--Fort Pr. George
"As soon as he (the great warrior) gave the signal, off went about
25 or 30 guns from the Indians that had concealed themselves under
the banks of the river before daylight, as we supposed. Shot Lieut.
Coytmore through the left breast, Ensign Bell slightly on calf of
the leg, Foster, the Inquisitor, in the buttock". sd: Alex'r .
Miln and John Bell. Page 226--Lieut. Coytmore died of wound.

BELL, JOHN--Petit Juror Edgefield 1789. List 13

BELL, JOHN--Dec'd. 26 June 1793. Old Index YY 313. Declarutive by
his Exor. Conc. sale of slaves.

BELL, JOSEPH--Gr. 150 Acres on Horn's Creek of Savannah River. 21 Feb. 1771. Archives Dept. Prev. Rev. Plats.

BELL, JOSEPH TUCKER of Wilson Co. Tenn. to his brother, John Bell, of Edgefield--P. A. 22 July 1811 to sell land. Deed by John Bell.To Joseph Ferguson. Land Gr. to Joseph Tucker Bell by Gov. Arnoldus Vanderhorst. Edgefield Deed Bk 30-373/4

BELL, LESSLIE--100 Acres Craven-Little River 18 July 1767. Bd. John Robinson and James Henning. Archives Dept. Prev. Rev. Plats

BELL, MARMADUKE--(or Duke) Archives Dept. Prev. Rev. Plats
Survey--100 A. SW side Wateree-Oct. 1750 Bd. John Mayrant. Gr. to James Parsons 1 Aug. 1758
1000 A. Craven 3 Nov. 1757 bd. James Kinlock and Albert Leneud
300 A. Santee bd. John Bell 7 May 1764
300 A. Craven, Lynches Creek 9 April 1765

BELL, MATTHEW--150 A. Long Cane and Rocky Creek 7 Oct. 1767.

BELL, PATRICK--100 A. Bounty Gr. on West Fork of Long Cane and Little Hog Skin Creek. 20 May 1767. Bd. Christopher Russel and vac. Prev. Rev. Plats

BELL, RICHARD--200 A. Fork Congaree and Wateree 1767. 300 A. N-S Congaree 1770. Prev. Rev. Plats

BELL, ROBERT--Bounty grants of 100 A. S-s Broad on Brown's Creek 1768
100 A. N. of Long Cane 1768. Prev. Rev. Plats.
-Thomas-Bell 200 A. on Brown's Creek 1760 (Same card)
250 A. on Long Cane 1768

BELL, SAMUEL--200 A. Enoree 1768 Prev. Rev. Plats
100 A. Reedy Branch 1770
250 A. Enoree 1773

BELL, SAMUEL -w- Peggy and Blewford, Jas, Wm. and Chas.--Heirs of William Holliday. Edgefield Receipt Bk. A-106 1831

BELL, STEPHEN -w- Mary-dower to Wm. Fluker 6 Dec. 1811 196½ Acres Bd: Sarah Bodie, Isaac Bell, Martin Fant, Nathan Bodie, Martin Wits. Edgefield Deed 31-16/7

BELL, COL. THOMAS--"Know all men whom it may concern thet I, the sub-senior, have sold to Thos. Yates of North Carolina, for the use, occupation etc, a tract of land, the property of Colonel Bell of Hard Lavour for two hundred pounds sterling. Currency to be paid to sd Colonel Thos. Bell at and before the third day of December in the year of our Lord 1768 and I do give the said Yates a free possession by Colonel Bell's orders to me for that purpose given November 14, 1767. James Mayson."
"Glasgow, 23 Sept. 1768--I hereby approve of the sale made by James Mayson, Esq. of 200 Acres of land lying on Wilson's Creek and hereby oblige myself to make title unto Thomas Yeats (sp?) Thomas Bell". Patrick Calhoun and Le Roy Hammond "Will accept with handwriting of Col. Thos. Bell----1789

BELL, THOMAS, WILLIAM, DAVID--of Franklin Co. Indiana to James Adams
14 Oct. 1814. Land pur. by Jesse Harrison and David Bell.
Edgefield Deed 32-206

BELL, VALENTINE--Archives Dept. Prev. Rev. Plats.
200 A. on Kings Creek, Craven 19 Feb. 1763. Gr. to Susan Brown
26 May. 100 A. Branch Turkey Creek, N-s Broad. Cert. 13 Dec. 1764
200 A. Turkey Creek of Broad 25 Sept. 1766 and 150 A. Turkey Cr.
12 May 1773.

BELL, WALTER--350 A. Granville-small Br. Sav. River 13 Mar. 1770
Prev. Rev. Plats. Edgefield File.

BELL, WILLIAM -"CAPTAIN"--100 A. Granville E-s Swamp of Sav. River.
Bd. Wm. Cochran and vac. Cert. 5 Mar. 1732/3 by Hugh Bryan, D. S.
150 A. on Pee Dee 23 June 1757, 300 A. on Deed Cr. Pee Dee 19 June
1767

BELL, WILLIAM--To his children 19 July 1793. Edgefield Deed Bk 8-306
Mary Bell   William Harrison Bell
Agnes Bell   Elizabeth Bell
Zachariah Bell   Locreacia Bell
Antimalia Tabitha Bell   Deed gift Per. Prop. to all.

BELL, ZACHARIAH--500 A. N E side Broad River on Bullock Creek and
Bell's Br. All vac. Cert. 12 Oct. 1758. Prev. Rev. Plats

BENDER, GEORGE--Former husband of Sarah Ardis-wife of Abram Ardis-
Will 1816. Edgefield

BENDER, ULRICK--"Son" of John Clarke, Sen'r.-Will 1821. (Think his
name is Ulrick Bender Clarke.) Edgefield

BENNETT, ANNE--Dau. of Peter Day-Will 1789. Edgefield

BERNARD, ROBERT--Of Horse Creek. Edgefield File. Misc. B-566
To Wife: Nancy   1 Oct. 1808 Deed Gift
Children: Ann Jervis-widow
          Elizabeth
          Sarah
          Jane-a minor--"his daus")
          Robert   )Thos. Galpin and Walter
          Justin   )Taylor, Trs.
          Ulisses (sp?)a minor--his sons

BERRY, ARNOLD--Dec'd. Order to sell personal estate at home of Nathaniel
Bolton. Ret. made by Mary Berry, Adm'x. Edgefield Ct. Min March
1795. January Ct. 1795--Mary Berry applied for letters Adm. on
estate of her husband, Arnold Berry. Granted-Bond 2,000 pounds.
S: Ogden Cockroft, Nath'l Bolten. Appr's: Henry King, Sam'l
Deloach, Wm. Burdit, Wm. Rotten. Oct. Ct. 1794--Arnold Berry,
Gdn. of the children of Henry Boalling, Dec'd.

BERRY, JOHN--et al -vs- Jane Berry, et al. Equity Bill 537. Edgefield

BERRY, MARTIN, E. to John Pollatty 72½ Acres adj. Jordan Holloway and
    Jacob Goleman. 20 April 1829. Edgefield Deed 44-245

BERRY, RICHARD--Gdn. for minor heirs of Michael Shaver. See Shaver
    card. Edgefield Rec. Bk. A-132. 1832

BERRY, SABETHA--Dau. of John Gorman-Will 1798. Edgefield

BERRY, THOMAS--Petit Juror Edgefield 1789. List 15

BERRY, THOMAS--Heir of Elizabeth Hill. See Hill card. Edgefield
    Rec. Bk. B-83. 1843

BERRY, THOMAS--Dec'd. R. E. Sold 1852. Edgefield Rec. Bk. B-213
    Dist: Nancy Berry-widow--1/3

Claborn Berry	1/8 of 2/3			
Jacob "	" " "			
Elijah "	" " "			
Thomas "	" " "			
Nancy "	" " "-Nancy Gdn. for all except			
George "	" " "	Claborn.		
Sarah Ann"	" " "			
William "	" " "			

BEXLEY, E. E.--Wife of James Bexley--Tombstone Little Stevens Creek
    Baptist Church, Edgefield. Born 1 Feb. 1816. Died 6 June 1883
    Dau. of Mrs. Anna Hammutal Lowey. See Lowey card.

BETTIS, BENJAMIN, ELIZA, AND HARRIETT--Heirs of Lucy Hatcher. See
    Hatcher card. Edgefield Rec. Bk. B-23. About 1848

BETTIS, JESSE--Will 11 April 1838. Edgefield

BETTIS, LUCY--Dau. of Lucy Hatcher-Will 1834. Edgefield
            Heir of Mary Tillman. See Tillman card. Rec. Bk.B-103
                                           1846
BETTIS, MATHEW -w- Winny, also Eliza and Elisha Bettis--Heirs of Sarah
    Lott. See Lott card. Edgefield Rec. Bk. A-138 1833

BETTIS, STEPHEN--Petit Juror 1787 Edgefield. List 8 and 16

BETTIS, WINNEFRED--Dau. of Sarah Lott-Will 1831 (Name possibly Betty-
    Will mentions Stephen Betty, dec'd. and his children.)

BICKERS, W. J. -w- Martha--Heirs of Lewis Youngblood. See Youngblood
    card. Edgefield Rec. Bk. B-89 1845

BIDDER, JENNET--Niece of Cradock Burnell-Will 1818. Edgefield

BIRD, DANIEL -w- Susannah to Solomon Bird-Deed. Ct. July 1787.
    Min. Book 1786-pg.93 Edgefield

BIRD, DANIEL -m- Sarah Oliver 25 Dec. 1806. Moses Waddell Marriages
    Lib. of Congress. Edgefield File.

BIRD, DANIEL--Petit Juror Edgefield 1794. List 21

BIRD, DANIEL--Apt. Clerk Ct. for Edgefield Dist--Bond: Jesse Blocker, Samuel Nicholson, Whit Brooks, Andrew Butler. Hist. Com. Misc. Rec. D-604 5 Feb. 1822

BIRD, DANIEL--"Of Edgefield Dist. and Beheathland Simkins"--relict of Jesse Simpkins of Edgefield. Marriage agreement. Whitfield Brooks, Trustee. Hist. Com. Misc. Rec. F-104. 17 Aug. 1827

BYRD, FANNY--Dau. of Charles Fooshe-Will 31 Mar. 1820. Abeville Wills 2-pg. 111

BIRD, FRANCIS--Dec'd. R. E. Sold 1848. Edgefield Rec. Bk. Pg.137
    Dist: William T. Bird   1/7 - $68.11
       Rebecca Bird   "
       S. J. Roberas -w- Eliza "   "
       John Cheatham-w- Mary   "   "   John dec'd.
       Timothy Reardon -w- Harsey   "
       Benj. Rearden -w- Abbey "   "
       Ch. of James Boyd -w- Susannah 1/7 viz:
          Thos J. Mayberry -w- Frances $\frac{1}{4}$ of 1/7 $17.02
          Sarah Amanda Boyd   "   "   "
          Thomas Boyd   "   "   "
          William Boyd   "   "   "
          Benjamin Boyd.

BIRD, PEGGY--Dau. of Drury Adams-Will 1814. Edgefield

BIRD, SOLOMON--Petit Juror Edgefield 1789. List 15

BITTLE, REBECCA -w- Andrew Bittle. Sister of James Lowry-Will 1815 -Rebecca Bittle--Heir of Daniel Braner, dec'd. Edgefield Rec. Bk. A-34 1834

BLACK, ELIZABETH--Dau. of Paul Abney-Will 1819. Edgefield

BLACK, JOHN H.--Will 7 Nov. 1840

BLACK, MARK -w- Mary--Heirs of William Bladon. See Bladon card. Edgefield Rec. Bk. A-258 1837

BLACK, REBECCA--Dau. of James Summer-Will 1826. Edgefield

BLACK, SARAH--Dau. of Edward Coleman and mentioned in Will of Matthew Wells-Will 1825. Edgefield. Sarah -w- Daniel Black

BLACKBURN, CERESSA--Sister of Henry W. Lowe-Will 1828. Edgefield

BLACKBURN, ELIAS--Exor. Estate Angus McDaniel. See McD. card. Edgefield Ct. Min. March 1795

BLACKBURN, JOHN--son of Elias Blackburn-Legatee of Angus McDaniel. Will 1795-Codicil. Edgefield

BLACKLEY, BENJAMIN--Petit Juror Edgefield 1786. List 5

BLACKWELL, STEPHEN F. -w- MARIAH of Va.--Heirs of Leuchen Winn. See Winn card. Edgefield Rec. Bk. A-64 1830

BLADON, WILLIAM--Dec'd. R. E. Sold 1857/8 Edgefield Rec. Bk. A-258
    Dist: John Bladon andJames Carsen sold their interest in the
           land to Mrs. Bladon, the widow, and therefore they are
           only entitled to their share of the interest in said
           lands--1/7 of the 3 shares to each.
           John Bladon   1/7 $124.64
           E. Walton   )
           Mark Black -w- Mary)   "   "
           James Carson   )
           Frances Carson)
           Sarah Carson   )   "   "
           Allen Corley -w- Winney of Washington Co. Ala. in 1844 1/7
           Martha Bladon)
           Tabitha Bladon)   1/7 $124.64
           James Bladon   "   "
           William Bladon   "   "
    Hardy White, Gdn. of Tabitha. John Bladon d. and his Adm. collected
    in 1844

BLAIR, CHRISTOPHER--Dec'd. See card Hannah Robinson. Edgefield Rec.
    Bk. A- 1830

BLAIR, C. L. -w- Huldah--Heirs of Thomas Jennings. See Jennings card.
    Edgefield Rec. Bk. B-211 1852

BLAIR, GABRIEL -w- Rebecca--Heirs of Jonathan Sullivan. See Sullivan
    card. Edgefield Rec. Bk. A-1 about 1820

BLAIR, JAMES--Dec'd. R. E. Sold 1848. Rec. Bk. B-175 Edgefield
    Columbus Blair, Applicant -vs- Sarah Blair and others, deft's.
    Settlement not shown.

BLAIR, PATSEY--Gr. dau. of Esther Howe (or Howle)-Will 1840 Edgefield

BLAIR, SARAH--Widow of C. Blair, Gabriel Blair, et al. Heirs of
    Bersheba Hill. See Hill card. Edgefield Rec. Bk. A-78 1832

BLAIR, WASHINGTON--Heir estate of Thomas Howle. See Howle card.
    Edgefield Rec. Bk. A-286. 1838
    -Washington Blair -w- Martha--Heirs of Nancy Odom. See card Odom.
    Edgefield Rec. Bk. B-99 1845
    -Washington Blair -w- Martha--Heirs Thomas Howle, Sen'r. See
    Howle card. Edgefield Rec. Bk. B-99 1845

BLALOCK, BUCKNER--Wit. John Blalock--Appr. Estate of Lewis Clark, Dec'd.
    See Clark card. Edgefield Ct. Min. March 1795

BLALOCK, CHARLES--Dec'd. R. E. Sold 1842. Edgefield Rec. Bk. B-69
    Dist: Shadrick Homes -w- ?   1/3 $157.66
           David Blalock   ¼ of 2/3 $78.83
           Levi   "   "   "
           William B. Blalock   "   "
           Martha A.   "   "   "

BLALOCK, DOLLY--Dau. of Edward Coleman-Will 1826. Edgefield

BLALOCK, MILLINGTON -w- Heirs of Ebenezer Hill. See Hill card.
    Edgefield Rec. Bk. A-280

BLALOCK, NANCY--Dau. of Lewis Clark-Will 1794. Edgefield

BLALOCK, SARAH--Dau. of Mary Hill-Will Rec'd. 1822. Edgefield

BLAND, B. F. -w- Elizabeth--Heirs of Marian Adams. 1842. See card. Edgefield Rec. Bk. B-61

BLAND, ELBERT C.--Legatee of Robert Cochran-Will 1838 Edgefield

BLAND, ELSEY -w- Demaris--Heirs of Mary Tillman. See Tillman card. Edgefield Rec. Bk. B-103 1846

BLAND, PRESLEY--Qualified as Constable Edgefield Ct. Min. Jan. 1795 -Presley Bland--Will 11 Feb. 1839

BLAND, ROBERT--Petit Juror Edgefield 1788. List 9

BLAND, WORMLY--Default in Road work. See Lodwick Hill. Edgefield Ct. Min. March 1795

BLEAZE, THOMAS -w- Bethany--Heirs of Francis Coleman. See Coleman card. Edgefield Rec. Bk. A-219. 1835

BLEDSOE, BARTLETTE--Petit Juror Edgefield 1788. List 9

BLEDSOE, BUD and wife--Heirs of estate of John Gorman. See Glrman card. Edgefield Rec. Bk. A-52. 1831

BLEDSOE, ELBERT AND HENRY--Heirs of Job. Thornton. See Thornton card. Edgefield Rec. Bk. B-63. 1843

BLEDSOE, JOHN--Default in road work. See Lodwick Hill. Edgefield Ct. Min. March 1795.

BLEDSOE, LYON--Dau. of John Douglass-Will 1799. Edgefield

BLEDSOE, WILLIAM--Son in law of Nicholas Lowe-Will 1843. Married Hannah-dau. of Testator. Edgefield

BLEWER, ELIZABETH M.--Dau. of James L. Jones-Will 1824. Wife John G. Blewer. Edgefield

BLOCKER, JOHN--Petit Juror Edgefield 1788. List 10

BLOCKER, JOHN and Thomas McGinnis--Apt'd. Gdns for Lydia Leech. See Leech card. Appl. Ct. 1790. Edgefield Min. Bk.

BLOCKER, JOHN, ESQ.--Produced certificate of his qualification as a J. P. for the County sd by Hon. Arthur Simkins. Edgefield Ct. Min. Jan. 1795

BLOCKER, JOHN--Surety for Adm. Bond Est. Samuel Edmunds. See Edmunds card. Jan. Ct. 1795--John Blocker Exor. of John Jacob Messersmith. See Messersmith card.

BLOCKER, JOHN--Dec'd. R. E. Sold 1833. Edgefield Rec. Bk. A-158
  Dist: Ben. F. Nicholson and wife   1/7 $82.78½
       Sophia Blocker, George, and Eliza beth S. "   " each.
       Caroline S. Blocker -m- M. W. Abney   "   " Rec. 1842
       Sarah S. and Emma E. Blocker   "   " each
  Rec't. from John Lake 1835-right of wife.
  Rec't. Felix Lake 1839
  Isabella M. Blocker Gdn. of Catherine E. and Sarah S. Blocker 1842

BLOCKER, LAURA A. AND ELIZA A.--Heirs of Lucy T. Moore-Will 1856.
  Edgefield Probate 178/9 1856

BLOCKER, MICHAEL--Dec'd. R. E. Sold 1st Mon. Sept. 1825. Bk A-14
  Dist: John Blocker ½
      Martha Marsh 1/3 of ½
      Samuel B. Marsh and wife 1/3 of 2/3 of ½
      John Buckholtz and wife 1/3 of 2/3 of ½
      James Blocker 1/3 of 2/3 of ½
  Shows Martha Marsh-widow.

BLONOM OR BLOXOM, HENRY -w- Elizabeth--Heirs of Hezekiah Noble. See
  Noble card. Edgefield Rec. Bk. A-274 1837
  -Heirs of Daniel Holloway. See Holloway card. Edgefield Rec.
  Bk. A-154. 1823

BOALLING, HENRY--Dec'd. Arnold Berry allowed 5 pounds per year for
  boarding and clothing of children of dec'd. Edgefield Ct. Min.
  Oct. Ct. 1794.

BOAROAM, WILLIAM--Grand Juror Edgefield 1794. List 20

BOBO, W. M.--Of Union -m- 21 July 1845 Martha L. Carey of Edgefield.
  Dau. of W. H. Carey, Dec'd. Archives Dept. Misc. N-196

BODIE, JOSHUA--Dec'd. R. E. Sold 1809. Edgefield Rec. Bk. A-308
  Dist: Mary Bodie-widow 1/3 $301.26
      Abraham Turner -w- Judith   )
      John Bodie   )
      Thomas Coburn -w- Eleanor   )
      James Smith -w- Mary   ) All 1/15 of 2/3 $40.16
      Simon Day -w- Sophia   )
      Nancy Bodie   )
      William Gulledge -w- Martha)
      Eliza, Allen, Lucy, Joseph, Jane--All minors. Same share
      Sarah, West Michael--Also minors-Solomon Cohen, Gdn. Same.
  Lucy -m- Silas Dabbs and lived in Harris Co. Ga. 6 Nov. 1843
  Simon Day -w- Sophia lived in Dallas Co. Ala. 14 Sept. 1840
  Rec't. Allen Smith in right of wife, Eliza Bodie Smith

BODIE, NATHAN and wife--Heirs of John Warren, Dec'd. See Warren card.
  Edgefield Rec. Bk. A-169 1834
  -Nathan Bodie Will 12 Aug. 1841.
  -Nathan Bodie -w- Edney--Heirs of James Eidson. See Eidson card.
  Edgefield Rec. Bk. B-125. 1847

BODY, ALLEN--Dec'd. R. E. Sold. Edgefield Sale and Div. Bk. A-92-96
    Dist: Ezekiel Jones -w- Elizabeth (widow of intestate) 1/3
        Abijah Body--Rec't. 7 Jan. 1832
        William Body
        Simeon--Rec't. 20 Jan. 1832
        Allsee Body--Philip McCarty, Gdn.
        Richard Dunkin (Duncan) and wife
        Elisha Whittle and wife
        James Newton -w- Sarah (Assigned to Nathan Berry)
        Mark Harrid -w- Barbbary
        Charon Body
        Lotha, Jane, Hester Body-Philip McCarty, Gdn.
        John Body's sole heir-Nancy Body by her Gdn.-James Whittle.
Widow's share--1/3 $190.52. Each of others 1/13 of 2/3 $29.31
Purchased by Ezekiel Jones.

BODY, ELLEN--Married Thomas S. Coburn and lived in Loundes Co. Ala.
    Dau. of or heir of Joshua Body-1834. Edgefield Rec. Bk. A-?

BODY, JOHN--Petit Juror Edgefield 1789. List 15

BODY, LOACHAMAH--Dau. of James Smith, Sen'r.-Will 1823. Edgefield

BOLES, EDY--Dau. of Frederick Word-Will 1803 Edgefield

BOLES, ISAAC--Adopted son of Caleb Holloway-Will 1840. Edgefield

BOLGER, ELIZABETH--Will 8 Aug. 1836. Edgefield 11

BOLGER, JOHN -w- Sarah--Heirs of Hezekiah Nobles. See Nobles card.
    Edgefield Rec. Bk. A-274

BOLGER, SALLY--Dau. of Hezekiah Nobles-Will 1830. Edgefield

BOLTER, GEORGE--Petit Juror Edgefield 1794. List 21

BOLTON, HENRY--Petit Juror Edgefield 1789. List 14

BOLTON, JOSEPH and wife--Heirs of estate of Jacob Green. See Green
    card. Edgefield Rec. Bk. A-171 1834

BOLTON, WILLIAM--Petit Juror Edgefield 1790. List 18

BONDS, THOMAS -w- Malinda--Heirs of Job Padgett. See Padgett card.
    Edgefield Rec. Bk. A-312 1839
BONES, JAMES--Will 4 Sept. 1841 Edgefield

BOONE, DANIEL--Pur. share estate of John Gorman. See Gorman card.
    Edgefield Rec. Bk. A-52. 1831

BOONE, SHADRACK--Dec'd. Sale R. E. 1829. Edgefield Sale Bk. A-48
    Dist: Daniel Boone 1/5 of 2/3 $18.78
        Wm. Williams and wife--same (wife-Ruth)
        Daniel Havard and wife--same Rec't. 2 July 1829 (wife-Matilda)
        Jno McCrary and wife--same(wife-Rebecca)
        Edna Boone--same (also Edeline)
        Mary Sandy, widow--1/3
        Rec't. assignment to Daniel Boone-Wm. Williams -w- Ruth
Mary Sanday assigned as gift her share to children. 12 March 1831

BOONE, THOMAS--Petit Juror Edgefield 1789. List 14

BOOTHE, AARON--Dec'd. Jesse Griffin produced Acct. See Griffin card.
    Edgefield Ct. Min. Jan. 1795

BOOTH, JAMES--Petit Juror Edgefield 1786. List 5

BOOZER, HENRY and wife--Heirs of William Sheppard. See Sheppard card.
    Edgefield Rec. Bk. A-156. 1833

BOSTICK, JOHN--Grand Juror Edgefield 1794. List 21

BOSWELL, DAVID--Petit Juror Edgefield 1787 List 6 and 19. Grand Juror
    List 20.

BOSWELL, MARY ANN--Dau. of William Quarles-Will 1821 Edgefield

BOWERS, ANN -w- Jiles Bowers and dau. of Samuel Burgen and Legatee of
    John Joacan Tobler. Edgefield Will 1810

BOWERS, BERY--Dec'd. Edgefield Ct. Min. Bk. 196. 14 July 1788
    "In the Court of Ordinary--ordered that the Executors of Bery
    Bowers have three months to make up their accounts."

BOWERS, DAVID--Petit Juror Edgefield 1786. List 3

BOWERS, DAVID, SEN'R.--Dec'd. "My interest in the R. E. of David
    Bowers, Sen'r. Dec'd." See Will of John Burgess 1829. Edgefield

BOWERS, DEBORAH--Wife of ? Bowers. Heir of Job Padget. See Padget
    card. Edgefield Rec. Bk. A-312 1839

BOWERS, JAMES--Legacy in trust for Maria, dau. of Casper Nail-Will 1833

BOWERS, MARY--Dau. of Benjamin Bowers of age to choose her Gdn. Chose
    Isaac Ardis. Ct. also apt'd. him Gdn. of Nancy Bowers.
    Edgefield Ct. Min. Oct. 1794

BOWERS, NANCY--Dau. of Catherine Bates-Will 1849. Edgefield

BOWERS, PHILEMON -w- Nancy--Heirs of Thomas Broom. See Broom card.
    Edgefield Rec. Bk. A-239 1835

BOWLES, LUCY AND BETSY--Gr. daus. of Jesse Holloway-Will 1818 Edgefield

BOWLES, SPENCER--Bro. in law of Elizabeth M. Ray-Will 1817. Edgefield

BOWLIN, ELIZABETH--Dau. of John Crowder-Will 1790. Edgefield Wills A-29

BOURGOIS, BENEDICT--Legatee (son?) of Hamutal Wilson (a woman)-Will 1806
    See also card on Fay. Edgefield

BOUKNIGHT, JAMES -w-Martha--Heirs of James Eidson. See Eidson card.
    Edgefield Rec. Bk. B-125

BOULWARD, HUMPHREY--Married Rachel Lark-dau of John Lark-Will 1822

BOYD, EDMOND--Petit Juror Edgefield 1787. List 7

BOYD, FRANCES--Sister of John Lyon-Will 1841. Also Nancy Boyd.

BOYD, JAMES -w- Susannah and their children--Heirs of estate of Francis
    Bird. See Bird card. Edgefield Rec. Bk. B-137 1848

BOYD, JOHN--Edgefield Will C-202 Bx. 5 Pk. 145
    Brother: Henry K. Boyd
    Sister: Mariah Williams and her son, John Henry Williams
    Uncle: Hezekiah Boyd and wife, Emma Ann. Daughters: Frances
        Martha Boyd, and Euselia Elvira Boyd
    Aunt: Martha Collier and her children: Higdon Borom and
        William T. Borom. Joseph and Ann Collier.
    Cousin: John Boyd-son of John
    Cousin: Winefred Williams and her children: Ogburn, Palsey
        and Elizabeth
    Same Card: John Boyd, Sen'r. Will
        Dau: Maria Boyd
        Son: Henry K. Boyd-no issue
            John Boyd-no issue
        Sister: Ann Boyd
        Brother: Robert and Hezekiah Boyd

BOYD, POLLY--Dau of Joseph Collier-Will 1818. Edgefield. Her ch:
    Augustus, John, Amy, Sarah, Sayntha Boyd

BOYD, SAMUEL--Proved Will of Featherstone Cross as a witness. Edge-
    field Ct. Min. 1795

BOYD, SARAH--Dau. of William Borrum-Will 1817.

BOYD, SEBELLAH--Dau. of Zadoc Bussey-Will 1822 Edgefield

BOYD, SUSANNAH--Dau. of Elizabeth Thurman-Will 1804

BOZEMORE, DAVID--Petit Juror List 20. Edgefield 1794 (Bazemore?)

BRACKETE, MRS. SUSANNAH--Advs. Taylor and Moore (she owed) Store Acct.
    Edgefield Ct. Com. Pleas 1809. Pg 283

BRACKNELL, JOHN and wife--Heirs of Stephen Martin. See Martin card.
    Edgefield Rec. Bk. A-36 1830

BRACKNELL, JOHN--Dec'd. R. E. Sold 1849. Edgefield Rec. Bk. B-176
    Dis: Elizabeth Bracknell, widow 1/3 $98.10
        William Bracknell 1/9 $21.80
        Daniel Bracknell   "   "
        Jane -w- Wm. Price assn'd. her share to H. T. Wright

BRADBURY, THOMAS -w- Nancy--Heirs of James Thomas. See Thomas card.
    Edgefield Rec. Bk. A-6 1826

BRADFIELD, JAMES--Dec'd. R. E. Sold 1839. Edgefield Rec. Bk. A-316
    Dist: Nancy Bradfield, widow 1/3 $6.38
          James Bradfield 1/11 of 2/3 $1.16
          Thomas Carter -w- Margaret--same
          William McCullough -w- Rebecca--same
          Robert, John, William, Toliver, Oliver, Emily, Mary Ann
          and Nancy Bradfield--All 1/11 of 2/3 - $1.16

BRADFORD, RANDOLPH--Son in law of Polly Low-Will 1830. Mary Elizabeth
    Bradford, Gr. dau. of Testator. A minor. Edgefield

BRANSON, ELI -w- Nelly, and William Branson et al--Heirs of William
    Holliday. See Holliday card. Also Thos. Branson -w- Polly.
    Edgefield Rec. Bk. A-106 1831

BRANSON, ELI--Will 30 May 1796. Abbeville Wills
    Wife: Keziah
    Son: John, Daniel, Thomas, Levi, Eli--Land in Newberry
    3 eldest daus: Rebecca Jones, Mary Jones, Naomi Ward

BRAZIL, MRS. RACHEL--Relinquished right to Adm. estate of her former
    husband, Benj. McKinney. See McKinney card. Edgefield Ct. Min.
    March 1795

BREED, NATHAN--B/S to Samuel Landrum for a Negro. Prov. by oath of
    Silas Sellers. Edgefield Ct. Min. 1785-90 Pg. 49

BREMER, MICHAEL--Dec'd. Intestate. Edgefield Equity Roll 5
    Widow: Rebecca -m- _____ Bittle
    Ch: Sally
         Daniel
         Mary -m- Tobias Prior

BRENAN, EUGENE--Gdn. of Miss Sally Dalty, minor. Edgefield Ct. Min. 1795

BRENAN, JAMES W.--Gr. son of Hannah McGennis-Will 1823. Gr. daus:
    Louisa and Martha Brenan. Dau: Nancy Brenan Edgefield

BROADWATER, CHARLES--Petit Juror Edgefield 1794. List 21

BROADWATER, GUY -w- Rachel--Heirs of estate of Edmond Flinn. See
    Flinn card. Edgefield Rec. Bk. B-121 1846

BROADWATER, PERMELIA--Dau. of John Griffis-Will 1838. Edgefield

BROADWATER, RODE--Dau. of William Flinn, Sen'r.-Will 1837

BROADWATER, SAMUEL -w- Martha P.-Heirs of Lewis Glanton. See Glanton
    card. Edgefield Rec. Bk. B-206 1851

BROADWATER, SCARBROUGH--Dec'd. R. E. Sold 1825. Rec. Bk. A-221
    Dist: Martha Broadwater, Widow--1/3 $96.66
          Ezekiel Broadwater 1/8 of 2/3
          Thomas Ford -w- Orphia--same
          Caleb and Guy Broadwater--same
          Peter Williams -w- Nancy--same
          Scarbrough Broadwater--same
                             -CONTINUED-

BROADWATER, SCARBROUGH--Continued
   The heirs of Samuel Broadwater, Dec'd.
     Rebecca Broadwater, widow 1/7 of 2/3
     Elizabeth Broadwater--same
     Thomas Broadwater--same
     Charles Tally -w- Martha--same
     James, Matilda, Ezekiel, and Mary Broadwater-minors-each
       1/7 of 2/3. Rebecca Broadwater, Gdn.
   The heirs of Josiah Broadwater 1/3
     Elizabeth Broadwater, widow 1/3
     James A. Broadwater 1/3 of 2/3
     Permelia -m- Robert E. Baskerville 1/3 of 2/3 Rec't. 1836
     Clementha -m- Metton or Melton--1/8 of 2/3

BROADWAY, NANCY--Heir of Abney Mays. See Mays card. Edgefield Rec.
   Bk. 192-B 1850

BROOKS, ABBA--Of Virginia--Step daughter: Martha White of Edgefield
   Conv. 1830 to dau. Lucy White. Edgefield Deed 31-369/70

BROOKS, ELIZABETH--Dau. of John Clark, Sen'r.-Will 1814. Edgefield

BROOKS, JACOB--Grand Juror Edgefield 1786. List 1 and 2

BROOKS, JACOB--Dec'd. Ct. Min. 14 July 1789. Edgefield Min. Bk.
   Estate being wasted. Citation issued for Vachel Clary and Mary
   his wife to appear at next court to answer the complaint. Made
   by John Gorman and James Cason, securities.

BROOKS, JAMES--Petit Juror Edgefield 1786. List 1 and 2
   Grand Juror 1786. List 6 and 18

BROOKS, LITTLETON A.--Son in law of Nicholas Lowe-Will 1843. Wife
   Lucinda-dau. of testator. Edgefield

BROOKS, MRS. MARY--Applied for Letters of Administration of Estate
   of Jacob Brooks, dec'd. She gave Bond. S: Benj. Cook, John
   Garman, James Carson. Appr's. Apt'd: Samuel Savage, James
   McKay, William Abney. Edgefield Ct. Min. Bk. 1787-pg. 98

BROOKS, MARY--Her heirs: William, John, Francis, et al--Heirs of
   Rebecca Ramey. See Ramey card. Edgefield Rec. Bk. B-75 1842

BROOKS, ROBERT -w- Mary--Heirs of Spencer Minor. See Minor card.
   Edgefield Rec. Bk. B-94 1846

BROOKS, SIMON--App'r. of Estate of Peter Buffington. See Buffington
   card. Edgefield Ct. Min. Jan. 1795

BROOKS, THOMAS--Son of Christian Limbecker-Will 1818. Edgefield

BROOKS, WILLIAM--Petit Juror Edgefield 1788. List 10 and 16

BROOKS, WHITFIELD--Heir or purchaser of Estate of Lewis Youngblood.
   See Youngblood card. Edgefield Rec. Bk. B-89 1845

BROOM, THOMAS--Dec'd. R. E. Sold 1835. Edgefield Rec. Bk. A-239
    James Broom 1/6 $4.75
    Dan'l Brener for Sam'l C. Brown, Dec'd.--same
    Philemon Bowers -w- Nancy--same
    Henry C. Peay -w- Mary--same
    Eliza Starr, widow of Geo. Starr 1/3 $153.00
        Minor children of Eliza Starr: Nancy, Mary, Thomas, Frances,
        Sarah, George--each 1/6 of 2/3 (1/6 equals $4.75)
    Ruth Broom, widow of Thomas Broom
        Minor children: Eliza, Mary, James, Thomas, Joshua-Ruth
        Broom, Gdn.--1/6

BROWN, ARATHUSIA (?)--Dau. of Walter Abney-Will 1827.

BROWN, JACOB--Petit Juror Edgefield 1786. List 5

BROWN, JAMES--Son in law of James Johnson-Will 1811. Edgefield

BROWN, JOICY--Heir of James Picket. See Picket card. Edgefield Rec.
    Bk. A-306 1839

BROWN, MARY M. W.--Gr. dau. of Robert Harrison-Will 1827. Edgefield

BROWN, REBECCA -w- Abner Brown--Heirs of Philip Jennings. See Jennings
    card. Edgefield Rec. Bk. B-186 1850

BROWN, WILLIAM--Petit Juror Edgefield 1788. List 9

BROWN, WILLIAM, BARTLETT AND JAMES--See card Joseph Addison 1789.
    Edgefield Min. Bk. Pg. 252 14 July 1789

BROWN, WILLIAM--Dec'd. John Abney, Adm'r. Am8. sale of estate
    returned and recorded, Jan. Ct. 1795. Order to sell personal
    estate of Wm. Brown 4th Sat. in Jan. next at home of John Abney.
    -Joel Brown--default in Road work.
    -Joseph Brown--default in Road work

BROWN, WILLIAM--Of Richmond Co. Ga. Married 22 Dec. 1842 Emily H.
    Joor of Edgefield. John Bones, Tr. Edgefield Misc. M-410

BROWNELL, JANE--Married Alexander Robertson of C. T. Edgefield Deed 7-241

BRUNER, DANIEL--Dec'd. R. E. Sold 1834. Edgefield Sale Bk. A-34
    Dist: Rebecca Bittle 1/3 of 1/2 $63.83
        Tobias Prior and wife 1/3 of 2/3 of 1/2 $42.55
        Horatio Collins and wife--same
        Dan'l M. Bruner--same
        Jno. I. Gray 1/4 of the whole $95.75
        William Dicks 1/8 of 1/4 of whole $1197
        Martha McKenna-- same
        Dave Meyer and wife--same
        Mary Thomas, John Williams, James Calvin, Nancy Pey, Ann
        Owens,-- 1/8 of 1/4 $11.97 each.
        James Calvin and Nancy Pey--1/8 of 1/4 $11.97

BRIANT, MARY--Dau. of Presley Bland-Will 1839. Edgefield

BRYAN, TABITHA--Sister of Henry Clark-Will 1840. Edgefield

BRYAN, TILLMAN--Dec'd. R. E. Sold 1826. Edgefield Rec. Bk. A-252
    Dist: Tempy Bryan, widow 1/3 $44.00
        John, Elizabeth, Julia, Edoline, Catherine and Nancy
        Bryan 1/6 of 2/3 each. Robert Bryan Gdn. of minors.

BRYANT, ROBERT--Son of Sarah Stevens-Will 1793. William Bryant another
    son. Edgefield

BRYANT, WILLIAM--Petit Juror Edgefield 1789. List 13

BRYANT, WILLIAM AND ELISHA--Nephews of William Tobler-Will 1806

BRUCE, HANNAH--Dau. of Samuel Satcher-Will 1813

BRUNER, DANIEL--See card of Thomas Broom, dec'd. Edgefield Rec. Bk-239
                                                                 1835
BRUNSON, HARRIET--Dau. of Beheathland Mims-Will 1836. Edgefield

BUCHANAN, JOHN -w- Sarah (late Milling)--See card of Lud Williams.
    Edgefield Judgements 1802

BUCHANAN, SAMUEL--Heir of Philip Jennings. See Jennings card.
    Edgefield Rec. Bk. B-185 1850

BUCKELEW, FREDERICK--Wit. deed 4 Oct. 1785. Edgefield Deed 5-174

BUCKELEW, GARRETT--Petit Juror Edgefield 1789. List 15
    -GEORGE--Petit Juror Edgefield 1788. List 12

BUCKELEW, JAMES--Petit Juror Edgefield 1788 List 10 and 18
    -Same card. Stray paper 10 June 1842--Orphan's Court held in
    Chambers Co.Ala.--Sarah Buckelew, widow of Wm. Buckelew applied
    for Gdnship of her children to wit: Robert F., Benj. W., Wm. D.,
    Susannah I., and Seaborn B. Buckelew. Surety: Abner Buckalew

BUCKELEW, JAMES--Default in Road work. See Lodwick Hill. Edgefield
    Ct. Min. March 1795

BUCKELEW, WILLIAM--Dec'd. R. E. Sold 1841. Edgefield Rec. Bk. B-27
    Dist: Widow: Sarah 1/3 $26.50
            Abner A. and Nancy A. Buckelew 1/7 of 2/3 moved
            to Alabama.
            Benj. W., Robert F., William D., Susan I., and
            Seaborn Buckelew 1/7 of 2/3 each

BUCKHALTER, JOHN--Petit Juror Edgefield 1786. List 3

BUCKHALTER, JOHN--Son in law of John Elam-Will 1824. Edgefield
    Gr. Children: James, Tandy, Christina E., Polly, Elizabeth,
              Martha, Susannah and Martin Buckhalter

BUCKHALTER, MICHAEL--Grand Juror Edgefield 1786. List 5 and 8

BUCKHOLTZ, JOHN and wife--Heirs of estate of Michael Blocker. See
    Blocker card. Edgefield Rec. Bk. A-14

BUFFINGTON, MARY--Dec'd. R. E. Sold 22 Oct. 1832. Edgefield Sale Bk.
Dist: James Jones and wife 1/6 $55.35   A-60
Elizabeth, Joseph, James, Henry, and Mary Buffington-same.
Rec't 12 March 1833 by James Shelby-Gdn. for shares of James and
Henry. Joseph Hearst--Purchaser at $320.00 and appears transferred
to Jas. S. Jeter or he pd. the money to the Ord. on 22 Oct. 1832

BUFFINGTON, PETER--Dec'd. S. May, Adm'r. Inv. returned. Edgefield
Ct. Min. March 1795. Jan. Ct. 1795-Per. estate to be sold 29th
inst. at his late dwelling.
-Peter Buffington, Dec'd.--Widow, Mrs. Buffington relinquished her
right of administration in favor of Samuel Mays and Rydon Grigsby
Bond 150 pounds. S: Russell Watson and Wm. Butler
Appr's. Apt'd.: John Moseley, Joseph Moseley, Simon Brooks and
Dannett (or Daniel) Abney.

BUFFINGTON, WILLIAM H.--Dec'd. R. E. Sold 1832. Edgefield Sale Bk. A-134
Dist: Elizabeth Buffington, widow--½
James Jones -w- Matilda 1/6 of ½ $29.63½
Hester Buffington -m- Wm. Jones or James
Joseph, James, Henry, and Mary-minors. Brothers and sisters
of half-blood to dec'd. each 1/6 of ½

BUIST, JAMES K. -w- Amanda--Heirs estate of William Ferguson. See
Ferfuson card. Edgefield Rec. Bk. B-208 1851

BUIST, PETER--Petit Juror Edgefield 1786. List 5. (Possibly Burt)

BULLOCK, DANIEL--Surety Adm. Bond estate of Pleasant Burnett, Dec'd.
See Burnett card. Edgefield Ct. Min. Oct. 1794

BULLOCK, HANNAH to Berry Watson 6 Dec. 1797 350 pounds sterling
for slaves, horses, etc. Wit: William Ogilvie, James Ogilvie
Edgefield Deed 14-506

BULLOCK, DANIEL to Thomas Bullock 7 May 1812 and 15 Aug. 1812--slaves
and 1000 acres land on Turkey Creek. Deed 31-352. (Thomas is son)
-Daniel Bullock -w- Hannah to son, David Bullock-Deed gift of land.
18 Oct. 1817. To dau. Mary Wooten-land after death of her mother.
Ch. of Mary Wooten: Mary, Martha J., John. Thos. Bullock, Tr.
Edgefield Deed Bk. 34-304
Book 38 Pg. 201 recites: John Bullock, dec'd. Will bequeathed to
children of Daniel and Jane Bullock. Daniel is living on the land.
His son: Daniel Bullock, Jr. conv. his interest to Zachariah
S. Bullock 1 March 1820. No dower.
Page 132--Daniel Bullock to his children: Zach'h, Daniel, Jr., Lucy
Deed Bk 40-268 Daniel -w- Hannah Dower 1822

BULLOCK, DANIEL--To wife, Hannah to have for life the 2 slaves "I have
given to my two daughters, Martha and Rachel Canfield. 7 Sept. 1824
Pg. 510 shows wives of James and Joseph Canfield. Hannah-formerly
widow of Burdett Eskridge-Pg. 3. Deed Bk. 2. See Eskridge card.

BULLOCK, ELIZABETH AND REBECCA--Nieces of John G. Slappy-Will 1830

BULLOCK, JOHN--Grand Juror Edgefield 1786 List 3, 8, and 14

BUNTING, BENJAMIN--Will 1823. Edgefield

BUNTING, RUTH--Dau. of Amos Richardson-Will 1809. Legacy--Land
where Benj. Bunting lives. Gr. dau. Eliza Bunting. Gr. son-
Isaac Bunting. Gr. dau.- Frances Bunting

BURCKHALTER, ELAM -w- Nancy--Heirs of Benjamin Doolittle. See
Doolittle card. Edgefield Rec. Bk. A-209 1835

BURDELL, JESSE--Letter from Henry Hart of Tennessee--"Jesse Burdell
has lately returned from the Creek Country".. See card James
Hart, dec'd. Edgefield Rec. Bk. A-110 1833

BURDEN, ABRAHAM -w- Elizabeth--Heirs of Valentine Young. See Young
card. Edgefield Rec. Bk. B-19

BURGES, AGNESS--Dau. of Charles Partin-Will 1796-Rec'd. 1813 Edgefield

BURGESS, JOHN--Will 1829. Edgefield

BURGESS, SAMUEL--Grand Juror Edgefield 1786. List 5,6, and 13

BURGESS, SAMUEL--All Legatees of John Joacam Tobler-Will 1810
Ann -w- Jiles Bowers
John Burgess
Samuel Burgess
Elizabeth -w- John Bush

BURK, JAMES AND WILLIAM--Orphan boys--On motion of Burges White, John
Frazier, Sam'l Landrum and Jeremiah Hatcher--ordered the two
orphans be bound out as apprentices. Edgefield Ct. Min. Oct. 1794

BURKHALTER, MARY--Dau. of John Fleke-Will 1798. Gr. son-John Burkhalter

BURKS, DAVID--Petit Juror Edgefield 1788. List 11 and 16
-Deed Bk. 3-245--David Burks -w- Jean conv. 3 Jan. 1788--Land on
Horn's Creek.

BURKS, JEAN -w- David Burks--Dower favor Drury Mims. Oct. Ct. 1787
Edgefield Min. Bk.

BURNET, ALEXANDER--Petit Juror 1787. Edgefield List 6

BURNETT, JEREMIAH and wife--Heirs of Marian Adams-1842. See Adams
card. Edgefield Rec. Bk. B-61

BURNETT, JOHN -w- Rhoda--Heirs of Catherene Butter. See Butter card.
(Possibly Butler). Edgefield Rec. Bk. A-298 1838

BURNETT, LURANY--Her children Legatees of Hezekiah Gentry-Will 1820

BURNETT, MARY--Dau. of Richard Quarles, Sen'r.-Will 1796. Edgefield

BURNETT, PLEASANT -w- Mary--Heirs of Sarah Dodgen. See Dodgen card.
Edgefield Rec. Bk. A-262

BURNETT, PLEASANT--See Will of Anna Tees-1827. She calls him "son"
   -Pleasant Burnett-Dec'd. Hezekiah Gentry appl'd. for Letters of
   Administration. S: Daniel Bullock and Dennett Abney. Appr's.
   Elijah Weatherington, James Nichols, Valentine Cowley, Anthony
   Leach.
   -Jan. Ct. 1795--Inv. Estate of Pleasant Burnett Ret'd.--Order to
   sell Personal property at House of Hezekiah Gentry 4th Mon. Jan.

BURNS, FRANCES--Former widow.--Heir of estate of Abraham Cruise. See
   Cruise card. Edgefield Rec. Bk. A-24 1825

BURNS, SARAH--Oldest dau. of John Oliphant-Will 1815. Edgefield
   -Sarah Burns--Sister of William Oliphand-Will 1827. Her children:
   William, John and Nancy Burns

BURRESS, ELIZABETH--Dau. of William Elam-Will 1805. Wife of John
   Burress. Edgefield

BURRELL, CRADOCK--Commissioned to build bridge. See card Abram Ardis.
   Edgefield Ct. Min. Oct. 1794
   -Cradock Burrell--Adm'r Estate of John Beddingfield, Dec'd. See
   Beddingfield card. Edgefield Ct. Min. Oct. 1794

BURRIS, SARAH--Dec'd. dau. of Ann Conner-Will 1824. Edgefield

BURT, FRANCIS--Justice of Quorum for Edgefield took dower of Nancy
   Gayle -w- John Gayle who sold lot in Sumterville. Dower 9 Nov. 1802
   Edgefield File Sumter Deed B-20

BURT, FRANCIS--Surety for Eugene Brenan as Gdn. of Miss Sally Dalty.
   Edgefield Ct. Min. Jan. 1795
   -Frances Burt-Dau. of Samuel Goode-Will 1800. Edward Burt, Exor.

BURT, MARY--Mother of Elizabeth Scott-Will 1831. Edgefield

BURTS, CATEY, SUKEY--Daus. of Aquila Miles-Will 1797. Exor's: Frank
   Burt, Harvard Burt, Philip Burt.

BURT, MATTHEW--Dec'd. Francis Burt one of Exor's. made return and
   Invoice. Francis Burt--Adm'r. of Moody Burt, Dec'd.--returned
   accounting of the sales of the crop.Edgefield Ct. Min. Oct. 1794
   -Same card: March Ct. 1795--Philip Burt one of Exor's. of Matthew
   Burt qualified as such.
   -March Ct. 1795--Robert Burt discharged as Security--Est. of James
   Coody, minor. See Coody card.

BURT, ARMSTED--Will 7 Aug. 1839

BURTON, ALLEN Y.--Will 4 June 1839 Edgefield

BURTON, JOHN--Grand Juror Edgefield 1787 List 6

BURTON, ROBERT--Surety for John Simkins as Gdn. of Miss Sally Dalty.
   Edgefield Ct. Min. Jan. 1795
   -Robert Burton -w- Martha--Heirs of Solomon Cox. See Cox card.
   Edgefield Rec. Bk. B-117 1846

BURTON, SARAH--Wife of Robert Burton--Legatees of Arthur Simlins-Will 182

BURTON, TABITHA--Gr. dau. of Elizabeth M. Ray-Will 1817. Edgefield
"and William Burton's four youngest children".

BUSH, AMOS and wife--Heirs of John Quarles. See Quarles card.
Edgefield Rec. Bk. B-73 1842

BUSH, BIBBY--Overseer of road from Lee's Bridge to the Pine House, that
part from his house to Christian Gomillian's in the room of Elisha
Barrinton--Excused.
William Bush--Oversear of road from the Court House to the Ridge.
That part from Brazil's to James Barrinton's--in the room of Adam
Stalnaker, excused. Edgefield Ct. Min. March 1795
Jan. Ct. 1795--License to Bibby Bush to keep Tavern. S: Frederick
Swearingen, John Williams

BUSH, ELIZABETH--Dau. of Thomas Deleach-Will 1810

BUSH, ELIZABETH -w- John Bush, and dau. of Samuel Burgess. Legatee
of John Joacam Tobler-Will 1810. Edgefield

BUSH, FEROBY--Dau. of Charles Powell-Will 1813. Rachel Bush another
daughter. Edgefield

BUSH, HERIN -w- Martha--Heirs of Sarah Lott. See Lott card.
Edgefield Rec. Bk. A-138 1833

BUSH, ISAAC--Will 18 March 1836. Edgefield 6
-Isaac Bush-dec'd. R. E. Sold 1836. Edgefield Rec. Bk. A-264/66/68
Dist: Richard Ward and wife   1/5 $243.31
        Mary Swearingen--same
        Susan Watson--same
        Thomas Deloach and wife--same
        John Whitlock and wife ½ of 1/5
        Isaac and Sarah Slaten ½ of 1/5
Receipt Jan. 25, 1838 from H. Winn "In right of my wife, Susan"

BUSH, JOHN--Brother of Nancy Carter-Will 1817 Edgefield
-John Bush--Will 29 Feb. 1844 Edgefield

BUSH, LEWIS -w- Elizabeth Chadwich and) Heirs of Thomas Howle, Sen'r
Levi -w- Nancy   ) Edgefield Rec. Bk. B-90 1845

BUSH, MARY--Dau. of Jacob Miller-Will 1775. Edgefield

BUSH, RICHARD--Petit Juror Edgefield 1787. List 7 and 15

BUSH, SARAH, SEN'R--Legatee of Millie Gillion-Will 1828 Edgefield

BUSH, WILLIAM--Will 18 July 1837. Edgefield
-William Bush -w- Heirs of John Morring. See Morring card.
Edgefield Rec. Bk. B-21 1849

BUSSEY, REV. CHARLES--Personal estate Stephen Glover to be sold at
his home. See Stephen Glover card. Edgefield Ct. Min Oct. 1794

BUSSEY, EDWARD--Petit Juror Edgefield 1787 List 8 and 18

BUSSEY, GEORGE--Petit Juror Edgefield 1786. List 4
        Grand Juror   "   "   " 21 (Sen'r.)

BUSSEY, JOHN--Dec'd. R. E. Sold 1834 Edgefield Rec. Bk A-195
  Dist: Frances Bussey, widow 1/3 $73.62
       Wm. Mallet -w- Caroline 1/4 of 2/3
       Nathan, Charles, and Frances Bussey--same
  Charles and Frances-minors. E. Morgan, Gdn.

BUSSEY, REBEKAH--Dau. of William Hagen-Will 1836 Edgefield 13
  -Rebecca Bussey--Dau. of William Hagens and Legatee of William
  Robertson-Will 1840. Sarah Bussey another dau. Wife of Tadeo Busse

BUSSEY, SUSAN--Dau. of William Robertson, Sen'r.-Will 1838

BUSSEY, SARAH--Dau. of John Bailey-Will 1842

BUTLER, BAHATHALIN -w- Maj. Gen. William Butler. Edgefield Wills 1818
  Sister of William Moore-Will 1818
  Her children: James Moore Butler   Andrew Pickens Butler
                William   "   Pierce Mayson   "
                Francis   "   Leantine   "
                George   "   Emily   "
  Wm. Moore left to George Butler land below Saluda, Old Town Branch
  which runs in river just below Flat Landing,"my present dwelling
  place". Bd. by Coleman Bladen and Patrick Mosely Walton. Pierce
  Mayson Butler got part of same plantation.

BUTLER, CATHERINE--Dau. Rachel -m- Wm. Adams. See Levi Adams card.
  Edgefield Rec. Bk. A-298   1838

BUTLER, CATHERINE--Dec'd. R. E. Sold 1838 Edgefield Rec. Bk. A-298
  Dist: David Butler   Edward Osborn -w- Nancy
       David Johnson -w- Elizabeth Milton Perkins -w- Catherine
       John Johnson -w- Alcy   Nancy Waits
       Henry Butler   Jane Butler
       Thomas Butler   Rachel Butler
       John Barnett -w- Rhoda   James Butler
       John Butler   Morris Fowler -w- Mary
  All received same share, 1/14 equal to $6.97. Receipt from Asa
  Fowler for shares of several heirs as agent.

BUTLER, ELIZABETH--Dau. of John Clacker-Will 1814 Edgefield

BUTLER, ELIZABETH--Dau. of James Goggins-Will 1843. Edgefield

BUTLER, FANNY--Dec'd. R. E. Sold 1841. Edgefield Rec. Bk. B-37
  Dist: Reuben Carpenter
       Reuben Carpenter and wife
       Martha Grisam
       Rhody Harris--Order to pay to her daughter, Nancy Harris
       Nancy Mosely
       Anna Danner
  Relationship to dec'd. not shown

BUTLER, JAMES--Dec'd. R. E. Sold 25 Feb. 1833. Sale Bk. A-124
    Widow--since dec'd
    John Butler--also since dec'd. Left widow and 6 children
    Heirs of Anthony Butler: John, Winny, Abner, Seth, Anna, James
        and Betsy--each received 1/7 of 1/6
    Heirs of Rebecca Valentine: Thomas Shaw and Jno Harrison ½ of 1/6
    Henry Waldrun and children:
        James Waldrun
        Nancy, Charles, William and Jno Waldrun
        Joseph Addison and wife
        Benjamin Addison and wife
        James Armstrong and wife
        Charles Limbeck and wife
        Edward Moseley and wife
    Rec't. S. W. Gardner -w- Elizabeth and from John Harrison for wife
    John Tally right -w- Mary   )
    James W. Moore right -w- Betsy) Heirs of Edward Moseley, Devisee
    John Forrest right -w- Patsy   ) of James Butler
    Anna Tally   )
    Robert Walker right his wife.

BUTLER, SAMUEL -w- JANE--Heirs of Reuben Carpenter. See Carpenter
    card. Edgefield Rec. Bk. B-77-79 1843

BUTLER, SARAH--Dau. of Joseph Morris, Sen'r.Will 1839

BUTLER, MRS. SUSAN ANN--Wife of Col. A. P. Butler died 22 inst. age
    19 years. Edgefield 28 May 1830

BUTLER, THOMAS--Petit Juror Edgefield 1787. List 8, 18, 20

BUTLER, WILLIAM--Grand Juror Edgefield 1786. List 4, 10, and 16

BUTLER, WILLIAM -w- MARY--Heirs of Presley Sullivan. See Sullivan card.
    Edgefield Rec. Bk. A-213 1835

BUTLER, WILLIAM--Will 20 Sept. 1839 Edgefield

BUZZEL, THOMAS--Petit Juror Edgefield 1787. List 8

CABANESS, LUCY--Dau. of Henry Kay-Will 1810

CAHILL, WILLIAM--Dec'd. R. E. Sold 1850 Edgefield Rec. Bk-B-178
    Dist: Bridgett Cahill, widow 1/3 of estate $143.08
        Richard, Thomas, Margaret, Paul, Catharine, William
        each received 1/6 of 2/3 of estate.

CALDWELL, ELIZABETH--Dau. of John Williams-Will 1794. Wm. Caldwell
    seems her husband. Edgefield

CALHOUN, ALEXANDER--Son in law of James Johnson-Will 1811. Gr. dau.
    Catherine Calhoun. Edgefield

CALHOUN, JOHN--Named as one of children of Eliza Hannah Simkins-Will 1837

CALHOUN, SUSAN--Dau. of Andrew Pickens-Will 1834. Wife of James Calhoun

CALLIHAN, JOHN--Petit Juror Edgefield 1788. List 9

CALLIHAN, MORRIS--Dec'd. R. E. Sold 1835. Edgefield Rec. Bk. A-229

Dist: William Callihan
William Kimbell -w- Sarah
Wilkerson Callihan
Joseph Summerlin -w- Mary
Wiley Collins -w- Jane
James Callihan (John Key, Gdn.)
John Callihan
Edmund Callihan

Name also spelled
Calliham

All received 1/8 of
estate.

CAMPBELL, JAMES--Petit Juror Edgefield 1789. List 15

CAMPBELL,MACARTAN--Dec'd. of Chatham Co. Georgia. Edgefield File
Widow: Sarah   Deed Bk 34 Page 1
Maria -w- Dr. Lemuel Killock
Sarah -w- Noble W. Jones
Edward F. Campbell   Plantation on Horse Creek
Martha G. Campbell   Deed 18 March 1795
Harriet Campbell

CAMPBELL, MARTIN--Father of Hellen Fitch, niece of Francis McCartan-
Will 1768. Son: McCartan Campbell. C. T. Wills

CANADA, JOHN--Petit Juror Edgefield 1788. List 11

CANADA, WHITTY--Child (son or dau?) of Elles Palmer-Will 1800

CANNON, MRS. ELEANOR--Sacred to the memory of Mrs. Eleanor Cannon who
departed this life on 2nd day of June 1829. Age 50 years.
Little Stevens Creek Baptist Church, Edgefield

CANNON, JOHN--Of Edgefield Co. to son, Wm. Cannon, born 8 May 1785
gift of goods received in -m- with Lucy Hatcher, widow of Benj.
Hatcher. Wit: Lud Williams and Sophia Harris. UU-451 Edgefield
Same card--Henry Cannon-Commissioned as Coroner Darlington Dist.
21 Mar. 1801.

CANNON, ROBERT A. -w- H. B.--Lost son, Allie on 2 Dec. 1864 age 9 mos.
Edgefield Adv.

CANNON, WILLIAM -w- Winefred--Heirs of Robert Rebuck. See Rebuck card.
Edgefield Equity Bill 30 1801

CANNON, WILLIAM H.--Dec'd. R. E. Sold 1851 Edgefield Rec. Bk B-215
Dist: Thomas Allawine -w- Margaret
Eli A. Cannon
Martha Ann -m- William Rish
George Cannon
J. A Cannon
David Cannon, father of dec'd. of Newberry Dist.
Each received 1/6 of estate. $26.70

CARLING, GEORGE--Dec'd. R. E. Sold 1 Feb. 1834. Edgefield Sale Bk A-42
    Dist: John Overstreet -w- 1/3 $2.51
           Mary Caroline   2/3 $5.03
    1829-1835--Receipt on page 88 Bk-2 shows John Overstreet married
    the widow. Peter Jumperd-Gdn. of minor. Receipt 5 Oct. 1835
    from Tarlton McClendon for share of his wife, Mary Caroline.

CARLTON, MOURNING--Dau. of Hezekiah Gentry-Will 1820

CARPENTER, ISHAM--Dec'd. R. E. Sold 1846. Edgefield Rec. Bk-B-199
    Dist: Nancy Carpenter, the widow 1/3 $143.00
           John Carpenter-a minor   1/3)
           Owen Carpenter-a minor   1/3) Gdn. Marion Coleman
    Rec't. 1 Feb. 1851 by Nancy Coleman for her share.

CARPENTER, MARY--Dau. of Reuben Carpenter married James Gray and
    moved to Mississippi. See Gray card. Edgefield Rec. Bk B 1843

CARPENTER, REUBEN and wife--Distributees of estate of Fanny Butter or
    Butler, dec'd. See card. Edgefield Rec. Bk B-37 1841

CARPENTER, REUBEN--Dec'd. R. E. Sold 1843. Edgefield Rec. Bk. 77/79
    Dist: Samuel Butler -w- Jane 1/9 $62.16
           Thomas and Reuben Carpenter-same
           James Gray -w- Mary of Chickosaw Co. Ala.-same
           Samuel Stalnaker -w- Abigail-same
           George Hancock -w- Elizabeth-same
           Martha Carpenter-same
           Heirs of Ellen Bardon: Thomas S. and _____ Barden-same
           Heirs of Frances Hill: Mary Ann and Unity Hill-same
           Rebecca Carpenter, widow--$55.95 her share
    Page 79--same estate and same heirs but different lands.

CARSON, HUGH--Petit Juror Edgefield 1786. List 3
    -James-   "   "   "   "   "   5

CARSON, JAMES--Dec'd. Edgefield Min. Bk. Pg-271. Oct. Ct. 1789
    Citation returned and John Gorman apt'd. Adm'r.
    -James Carson--Legatee of James Hollingsworth-Will 1818. Sarah
    Carson is daughter.
    -James, Thomas and Sarah Carson--Heirs of William Bladen.
    Edgefield Rec. Bk. A-258 1837

CARSON, SAMUEL--Dec'd. Edgefield Min. Bk. Pg 255. 14 July 1789
    Ordered citation issue to show cause why John Gorman should not
    be granted Adm.

CARSON, WILLIAM--Petit Juror Edgefield 1786. List 5
    -William Carson--Will 5 Jan. 1842. Edgefield

CARTER, BENJAMIN--Gr 2 Feb. 1735. Died intestate. Eldest son-Henry
    and wife, Elizabeth. Land conveyed 6/7 March 1765 to son.
    Henry Whetstone-men. Page 59 men. of Robert Carter's Gr. on
    N. Br. of Black River. Gr. 1 Aug. 1758.Archives Dept. Mem 9-463

CARTER, DANIEL, SEN'R, JOHN JR., AND WILLIAM JR.--Wit. Will of
    Jacob Earnest 22 May 1824. Edgefield

CARTER, DUDLEY--Petit Juror Edgefield 1788   List 9

CARTER, ELIZABETH--Dau. of Henry Tate-Will 1836.   Amanda M. Carter
   another dau.
   -Elizabeth Carter--Sister of Rachel Wise-Will 1842

CARTER, ENOCH -w- Nancy and Wm. and L. G. Carter--Heirs of Abney Mays.
   See Mays card. Edgefield Rec. Bk. B-192 1850

CARTER, JANE--Dau. of Pleasent Thurmone-Will 1830

CARTER, JOHN, JR. and wife--Heirs of Sugar I Matthews. See Matthews
   card. Edgefield Rec. Bk. A-38 1831

CARTER, LYDIA--Dau. of Alexander Edmunds-Will 1821. Also wife of
   William Clark
   -Lydia Clark and child--Heirs of Lydia Edmunds and of John Cogburn.
   See Cogburn card. Edgefield Rec. Bk. A-225 1834

CARTER, MARY B.--Dau. of Mrs. Wormley. See Wormley card. Edgefield
   rec. Bk. B-71

CARTER, NANCY--Dau. of Bibby Bush-Will 1812. Edgefield
   -Nancy Carter, Dec'd. Edgefield Wills A-379
            Dau. in law: Charlotte Carter
            Dau: Mary, Loving, and Nancy Carter
            Son: William Carter
            Dau: Sarah Carter
            Bro: John Bush   Will 29 May 1817 Rec'd 18 July 1817

CARTER, PHEBE--Dau. of Joseph Bishop-Will 1802

CARTER, REBECCA--Dau. of William Ogle-Will Rec'd 1803. Gr. son: Wm.Carte:

CARTER, ROBERT--Dec'd. Abbeville 96 Dist. Rec.--"John Sharp and Patty
   his wife, took a citation from John Thomas, Esq. (Ord. of 96 Dist.)
   on the estate of Robert Carter, late of said District, dec'd, as
   next of kin. The same certified by the Rev. Arthur Muhlin, was
   read and published after Divine Service 27 Sept. 1786." Granted
   Letters Administration 21 Oct. 1786.

CARTER, SAMUEL--Apt'd and qualified as Constable for Edgefield Co.
   Also--S: for John Adams-Tavern Keeper. See Adams card.
   Edgefield Ct. Min. Oct. 1794

CARTER, SARAH--Dau. of Reuben Cooper-Will 1824. Edgefield

CARTER, SARAH--Dec'd dau. of Elizabeth Cooper-Will 1831

CARTER, THOMAS--Petit Juror Edgefield 1786   List 1 and 2
                  Grand   "   "   "   " 21

CARTER, MAJOR THOMAS--Dec'd. 24 Jan. 1802 Edgefield A-504 Bx-35 Pk-1305
   Present: Col. John Carter
   Witnessed by: Freeman Hardy, Adrah Howard, and Sarah Gentry
   Legatees: "All my children".   (Nuncupative Will)

CARTER, THOMAS -w- Margaret--Distributees of estate of James Bradfield
   See Bradfield card. Edgefield Rec. Bk. A-316 1839

CARTLEDGE, EDMOND--Of Edgefield. Deed gift. Hist. Com. Misc. F-357
   To Dau. in law: Margaret Cartledge
   Gr. Children: Malcomb, Joseph and Sarah Ann Cartledge
   Plantation "I now live on". S W Stevens Creek. Samuel Cartledge
   and John Tompkins, Trustees. 31 Oct. 1825. Reserved life estate
   to himself.

CARTLEDGE, EDMUND and wife--Heirs of Ebenezer Hill. See Hill card.
   Edgefield Rec. Bk. A-280 1837

CARTLEDGE, JOSIAH--Dec'd Edgefield Sale Bk. A-3
   Dist: Sarah Cartledge, widow 1/3 $204.33
       Samuel, Joshua V., Elizabeth A., William J., Mary Ann--
   1/5 share each
   Receipt from John and Sarah Addison for $204.33. Widow evidently
   married again.

CARTLEDGE, MARGARET--Dau. of Joseph Cunningham-Will 1825. Wife of
   E. J. Cartledge. Legacy: Samuel Cartledge, Jr. Also dau: Sarah
   Cartledge. Exor: Samuel Cartledge. Edgefield
   -Margaret and Sarah Cartledge--Daughters of Sarah Cunningham Will
   1841. Edgefield

CAREY, ANN--Wife of Wm. Carey and dau. of David Bowers-Will 1833

CAREY, WILLIAM H.--Bro-in-law of Thomas G. Lamar-Will 1830
   -William Carey--Will 1 April 1836. Edgefield 17

CASON, MARY--Dau. of Joseph Tolbert.-Will 1793

CASON, WILLIAM--Petit Juror Edgefield 1790. List 11

CATER FILE--Edgefield Wills 20 March 1812. Will of Bibby Bush
   Wife: Mary Bush   Son: John William Bush
   Son: Richard Bush   Arthur Sacher Bush
   Dau: Phereby Bush   Dau: Nancy Carter

CATTONET, PETER--Mentioned as Judgement creditor of John J. Gray-
   Will 1838. Edgefield

CAWDREY, WILLIAM D.--Nephew of Washington Bostick-Will 1817

CAWLEY, ABNER--Petit Juror 1794 Edgefield List 20

CAWLEY, R.--Petit Juror Edgefield 1794. List 20

CAWLEY, VALENTINE--App'r. estate of Pleasent Burnett, dec'd. See
   Burnett card. Edgefield Ct. Min. Oct. 1794

CENTER, SAMUEL--Overseer Road from the Widow West's to the inter-
   section of the Chas'n road. From Lee's Bridge to Cloud Creek--
   in room of William Ethridge-excused.

CHADWICK, ELIZABETH and her heirs--Heirs of Thomas Howle, Sen'r. See
   Howle card. Edgefield Rec. Bk. B-99 1845 (about)

CHADWICK, JOHN AND WILLIAM--Heirs of Thomas Howle. See Howle card
    Edgefield Rec. Bk. A-286 1838

CHADWICK, LAZARUS--Dec'd R. E. Sold. Edgefield Sale Bk. A-86
    Distributees--1/12 each or $28.80
    James Chadwick--Rec't 17 Jan. 1831
    Terrill Goff -w- Lucy--Rec't 10 Aug. 1831
    Jno Chadwick
    Rachel Chadwick--Rec't 4 Aug. 1832
    Edmund Chadwick--Rec't 17 Jan. 1831
    Robert Chadwick
    Thomas E. Tanner and wife
    Sarah Chadwick--Rec't 10 Aug. 1831
    Lively Chadwick--Rec't 10 Aug. 1831
    Jas. Peak and wife
    Stephen Chadwick--affidavit that he is 21 years of age. Not dated.

CHADWICK, STALY--Gr. dau. of Esther Howle-Will 1840. Also Esther
    Chadwick.

CHADWICK--See Shadwick

CHADWICK, WILLIAM and wife--Heirs of estate of Presley S. Dagnal. See
    Dagnal card. Edgefield Rec. Bk. A-272 1837

CHAMBERLON, SARAH--Sister of Joseph Day-Will 1789

CHANDLER, JOEL--Petit Juror Edgefield 1787. List 6
    -Joel Chandler--Surety on Bond West Harris-Tavern Keeper. See
    Harris card. Edgefield Ct. Min. March 1795

CHANEY, BAILEY -w- Sarah--Distributees estate of Joseph Barton. See
    Barton card. Edgefield Rec. Bk. A-296 1838

CHANEY, JOHN--Petit Juror Edgefield 1788 List 10
            Grand Juror   "   "   "   12 and 20

CHAPMAN, BARTHENY--Dec'd. and her children; John, Mary, and Caroline
    Heirs of Philip Jennings. See Jennings card. Edgefield Rec.
    Bk. B-185 1850

CHAPMAN, ELIZABETH--Dau. of Joshua Martin-Will 1827. Edgefield

CHAPMAN, WILLIAM--Dec'd. R. E. Sold 1833. Rec. Bk. A-160 Edgefield
    Dist: Wm. Powers -w- Elizabeth 1/3 $7.00
           Elijah M. Chapman 1/7 of 2/3 $2.00
           Moses Chapman-same
           Jno Rogers -w- Mary Ann-same
           William Chapman-same
           Geo. W. Reynolds -w- Elizabeth-same
           Joseph Chapman-same
           Jacob Chapman-same
    Elijah Chapman and Geo. Reynolds -w- Elizabeth of Henry Co. Ga.

CHAPPELL--See Will of Amos Banks-1842-who had son Thomas Chappell Banks

CHAPPELL, CAROLINE ANN wife of Thomas H. Chappell who died June 22, 1858. Age 29 years.
Tomb beside above: To the "Infant children of Thomas H. and Caroline Ann Chappell".
Little Stevens Creek Baptist Church, Edgefield

CHAPPEL, THOMAS--Petit Juror Edgefield 1786. List 1 and 2

CHATTEEN, PETER--Petit Juror Edgefield 1786. List 4

CHENEY, JAMES--Dec'd. John Cheney, Adm'r. Returns made and acc'ts filed. Edgefield Ct. Min. Jan. 1795

CHENEY, ROBERT, JOHN, BETSY--96 Dist. Rec. Index

CHENEY, DAVID--Of Granville--Will 13 Dec. 1762 Edgefield File.   C. T.
Sister: Mary McCleland -w- James MacCleland   Wills
Wit: Thomas Wire, Richard Cole, Benjamin Degard

CHEATHAM, CAROLINE--Gr. Dau. of Pleasent Thurmond-Will 1830 Edgefield
Dau. Elizabeth Cheatham
Gr. Dau. Elizabeth Thurmone-Will 1804

CHEATHAM, JOHN--Will 3 Sept. 1840 Edgefield

CHEATHAM, JOHN -w- Mary--Heirs of estate of Francis Bird. See Bird card. Edgefield Rec. Bk. B-137   1848

CHEATHAM, SARAH--Dau. of Ann Maria Terry-Will 1823 Edgefield

CHEATHAM, SUSANNAH--Dau. of Josiah Langley-Will 1826

CHILDS, JOHN--Grand Juror Edgefield 1786 List 4, 8, and 16
-WILLIAM--Grand Juror Edgefield 1786 List 5, 12, and 16

CHRISTEE, EMILY--Dau. of Presley Bland-Will 1839

CHRISTIE, ROBERT--Petit Juror 1786 Edgefield List 3

CHRISTIE, SUSANNAH-Will 10 Aug. 1842

CHRISTIAN, JESSE--Will 13 Oct. 1836

CHRISTIE, JOHN and wife--Heirs of Sugar I. Mathews. See Mathews card. Edgefield Rec. Bk. A-38 1831

CHRISTIAN, JOHN--Heirs of Sugar I Matthews. See Matthews card. Edgefield Rec. Bk. A-38 1831

CHRISTIAN, SAMUEL and wife, Rebecca--Heirs of John Kay. See Kay card Edgefield Rec. Bk. B- 1849

CHRISTMAS, MARY--Sister of William Robertson-Will 1840

CHRISTMAS, RICHARD--Apt'd Overseer on the Martin Road from Coody's Old Mill to Mat. Martin's. Edgefield Ct. Min. Oct. 1794

CLACKLER, JOHN, JR.--Petit Juror Edgefield 1787 List 6 and 18

CLACKSTON, LYNN CELIA--Dau. of John B. Bush-Will 1844

CLAIG, ELIZABETH--Gr. dau. of Wm. Holloway--Will 1838

CLARKLER, MARY -w- John Clarkler and dau. of Jacob Fudge, Sen'r.--Will
     1789. (name possibly Clackler)

CLARK, DR. ADAM--Heir Lucy T. Moore-Will 1856. Edgefield Wills Bx-178

CLARK, DAVID--Petit Juror Edgefield 1788 List 11

CLARK, ELIZABETH--Heir of Jesse Stone. See Stone card. Edgefield
     Rec. Bk. B-45 1842
     -Elizabeth Clark, Heir of Philip Lightfoot. See Lightfoot card.
     Edgefield Rec. Bk. B-65 1842
     -Elizabeth Clark--Dec'd. R. E. Sold 1849 Rec. Bk. B-191
     Dist: Philip , Ellington, and Jesse Clark 1/5 $65.80 each
            Jesse Wallace -w- Frances--same
            Westby Reynolds -w- Elizabeth--same

CLARK, HENRY--Will 8 April 1840 Edgefield

CLARK, JOHN, ESQ.--To adm. cow and 2 calves tolled by Nath'l Howel
     Edgefield Ct. Min. Oct. 1794
     -John Clark-Dec'd. Heirs: James Maynard and wife
                        Denny and Ellen Clark-James Maynard-Gdn.
     Edgefield Box 7 Pkg. 219 1822
     -John Clark, Dec'd. Edgefield Sale Bk. A-5 1827
          Dist: Mary -w- James Maynard
                 Ellen Clark
                 Caleb Walton and wife 1/3 each
     Receipt 21 June 1830 fos portion of Toliver Towlen -w- Ellen

CLARK, MILBURY--Step dau. Aaron Etheredge-Will 1811. Also dau. Josiah
     Allen. Edgefield

CLARK, MOSES-Gdn. Jane Hearst   ) Edgefield Rec. Bk. A-260 1837
       JAMES-Gdn. Elizabeth Hearst) Minor children of Silas Hearst,
       AARON-Gdn. Claresy Hearst) Dec'd. See Hearst card.

CLARK, MRS. ZILPHY -w- of ____? Dower favor Samuel Walker.
     Edgefield Min. Bk. Oct. 1788

CLARKE, ANN--Sister of Ulric Tobler-Will. Her dau: Helena Howell and
     her children. Her dau: Margaret Reddick and her children.

CLARKE, FRANCES--wife of Alexander Clarke-Heirs of John Morring. See
     Morring card. Edgefield Rec. Bk. B-21 1841

CLARKE, ULRICA B.-son John Clark. Legatee of Ulric Tobler-Will 1815

CLARKSON, LUCY--Heir of Mary Ann Moreton. See Moreton card. Edgefield
     Rec. Bk. A-90 1825

CLARKSON, LUCY--Heir of Wm. R. Moreton. See card. Edgefield Bk. A-98
                                                              1831

CLARY, DANIEL--Dec'd. R. E. Sold 1838 Edgefield Rec. Bk. A-288
      Dist: William Clary 1/6 $45.30
             Wiley Clary-same
             Jordan Hurst -w- Martha-same--Of Upson Co. Georgia
             Ira E. Clary-same--Minor
             Nancy Clary-same--George W. Ray, Gdn.
             Martha W. Clary-same

CLARY, VACHEL -w- Mary--Citation issued for them to appear in court
      in regard estate of Jacob Brooks. See Brooks card. Edgefield
      Min. Bk. 1789

CLAXTON, THOMAS -w- Rebecca--Distributees estate Hezekiah Almon, Sen'r.
      See Almon card. 1830. Edgefield Rec. Bk. A-62

CLEARLING, JAMES--Dec'd. Rene Clearling, Adm. Return made. Edgefield
      Ct. Min. Jan. 1795

CLEGG, JACOB--Dec'd. R. E. Sold (no date) Edgefield Sale Bk. A-46
      Dist: Uticey Clegg 1/3 $28.83
             Holloway, Peggy, Eliza, Louisa, and Abner Clegg 1/5 of
             2/3 each. $11.53. Wm. Holloway, Adm. Rec. 11 Sept. 1829

CLEMENT, OBEDIAH--Edgefield Wills A-171   2 March 1799
      Wife: Sarah
      "my children": ?
      Wit: Simon Clement, Di Clement, Stephen Clement, Wm. Strom

CLEMENT, PHENIAH--Son in law of Leana Jones-widow-Thos. Jones-Will 1822

CLERK, JAMES--Dec'd. Adm. gr. to Margaret Clerk. Bond 100 pounds
      S: Thomas Adams. Edgefield 13 April 1789. Min. Bk. page 249

CLERK, JOHN--Grand Juror Edgefield 1786. List 4, 8, and 14

CLERK, LEWIS--Petit Juror Edgefield 1787. List 6, 12, 20

CLERK, LEWIS--Dec'd. Invoice recorded. Edgefield Ct. Min. Mar. 1795
      Jan. Ct. 1795: Will of Lewis Clark proved by oaths of Ben Clark
      and Joseph Walker, Buckner Blalock, and Silphe Clark. Qual. as
      Exor's. Appr's: Shadrack Deas, John Blalock, Isaac Goreman and
      V. Swearingen.

CLERK, WILLIAM, SEN'R.--Petit Juror Edgefield 1787. List 17 and 7

CLEVELAND, MRS MILLA -w- Jacob Cleveland. Dower favor John and Benj.
      Ryan. July Ct. 1786. Edgefield

CLEVELAND, RICE--His heirs Legatees of John Cogburn-Will 1810

CLISBY, JOHN -w- Emily D. (nee Hughes) of Alabama--Heirs of Mary
      Tillman. See Tillman card. Edgefield Rec. Bk. B-103 1846

CLOUD, MARY--Dau. of Phillip Shipe-Will 1817

CLOUD, NOAH--Will 6 July 1834 Edgefield

COATES, JAMES--Son in law of James Scott-Will 1804. Gr. Dau: Elizabeth
      Coates. Edgefield

COATES, JOHN--Dec'd. Edgefield Min. Bk. Pg-155 14 Jan. 1788
"Ordered that citation issue to summons the nearest kin of John
Coates, dec'd--if any do appear next court- otherwise the Admin-
istration will be granted to George Cowan."

COATS, WILLIAM--Son in law of Hendley Webb-Will 1826 Edgefield

COBB, ELIZABETH--Gr. dau. of Catlett Corley-Will 1827. (Gr. has line
through it. Possibly Elizabeth is dau. of Catlett Corley)

COBBS, JAMES, JR.--Grand Juror Edgefield 1794. List 20

COBB, JOHN S. and Jane--mentioned in Will of John Ryan-Will 1827

COBB, NANCY--Dau. of Nathaniel Evans-Will 1824. Edgefield

COBB, THOMAS A.--Will 20 May 1840. Edgefield

COBURN, THOMAS -w- Eleanor--Dist. estate of Joshua Bodie. See Bodie
card. Edgefield Rec. Bk. A-308. 1839

COCHRAN, NANCY--Dau. Elizabeth Miller-Will 1808

COCHRAN, ROBERT--A Commission to build a bridge. See card Abram Ardis.
-Edgefield Ct. Min. Oct. 1794. Robert Cochran Will 5 April 1838

COCK, MARTIN--Brother of Elizabeth Burnett-Will 1820 Edgefield.

COCKAROS, MARY--Dau. of John Still-Will 1797 (name possibly Cochran)

COCKBURN, HANNAH -w- John Cockburn. Dower favor Frederick Tilman.
July Ct. 1787. Edgefield Min. Bk.

COCKBURN, JOHN--Petit Juror Edgefield 1788. List 11

COCKCROFT, SUSANNAH and MARY--Legatees of Elizabeth McCoy-Will 1817
Wit: William Cockcroft and Thomas Cockcroft

COCKEROFF, JOHN--Dec'd. R. E. Sold-tract #3. Edgefield Sale Bk A-26
MARY--Dec'd.
Dist: Each 1/9 share equal to $16.00
Thomas H. Loveless and wife
Benjamin
Henry
Sarah -m- John Martin
Thomas Cockeroft (listed 2nd)
William Rotton -w- Catherine
William, John, and David Cockeroft--minors-Thos. H. Loveless, Gdn.
Rec't. 31 Dec. 1827 from John Martin for share "to which myself
and wife are entitled".
Rec't. 31 Dec. 1829 from Wm. L. Rotton for share "to which myself
and wife are entitled".
Page 28--Sale Tract #4--same heirs.
Rec't from John Martin for self and wife, sarah 31 Dec. 1827
Rec't from B. L. Cockeroft for self and a minor-John 18 Dec. 1830
Page 30--Sale Tract #2--same heirs
Rec't from Wm. L. Rotton -w- Catherine 31 Dec. 1829

COCKEROFF, OGDON--Petit Juror Edgefield 1788. List 11 and 16
-Edgefield Ct. Min. March 1795--Ogdon Cockeroff--Surety for Thos.
Banks as Tavern Keeper.

COCKRAM, BENJAMIN--Dec'd. Edgefield Min. Bk Pg-328 April 1790
"On motion of Sarah Cockram, stating that her husband, Benjamin
Cockram made a Will on the 28th of August last to which Will or
Testament James Gray was a subscribing witness; that the said
Gray hath been applied to, and will not attend Court to prove
aforesaid Will, whereupon, it is ordered that Hugh Middleton, Esq.
oblige the said James Gray by attachment or other legal means to
come before him and give such evidence as he may be able respecting
the execution of the said Will" By Benjamin Cockram and return
the testimony so taken to the next court.

CODLE, DUAN AND JOHN--S: for Paul Abney. See Abney card. Edgefield
Ct. Min. March 1795

COGBURN, HANNAH--Will 14 April 1835

COGBURN, JOHN--App'r estate of Angus McDaniel. See McDaniel card.
Edgefield Ct. Min. March 1795

COGBURN, JOHN--Dec'd. R. E. Sold 1834. Rec. Bk. A-225 Edgefield
Dist: Hannah Cogburn, widow--1/9 equal to $34.40
       John Cogburn
       William Hagins and wife
       Moses Cogburn
       Heirs of Amy Addison, dec'd. to wit: 1/8 of 1/9 each
          Joseph Addison
          Batt Howard and wife
          Benjamin Addison
          George Martin -w- Harriet
          John Addison
          Washington Wise -w- Teresa
          Samuel Addison
          David Addison
       Heirs of Aaron Cogburn, Dec'd. 1/6 of 1/9 each
          Jonathan Tillman -w- Tabitha
          Wright Nicholson -w- Harriet
          John Cogburn
          Benjamin Roper -w- Emily
          Vincent Cogburn
          Hannah Cogburn
       Heirs of David Cogburn, Dec'd. 1/6 of 1/9 each
          Charlotte,   David   Harriet
          John Michael   Eliza   Martha
          Their mother, Margaret Bates, Gdn.
       Heirs of Lydia Edmunds, Dec'd. 1/2 of 1/9 each
          Samuel Edmunds
          Lydia Carter and child
       Heirs of Jesse Cogburn, Dec'd. 1/3 of 1/9 each
          John Lott -w- Charlsey
          Marshal Lott -w- Sarah
          John M. Cogburn.
   Receipt 27 Jan 1835 by Geo. Martin for share of his wife.

COGBURN, LETTY AND ELIZABETH--Dau. of John Cogburn. Legatees of
Elizabeth McCoy-Will 1817 Edgefield

COGBURN, MALACHI -w- Luiza--Heirs of Wiley Posey. Edgefield Rec.
Bk. B-20 1850

COGBURN, SALLEY--Dau. of John Huff-Will 1815

COLE, JANEY--Dau. of Thomas Berry-Will 1819 Edgefield

COLEMAN, AMEY--Dau. of John Bullock-Will 1799

COLEMAN, EDWARD--Provisional Legatee of Matthew Wills-Will 1825. Except
Sarah Black. Edgefield

COLEMAN, ELIZABETH--Heir of Peter Robertson. See Robertson card.
Edgefield Rec. Bk. B-33 1841

COLEMAN, FRANCIS--Dec'd. R. E. Sold 1835. Edgefield Rec. Bk. A-219
Distributees: Ann Coleman, widow--1/3 $192.82
               Thomas Wood -w- Sarah 1/10 of 2/3 $38.56
               Thomas Bleeze -w- Bethany-same
               John Crawford -w- Elizabeth-same
               Heirs of Reuben Lee, dec'd.
                  Ann Lee, Widow--1/3   )1/10of
                     Robert, Bethany, Mary, agnes-each 1/3 of 2/3)2/3
Robert, Jesse, Matilda, Pollard, Orra, and Francis M. Coleman--
Minors--Ann Coleman, Gdn. Each 1/10 of 2/3

COLEMAN, JOHN and wife--Heirs of James O'Gilvie. See O'Gilvie card.
Edgefield Rec. Bk. A-30 1838

COLEMAN, JOHN AND THORNTON--Heirs of Philip Jennings. See Jennings card
Edgefield Rec. Bk. B-185 1850

COLEMAN, MARGARET--Dau. of Elizabeth Cooper-Will 1831 Edgefield
-Margaret Coleman--Gr. Dau. of Reuben Cooper

COLEMAN, MARION AND NANCY--Heirs of Isham Carpenter. See Carpenter
card. Edgefield Rec. Bk. B-199 1846

COLEMAN, MATTHEY--Will 11 March 1840 Edgefield

COLEMAN, POLLYy-Dau. of Bryant Green-Will 1794

COLEMAN, THOMAS E. and wife--Heirs of Marian Adams 1842. See Adams
card. Edgefield Rec. Bk. B-61

COLLIER, ABSOLLOM--Wit. Deed for Thomas Adams -w- Mary to James
Harrison, Jr. 30 Oct. 1805. Edgefield Deed 26-341.

COLLIER, B. S.--wife ___ ? dau. of Joseph P. Jones, Dec'd.
Children: Perrin, Mary, Georgianna, and John Collier
Edgefield Rec. Bk. B-105. 1846 Wife also dec'd.

COLLIER, EDWARD and wife--Adv. James Robertson, et al--Partition
   alleges George Robertson made a Will in 1817. His widow married
   Edward Collier in 1821. Edgefield File. Hills Eq. Rep. Vol. 1
                                                            Pg-253
COLLIER, FRANCIS--Dau. of William Quarles-Will 1821

COLLIER, HAMILTON--Wit. Will of Betty Martin 20 March 1797. Edgefield Wills A-127

COLLIER, HILLARY M.--Will 7 June 1841. Edgefield

COLLIER, JOSEPH--Grand Juror Edgefield 1786 List 4
               Petit Juror 1786 List 9 and 18
  -Equity Bill shows he died 2 Feb. 1819. Will 26 Dec. 1818
  Wife: Amy
  Gr. Dau: Mary Magdalene Chasteen Garrett
  "   "   Amy Wilborn
  "   Son   Joseph Collier)
  "   Dau: Annah Collier)Brother and sister.
  Son: Hillary Collier
  Son in law: Samuel Boyd -w- Polly
  Dau: Patsy Collier
  Dau: Catherine Collier
  Dau: Polly Boyd and her 6 children
       Augustus, Joseph, John, Amy, Sarah, Sayntha Boyd
  Gr. Son: Edward Collier
  Dau: Sarah Coombs
  Son: Abialvun (sp?) Collier
  Son: Thomas Collier
  Dau: Amy Farrer
  Dau: Nancy Talbert

COLLIER, JOSEPH--Wit. Will of Richard Lowry. 16 April 1787. Edgefield Wills

COLLIER, JOSEPH--"Thomas Beckham came into Court and acknowledged
   his deeds of lease and release for 150 Acres of land to Joseph
   Collier which was ordered to be recorded. Edgefield Ct. Min.
   Jan. 14, 1788. Min. Bk. Pg-141

COLLIER, LUCY--Dau. of Thomas Key-Will 1820. Wife of Edward Collier

COLLIER, MARTHA--Aunt of John Boyd-Will 1825. Her children:
  Higdon Bourom   Joseph Collier
  William T. Bourum   Ann Collier

COLLIER, PERRIN, MARY, GEORGIANA, AND JOHN--Gr. children and heirs of
   Jospeh P. Jones. See Jones card. Edgefield Rec. Bk. A-105 1846

COLLIER, THOMAS--Dec'd. Edgefield Bill 914 and 975
  Widow: Catherine -m- Wyett Holmes
  Son: Edward M.--Minor in 1818. 21 in 1832. Died intestate 1839
       Widow of Edward, Ann, married in 1811 Lewis Collins d. 1851
       Dau: Eliza -m- Thos. Tally   Several children.
       Edward H.
       Thomas M.

COLLINS, MRS. ELIZABETH -w- Col. Collins. Dower favor of Charles
Broadwater. Edgefield Min. Bk. April 1787

COLLINS, HORATIO and wife--Heirs of Daniel Bruner. See Bruner card.
Edgefield Rec. Bk. A-34 1834

COLLINS, JAMES,--Son of Gibson Collins. Legatee of Hezekiah Nobles.
Will 1830. Edgefield

COLLINS LEWIS -m- Ann Collier widow of Edward Collier d. 1834
Edgefield Bills 914 and 975

COLLINS, WILEY -w- Jane--Heirs of Morris Callihan. See Callihan card.
Edgefield Rec. Bk. A-229 1835

COLVIL, JAMES--Heir of Daniel Bruner. See Bruner card. Edgefield
Rec. Bk. A-34 1834

CON, JEROME -w- Louisa--Heirs of James Picket. See Picket card.
Edgefield Rec. Bk. A-306 1839

CONNER, LUCY--Dau. of Daniel McKie-Will Rec'd 1819

CONNER, MARGARET--Dau. of William Robinson-Will 1820

COODY, JAMES--Minor. John Williams, Gdn. Robert Burt, Security-
Discharged. Edgefield Ct. Min. March 1795

COODY, SUCKEY--Widow--Reimbursement. The prosecuting witness, The
State -vs- Robert Stark, Clerk Edgefield Court. Illegal Fees.
Edgefield Min. Bk. 320. Jan. 1790

COOK, BENJAMIN--Grand Juror Edgefield 1786. List 5, 6, and 12

COOK, JEREMIAH--Son in law of Fereby Whatley-Will 1840. Edgefield

COOK, JOHN G.--Surety on Bond John Hall, Tavern Keeper. See Hall card.
Edgefield Ct. Min. March 1795

COOK, JOSEPH--Petit Juror Edgefield 1788. List 9

COOK, REBECCA -w- John Cook. Dower favor of Charles Goodwin. July Ct.
Edgefield Min. Bk.

COOK, PEGGY--Heir of Sollomon Cox. See Cox card. Edgefield Min. Bk.
B-117 1846

COOK, SUSSIAH (OR SUSANNAH)--Dau. of Jacob Fudge-Will 1789 and the
two children she bore to William Jones. Edgefield

COOK, WEST--Deed. Adm'x: Prudence Martin -w- Charles Martin
Adm'r: George Y. McMac -vs- Thomas Key. Edgefield Ct. Com.
Pleas 1809. Pg-355
-Widow, Prudence Cook -m- Chas. Martin

COOMBS, SARAH G.--Dau. of Joseph Collier-Will 1818. Son in law:
John S. Coombs. Edgefield

COOPER, ANTHONY--Petit Juror Edgefield 1794. List 21

COOPER, REUBIN--Father in law of Robert Butler-Will 1803. Edgefield

COOPER, TIMOTHY--Apt'd to be Overseer of the Newmarket Road from
Gunnels Creek to Horns in room of Daniel Marcus. Excused.
Edgefield Ct. Min. Oct. 1794

COPS, MATHEW--Petit Juror Edgefield 1794. List 21

CORLEY, AGNES--Heir of Est. William Ferguson. See Ferguson card.
Edgefield Rec. Bk. B-208 1851

CORLEY, ALLEN -w- Winney--Moved to Alabama--Heirs of William Bladon.
See Bladon card. Edgefield Rec. Bk. A-258 1837

CORLEY, CEALY--Dau. of Joshua Martin.-Will 1827. Edgefield

CORLEY, MICHAEL and Dicey, dec'd. and their children: Betsy, Wilson
McCreless.and Milly Corley--Heirs of John McCreless. See
McCreless card. Edgefield Rec. Bk. A-130 1836

CORLEY, MICHAEL--Dec'd. R. E. Sold 1833. Edgefield Rec. Bk. A-144-6
Dist: McCreless Corley 1/4 equals $19.65
        Mildred Corley
        Elizabeth Corley -m- Henry Garrett
        Simp. W. Corley-minor John Trapp, Gdn.

CORLEY, PHEEBE--Dec'd. Mason Ezzard, Adm'r. -vs- Benjamin Corley.
Alleges Sherwood Corley -m- Pheebe Ezzard, a widow, and then he
had a bastard by Elizabeth Hanna. Bastard called Benjamin Corley.
And Sherwood Corley conveyed land to Benjamin Corley. Sherwood
died and left Pheebe a widow--who died intestate, leaving said
Mason and Lewis her children. Edgefield Ct. Com. Pleas 1807-10 113

CORLEY, ROBERT--Dec'd. R. E. Sold.. Edgefield Sale Bk. A-82. No date
Dist: Agnes Corley, widow--1/3
        F. A. I. Corley--1/4 of 2/3
        R. H. Corley-same
        Jane Corley-same
        Jon (Jno-(John)B. Corley-same. D. H. Cogburn Pur. at $271.00

CORLEY, SALLY--Legatee of Ezekiel Perry-Will 1833

CORLEY, SHERWOOD--Purchased R. E. of William Gray, Dec'd.
Edgefield Sale Bk. A-40 about 1829
-Sherwood Corley--Heir estate of William Gray. See Gray card.
Edgefield Rec. Bk. A-40 1829

CORLEY, THOMAS -w- Lucy--Heirs of James Picket. See Picket card.
Edgefield Rec. Bk. A-306 1839

CORLEY, WILLIAM--Petit Juror Edgefield 1794. List 21

CORNAHAN, JOSEPH -w- Elizabeth--Heirs of estate of Ransom Hamilton.
See Hamilton card. Edgefield Rec. Bk. B-107. 1846

COSEY, SUSANNAH--Dau. of Jesse Hill-Will 1818

COTTEN, CHARITY--Dau. of Martha Odom-Will 1817. See Odom card

COTTON, JONATHAN--See card Aaron Moore. Edgefield Deed 31-77

COTTON, THOMAS--Petit Juror Edgefield 1786. List 1 and 2

COTTER, JOHN -w- Mary Ann--Heirs of Joseph P. Jones. See Jones card
Edgefield Rec. Bk. B-105 1846

COTTRELL, LADOCK -w- Eliza--Heirs of James O'Gilvie. See O'Gilvie
card. Edgefield Rec. Bk. A-318 1839

COUCH, EDWARD--Petit Juror Edgefield 1786. List 5 and 16

COURSEY, JAMES--Grand Juror Edgefield 1786. List 3, 6, 14, and 20

COURSEY, JOHN--Petit Juror 1788 Edgefield. List 11

COURTNEY, ROBERT--Petit Juror Edgefield 1788. List 9 and 17

COUSIN, GEORGE--Grand Juror Edgefield 1786. List 2

COVINGTON, JOHN--Petit Juror Edgefield 1789. List 14
                 Grand   "   "   "   "   21

COVINGTON, JOHN--Appr. Estate of Mary Fagna. See Fagna card. Jan.
Court 1795--Wm. Covington proved Will of Charles Hammond as
witness. March Court 1795--Wm. Covington Adm'r. of Allen Hinton.
See Hinton card. Edgefield Ct. Min. Oct. 1794

COVINGTON, JOSEPH--Petit Juror Edgefield 1789. List 14

COWAN, ALEXANDER--License to keep Tavern. S: John Fuller and Richard
Quarles. Edgefield Ct. Min. March Ct. 1795

COWAN, GEORGE--Grand Juror Edgefield 1787. List 8 and 18
-George Cowan Apt'd Adm. estate of Richard Stags. See Stags card.
Edgefield Min. Bk. 1788
-George Cowan--Applied Letters Adm. Estate of John Coates. See
Coates card. Edgefield Min. Bk. 1788
-George Cowan--Dec'd. Per. estate to be sold at house of LeRoy
Roberts last Thursday in March. March Ct. 1795--Edward Whatley
apt'd. Adm. Bond 200 pounds. S: John Swilliven and Daniel
Marcus. Appr's: John Martin, Sam'l Doolittle, Shearly Whatley, Sr.
Absolum Roberts. March Ct. 1795 Am't. sale returned.

COWLEY, ALEXANDER--Petit Juror Edgefield 1787. List 8

COWLEY, CATLETT--Petit Juror Edgefield 1787. List 8

COWLEY, JOHN--Petit Juror Edgefield 1786. List 5
John, Jr. Petit Juror Edgefield 1786. List 17 (Corley?)

COWLEY, NATHAN--Petit Juror Edgefield 1788. List 11 and 16. (Cawley)

COWLEY, RICHARD--Petit Juror Edgefield 1787. List 7

COWLEY, SHERWOOD--Petit Juror Edgefield 1787. List 7
    -On same card--Sherwood Corley-Petit Juror Edgefield 1787. List 16

COX, CHRISTOPHER--Petit Juror Edgefield 1788. List 10

COX, EDWARD--Petit Juror Edgefield 1786. List 3

COX, JAMES--Petit Juror Edgefield 1787. List 6

COX, JOEL--Petit Juror Edgefield 1788. List 9

COX, MARTHA--Legatee and seems a dau. of Wm. West-Will 1779 Edgefield

COX, NANCY--Dau. of Mary Hill-Will Rec'd. 1822
    -Nancy Cox--Heir of Ebenezer Hill. See Hill card. Edgefield Rec.
    Bk. A-280. 1837

COX, SOLLOMON--Dec'd. R. E. Sold 1846. Edgefield Rec. Bk. B-117
    Distributees 1/9 equal to $4.33 each
    Odum Cox-died
    Calvin Cox
    Children of Nancy Ford
    Peggy Cook
    Odum Cox-son of Gillman Cox
    Robert Burton -w- Martha
    Catherine, Sally, and Elizabeth Cox
    Deed Gift-29 March 1847 From Calvin Cox -w- Patsy of Copeak Co.
    Miss. to Miss Sarah Cox and Elizabeth Cox of S. C. Edgefield Dist.
    Love and affection for "sister", their interest in share of
    Dec'd. brother, Odom Cox.

COX, TOLIVER--Petit Juror Edgefield 1786. List 5

COX, WILLIAM--Petit Juror Edgefield 1789. List 13

CRAFTON, LUCINDA--Dau. of Susannah Barksdale who was a dau. of Robert
    Ware-Will 1817. Edgefield

CRAFTON, MARY--Dau. of Thomas Meriweather-Will 1831

CRAFTON, SAMUEL--Grand Juror Edgefield 1786. List 4, 6, 14. (Crofton?)

CRAIN, AMBROSE--Dec'd. R. E. Sold 1st Mon. May 1828. Sale Bk. A-23
    Dist: Ann Crain, widow--1/3 equal $15.00
           Elizabeth Crain-same
           George A. Crain-same.
    David Crain, Adm'r. Receipt by Ann Crain for her share 1 June 1829
    Second sale on page 25. Same heirs.

CRANE, VARY--Dau. of Benjamin Lindsey-Will 1841. Wife of David Crane
    Edgefield

CRANE, VARY--Sister of William Lindsey-Will 1827

CRAFFORD, ELVIRA--Gr. dau. of Patience Carter-Will 1823 (Crawford?)

CRAWFORD, HETTY--Dau. of Patience Carter-Will 1823

CRAWFORD, JOHN -w- Elizabeth--Heirs of Francis Coleman. See Coleman
card. Edgefield Rec. Bk. A-219 1835

CREED, ALLEN -w- Sally--Heirs of William Scott. See Scott card.
Edgefield Rec. Bk. B-53 1841

CRESWELL, JOHN--Dist. of Estate of Abraham Cruise. See Cruise card.
Edgefield Rec. Bk. A-24. 1825

CRISTOPHER, JAMES--Petit Juror 1787 Edgefield. List 6

CROFT, DRURY--Petit Juror Edgefield 1787. List 6

CROLEY, JOSIAH--Dec'd. R. E. Sold 1847. Edgefield Rec. Bk. B-133
Dist: Sarah Croley, widow--1/3 equal to $130.75
John Fendley -w- Tabitha 1/9 of 2/3 equal to $29.05
Mary   Eliza
Delaney   Sarah
James   Josiah
John   Margaret A. All 1/9 of 2/3
P. A. by: Sarah Croley, the widow, Tabitha Fendley, James Croley,
Franklin E. Morgan, and Mary Croley--All of Chickasaw
Co. Miss. Power Attourney granted 11 Nov. 1847

CROSS, SARAH--Dau. of Wm. Jeter-Will 1793

CROUCH, ALCY--Dec'd dau. of Susannah Matthews-Will 1839 Edgefield
Gr. sons: Hillary Hardy and Howell Crouch

CROUCH, BETSY--Dau. of John B. Bush-Will 1844

CROUCH, JOHN--Will 22 Jan. 1790. Edgefield Will Bk. A-29
Wife: Margaret, Exe'x.
5 children: John Crouch
Elizabeth Bowlin
Toliver, Isaac and Birley Crouch
Exor's: John Saulter, and Robert Allen, Jr.

CROUCH, NANCY--Legatee of Nathan Melton-Will 1805

CROZIER, ANDREW--Deed Bk 43-47. Edgefield
Agnes--Her grant to oldest son-James Crozier to his oldest
son-Samuel Crozier, conv. to Andrew Crozier thence to Josiah
Langley, his heirs--this deed.

CROZIER, ANDREW--Petit Juror Edgefield 1786. List 5

CRUISE, ABRAHAM--Dec'd. R. E. Sold 4 April 1825. Sale Bk A-24Edgefield
Dist: Frances Burns, widow--1/3 equal to $323.86
Stanley Cruise 1/2 of 2/3 equal to $323.86
Susan Cruise 1/4 of 2/3 equal to $161.93
Joseph Griffin-Purchaser of share of Jordan_____? same.

CRUZE, ELIZABETH--Dau. of William Jeter-Will 1793
-Elizabeth Crews--Gr. Dau. of William Jeter-Will 1793

CULBERTSON, ELIZABETH--Dau. of Martha Moore-Will 1822
-Elizabeth Culbertson--Dau. of Martha Moore-Will 1825

CULBERTSON, LARKIN and wife--Heirs of William Holliday. See Holliday
card. Edgefield Rec. Bk. A-106 1831

CULBREATH, EDWARD--Bro. in law of John Maynard-Will 1829

CULBREATH, JOSEPH--Petit Juror Edgefield 1786. List 1, 2, and 12

CULBREATH, KEZIAH--Legatee of John Whitley-Will 1811

CULLUM, JOHN P.--Purchased 2 shares estate of Joseph Barton. See
Barton card. Edgefield Rec. Bk. A-296 1838

CULPEPPER, BENJAMIN--Legatee of Elizabeth Mason-Will 1822. Edgefield
-Benjamin Culpepper--Deed settlement of property on them
Wife: Joyce   George Strother, Tr.
Daughter: Joyce.   Edgefield Misc. C-123

CULPEPPER, JOICY--Will 16 Aug. 1837. Rec'd. 10 April 1841
Gr. Son: Wm. A. Strother, David R. Strother, George I Strother
Gr. Dau: Frances C. Devore
Gr. Son: George I. Sheppard
Dau. in law: Mrs. Charlotte Peterson
To: Letty -w- Drury Culpepper
To: Nancy Lockhart -w- John Lockhart
To: Patricia Dodger--$50.00
Son in law: James Sheppart
        Joel Culpepper   )
        Drury Culpepper   ) To have proceeds from sale of Negro-
        Benjamin Culpepper) Doublin
        Mary Gilder   )
        Frances Sheppard   )

CUMBO, HAMMOND -w- Polly--Heirs of William Scott. See Scott card.
Edgefield Rec. Bk. B-53 1841

CUNNINGHAM, JOHN--Petit Juror Edgefield 1788. List 10 and 16
        JOSEPH- "   "   "   1786   " 14 " 20

CUNNINGHAM, ROBERT--Dec'd. R. E. Sold. Edgefield Sale Bk. A-16
James Jennings Gdn. of John C. Cunningham, sole heir.
2 Receipts by James Jennings, Gdn. 4 Sept. 1826 and 5 Nov. 1829

CUNNINGHAM, SARAH--Dau. of John Hardy-Will Rec'd. 1799. Edgefield
-Sarah Cunningham-Will 5 May 1841

CUNNINGHAM, WILLIAM--Dec'd. R. E. Sold 1833. Edgefield Rec. Bk. A-140
Dist: Samuel Cartledge -w- Sarah 1/6 equal to $139.75
        Sarah Cunningham-same
        Elisha Cartledge -w- Margaret-same
        James Cunningham-minor
        Geo. Robertson and Jno. Tomkins -w- Polly-Rep's. of 1/6
        Jno Cunningham sole heir of Rob't. Cunningham--1/6
        Betsy Robertson, Dec'd.

CURRY, HARRIET--Dau. of Martha Hancock-Will 1827. Husband: John
    Curry. Edgefield

CURRY, JOEL -w- Elizabeth--Heirs of William Thomas-See William
    Thomas card. Edgefield Rec. Bk. A-18 1826

CURRY, JOHN--Petit Juror Edgefield 1789. List 15
    -John Curry--App'r estate of Mary Fuqua. See Fuqua card.
    Edgefield Ct. Min. Oct. 1794

CUTTER, JOHN F.--Son in law of Richard Hampton-Will 1837. Edgefield

DABBS, SILAS -w- Lucy--Res. Georgia. Dist. of estate of Joshua Bodie.
    See Bodie card. Edgefield Rec. Bk. A-308. 1839

DAGNEL, CHARLES--Heir estate of Thomas Howle. See Howle card.
    Edgefield Rec. Bk. A-286 1838

DAGNEL, CHARLES H.--Will 8 July 1843. Edgefield

DAGNELL, ELIZABETH--Gr. dau. of Esther Howle-Will 1840.

DAGNOL, PRESLEY S.--Dec'd. R. E. Sold 1837. Edgefield Rec. Bk. A-272
    Dist: Wm. Chadwick and wife 1/2 equal to $171.42
           Frederick Danaol, minor-same. A. Sharpton, Gdn.

DAGNOL, ROBERTSON and wife.--Heirs of Jonathan Sullivan. See Sullivan
    card. Edgefield Rec. Bk. A-; about 1820

DALTON, MARY--Dau. of Michael Vessells-Will 1805. Gr. dau: Eliza Dalton

DALTON, MARY--Will 12 March 1837

DALTY, MISS SALLY--Minor--of age to chose her guardian. Chose Eugene
    Brenan-Bond 500 pounds. S: John Simkins and Francis Burt.
    Oct. Ct. 1794--Order that estate of Sally Dalty by in hands of
    John Simkins as Gdn. Bond 500 pounds. S: Robert Burton and
    Britton Mims.

DANIEL, CHESLEY -w- Judith of Granville Co. N. C. Grant to Champress
    Terry conveyed to said Chesley Daniel 1774. Edgefield Deed 3-114
    4 Feb. 1789

DANIELL, JOSIAH L.--Will 27 Nov. 1813. Edgefield Probate 9-310
    Wife: Mary-Ex'x.   Prov. 14 Jan. 1814
    Son: William Francis Daniell-minor
    Exor's: Philip Raiford and Jesse Daniel
    Wit: William Daniel and Allen Robison
    Shows: "Pd. Philip Raiford, Jr. 15 Nov. 1816" by Philip Raiford, Ex.
    -Same card--Jesse Daniel-Dec'd.   Edgefield 9-311
    Martha Daniel, Adm'x Bond 6 June 1816
    S: John P. Bond and Philip Raiford-asked to be excused in 1827
    -Final shows: Martha S. Spann -w- Henry Spann 1818 paid W. Daniel
    Dist. share. Paid Walter S. Daniel full Dist. share 1834 and
    Thomas S. Daniel in full Dist. share 1836.
    To Boarding: John W. Daniel, 1 year
                  Sumter Daniel, 1 year.
                  Walter Daniel, 1 year
    H. H. Hill Adm'd. in 1833 "in right of his wife"

DANIEL, WILLIAM, ESQ.--Produced cert. as to his qualifications as
Justice of Peace for Edgefield Co. Said: Arthur Simkins, Esq.
Edgefield Ct. Min. Jan. 1795
-William Daniel of Edgefield, dau. Catherine -m- Llewellyn Three-
wits. Of Lexington Dist. Richland Eq. Roll 71. 1811
-William Daniel, Dec'd. Deed 31-451 Edgefield
    Heirs: John, James, and Jesse Daniel
           Bryant Marsh
    Release their claim in the real estate given to his son in
    law, Philip Raiford. 16 Aug. 1813.
-William Daniel, Gdn. S: Stephen Daniel and Jeremiah Hatcher
    Lucretia Daniel
    Mary Daniel
    William Washington) Children of Mary Daniel. Consent
    Martha S. Washington) 8 Jan. 1823.
Entitled to property from their grandmother "Mrs. Brooks".

DANT, JOHN -w- Clarissa--Heirs of Henry J. Kemp. See Kemp card.
Edgefield Rec. Bk. B-131 1847

DANTON, SARAH ELIZA--Gr. dau. of Peter LaBorde (sp?)-Will 1820
Dau: Zelina Danton   Son in law: Hollis Danton

DARBY, BENJAMIN--Petit Juror Edgefield 1787. List 7 and 16

DARBY, BENJAMIN and JONATHAN WRIGHT--S: for Jacob Foreman as Gdn of
his children. See Foreman card. Edgefield Ct. Min. Bk-310
Jan. Ct. 1790

DERBY, FANNY--Dau. of Nathaniel Bacon-Will 1805. Wife of Jeremiah
Derby. (With Darby cards}

DARBY, WILLIS--Dec'd. R. E. Sold. Edgefield Rec. Bk. A-203 (no date)
Dist: Susan Darby, widow 1/3 equal to $224.27
      William and Benjamin Darby
      Wiley White -w- Frances
      John T. White -w- Civil
      Jeremiah Darby   Each received $56.06 as
      Eli Henderson -w- Mary   his share.
      Reuben B. Evans -w- Eliza
      Willis Darby

DAVIS, CAROLINE--Heir of Charity Johnson-See Johnson card.
Edgefield Rec. Bk. B-161 1849

DAVIS, HARRIET--Wife of Hightower Davis and Dau. of Mary Dalton-Will
1837. (Also written Davies)

DAVIS, JAMES--Petit Juror Edgefield 1788. List 9

DAVIS, JOHN--Petit Juror Edgefield 1789. List 13
-Edgefield Rec. Bk. A-90 1832--John M. Davis -w- Rhoda--Heirs of
John Marchant. See Marchant card.

DAVIS, MARY--Dau. of John Elam-Will 1824. Edgefield

DAVIS, NANCY--Dec'd. dau. of Catlett Corley-Will 1829.

DAVIS, RHODA--Dau. of John Marchant-Will 1830

DAVIS, SUSANNAH--Dau. of Thomas Berry-Will 1819

DAVIS, WILLIAM -w- Sarah--Late Sarah McQueen, widow. Deed Bk. 2-8

DAVISON, JOHN, Dec'd. Edgefield Min. Bk. Pg. 233 12 Jan. 1789
Ordered citation be issued to show cause why Adm. should not be
granted to Edward Keating.
Page 258--Granted to Edward Keating and Samuel Willison as creditors of the dec'd.

DAVISON, LEMUEL--Bro-in-law of George Hagood-Will 1827. Edgefield

DAVISON, RACHEL--Dau. of Robert Mosley-Will 1796

DAWSON, JAMES E.--Will 9 July 1835

DAWSON, JOSEPH--Grand Juror Edgefield 1794. List 20

DAWSON, REPSY--Dau. of Wright Nicholson-Will 1807 Edgefield

DAWSON, SAMUEL G.--Son in law of Jonathan Glanton-Will 1823

DAWSON, WILLIAM and JOHN--Sureties for John Gibson, minor's Gdn. See
Gibson card. Edgefield Ct. Min. 14 July 1788

DAY, CLARA -w- _____? Day. Dau. Robert Roebuck. Edgefield Eq. Roll
#30. 1801. See Roebuck card.

DAY, EDWARD--Wit. Will of John Longmire 11 Sept. 1817. Edgefield
Wills A-394
-Edward Day--Wit. Will of Thos. Thornton 27 May 1821

DAY, EMERY AND JOHN--Sec. for William Day to keep them. Jan. Ct. 1790
Min. Bk. Pg. 302 Edgefield

DAY, HENNY--300 Acres in Granville on Stephen's Creek. 20 Jan. 1773
Royal Grant Vol. 28-57 1773
-Henny Day--Mentioned in Will of Robert Gardner-Will 2 Aug 1806.
"Part of the tract that Henny Day made me title to".
Edgefield Wills A-225

DAY, JAMES--Married widow of William Hall, Elizabeth. William Hall
died 1812. Elizabeth died 1820. John Day, Adm. of James Day was
brother. Children of William Hall, wife of John H. Garrett, et al,
sued John Day for partition of estate of William Hall. McCords
Equity Vol. 2-352. State Law Library, Columbia

DAY, JAMES -m- Elizabeth Roebuck or Clara Roebuck. Filed 1st June 1815
Edgefield Equity Bill No. 30
Sanders Day -m- Frances Green

DAY, JAMES--Exor. Will of Elizabeth Napper 1816. Edgefield

DAY, JOHN--400 Acres Colleton--Buckhalter's Creek. 5 May 1773
Royal Grant Bk. Vol 29-212

DAY, JOHN--To John Hancock, Deeds Proved Oct. 1787 Edgefield Min. Bk
16½ acres. 240 Acres from John Hancock to John Day. Prov.

DAY, JOSEPH--Petit Juror 1786 Edgefield. List 3
-Joseph Day-Dec'd. Edgefield Rec. Bk. A-242
  Dist: Richard Jones -w- Rebecca 1/3 equal to $89.37
        The heirs of Sarah Hill, Dec'd.
           Martin Hill 1/4 of 1/3   )
           Charity Delaughter 1/4 of 1/3   ) 1/3
           Charlotte Lee 1/4 of 1/3   )
           Heirs of Mary Rhodes, dec'd. 1/4 of 1/3)
        The heirs of Nancy Bennett
           James Rodgers 1/4 of 1/3   )
           ~~Charlotte Rodgers~~ (struck out) 1/4 of 1/3) 1/3
           Lucy Bennett 1/4 of 1/3   )
           Mary Bennett 1/4 of 1/3   )
  Note: "The children of Charlotte Rodgers said to be illigitimate
and Lucy Bennett and Mary Bennett were never married.
Martin H. Day gave receipt for part of James Rodgers, and for
share of Philip Frazier -w- Lucy.

DAY, PETER--"The Elder"Will 26 Oct. 1789.   Edgefield Wills
  Son: Joseph
  Sister: Sarah Chamberlain
  Dau: Sarah Hitt (Another card also mentions John Hitt)
       Ann Bennett
       Rebecca Jones
  Gr. Dau: Charlotte Rogers
  Gr. Dau: Mary Jones
  Exor's: John Hitt, John Hardy and Joseph Day.

DAY, PETER--To Joseph Cunningham-95 Acres Land. Deed Proved
  Oct. 1787. Edgefield Min. Bk.
  -Peter Day--Petit Juror Edgefield 1787. List 14

DAY, SIMON -w- Sophia--Distributees of Joshua Bodie. See Bodie card.
  Edgefield Rec. Bk. A-308. 1839

DAY, STEPHEN--Grand Juror Supreme Ct. Augusta, Ga. Minutes ? Term
  Oct. 1786

DAY, SUSAN,--Dec'd. R. E. Sold 1849. Edgefield Rec. Bk. B-164
  Distributees: Mayson Day-Husband 1/3 equal to $260.66
               Thomas J. Day   )
               Caroline F. Day)Each received 1/3 of 2/3
               Lucinda J. Day)

DAY, WILLIAM--Of New Windsor, "Gent" to Robert Vaughn. Edgefield
  Mortgage Bk. 000-1739-1740 Pg. 469
  -WILLIAM DAY--Of New Windsor, Gent. to Robert Vaughn, Storekeeper
  of the same place, Negro Slaves-Cambridge and Catarena. Wit:
  James Thomas and James Seals--Misc. Mtg. 10 April 1740. 000-469
  -William Day of New Windsor and Robert Vaughn, Storekeeper of same
  place--300 pounds paid to Wm. Day. Slaves Mtg'd. 10 April 1740
  Wit: James Thomas and James Seales. Receipt for money by Wm. Day.

DAY, WILLIAM--)f New Windsor to Daniel Pepper of same place--Mtg.
slaves--Cambridge, Catherine and her son, Cato. 23 March 1743
Wit: Sarah Ramsay, Row. Loundes. Misc. Mtg. 1741-471
-William Day--Of Edgefield Co. 96 Dist. from John Randal ofWinton
Co. Orangeburg Dist. 5 June 1786. 50 Acres on Shaw's Creek,
Edgefield Co. Waters of Edisto River. Wit: Daniel Day, Isham
Mathews, Peter Day. Edgefield 12 Nov. 1787. Deed Bk. 2-28
-William Day--"On application permission was granted to William
Day to keep a Tavern. Money paid Securities. Emory Day, and
John Day. Edgefield Ct. Jan. 1790. Min. Bk. 302
-William Day of Edgefield Dist. to Joshua Body--150 Acres-part of
818 acres surveyed for and gr. Wm. Day, 5 Aug. 1793--on Shaw's
Creek of South Edisto River. Sd. William Day.
Wit: Daniel Day, Thos. Franklin, Eason C. Drake--No dower.
-William Day to Ephraim Franklin--100 Acres, part of grant 5 Aug.
1793 of 800 acres on Shaw's Creek. Wit: Daniel Day, and Jacob
Lukes. Deed Bk. 15-526. Edgefield. Page 528--John Day to
Ephraim Franklin--100 acres--part of 200 acre grant 7 May 1787
on Shaw's Creek. Wit: Daniel Day, James Day, Silas Green
-William Day--818 Acres 96 Dist. on Shaw's Creek 5 Aug. 1793
Charleston Grant Vol. 35-58 1793 Archives Dept.
William Day of Edgefield -w- Fanny Day--Dower to John Fox of
Richmond, Co. Ga. 191 Acres on Chaves's Creek. 28 Feb. 1809
Edgefield Deed Bk. 29-426

DEAN, JOSHUA--Petit Juror Edgefield 1786. List 5

DEAN, JULIUS--Petit Juror Edgefield 1789. List 13

DEAN, NANCY--Dau. of Sarah Stevens-Will 1793

DEAN, RICHARD--Petit Juror Edgefield 1786. List 1, 2l and 11

DEEN, SAMUEL -w- Amey--Heirs of James Rushton. See Rushton card.
Edgefield Rec. Bk. A-248. 1836

DEEN, SMITHY--Dau. of John Dean and Legatee of Thomas Lakey-Will 1815

DEEN, THOMAS--Will 10 Jan. 1845

DEAN, WILLIAM--Petit Juror Edgefield 1790. List 18

DEEN, WILLIAM, SEN'R-- and Sarah Adams marriage agreement. Both of
Edgefield. 12 Sept. 1828. Misc. F-359 Hist. Com.

DEAN, WILLIAM--Edgefield Wills C-320 Box 8 Pkg-295
Son: Robinson
Wife: Sally
Dau: Margaret Holloway
Gr. Son: Robert M. Smith
Dau: Isbal Youngblood
Sons: Thomas, William, Bryan and Simeon
14 July 1829   Prov: 22 Sept. 1830
Wit: Benj. Stevens, Robert Bryan, and Thomas S. Carter

DEEN, WILLIAM -m- Mary Ann Adams--Heir Charles Adams. See Adams card
1832. Mrs. Sarah Deen, Gdn. same card. Edgefield R. E. Bk.A-58

DEES, BENJAMIN--From Nathaniel Fooshe--Edgefield Deed Bk. 25-41 1804
  -Benjamin Dees to Jacob Whithead--Edgefield Deed Bk. 29-233 1808

DEES, BOWLING -w- Amy of Edgefield--To Henry McClendon--P. A. to collect
  in Wayne Co. N. C. and especially of William Readford-father of Anne.
  31 Oct. 1796. Edgefield Deeds 13-395

DEES, BOLEN--To Ebenezar Sharp--Edgefield Deed Bk. 13-605 1796

DEES, BOWLING--From Rolan Williams--Edgefield Deed Bk. 13-342. 1796
  -Bowling Dees from William Smith--Edgefield Deed Bk. 17-230 1797
  -Bowling Dees to Absolom Radford--150 Acres on the road leading
  from the Ridge to Augusta--on the drains of Edisto and Mine Creek.
  14 Feb. 1800 Edgefield Deed Bk. 18-244
  -Bowling Dees from Mary Lewis--Edgefield Deed Bk. 21-78 1802

DEES, DANIEL--From Elizabeth Wimberly, et al. Edgefield Deed Bk. 36-298
                                                                    1819
DEESE, DANIEL--Of Butler Co. Alabama from Lewis Holmes of Edgefield
  Dist--Negro slave-Seaborn 23 Sept. 1842. Wit: S. F. McDowell
  Gabriel Holmes. Edgefield Deed Bk. CCC-170
  -Same card: Shadrack Dees of Edgefield Co. Will 1797 March 7
  Wife: Grace
  Brother: Bolling Dees
  "my children"
  Wit: Joel Deese, and Nehemiah Possey. Prov. July 1797
  Receipt 13 Dec. 1831 to Lewis Holmes by:
    Joel Dees, Jr   James Dees
    Susan Dees   Martha Dees

DEES, GRACE and BOWLING--To John Frederick. Edgefield Deed Bk. 25-302
  -Grace Dees, et al to Wm. McClendon. Deed Bk. 39-300-1822 1805
  -Grace Dees to George Huiet. Deed Bk. 41-208 1826

DEES, JOEL--From Benjamin Jernegan--Edgefield Deed Bk. 14-117 1797
  -Joel Dees from James Whitehead--Edgefield Deed Bk. 31-296 1811
  -Joel Dees, Sr. to Joel Dees, Jr. Deed Bk. 31-298 1811
  -Joel Dees from Richard Bush--Edgefield Deed Bk. 31-298 1811
  -Joel Dees, Sr. to Tabitha Dees--Deed Bk. 32-184 1814
  -Joel Dees, Sr., Tabitha Dees, and Joel Dees to Keziah Almon.
  Edgefield Deed Bk. 35-204 1813
  -Joel Dees, Jr. to James Muirhead--Edgefield Deed Bk. 35-51 1818/9
  -Joel Dees and wife, James Dees and wife--Heirs of Roland Williams,
  Jr. See Williams card. Edgefield Rec. Bk. A-76 1830

DEAS, NOAH--From Benjamin Seals--Edgefield Deed Bk. 22-337 1802(4 or 7)

DEAS, SHADRACK--App'r estate of Lewis Clerk, dec'd. Edgefield Ct.
  min. March 1795
  -Shadrack Dees of Edgefield. Will. Edgefield Wills A-130
  Wife: Grace
  Brother: Bolling
  "My children-not named
  7 March 1797 Rec'd. July 1797. Wit: Joel Dees, Nehemiah Pilsey (?)
  -Shadrack Dees -w- Selah--Heirs of Jonathan Gregory. Edgefield
  Rec. Bk. A-187-9 1834
  -Shadrack Dees--Will dated. Edgefield Will Box 37-1396
  Nothing else in file. Only Dees on Probate book.

DEES, WILLIAM--Edgefield Petit Juror 1788. List 10
-William Dees--Son in law of Sarah Stevens-Will 1793 Edgefield

DENDY, THOMAS N.--Marriage settlement 9 March 1843 to Harriet Elizabeth
Ann Still--John Curry, Tr. Edgefield Misc. N-89

DELAUGHTER, CHARITY--Heir of Sarah Hill, dec'd. and of Joseph Day.
See Day card. Edgefield Rec. Bk. A-242 About 1830

DELAUGHTER, DRUSILLA AND RANDALL--Gr. children of James Carson, Sen'r.
Will 1822. Edgefield

DELAUGHTER, GEORGE--Petit Juror Edgefield 1787. List 8 and 16
-George Delaughter died intestate 1844. Edgefield Pro. Roll 976
Wife: Elizabeth died intestate 1848
Dau: Susan Ann age 12--Pet. Gdn.
      James Swearington--her brother in law apt'd. Gdn.
Susan Ann Delaughter sued James Swearington for settlement

DELOACH, DORCAS--Dau. of John Still-Will 1797

DELOACH, MICHAEL--Petit Juror Edgefield 1788. List 9

DELOACH, SAMUEL--Petit Juror 1787. Edgefield List 6

DELOACH, SARAH--Dau. of Isaac Bush-Will 1836. Thomas Deloach, Exor.

DELOACH, THOMAS and wife--Heirs of Isaac Bush. See Bush card.
Edgefield Rec. Bk. A-264 1836
-Thomas Deloace--Petit Juror Edgefield 1786. List 1, 2, 10, and 16

DELOACH, WESTLEY AND JAMES--Heirs of estate of James Eidson. Edgefield Rec. Bk. B-125 1847

DENNY, WILLIAM--Dec'd. R. E. Sold 1835. Edgefield Rec. Bk. A-205
Dist: John Denny and wife)
       Arthur E. Denny   ) 1/3 each
       John Denny   )
DESHASE, ROBERT--Petit Juror Edgefield 1788. List 9

DESHZIER, JOHN -w- Anna--Heirs of Philip Jennings. Edgefield Rec.
Bk. B-185. 1850 See Jennings card.

DEVORE, ELIZABETH--See Will of John Clackler, Sen'r. 1790. Edgefield

DEFORE, FRANCES C--Gr. dau. of Joicy Culpepper-Will 1837. Edgefield
Wills D-126

DEVORE, JONATHAN--Dec'd. R. E. Sold 1830. Edgefield Sale Bk. A-54
Distributees: The widow   1/3 equal to $262.65
               Jesse Hobbs -w- 1/6 of 2/3
               Rebecca, Elbert, Julian, James, and Mary Ann
               Devore 1/6 of 2/3 each. Receipts--13 Oct. 1831

DEVORE, MARY--Dau. of Drury Adams-Will 1814. Jonathan Devore, Exor.

DEVORE, MATTHEW--Petit Juror Edgefield 1786 List 1, 2, and 13

DEVORE, REBECCA -w- Matthew Devore, Jr.--Dower favor Christian Limbacker.
Edgefield Min. Bk. Oct. 1787

DICK, JOHN--Will 24 April 1776 of Granville Co. 96 Dist. Bk. Abbeville
Wife: Mary and her small children
Son: Joseph, William, John, and Thomas. Son Joseph to support
minor sisters

DICK, JOHN AND WILLIAM--Minor children of Thomas Dick--Joseph Dick
Apt'd. Gdn. Edgefield Ct. Min. 12 Jan. 1789

DICK, JOSEPH--One of the executors of the last Will and Testament of
John Dick, deceased--was qualified as such. Edgefield Min. Bk.
Page 212. 13 Oct. 1788

DICK, JOSEPH--Petit Juror Edgefield 1789. List 14
-Joseph Dick applied for permission to keep Tavern. S: Isaac
Ardis and Jacob Zin. Edgefield Ct. Min. March 1795

DICKENS, NIMROD and children, Mary and Serena--Heirs of John Roberts
See Roberts card. Edgefield Rec. Bk. A-120 About 1830

DICKENSON, RICHARD--"Richard Dickenson, Esquire, produced his credentials
as an attorney which were read in open Court, and the said Dickenson is hereby enrolled as Att'y. of this Court". Edgefield
min. Bk. Pg. 261. Oct. 1789

DICKEY, JOHN--Married Agnes Baird 21 Nov. 1816. Edgefield File.
Library of Congress. Moses Waddell Mar.

DICKS, WILLIAM--Heir of Daniel Bruner. See Bruner card. Edgefield
Rec. Bk. A-34. L834

DICKSON, ARTHUR--Of "96". Will 17 July 1780. Edgefield File C.T. Wills
Wife: Hannah
Sister's oldest son-Arthur--The land
Friend: David Lorimore, Exor.

DILLARD, ARTHUR--Legatee of William Hogans-Will 1805. Edgefield
-Arthur Dillard--Legatee of John Abney-Will 1812

DILLARD, NICHOLAS--Petit Juror Edgefield 1788. List 10

DINKINS, ELIZA--Dau. of Margaret Miles-Will 1834

DINKINS, RICHARD and wife--Heirs of Richard Miles. See Miles card.
Edgefield Rec. Bk. A-241 1836

DOBY, ELIZABETH--Dau. of John H. Mealing-Will 1823

DOBY, LUKE--Dec'd. R. E. Sold 1836. Edgefield Rec. Bk. A-223
Dist: David W. Moore 5/9
Frances and Susan Doby-minors-Martha Doby, Gdn. 2/9 each.

DOBY, MALINDA--Dau. of Elizabeth Cooper-Will 1831

DOBY, MATILDA--Dau. of Reuben Cooper-Will 1824

DOBY, NANCY--Dau. of William Murfey-Will 1794. Rec'd. 1801

DOBY, WILLIAM -w- Ann--Dower favor John Oliphant. Mrs. Nancy Doby,
   -w- William Doby--Dower favor Absolom Shearly. Jan. 1788
   Edgefield Min. Bk.

DODGEN, PARTHENIA--Legatee of Joicy Culpepper-Will 1837. Edgefield

DODGEN, SARAH--Dec'd. R. E. Sold 1837. Edgefield Rec. Bk. A-262
   Distributees: Sheppard Dodgen 1/4 equal to $79.51
   Pleasant Burnett -w- Mary-same
   Bethany and Preston Dodgen-minors-1/4 each.

DON, ANNA and her children and Nancy, stepmother,--Heirs of John Hester.
   Edgefiåd Rec. Bk. A-278. 1837 (Nancy, stepmother of Anna's children

DON, JAMES--Dec'd. R. E. Sold 1847. Edgefield Rec. Bk. B-113
   Dist: John Don 1/9-sold to Moses Kirkland
      Wm. Whitehead -w- Rachel 1/9
      Nancy Don, the widow 1/3 equal to $140.22
      Adaline-a dec'd. dau.
      Louisa, Clarinda, and James Don

DON, JANE AND NANCY--See card Jacob Whitehead, Sr. Dec'd. Edgefield Rec. Bk. A-278

DON, JOHN -w- Matilda--Heirs of Jordan Holloway. See Holloway card.
   Edgefield Rec. Bk. A-270 1837

DONNER, ANNA--Dist. Estate of Fanny Butler, dec'd. See Butler card.
   Edgefield Rec. Bk. B-37 1841

DOOLITTLE, AGNES--Dau. of William Howle, Sen'r. Will 1830

DOOLITTLE, BENJAMIN--Dec'd. R. E. Sold 1835. Rec. Bk. A-209 Edgefield
   Dist: Rhoda Doolittle, Widow 1/3 equal to $126.70
      Lewis Murrah -w- Sarah 1/10 equal to $20.34
      James R. Kimbrell -w- Martha--same
      William Thurmond -w- Henrietta-same
      Pleasant Doolittle-same
      Elam Burckhalter -w- Nancy-same
      Rhoda Ann, William P., Julia A., Francis Doolittle-minors
         each 1/10

DOOLITTLE, JOSEPH--Dec'd. Box 9-308
   Ephram Doolittle, Adm'r.
   Sale Pur: Sarah Doolittle
      Ephram Doolittle
      Benjamin Doolittle
      Terrell Goff-3chs.

DOOLITTLE, JOSEPH--200 Acres supposed to be in Pellsey Evania Prov. Va.
   Granted Joseph Doolittle 23 Dec. 1768 by Gov. Wm. Tryon and conv.
   to Wm. Motte on 23 June 1773. Both sides Doolittle Creek and Broad
   River. North Carolina Grant. Mem. 12-450

DOOLITTLE, MRS. NANCY -w- Samuel Doolittle--Dower favor of Wm. Jeter
April 1787. Edgefield Min. Bk.

DOOLITTLE, POLLY--Dau. of Roger M. Williams. See Williams card.
Edgefield Wills D-17 1828

DOOLITTLE, SAMUEL--App'r. estate of George Cowan, Dec'd. See Cowan
card. Edgefield Ct. Min. March 1795

DOOLITTLE, SAMUEL'S LEGATEES -vs- Richard Newman, et al--"Premises
and Assumptions". Inv. Bk. A-1800-1803 orig. pg. 25
Estate Samuel Doolittle, Inv. and App'l. 3 July 1800 by Drury
Adams, Roger Williams, and Thomas Palmer, and Wm. Miller.
Val. Personal Prop. $2,665.87½ and 8 slaves. Edgefield Ct.
Com. Pleas. Docket. 1800 - 1801
-Same card--Benj. Doolittle purchased 2 sides leather at estate
of Jesse Puckett and Roger Williams purchased 2 large basons.
12 May 1800

DOOLY, PATRICK -w- Ann-Grant 20 Aug. 1767 to Mackerness Goode-late
of Va., Planter, now of 96. 11 Dec. 1767. 300 Acres on 96 Creek.
Edgefield Deeds 8-119
Page 127--John Dooly--Gr. 100 Acres on 96 Creek to Samuel Goode
19 Sept. 1771. Bd. Rob't. Mitchel.

DORN, EMILY--Dau. of Wm. Dean, Jr.-Will 1834

DORN, SARAH, JOHN, et al -vs- Robert Don, et al. Equity Bill 738

DORN, WILLIAM -w- Mary to George Dorn--96 acres on waters of Sleepy
Creek. Part tract of land laid out for John Coursey and the
above 96 acres being the shares of 2 Legatees of John Harling,
dec'd. Bd. by John and David Harling lands. Wit: Geo. Quattlebaum,
Oliver Moore. Edgefield Deed Bk. 48-479 18 Dec. 1832

DORN, WILLIAM -w- Polly--Heirs of estate of Elizabeth Falkner. See
Falkner card. Edgefield Rec. Bk. B-182 1850

DORRIS, REBECCA AND LUCY--Daus. of Josiah Langley-Will 1826. Edgefield

DOSBY, BENJAMIN--Petit Juror Edgefield 1794. List 20

DOUGLAS, SALLEY--Dau. of Elizabeth Mackquister -w- Moses Mackquister-
Will 1797. Edgefield

DOWNER, ALEXANDER--Petit Juror Edgefield 1786. List 5
-Alexander Downer--sale at his house of personal property of Estate
of John Beddingford, dec'd. Edgefield Min. Oct. 1794

DOZIER, CAROLINE--Dau. of Gilson Yarbrough-Will 1839. Edgefield

DOZIER, ELIZABETH--Dau. of Elias Blackburn-Will 1821. Edgefield
Gr. daus: Eliza, Caroline, Charlotte, Augusta, Frances Dozier

DOZIER, JAMES A. -w- Sallie--Lost infant son, Wm. Allen Dozier
Died 9th. age 2 years 5 mos. Edgefield Adv. Dec. 1864

DOZIER, POLLY--Dau. of Lucretia Gayle-Will 1808. Edgefield

DOZIER, REBECCA--sister of Albert Dozier. Legatee of John Fox-Will-1837

DOZIER, THOMAS--Grand Juror Edgefield 1786. List 5, 10, and 14

DOZIER, WILLIAM and RICHARD M.--Permission to keep Tavern. S: Russel
Wilson, and Sampson Butler. Edgefield Ct. Min. March 1795

DOZIER, WILLIAM -w- Elizabeth--Heirs of John Rogers. See Rogers card.
Edgefield Rec. Bk. A-324. 1839

DRAKE, HARVY, REUBEN, WM. A., AND ELIZA--Children of Martha Robihson-
Will 1832. Edgefield

DRAKE, MARY--Dau. of Benj. Frazier. A Legatee of Sarah Lott-Will 1831

DRAKE, REUBEN -w- Mary--Heirs of Sarah Lott. See Lott card. Edgefield Rec. Bk. A-138 1833

DRUMBELL, ALEXANDER -w- Rebecca--Heirs of Philip Lightfoot. See Lightfoot card. Edgefield Rec. Bk. B-65 1842

DRUMMOND, NANCY--Dau. of Ann Conner-Will 1824

DRYSDALE, ALEXANDER--Of Savannah, Ga.--Legatee-Gold watch-of Robert
Watts-Will 1839. Edgefield

DUCK, ROLON A. -w- Mary (formerly widow)--Heirs of William Pussell.
See Pussell card. Edgefield Rec. Bk. A-320 1839

DUFFY, HUGH--Son in law of Raynol Gentry-Will 1826. Edgefield

DUNBAR, SARAH -w- George and dau. of David Bowers-Will 1833.

DUNCAN, RICHARD and wife--Heirs of Allen Body. Edgefield Rec. Bk. A-92
1832

DUNCOMB, ABIGAIL--and her children: Elizabeth, James, Jennett, John
Wiley, Ailsey Duncomb--dau. and gr. children of John Jackson-
Will 1787. Edgefield

DUNKIN, REBECCA--Dau. of John Rinehart-Will 1828. Edgefield

DUNLAP, WILLIAM -w- Hulda--Heirs of James Martin. See Martin card.
Edgefield Rec. Bk. A-72 1831

DUNSTON, SILVESTER--Heir of Bates Wrenn. See Wrenn card. Edgefield
Rec. Bk. B-95 1846

DUNSTON, MARY L.--Will 10 April 1841. Edgefield

DUPEES, SARAH--Of Georgia--Dower Dedimus. July Ct. 1786

EAVE, OSWELL--Commissioned to build a bridge. See card Wm. Anderson
Edgefield Ct. Min. March 1795

EDDY, WILLIAM--Of Granville Co. Will 6 July 1767. Edgefield File
Wife: Mary--Pregnant
3 sons: Charles, Thomas and John Eddy (John listed first)
4 Daus: Margaret, Elizabeth, Ann and Hannah.

EDDY, WILLIAM--Another card. Edgefield File. C. T. Wills. Same Heirs.
Exors: John McGill, Alexander McAlpen
Wit: William Harris, James Garret, Robert Caton
Dedimus to John Pickins. Prov. 28 Dec. 1767

EDGEWORTH, MARIA--Dau. of Eliza Hannah Simkins-Will 1837
EDINGS, ABRAHAM--Dec'd. Warrant to divide his estate to John Jackson
14 March 1745. Old Indes. Misc. Vol. Arch. Dept. F. F. 392

EDDINS, ABRAHAM--from James Bean and Alexander Bean, James Still
and Joseph Still, John Lee, Thomas Youngblood, Christian Bean
16 May 1812. Wit: William Eddins, Sen'r. 5 Sept. 1812
Edgefield Deed 31-200/1

EDINGS, BENJAMIN--Of·Edisto Island. Arch. Dept. Misc. 6G-330
William Edings tr. for
Wife: Susan Howard Edings (Benjamin's wife)
-Children: William, Mary, and Julian C. Edings. 15 Feb. 1755
-Same Card: Sarah Edings of Edisto to Gr. Dau. Charlotte P.
Edings and Gr. son, Joseph Edings--28 Jan. 1854. 6G-237/8
Page 235--John Evan Edings-Tr. in 1852 Mary W. Edings -m-
27 June 1842 Optimus E. Hughs

EDDINS, BENJAMIN -w- Elizabeth to Alexander McCrary and Thomas McMaster
of Newberry Dist. Various tracts property . Wit: Wm. Eddins
Jesse Forrest 23 Oct. 1811. Edgefield Deed 31-112/3

EDDIN, JOHN--102 Acres Orangeburg Nov. 8, 1798. Loose Plat 55-163

EDDINS, JOHN -w- Mary-Dower to James Long of Fairfield Dist 25 Dec.
1810. 416 Acres on waters of Long Creek. Pt. 964 acres surveyed for Andrew Broughton on 24 Aug. 1774. Edgefield Deed 31-230

EDDINS, JOSEPH -w- Elizabeth--Conv. part several grants "Where the said
Joseph Eddins lately lived". Plat on Horn's Creek. Edgefield
Deed Bk. 31-429 1813
-Joseph Eddins. Child: Benjamin L. Arch. Dept. Misc. 5P-80
-w- Wm Seabrook. Joseph D. Eddings, William Eddings--?

EDDINS, MARY--Widow of Edgefield Dist. Married 6 March 1826, Thomas
Chiles of Green Co. Alabama. Wit: Benj. Frazier, Wm. Eddins,
George Tillman. Edgefield Deed Bk. 42-161

EDDINGS, NANCY--Dau. of Abraham Taylor-Will 1805. Edgefield

EDDINS, THEOPHILUS, and Henry Anderson-his land- to Bennett Kettle.
Bond and Mtg. 5 Oct. 1808. ½ Gr. to Geo. Fellman 24 Dec.
1764. Mtg. 1 March 1810. Edgefield Deed 30-171/3
-Same card--Wm. Donoho to Theophilus Eddins 29 Sept. 1803. 24-206
1. Gr. to John Jacob Messersmith. 2. Gr. to James Miller
100 acres part grants.

EDDINGS, WILLIAM--Archives Dept. Mem. 3-277
1820 Acres Colleton 23 May 1733
532   "   "   24 Oct. 1743--Mem. 7-412
1. 200 acres part 350 acre grant Benj. Sealy in 1700--Bd. by
Moses Watson and Edisto Creek. Purchased from John Sealy
20/21 Jan. 1737.

EDDINGS, WILLIAM--CONTINUED
    2. 332 acre-grant John Dedcott, son of Benj. Dedcott--in 1705
        at head of Tooloodoo Creek. Sold to Wm. Eddings.
    1903 Acres Colleton 14 June 1765. Mem. 6-447
    415 acres Abbeville. July 4, 1798. After Rev. Loose Plats.
        Bdle. 55-164
    William Eddings, the Elder. Mem. 10-484/5
        Grant 22 May 1736, purchased from John Sealy, son Benj. Sealy.
    Heirs of Wm. Eddings, the Elder:
        Mary Russell--Will
        William Eddings, the younger, and son, Benjamin. All on
        Edisto Esland--Mem. 8 Sept. 1796
    William Eddings, son of William. 1709. Mem. 6-447
    460 Acre gr. Henry Bower 1711
    136 "   "   "   "   "
    150 "   "   "   "   "   1710--divided by sd Henry Bower between:
    Wm. Eddings, Sen'r. father of mentioned and Joseph L. Russell
    60 A pt Gr. to Henry Bower   )
    200 A. gr. Benj. Sealy 1700) All owned by Mary Russell, Aunt
    340 A. gr Laurens Dennis 1710) of William Eddings, Senior.
    57 A. Gr. to Wm. Eddings 1736)

EDENS, WILLIAM--Legatee of Henry Chiles-Will 1791

EDDINS, WILLIAM--Of Pendleton to Benjamin Eddins, Sen'r. of Edgefield
    28 Dec. 1798--1/2 interest in 133 Acres Abbeville Co. on Hard
    Labor--which they had purchased jointly. Wit: Joseph Eddins
    John Eddins. Deed 16-261 Edgefield.

EDDINGS, WILLIAM--Dec'd. Will 20 May 1834. Died April 1836
    Dau: Eliza -m- 30 Mar. 1819 Benjamin Whaley. Eliza died 26 June
        1823. Only issue: Wm. J. Whaley and Benj. S. Whaley.
        Benjamin Whaley -m- 2nd in 1825 and had 3 other children.
        He died 11 Ma rch 1832.
    Dau: ? -m- Fripp
    Dau: ? -m- Chisolm
    Beaufort people. Speers Law Rep. Vol 1-210

EDINS, ZELPHA--Lexington Ct. Com. Pleas Journal Page 34.
    Son: James A. Edins) Deed Gift Land. 20 Feb. 1816
        William D. Edins)
EDMUNDS, ALEXANDER--Dec'd. Inv. Ret. Edgefield Min. March 1795

EDMOND, LYDIA--Gr. dau. of John Cogburn-Will 1810
    -Lydia Edmunds, dec'd. and Samuel Edmunds-Heirs of John Cogburn.
    See Cogburn card. Edgefield Rec. Bk. A-225 1834

EDSON, ELLENOR--Dau. of John B. Bush-Will 1844. Edgefield

EDWARDS, ANNA and MARY--Daus. of John Huff-Will 1815. Edgefield

EDWARDS, FRANCES--Dau. of Mackerness Goode-Will 1793. Formerly widow
    of William Martin. See Martin card. Edgefield

EDWARDS, HEZEKIAH and wife-Heirs of Rebecca Ramey. Edgefield Rec. Bk.
    B-75 1842

EDWARDS, JOHN--Living on Saluda. Archives Dept. Edgefield File Misc.
22-17 1773

EDWARDS, JESSE and wife--Heirs of estate of William Ferguson. See
Ferguson card. Edgefield Rec. Bk. B-208 1851

EDWARDS, MARY--Dedimus to Wm. Anderson to take her dower to land conv.
by her husband to William Hill. Edgefield Min Bk. 12 Jan. 1789

EDWARDS, PETER--Dec'd. His dau. Anne E. Murray mentioned in Will of
John Fox 1837. Edgefield

EDWARDS, THOMAS--Petit Juror Edgefield 1789. List 13

EDWARDS, URIAH--Edgefield Deed 31-447
Son: John Edwards of Franklin Co. Kentucky to Covington Coleman
P. A. to collect in part of estate of Uriah Edwards in N. C. and
S. C. and Georgia. 22 Oct. 1812. Page 448--Francis Coleman
died Harrison Co. Kentucky.Adm'x: Elizabeth R. Coleman 1813.
Page 449: Elizabeth R. Coleman to Covington Coleman-P. A. 1813
Page 449/50--Cert. by Clerk of Court at Spotsylvania Co. Va.
dated Nov. 2,1784 that Alexander Spencer Head, Benjamin Head,
and John Sorrell made oaths that John Edwards is the oldest son
of Uriah Edwards, dec'd.

EFFURT, ADAM -w- Lucy to Reason Wooly--140 Acres on Cloud's Cr.
10 Aug. 1804. Edgefield Deed Bk. 27-395

EGLISTON, ELIZABETH--Heir of.Mrs. Wormley. See Wormley card. Edgefield rec. Bk. B-71

EIDSON,JAMES--Dec'd. R. E. Sold 1847. Edgefield Rec. Bk. B-125
Dist: The following received 1/15 equal to $17.25 each
James Eidson   Rowland Eidson
James Redgers -w- Sarah   Larkin Norwood -w- Elizabeth
Marsey Eidson   Benjamin Rushton -w- Harriet
Samuel Eidson   Martha Eidson
Boyce Eidson   Edward Eidson
William Eidson   Humphrie Eidson
James and Westley Deloach received ½ of 1/5 equal to $8.62½ each
The following received 1/6 of 1/5 each, equal to $2.87
William Rodgers -w- Sarah   John Gillon -w- Polly
Jackson Salter   Gideon Salter
Samuel Salter   William Salter
The following received 1/10 of 1/5 each, equal to $1.72
Wiley Eidson   Nathan Bodie -w- Edney
Allen Eidson   Lewis Watson -w- Matilda
Malon Eidson   Josey Howell -w- Sarah
Russell Eidson   Malon Padgett -w- Polly
Catherine Eidson   James Bouknight -w- Martha
Receipt by J. H. Howell 19 Aug. 1847 for Howell, Padgett and
Bouknight
Receipt 23 May 1847 by Martin McCarty for part of his wife Cyntha
formerly Cyntha Rodgers in estate of James Rodgers -w- Sarah, Dec'd.

EIDSON, PATIENCE--Dau. of Arthur Watson-Will 1804 Edgefield

ELDER, SILVESTER--Dec'd. Adm. produced Inventory which was ordered to
be recorded. Edgefield Ct. Min. Bk. 271 Oct. 1789
-Edgefield Min. Bk. 15 July 1789--Page 259--Letters Adm'n. granted
John Hammond and Ephraim Hendren.

ELLIOT, ALLEN -w- Mary, dau. of Lucy Parten--Heirs of Philip Jennings.
See Jennings card. Edgefield Rec. Bk. B-186 1850

ELIOT, WILLIAM--Gr. son of Elisha Robertson-Will 1792

ELLETT, WILLIAM -w- Sarah Ann of Ala.--Heirs of Littlebury Mitchell.
See Mitchell card. Edgefield Rec. Bk. A-22 1826 (or Elliott)

ELUM, JOHN--Petit Juror Edgefield 1787. List 7 and 20
-John Elum -m- Mary Minter, dau. of Joseph Minter-Will 1780. See
Minter card. Edgefield

ENGLISH, THOMAS--Dec'd. Edgefield Box 24-823 1792
Adm'r: Joshua English   Bond: 22 Oct. 1792
S: Wm. Bond and Richard Stratford

ESKRIDGE, BURDETT--Of Colleton Co. Will 23 Mar. 1779. 96 Dist. Abbevill
Wife: Nanie
Son: Samuel
      Grigesby
      Richard
-Burdett Eskridge--Dec'd. Will Edgefield Deed 2 Page 3
Jacob Smith and Enoch Grigsby, Exor's.
To: Daniel Bullock -w- Hannah, late widow of dec'd. 1/3
9 Oct. 1787

ESKRIDGE, SAMUEL--A youth of age to choose Gdn. Chose John Thomas.
Apt'd. Edgefield Ct. Min. 8 Oct. 1787

ESKRIDGE, JOHN--Petit Juror Edgefield 1794. List 20

ESKRIDGE, LOT--Petit Juror Edgefield 1788. List 10

ETHERIDGE, AARON--Petit Juror Edgefield 1787. List 6

ETHERIDGE, BENJAMIN -w- Elizabeth and Martha -w- _____ ? Etheridge--Heirs
of Philip Jennings. See Jennings card. Edgefield Rec. Bk. B-185
                                                              1850

ETHERIDGE, LEWIS--Petit Juror Edgefield 1787. List 7 and 21

ETHEREDGE, ROBERT--Dec'd. R. E. Sold 1834. Rec. Bk. A-173 Edgefield
Dist: Jesse Thornton and wife 1/3 equal to $93.90
      (David Etheredge   Manley Etheredge)
      (Martha   "   William   "   ) 1/10 of 2/3 each
      (Elisa   "   Sampson   "   )
      (Betsy   "   Robert   "   )
      (James   "   Sarah   "   )
Shows by receipt: Jesse Thornton -m- widow
                  Martha -m- James Rampey
                  P. A. Robert Etheredge of Abbeville to Wade E.
                  P. A. Sarah Etheredge Greenville Co. to Robert E.

ETHERIDGE, WILLIAM--Excused as Overseerof road--Lee's Bridge to Cloud's
Creek--Samuel Center apt'd. in his place. See Center card.
Edgefield Ct. Min. March 1795

EVANS, CAD--Dec'd. R. E. Sold. Edgefield Sale Bk. A-100
Dist: Mary Evans, widow--¼ equal to $52.94½
Daniel Evans 1/5 of 1/2 equal to $10.59
Robert Evans-same
Hamlin Freeman, et ux-same
James Lamkin, et ux-same
Dinwiddie Evans-died-W. Belcher Adm'r.-same
Rec't. 2 July 1832 by M. G. Adams-who -m- 2nd Adams. John Key
Trustee or Agent.

EVANS, DANIEL -w- Nancy--Heirs of Bates Wrenn. See Wrenn card.
Edgefield Rec. Bk. B-95 1846

EVANS, ELIZABETH--Aunt and Heir of Wm. R. Morton. See Morton card.
Edgefield Rec. Bk. A-98

EVANS, ELIZABETH--Heir of Mary Ann Moreton- See Moreton card.
Edgefield Rec. Bk. A-90 1825

EVANS, ISAAC--Petit Juror Edgefield 1789. List 14

EVANS, JANE--Widow Asa Evans--Heir of Philip Jennings. See Jennings
card. Edgefield Rec. Bk. B-105 1850

EVANS, MARTHA--Dau. of George Bussey, Sen'r. Will Prov. 1797.

EVANS, MARY -w- Caldwell Evans. Gr.-dau. of Elizabeth Bassett-Will
1827. Also dau. of Hannah Longmire.

EVANS, REUBEN B. -w- Eliza--Heirs of estate of Willis Darby. See Darby
card. Edgefield Rec. Bk. A-203 About 1828

EVANS, WILLIAM--Will headed Abbeville. Edgefield Stray
Son: Peter, William, and Harvey Evans
Daus: Polly, Elizabeth, Martha White.
Exor: Son in law--Blumon White. 17 June 1836
Will filed in case of Suit over a slave alleged given to Antonett
White, a sister of Francis M. White, who so testified. Stated he
left S. C. in 1836 and lived in Sumter County, Alabama.
Case: John Lyon, Adm'r. of Wm. Evans -vs- Stephen White.

FAIR, JOHN -w- Mary--Heirs of Lucy Hatcher. See Hatcher card.
Edgefield Rec. Bk. B-23 about 1840

FALKNER, ELIZABETH--Dec'd. R. E. Sold 1850
Dist: Joseph Parkman -w- Peggy 1/9 equal to $77.38
William Dorn -w- Polly-same
Ransom Holloway -w- Matilou-same
James McCreless -w- Delilah-same
Blake Falkner -w- Elizabeth-same
Elijah and Marshal Falkner 1/9 each
John and David Harling 1/9 each
Edgefield Rec. Bk. B-182

FANNING, ABRAHAM--Petit Juror Edgefield 1789. List 14

FARROR, ANNY--Dau. of Joseph Collier-Will 1818. Wife of George
    Farrow--see Equity Bill filed 22 April 1822. Hugh Cameron
    and wife -vs- John Talbot, John Coombs, and Hillary Collier, Ex.

FARROR, BENJAMIN--Chain title on Handy Creek-Saluda River near Cam-
    bridge. 200 Acre gr to Thomas Brown. Desc. to Richard Brown
    who conveyed to Benjamin Farrer. 6 Nov. 1802 who conv. to
    Taciter Gaillard. Isaac Gaillard to Richard Eskridge, exor. and
    heir of the Mississippi Territory. Edgefiell Deed Bk. 23-81

FARROR, CHESLEY--Wit. Will of Dolly McCary 4 Feb. 1810.

FARRAR, ELIZABETH--Sister of William Martin-Will 1801. Other heirs;
    Mother of testator, Grace Martin. Wit: John, Nathaniel, and
    Nancy Martin. Exor: Matt. Martin. Edgefiell Wills A-453

FARRAR, ELIZABETH--Formerly E. Howard. Dau. of Thomas Key-Will 1820

FARROR, GEORGE -vs- Thomas Bibb. "Ordered that the deposition of
    Hickerson Barksdale be taken in this case." Min. Bk. Page 310
    Jan. 1790.
    April Court, Page 345--"The verdict of the same Jury as before
    say that Thomas Bibb pay twelve pounds with interest and costs."

FARRAR, GEORGE--Died. Edgefield File. McCord's Rep. 1-387 May 1819
    Widow: Peggy   Only child: Haddaway Farrar-minor
    Widow apt'd. Adm'x 5 July 1802. S: Davis Williams, H. Parkman
    and John Gibson. Letters Adm. Joseph Collier 11 March 1803

FARRAR, PETER--From John Longmare -w- Hannah all of Edgefield 50 Acres
    on Stephans Creek. Orig. gr. to David Bell. Edgefield Deed Bk.
    22-280. 10 May 1802

FARROW, CHANEY--Of Sptg. to Wm. Mays of Edgefield--Land on Horn's Cr.
    2 shares purchased of Mrs. Rebecca Beames and Jos. Eddins. Wit:
    John S. Glascock, W. H. Farrar. Edgefield Deed Bk. 33-317
    21 Dec. 1816

FARROW, CHANEY -m- Dau. of Samuel Walker of Edgefield. Edgefield File
    McCord's Rep. 1818.

FARROW, PETER, SEN'R AND JUN'R.--See card Stephen Garrett -vs-
    Jeremiah Wilborn. Edgefield Eq. Bills No. 14 Filed 19 April 1817

FARROW, VASHTI--Sister of William Lindsey-Will 1827
                 -Dau. of Benjamin Lindsey-Will 1841

FARQUHOL, MARY--Niece of Mary McFarland-Will 1805. Also Elizabeth
    and Margaret Farquhol. (Possibly Farquhar.)

FARQUIER, JAMES--Petit Juror Edgefield 1788. List 12

FAY, WILLIAM, JAMES, LOUISA, HAMUTAL, AND FREDERICK--Children of
    Hamutal Wilson(a woman)-Will 1806

FERGUSON, MARY--Dau. of Jarrott Edwards-Will 1822

FERGUSON, WILLIAM--Will 25 Dec. 1831. Edgefield
WWilliam Ferguson, dec'd.   R. E. Sold 1851.   Rec. Bk. B-208
Dist: Zedekiah Watkins -w- Jane 1/7 equal to $103.03
        John Ferguson-same
        Agnes Corley-same
        Jesse Edwards and wife-same
        Anna Reaves and children-same
        Children of Hiram Ferguson-same
        Children of William Ferguson-same
        James K. Buist -w- Amanda among heirs.
        James Wood an heir.

FENDLEY, JOHN -w- Tabitha--Heirs of Josiah Croley.   Edgefield Rec.
        Bk. B-133

FIKE, TIRE--Petit Juror Edgefield 1794.   List 21

FINCH, AMY--Dau. of George Martin-Will 1817

FINDLEY, CHARLES P. -w- Rachel--Heirs of John Marchant, dec'd.   See
        Marchant card.   Edgefield Rec. Bk. A-90 1832

FINLEY, JOHN--Petit Juror Edgefield 1794.   List 20

FLANGANE, HANNAH--Dau. of John Still-Will 1797.   Edgefield

FLECK, HANNAH--Now wife of Abram Taylor.   Conv to Harvey Blassengame
        her grant.   20 Dec. 1779.   Edgefield Deed Bk. 3-133

FLINN, EDMUND--Dec'd.   R. E. Sold 1846.   Edgefield Rec. Bk. B-121
Dist: Mary Flinn, widow   1/2 equal to $125.95
        Guy Broadwater -w- Rachel 1/8 of ½ equal to $16.05
        David Rush and wife
        William, David, Abraham, George W., Anderson T., Nancy
        Received 1/8 of 1/2 share each. $16.05
        Joseph, Franklin and William Rush received 1/3 of 1/8
        share each. $5.35

FLIN, WILLIAM -m- Elizabeth Adams-dau. of James Adams-1801.   See
        Adams card.   Edgefield Judgement-1801
        -William Flin--Will 25 March 1837.   Edgefield

FLOY, MARY--Heir of John Roberts-See Roberts card.   Edgefield Rec.
        Bk. A-120 About 1830

FLOY, SIRAS -w- Sarah--Heirs of Martha Hancock.   See card Jane Odom.
        Edgefield Rec. Bk. B-25 1839

FLOYD, SIRAS -w- Mary Ann--Heirs of Martha Hancock.   See Hancock card.
        Edgefield Rec. Bk. B-25 1840

FORD, NANCY--Heir of Sollomon Cox.   See Cox card.   Edgefield Rec.
        Bk. B-117 1846

FORD, THOMAS -w- Orphia--Heirs of Scarbrough Broadwater.   See Broadwater
        card.   Edgefield Rec. Bk. A-221 1835

FOREMAN, ANN, DAVID, ISAAC, AND ZELPHA--"The children of Jacob Foreman, minors. The said children appeared in Court and the Court appointed Jacob Foreman guardian, whereupon the said Foreman entered into Bond of 3000 pounds with Jonathan Wright and Benjamin Darby. as securities." Edgefield Jan. 1790. Min. Bk. Pg. 310
Page 313--"On application of Isaac Foreman, ordered that the Com'rs. who let a part of this building to him do view the same and report to next Court whether he has done his work according to contract.

FOREMAN, GEORGE--Petit Juror Edgefield 1786. List 4

FOREMAN, ISAAC--Petit Juror Edgefield 1787. List 7 and 17

FOREMAN, JACOB--Dec'd. Edgefield Ct. Min. 1785/90 311 12 Jan 1790
Children: Ann, David, Isaac, Zelpha Foreman-minors. Isaac Foreman apt'd. Gdn.

FOREMAN, MARY--Dec'd. Edgefield Ct. Min. March 1795. Isaac Foreman, Exor. Inv. returned. Jan. Ct. 1795.
Will of Mary Foreman prov. by oath of John Perry and Isaac Foreman as exor. App'rs: Sam'l Walker, John Gray, Wm. Harden.

FORREST, GEORGE--Grand Juror Edgefield 1786. List 5 and 10

FORREST, JOHN -w- Patsy--Heirs of Edward Mosely, a devisee of James Butler. See Butler card. Edgefield Rec. Bk. A-165. 1834

FORT, NATHAN--Petit Juror Edgefield 1786. List 4

FORTNER, WILLIAM, SEN'R.--Will 25 Mar. 1843. Edgefield

FOWLER, MORRIS -w- Mary--Heirs of Catherine Butler. See Butler card. Edgefield Rec. Bk. A-298

FOX, JOHN--Of Marchmont, Richmond Co. Augusta, Georgia. Will in File
Niece: Mrs. Catherine Beale -w- Charles T. Beale of Columbia Co.
Mrs. Charlotte McGehee -w- John McGehee of Florida
Albert Dozier and Rebecca Dozier-Brother and sister
The 2 surviving daus of Anne E. Massay-dau. of Peter
Edwards, dec'd. late of New Providence
Legacy: Lydia Edwards-dau of Peter Willy Fox Edwards, son
of John Young of Alabama, son of late Col. Wm. Young.
Will in File 20 March 1837. Mrs. Caroline Patterson, formerly Caroline Young.

FOX, JOHN B. -w- Sophia--Heirs of Mrs. Wormley--See Wormley card. Edgefield Rec. Bk. B-71

FOX, JOHN--Will 31 Jan. 1837. Of Richmond Co. Georgia. Edgefield

FOY, WILLIAM and wife--Heirs of James O'Gilvie. See O'Gilvie card. Edgefield Rec. Bk. A-317 (or 9) 1839

FRANCES, REBECCA--Dau. dec'd. Elizabeth Clark-Will 1827. Edgefield

FRANKLIN, BARTLETT -w- Alpha--Heirs of William Scott. See Scott card.
Edgefield Rec. Bk. B-53 1841

FRANKLIN, BERRY and wife--Heirs of John Hester. See Hester card.
Edgefield Rec. Bk. A-278. 1837

FRANKLIN, EDMUND--Petit Juror Edgefield 1786. List 3

FRANKLIN, JOHN--Brother of Dicey Barton-wife of Thomas Barton-Will 1825

FRANKLIN, WILLIAM -w- Nancy and JAMES -w- Margaret--Heirs of Valentine
Young. See Young card. Edgefield File.

FRANKS, SALLY--Dau. of Solomon Bird.-Will 1810

FRAZER, ALEXANDER--Petit Juror Edgefield 1786. List 5

FRAZIER, BENJAMIN--Legatee of Aaron Allen-Will 1823 Edgefield
FRAZEER, BENJAMIN and his two daus: Mary Drake and Martha Frazeer-
    The daughters of Sarah Lott-Will 1831. Edgefield
-Benjamin Frazier--Heirs of Livingston Mims, dec'd. See Mims card.
Edgefield Rec. Bk. A-304 1839

FRAZIER, JAMES, ABSOLOM WILLIAMS, ABNER PERRIN--Comm'rs to view ground
    for a new road from Abbeville Co. line near Murrays old store to
    intersect the Martinton Road.near Joseph Collier's. The section
    from Co. line to Stephen's Creek and to Turkey Creek. Jas. Sanders,
    John Talbott, Wm. Evans-to view there to Joseph Colliers and on
    the Martinton road near Joseph Colliers. John Martin, Joseph
    Collier and David Thompson. Edgefield Ct. Min. March 1795

FRAZIER, JOHN--See card James Burk. Edgefield Ct. Min. Oct. 1794.
-John Frazier--Will 14 Sept. 1799. Edgefield Records A-359
    Wife: Lydia
    Children: Benjamin, James, John, Jesse Frazier
              Ann Oliphand
              Rosamond Jester
              Elizabeth Gunnels
              Margaret Gomillion

FRAZIER, JOHN M. --Of Edgefield Dist. to Martin Stidham Jan. 16, 1826
Mtg. or B/S slave-Joe, age about 14. Edgefield Deed 42-130
Vol. 45.59 E. B. Belcher, Shff. to John M Frazier-Trans. Title.
100 acres on Sleepy Creek. 1830

FRAZIER, MARTHA--Heir of Sarah Lott-See Lott card. Edgefield Rec. Bk.
    A-138 1833

FRAZIER, WILLIAM--Dec'd. Edgefield Ct. 13 Jan. 1789. Min. Bk. Pg-236
"On application of James Frazier, ordered that a citation issue to
show cause why Adm. should not be granted said James.

FREDERICK, JOHN AND JAMES--S: For Elizabeth Manse, Adm'x. estate of
John Watsman. See Watsman card. Edgefield Min. 1788

FREDERICK, LEWIS -w- Mary--Heirs of Samuel Medlock. See Medlock card.
    Edgefield Rec. Bk. A-74 1829

FREEMAN, FREDERICK, JUN'R.--Petit Juror Edgefield 1794. List 21

FREEMAN, HAMELIN and wife--Heirs of estate of Cad Evans, dec'd. See
    card-Evans. Edgefield Rec. Bk. A-100 1832

FREEMAN, REBECCAT.--Gr. Dau. of Rebecca Wilson-Will 1804

FREEMAN, THOMAS--To his children. Pet. 10 Dec. 1823. Deed Bk 40-269
    1st wife: Kizziah -w- James Garrett
    2nd wife: Garrett Freeman
        James
        Cilla -w- John Martin
        Allah -w- Pleasant Searls
        Rebecca -w- Covington Seals
        Samuel and Willy Freeman
    3rd wife:Nancy
        Thomas L. Freeman
        Narcissa Freeman.
    Pet. Court to give him back part of property he gave his elder
    children.
    -Thomas Freeman--Petit Juror Edgefield 1787. List 8 and 18

FRENCH, AMY--Dau. of George Martin-Will 1817. (or Finch)

FRASTER, CEILIA--See Will of Elizabeth Burnett-1820. Edgefield

FUDGE, ELIZABETH--Dau. of Michael Buckhalter-Will 1804 Edgefield

FUDGE, JACOB, SEN'R.--Petit Juror Edgefield 1787 List 6
    JACOB, JUN'R.-- "   "   "   "   " 15

FUDGE, MRS. MARGARET -w- Jacob Fudge--Dower Oct. Ct. 1786 favor Benj.
    Cook. Edgefield Ct. Min.

FUDGE, WILLIAM--Road Overseer excused--William Griffin apt'd. See
    Griffin card. Edgefield Ct. Min. March 1795

FULFORD, PERMELA--Heir of Martha Hancock. See card Jane Odom.
    Edgefield Rec. Bk. B-25 1839

FULLER, JOSEPH--Overseer of road from John Hammond's Ferry to Pretty
    Run Bridge and from intersection of sd road and the Cherokee Ponds
    road to sd Ferry--which leads to Maj. Pardue's-in the room of
    John Hammond. Excused.
    March Ct. 1795--John Fuller surety for Alexander Cowan as Tavern
    Keeper
    James Fuller Proved Will of Mary Meyer, dec'd. March 1795. See
    Meyer card.

FULMER, DICEY--Dau. of Daniel Self-Will 16 Nov. 1836

FULMER, MARY--Dau. of George Long-Will 1815. Edgefield

FURMAN, JOHN--Grand Juror Edgefield 1786. List 5

FUQUA, MARY--Dec'd. Will Prov. by oath of Wm. Weems, James Baker Qual. as one of exors. Appr's: John Covington, John Hardy, Tichard Hardy, and John Curry. Edgefield Ct. Min. Oct. 1794

GAINES, ELIZABETH--Dau. of Hamutal Wilson-Will 1806. See also card on Fay. Edgefield

GAINES, SALLY--Dau. of William Cain-Will 1796

GAINES, WILLIAM--Default in road work. See Lodwick Hill. Edgefield Ct. Min. March 1795

GALLMAN, BENJAMIN and wife--Heirs of John Ryan. See Ryan card. Edgefield Rec. Bk. B-81 1843

GALLMAN, CASPER--Apt'd. Road Overseer. See card John Addison. Edgefield Ct. Min. Jan. 1795

GALLMAN, FRANCES -w- William J. Gallman and dau. of William S. Johnson Will 1834. Edgefield

GALLMAN, JASPER--Petit Juror Edgefield 1788. List 9

GALLMAN, SALLY -w- Benjamin Gallman and niece of John Ryan-Will 1827 Wm. G. Gallman--a Legatee. Also: Susan H, W. F., R. A. V., and Lucretia Burr Gallman. Edzey F., Rachel N., Priscilla H., and America Gallman. Edgefield

GALPHIN, GEORGE--Of Silver Bluff. Will 6 April 1782. Abbeville 96 Dist. Bk.

GALPHIN, THOMAS--Grand Juror Edgefield 1786. List 3, 10, 14, 18, 19.

GANER, ARGE--Applied for permission to keep Tavern. S: Daniel Huff and Robert Wright. Edgefield Ct. Min. March 1795

GANTT, SARAH--Dau. of Richard, Legatee of Wilson Woodroof-Will 1809

GARDNER, BETSY--Heir (dau.) of Roger M. Williams. See Williams card. Edgefield Wills D-17 1828

GARDNER, MARY -w- Samuel Gardner. July 1786. Edgefield Ct. Min.

GARDNER, RACHEL--dec'd. dau. of Daniel Parker-Will 1806. Edgefield Gr. Children: Salina and John Gardner

GARDNER, SAMUEL--Petit Juror Edgefield 1788. List 12
-Samuel Gardner--Grandfather of the children of William Quarles. Quarles Will 1821. Edgefield
-Samuel Gardner--Legacy in trust for Rebecca, dau of Casper Nail-Nail Will 1833. Edgefield

GARDNER, S. W. -w- Elizabeth--Heirs of James Butler. See Butler card. Edgefield Rec. Bk. A-124 1833

GARDNER, WILLIAM--Gdn. minor heir of Ellen Sullivan. See Sullivan card. Edgefield

GARNER, LYDIA--Dau. of Elisha Robertson-Will 1792. Edgefield

GARNER, SAMUEL--Petit Juror Edgefield 1789. List 16

GARRETT, CAROLINE -w- John W. Garrett. Dau. of John Middleton.
Edgefield Misc. M. 15

GARRETT, DELILAH--Dau. of William Jeter-Will 1793. Edgefield

GARRETT, EDWARD--Will 24 Sept. 1836. Edgefield

GARRETT, ELIZABETH--Dau. of Henry Ware. Will 1801
-Elizabeth Ware--Will 9 March 1843. Edgefield

GARRETT, HENRY--Widow-Ann. Edgefield Deed 29 Dec. 1797 Bk. 20-23
Joseph Garrett, carpenter, of Georgia conveyed 29 Dec. 1797 to
Hugh Middleton for Agatha Middleton 128 acres. Part 640 acre
grant Francis Bremen "Whereon Ann Garrett now lives". Wit: John
Middleton, Joseph Lewis, Georgi Garrett. Is dower.
Page 32-George Garrett of S. C. to same for same. Willed.

GARRETT, HENRY W. --Dec'd. R. E. Sold 1841. Edgefield Rec. Bk B-31
Dist: Susan Garrett, widow 1/3 equal to $91.83
Richard M. Johnson and wife 1/8 of 2/3
John, Mary, Sarah, Teresa, Susan, Martha, and Catherine
Garrett--all minors. 1/8 of 2/3 each. John A. Houstin,Gdn.

GARRETT, HENRY -w- Elizabeth--Heirs estate of Michael Corley. Edgefield Rec. Bk. A-144/6 1833

GARRETT, JAINUSARY--Gr. dau. of John Calliham of Luninburg, Va. Deed
gift to her of Slave-Milly. 1 April 1793. Wit: John Usary,
Ambrese Grisome. Edgefield Deed Bk. 34-112

GARRETT, JAMES--100 acres on Long Cane. Bd. Mr. Wood and vac.
Surveyed: 7 Aug. 1764   Grant: 27 Aug. 1764
-James Garrett and Thos. Flint--Bond 27 Dec. 1783 Samuel Watson
Old Index VV-55 Edgefield
-James Garrett, dec'd. Cit: 8 March 1800. Wm. Garrett, Adm'r.
Edgefield Record Bk. A-1800 Page 21. Pages 69 to 84- Inv. very
long.

GARRETT, JOHN--148 acres Craven Co--Indian Creek of Broad River.
Cert: 8 July 1774   Grant 19 Aug. 1774 to mentioned. Mem. 13-263
-JohnGarrett of 96 Dist to Comm'rs. of Treas. 12 July 1783
Recites: John Garrett and Samuel Hammond gave Bond 9 July 1783.
Mtg.--3 adjoining plantations in 96 Dist. Late the property of
the Chehesaw Indians. Described in the general plat of said land
as nos. 19-20 and 72 in the whole, 517 acres. Bd. Ralph Philips
and Savannah River. C. T. Deed M-5 173
-John Garrett--Original Will. Abbeville Bx. 39-865. 1784
Will 23 Oct. 1784   Prov: 6 Jan. 1785
Wife: Not named
Dau: Frances Longmire and her dau. Suckey Longmire
       Elizabeth Long of state of Va.
       Martha Ware of state of Ga.
       Lucy Lowry
       Dolly Ware
Exors: Henry Ware, Sr. of Georgia, Henry Ware, Jr. of S. C.

GARRETT, JOHN--Petit Juror Edgefield 1786. List 1 and 2

GARRETT, JOHN--Late of Ireland. Naturalized 13 July 1795 at Charleston. Has been in U. S. 5 years. Archives Dept. Misc. 3-E-564

GARRETT, JOHN CATLETT -w- Elizabeth to John Martin 19 July 1809 85 A. in Edgefield. Part of Richard Lowry's land. Deed Bk. 31-134 Page 135--Gen. John Martin -w- Mary Ann of Abbeville to Edmund Bacon of Edgefield--Same land.

GARRETT, LUCY, THOMAS, WILLIAM, STEPHEN--Children of Mary Rivers-Will
1802
GARRETT, MAYSON -w- Nancy conv. 23 March 1811 to Richard Covington Interest in 62 acres on Stephen's Creek which Nancy got from her father, John Covington, dec'd. She being entitled to 1/6 part. Edgefield Deed Bk. 30-387/8

GARRETT, MARTHA--Dau. of Amsted Burt-Will 1839. Edgefield

GARRETT, MARY MAGDALINE CHASTEEN--Gr. dau. of Joseph Collier-Will 1818

GARRETT, MARY--Dau. of John Clackler-Will 1814

GARRETT, RICHARD -w- Martha Pickett, dau. of James Pickett, dec'd. Edgefield Rec. Bk. A-306
-Richard Garrett -w- Martha--Heirs of James Picket. See Picket card. Edgefield Rec. Bk. A-306   1839

GARRETT, ROBERT. Mem 13-264. Edgefield. 1450 acres. Grant in 1774 in Granville County on Stephens Creek. Bd: John Davis, Joseph Dupea, Thos. Keys, Bussey and Morris, Rigg Manor,Robert Garrett. Nathan Reid, Samuel Wharton and John Clark.

GARRETT, ROBERT--Of Granville Co. Abbeville Box 39-856. Orig. Will
Wife: Mary--100 A. at mouth of Lloyd's Cr.   21 June 1781
          "Until the children I had by her come of age".
Son: Thomas-next inherits
"my 7 children"--Peggy, William, Stephen, James, Mary, Betsy, and
                  Thomas--Pet. for Gdn. 1786. Jones Rivers, Apt'd.
"My eldest children"--Frances Keay -w- Thomas Keay
                  Ann Good
                  John Garrett
                  John Catlett Garrett
                  Betsy Garrett
Wit: John Garrett, Lucy Lowry, Francis Longmire.
Debts due by: Mr. Breedlove, Catlett Garrett, John Garrett, Obediah Henderson, Mr. Rivers, John Smith, George Cowan, Matthew Dalton, Benj. Brooks, John Purvis, James Scott
-Robert Garrett, dec'd. Edgefield Deed 1-76. Exor's: John Garrett, Jones Rivers To: 1789 John Canady 100 A. on waters of Stephens Creek. Part of 1450 acre original grant Robert Garrett. Wit: John C. Garrett, Wm. Garrett, Elisha Palmer.
-Robert Garrett, Dec'd. Edgefield Deed Bk 1-76-81.
Exor's: John Garrett and Jones Rivers--Conv. to John Canady in 1789 100 A. on waters of Stephens creek. Wit. etc. as above.
-Book 1-156--Exor's (same as above) to Daniel McKey, Sen'r. 510 acres on Stephens Creek. Bd. John Garrett. Wit: Dan. Barksdale, John C. Garrett. 11 July 1789

76

GARRETT, ROBERT--Dec'd. Edgefield Min. Bk. Page 332. April 1790
"Ordered that the lands of Robert Garrett, dec'd. be sold
agreeable to his Will on the second Thursday in May next at
the house of Jones Rivers, in four equal divisions. Jones
Rivers and his wife, Mary Rivers Ex'x, to make titles.
-Robert Garrett--Grant on Lloyd's Cr. of Stephens Cr. and part of
another tract. Sale by Benj. McCary 2 Feb. 1821--1/2 interest.
To William Garrett. Edgefield Deed Bk. 39-17
-Recites Will of Benj. McCary -w- Dolly 25 May 1803. Son-Benjamin,
a minor and youngest son. Wit: John C. Garrett and Henry W. -
Garrett. (This information on same card.)

GARRETT, SALLEY--Dau. of Jesse Hill-Will 1818. Land where Thomas
Garrett lives.

GARRETT, SETH--To Jno McCord 2 March 1767 B/S one slave. Archives
Dept. Misc. MM-611

GARRETT, STEPHEN--Son in law of John Hammond.-Will 1800. Dau. Elizabeth
Garrett. Edgefield
-Record Bk. A-1820-364--Stephen Garrett-son in law and legatee of
John Hammond, wife, Elizabeth, dau. of John Hammond-Will 7 June 1800
Lot of land in Campbelltown with the buildings thereon "now in
occupation of John Longmire".

GARRETT, STEPHEN -w- Elizabeth Stephen Garrett of Stephens Creek
2 Feb. 1808 and Charles Hammond -w- Mary, Abraham Martin Wade -w-
Martha Patsy, Robert Livingston -w- Lucy--Children of Robert
Garrett of Granville Co. 96 Dist. Dec'd. To: William Garrett-
son of Robert Recites Will of Robert Garrett -w- Mary--land for
life. Then to son Thomas Garrett who died 1 Oct. 1804, age 24
last. Grantors are his brothers and sisters.

GARRETT, STEPHEN--Equity Bill Filed 19 April 1817 No. 14 -vs- Jeremiah
Welborn--Alleges: Peter Farrer, Sen'r. mtg'd. to him a negro
named London. That Jeremiah Willborn as Adm'r. of estate of
Peter Farrow, Jr. brought action alleging Peter Farrow, Sen. gave
the negro to his gr. son, Peter Farrow, Jr. about 30 years ago
as the slave was in his possession at the house of his grandmother, Mrs. Rivers.

GARRETT, STEPHEN--Will 1 Dec. 1823. Edgefield Bill 846 (46?)
Widow: Elizabeth S.
6 young children: James R. Garrett
                  William   "
                  Charles S.   "
                  Thos. S.   "
                  Stephen J.   " -widow Caroline -m- Abraham Martin
                                  Moved to Montgomery, Alabama
                  Mary Ann -w- Button (or Burton) Mims
Elder son: John H. Garrett-widow, Mary and 6 children:
           William H. Garrett
           Elizabeth -w- Augustus Bush
           Mary Ann -w- B. C. Sparks
           Susan B. Garrett
           Charley H. "
           John H.   "
Charles G. Garrett's widow, Caroline -m- Jas. P. Thurmond
           1 child, died in infancy.

GARRETT, SUSAN--Sister of Henry W. Lowe-Will 1828

GARRETT, THOMAS--Paid on 204 acres Craven, N. C. Grant paid up to
25 March 1768. 1770 Equity 1758-332 Int. Rent. Arch. Dept.
-Thomas Garrett--100 Acres in Craven on small branch of Indian Cr.
Cert. 6 April 1773. John Caldwell, D. S.
Grant 5 May 1773   Mem: 18 Aug. 1773 del to John
Armstrong. Mem. 12-382
-Thomas Garrett -w- Sarah-dau. of Jesse Hill, Deed Gift. 130 A.
on Stephens Creek 4 Feb. 1820. Dower, Elizabeth Hill. Edgefield
Deed Bk. 38-309
-Thomas Garrett -w- Nancy of Alabama-Heirs of Rebecca Ramey. See
Ramey card. Edgefield Rec. Bk. B-75 1842

GARRETT, WILLIAM--Adm. estate James Garrett 1800. Inv: $9,798.08
Edgefield A 21-69-244

GARRETT, CAPT. WILLIAM--Brother of Polly Hammond, wife of Charles
Hammond-Will 1836. Edgefield

GARRETT, WILLIAM--Dec'd. R. E. Sold 1850 Edgefield Rec. Bk. B-192
Dist: Harriet Garrett, widow 1/3 equal to $529.39
       Mary Ann -w- Daniel M. Hart 1/9   )
       Thomas L. Garrett   )
       Jane E. -w- John J. Hart   ) each received
       George W. Garrett   )   1/9
       Oliver S. Garrett   )
       James W., Wm. H. H., Nancy, John H.--minors)

GAWMAN, JOHN--Grand Juror Edgefield 1787. List 6

GENTRY, CAIN -m- Liddy Youngblood-dau. of Peter Youngblood. See
Youngblood card. Augusta Georgia deed. Edgefield File

GENTRY, ELISHA--Petit Juror Edgefield 1787. List 7

GENTRY, ELIZABETH--Sister of John Lyon-Will 1841. Edgefield

GENTRY, EZEKIEL--Petit Juror Edgefield 1786. List 5
HEZEKIAH-   "   "   "   "   " 17

GENTRY, HEZEKIAH--Adm'r. Estate of Pleasant Burnett, dec'd. See
Burnett card. Edgefield Ct. Min. Oct. 1794

GEORGE, DAVID -w- Milly--Heirs of James Picket. See Picket card.
Edgefield Rec. Bk. A-306 1839

GETSEN, SAMUEL P. -w- Mary A.--Heirs of Ellen Sullivan. See Sullivan
card. Edgefield Rec. Bk. B-111 1847

GIBSON, ELIAS--Petit Juror Edgefield 1788. List 10

GIBSON, JOHN--Minor son of Samuel Gibson. Edgefield Ct. Min. 14 July
Wm. Dawson, Apt'd. S: John Dawson, Richard Johnson   1788

GIBSON, SUSANNAH--Dau. of William Hudson-Will1809

GILDER, MARY--Legatee of Joicy Culpepper-Will 1837 Edgefield Wills
                                                        D-126

GILDERT, SOPHIA and her children--Heirs of Mrs. Wormley. See Wormley
    card. Edgefield

GILLIARD, THOMAS -w- Dione--Heirs of William Richardson-See Richardson
    card. Edgefield Rec. Bk. A-254. 1836

GILLION, PATSY--Dau. of Jarrott Edwards-Will 1822 Edgefield

GILLON, JOHN -w- Polly--Heirs estate of James Eidson-See Eidson card.
    Edgefield Rec. Bk. B-125 1847

GIMBRELL, ALSAY--Dau. of John Jackson-Will 1787. Edgefield

GITTY, JOHN--Dec'd. R. E. Sold 1847. Edgefield Rec. Bk. B-119
    Dist: Patsy Spikes, a sister 1/5 equal to $152.59
           Anna Spikes " " -same
           Henry Stott, son of dec'd. sister-same
           Stamford F. May and wife 1/2 of 1/5 equal to $76.29
           Susan Skillen -w- of ? 1/2 of 1/5
           Children of dec'd sister: Tabitha Moore
             John R. Moore   Eliza   "
             Cornelia "   William " 1/7 of 1/5
             Drayton "   Henry   " each.
    P. A. by William Spikes of Chambers Co. Ala. for part of his
    wife, Anna, to Henry M. Spike of Abbeville Co. S. C.

GITZEN, MARY--Dau. of John Sullivan-Will 1836. Edgefield

GLANTON, ANN--Dau. of Elizabeth Bolger-Will 1836

GLANTON, CHRISTOPHER--Petit Juror Edgefield 1789. List 13

GLANTON, JENCY--Dau. of John Kilcrease-Will 1829. Her daus: Mary
    and Martha. Edgefield

GLANTON, JOHN--Dec'd. R. E. Sold 1833. Edgefield Rec. Bk. A-181
    Dist: Lewis Glanton
           John Glanton
           Abner Glanton
           James Hardy and wife
           Children of Wm. Glanton: William, Jno. I., Julian, B. F.
   -Another card: states each received 1/5 equal to $96.98 each.
   The children of Wm. Glanton, dec'd each 1/4 of 1/5 $24.49
   Widow of Intestate relinquished her right and interest.

GLANTON, LEWIS--Dec'd. R. E. Sold. 1851. Edgefield Rec. Bk. B-206
    Dist: Mary Glanton, widow 1/3 equal to $161.75
           Mary Ann -w- Henry Parkman 1/11 of 2/3
           Martha P. -w- Samuel Broadwater-same
           Charles R. Glanton   Edward Glanton
           John W. Glanton   Sarah E. Glanton
           Benjamin F. Glanton   Lewis L. Glanton
           Abner M. Glanton   Caroline J. Glanton
           Patrick H. Glanton   1/11 of 2/3 each equal to $29.41

GLANTON, SARAI, EMELINE, MARTHA CAROLINE, WM. CHURL--Gr. children of
Elizabeth Weaver-Will 1830

GLASCOCK, BETSY--Dec'd. dau. of John Simkins-Will 1832. Gr. children:
Arthur and Ann Elizabeth Glascock.

GLASCOCK, WILLIAM--Dec'd. Was Surv. exor. of John Benningfield.
Abraham Jones qualified on estate of Benningfield. Cradock
Burnett to appear and show cause why his Adm. should not be set
aside. Edgefield Ct. Min. Jan. 1795. (Name possibly Beddingfield)

GLASSCOCK, WILLIAM -w- Lucinda--Heirs of James Martin. See Martin
card. Edgefield Rec. Bk. A-72 1831

GLASGOW, JOHN--Dec'd. Edgefield Box 41-920 Cit. missing
Bond: 15 Sept. 1828 $2000.00
Adm'r: Giles W. Glasgow   S: Joseph Williams, Jas. Williams
App'r: 15 Sept. 1828--James Morrow, Isiah Johnson, James Williams,
Oswell Heuston, Benjamin Hill. Sale Bill 8 Oct. 1828
Purchasers: James Glasgow   James Alexander
           Jane   "   Samuel Baker
           Elizabeth "   William M. Calhoun
           Giles   "   William Chapel
           John B. Williams   John Arnold
           Joseph Williams   James Williams, Sen'r.
           James T. Williams   O. Houston

GLASGOW, JOHN--Dec'd. Abbeville Part. and Sale R. E. Page 57
Summons 7 Dec. 1830 to:
Giles Glasgow   Dance Mullin -w- Elizabeth
Lewis Arnold -w- Ruth   Samuel Glasgow-dec'd.
David M. Daniel -w- Mary?   Winey)
John Glasgow   James) Minors. John Dale-Gdn.
Joseph Williams -w- Nelly   Jane)

GLASGOW, JOHN--Original Will 2 Dec. 1842 Edgefield Box 41-929
Wife: Eliza Ann
Sister: Jane McCalister the 166 acres where James McCallister lives.
Exor: Friend-Robert A. Martin
Wit: Robert McComb, George Cochrin, M. A. Smith
Child born shortly before his death.   Prov: 23 Oct. 1843

GLASGOW, JOHN DAVID--Minor under 14. Edgefield Box 41-933
Mother, Elizabeth A. Glasgow, consents to appointment of A. Kennedy
as his Gdn. Apt'd. 1 Jan. 1845. Son of John Glasgow, Will Prov.
23 Oct. 1843. R. A. Martin, Exor. Bond of Archibald Kennedy
1 Jan. 1845. S: A. Kennedy, James Lessly, James A. Foster

GLOSSIER, JACOB--Dec'd. R. E. Sold 1846. Edgefield Rec. Bk. B-141
Mary Glossier, the widow 1/3 equal to $156.10
John F. L. Glossier-the remaining 2/3

GLOVER, ALICE--Dau. of Christian Rountree-Will 1799. Wife of Andrew
Glover. Edgefield.

GLOVER, CHARLES I. -w- Martha--Heirs of Sarah Lott. See Lott card.
Edgefield Rec. Bk. A-138 1833

GLOVER, DAVID--Overseer of Road from Martinton to Augusta, that part
from Mill Creek to Sweet Water in room of John Curry, excused.
John Glover, Overseer of Road from Cloud's to Adam's Ferry, part
from Toundtree's Old Mills to sd Ferry. Edgefield Ct. Min. March
1795

GLOVER, ELIZABETH SARAH--Wife of Wiley Glover, Dau. of John Burgess-
Will 1829. Edgefield

GLOVER, FREDERICK--Grand Juror Edgefield 1786. List 1 and 2

GLOVER, REBECCA--Dau. of William Jeter-Will 1818. Gr-dau. of Charlotte
Elvira Glover. Edgefield

GLOVER, STEPHEN--Dec'd. Inv. Returned. Edgefield Ct. Min. Oct. 1794
Personal estate to be sold at house of Rev. Charles Bussy on 1st
Thursday, Nov. next.
March Ct. 1795--Amount sale returned by Charles Bussy. Recorded

GLOVER, WILEY, Dec'd. Exors: Nathan Lipscomb and James Bullock
(also Jemime Lipscomb -w- Nathan). Adv. Lewelling Goode, Adm'r.
of Samuel Williams. Ct. Com. Pleas 1807-10-225. Ct. Min. 1829
Page 201--John F. Glover, John Bullock, Wiley Glover-note to
estate of Samuel Williams. 3 Dec. 18__.

GLOVER, WILLIAM--Grand Juror Edgefield 1788. List 10, 16, 21.
-William J. Glover-Will 16 Sept. 1842

GLOZIER, NICHOLAS--Petit Juror Edgefield 1789. List 14

GOFF, ELLIS H. -w- Nancy--Heirs of Ahile Holsenbake. See Holsonbake
card. Edgefield Rec. Bk. B-35 1841

GOFF, TERRILL -w- Lucy--Heirs of estate of Lazarus Chadwick. See
Chadwick card. Edgefield Rec. Bk. A-86 1831

GOGGINS, JAMES-Will 8 May, 1843. Edgefield

GOLDING, JAMES, WILLIAM, ANTHONY, JR.--Children of Anthony, Sen'r.
Gr.-children of James Magill. See Magill card. 96 Dist. Bk. 1799

GOLDMAN, SARAH--Niece of Benjamin Ryan-Will 1808. Edgefield

GOLEMAN, ISABELLA--Niece of Caleb Holloway-Will 1840

GOLEMAN, JACOB, Dec'd. R. E. Sold 1841. Edgefield Rec. Bk. B-39
Dist: Isabella Goleman 1/3 equal to $161.62
        Henrietta F., and James R.,--minors--1/3 each
Lewis Runnels Gdn. of minors.
Another dist. on page 41-same heirs-$61.10 each
   "   "   "   "   43- ",   " $29.03 "

GOLIGHTLY, WILLIAM --Of Fairforest, 96 Dist. Will 18 Jan. 1872
  Wife: Amy   96 Dist Bk. Page 1 Abbeville
  Sons: Christopher, William and David
  Daus: Clarimon and Mary
  Bro: David

GOLMAN, RICE -w- Drucills--Heirs estate of James Rhodes-See Rhodes
  card. Edgefield Rec. Bk. A-56. 1831

GOMILLION, CHRISTIAN--His residence on road from Lee's Bridge to the
  Pine House. Bibby Bush apt'd. Overseer. See Bush card.
  Edgefield Ct. Min. March 1795

GOMILLION, CHRISTIAN--Petit Juror Edgefield 1787. List 17
           CHRISTOPHER "   "   "   "   " 16

GOMILLION, JOHN--Legatee of John Frazier-Will 1824. Edgefield

GOMILLION, MARGARET--Dau. of John Frazier-Will 1799. Rec'd. 1801

GOOD, ADAM--To John Rutledge 22/23 Aug. 1788 Charleston Deed Y-5-541
  Plantation called Beresford Hall--348 acres St. Thomas and St.
  Dennis Parish. Berkley CO. Bd: James Roulain, David Maul,
  Watcod Creek, John Howell, John Moore and Creek out of Cooper
  River Marsh.

GOODE, ADAM--Orangeburg, Savannah River 1796   PLATS-ARCHIVES DEPT.
  EDWARD--On Saluda R. Toney's Cr. 1784 (2)
  JOHN--Between Broad R. and Bullock Cr. 1795
  LEWELLING--Edgefield 1791, (3)
  MAJ. LEWELLING--26 Mi. Cr. of Keowee 1828 (2)
  RICHARD--Golden Grove Cr. 1784
  ROBERT--Barnwell--1828
  COL. ROBERT--On Great Saltcatchers-1828

GOOD, ADAM--Indent Q-480. Rev. AA2935-A Archives Dept.

GOODE, ANN, Dec'd. Ordered citation to be issued to show cause why
  Adm. should not be granted to William Longmire. Edgefield Min.
  Bk. Page 213. Oct. 1788

GOODE, DELANSON -vs- James Bullock. Conf. Jdg. $379.00. Note given
  Lewelling Goods. Sold note to Delanson Goode. Edgefield Ct.
  Com. Pleas-1807-1810 235

GOODE, ELIZA--Adm'x--Alleges: John Ramsay-orator contracted with
  Mackerness P. Goode, now dec'd. for purchase of tract of land--
  said Mackerness Goode died 1818 intestate--Left Wife, Eliza
  Goode and 1 child. Edgefield Equity Roll 66.

GOODE, GARLAND--Apt'd. Gdn of Wiley Martin and Rieves Martin. S: on
  Bond: Wm. Mathews and Drury Mathews. Ct. 11 Oct. 1787. Edge-
  field Ct. Min. 1785-90. Pg. 133
  Page 133/4--Samuel Goode, et al apt'd. Appr of Estate of William
  Martin, Dec'd.
  Page 156--Cit. issued to grant Adm. to Barkley Martin.

82

GOODE, GARLAND--Of Edgefield to Robert Thomas 27 Feb. 1795 272 Pounds.
320 acres on waters of 96 Creek. Bd. Luallen Goode, Samuel Goode.
Bequeathed to said Garland Goode by Mackerness Goode, his father.
By Will 1794. Edgefield Deed 12-359
Page 360--Garland Goode to Robert Thomas 1 March 1795 320 Acres
Willed by his father, Mackerness Goode. Dower: Elizabeth Goode
widow of Garland Goode. 12 Oct. 1795
-Garland Good from David Burns, Sen'r. 2 March 1795--250 acres on
head of 96 Creek. Bd. Mackerness Goode, Jane Brownlee, Robert
Duke. Edgefield Deed 12-89

GOODE, GARLAND--Dec'd. Will 10 July 1795. Prov: Oct. 1795
Edgefield Probate Box 38. Package 1490
Wife: Elizabeth
"My children": Susanna Phillips
               Mackerness Pope
               LewellingGoode
          Son: Philip Goode-at age 21
     Ex: Bro: Samuel Goode, Drury Mathews and John Pope

GOODE, GARLAND, et al--Alleges Philip Goode died intestate in 1817.
Three minor children: Garland, Duke and Philip.
Widow: Caroline Matilda -m- Wm. Paine, Jr.
Edgefield Equity Roll 120

GOOD, JOHN--Of Prince William Parish to John Mackenzie and Matthew
Roche--300 Pounds. Pend. 600 Pounds. Mtg. 3 Negro boys:
Prince, Jupiter and Paul
50 Cattle, 30 Sheep, 3 Horses, 3 Mares. Dated at Combahee
24 March 1746. Wit: Cha's. Stevenson
Archives Dept. Misc. Mtg. 1746-1748-139
-John Goode--Archives Dept. Mem 13-14
200 acres Granville County on S-side Stevens Creek. Bd.-All vac.
Cert. 10 Dec. 1772. Grant-7 May 1774. Men. 16 Sept. 1774
Del. to Henry Key. (Next is Philip Goode, same location.
-John Goode to C. Johnson 14 May 1773. Mtg. slaves. Arch. Dept.
Misc. Mtg. 3C-277
-John Goode--Order to deliver Indent to John Bankhead. Oct. 1786
Zachariah Bullock, J. P. Rev. AA-2940 Archives Dept.
-John Goode--Of Winton Co. -w- Joice to Thomas Dalton 2 Nov. 1787
150 acres Edgefield below mouth of Bedingsfield's Creek on Sav.
River. Part grant to Richard Cannady 1 Dec. 1772. Wit: William
Goode, Thomas Morris, Nathaniel Sands. Edgefield Deed 10-27
-John Goode to William Robertson 30 Nov. 1789--200 acres Granville
Co. S-side Stephens Creek. Grant to John Goode, 7 May 1774.
Edgefield Deed 11-284

GOODE, JOHN, SEN'R.--Will 19 Oct. 1805. York Wills Bk-A 238 File 167
Wife: Not named--Life Maintainance   Case 56
Sons: John Goode, Jr., Jones B. Goode--Land
Daus: Ann Goode-NM. Her Will Bk. G-543
       Mary Bratton   Wit: Henry Goode, George Goode, John McKenny
       Jane Hemphill   Prov: 18 April 1807
Mentioned under Will Ann Goode-Brother, John. James B. ? and
Mary Waller. 5 April 1832. Niece: Patsy Plexico. Jean He___? __

GOODE, JOHN--Dec'd. CONTINUED:-
   Will of Wm. Bratton devises land "I purchased of Henry Goode"
   27 Dec. 1813
   John and James Goode Wit. Will of Jean Hamilton 22 Nov. 1807
   John Good Wit. Will of Wm. Nelson 13 Aug. 1805
   James B. Goode Wit Will of Wm. Thompson 26 Oct. 1822
   John Goode Wit. Will of Martha Bratton 4 May 1827
    "   "   "   "   of John Roberts 21 March 1835
   John H. and Wm. J. Goode Wit. Will of Joseph Jameson 21 May 1842

GOODE, JOHN--Dec'd. Cit. 10 Nov. 1815 -w- Permelia -m- Daniel Williams
   Adm. Bond 1 Dec. 1815   Adm'x: Permelia Goode
   Adm'r. Mackerness Goode   S: Philip Good and Martin Palmer
   Edgefield Box 12 398

GOODE, JOSEPH--350 Acres on Black River. Cert. 10 March 1735.
   Pre. Rev. Plats. Archives Dept.

Goode, Lew. of Edgefield to Lewelling Goode, James McCracken. Mtg.
   for 3,847--696 Acres on which side Lew Goode resides. Bd. Est.
   Garland Goode, dec'd. To secure Gdnship Bond. Degree Williams,
   son of Samuel Williams and Wife, Catherine, of Abbeville, S. C.
   Edgefield Deed 30-350

GOODE, LEWELLING--Dec'd. Will 11 Sept. 1812r(Original) Prov. 25 Sept.
   Wife: Elizabeth--The home place   1812
   To: James Matthews--100 acres.
   To: Williamson Williams (nephew) a minor
   To: William Hargrove--a horse
   To: Michael Wood--a Horse. Edgefield Pro. Box 12-406

GOODE, LEWELLEN--Step son of Lewis Matthews-Will 1824. Freeman Goode
   a Wit. Edgefield

GOODE, MACKERNESS, JR.--100 acres on waters of Little River. Bd.
   Daniel Osborn, Mackoness Goode, Sen'r. Cert. 21 June 1765
   Prev. Plats.

GOODE, MACKERNESS--3 March 1767--500 acres on Br. Little River called
   Beaver Dam Branch. Bd. Col. Cargill, David Craddock, John Box,
   William Arthur. Prev. Rev. Plats

GOODE, MACKERNESS--Minor--Pet. Peter Morgan as Gdn. 12 Jan. 1790.
   Stray paper. Edgefield

GOODE, MACK--of Charlotte Co. Va. to John Thurmond of Edgefield--Land
   on Beaver Dam of Turkey Creek. Bd. lands, estate of Thomas Goode
   dec'd. David George, John Elam. Edgefield 15 March 1790 Deed 1-265

GOODE, MACKERNESS--Dec'd. Will proved by oath of Paul Holloway.
   Edgefield Ct. Min. March 1795

GOODE, MACKERNESS--From Jeremiah Hatcher-Shff.--Land sold in care of
   John Beckum and Reuben Beckum. On old road from Augusta to
   Cambridge. Edgefield Deed 13-380

GOODE, MACKERNESS--From Hezekiah Oden 22 Sept. 1798--116 acres on
Leyds Creek of Stephen's Creek. Edgefield Deed 16-102

GOODE, MACKENESS--Dec'd. Orig. Will 31 Aug 1793. Prov. 12 March 1795
Sons: John and Garland Goode
Ex: Lewwilling and Samuel Goode
Dau: Frances Eubanks formerly widow of William Martin. 1 child
Reeves Martin. Wesley Martin? Box 12. Pkg. 405
Cit: 26 Jan. 1818
Eliza Goode, Adm'x.
Paid Thos. Smith "in right of wife". Rec'd. of Permelia Goode

GOODE, MACKERNESS--7 March 1769--200 Acres Berkley on Beaver Dam. Bd.
Wm. Martin , Wm. McLaughlin, Benj. Eaton. Cert: 13 June 1769

GOODE, MACKENESS--Horse lost 1781. Rev. AA 2936

GOODE, MACKINESS--Dec'd. Edgefield Deed 31-232 Edgefield
Adm'x: Eliza Goode
Child: Susan-minor
Alleges: John Ramsey, Plantation sold to Mackiness Goode. 355
acres Bd. James Adams, Jesse Paul, Philip Goode, dec'd., Douglas
Holloway, Joseph Stalworth. Mackiness Good died without making
title. See Dooly

GOOD, MARY--Wit Will of Jane Wallis of St. Bartholomew's Parish
1 Nov. 1743 C. T. Wills
Dau: Mary Lawson (Dau. of Jane Wallis)
Gr. D.Ann Lawson
Gr. D.Mary Lawson
To: Joseph Madey, Jane Madey, John Lawson, Alexander Lawson

GOODE, PERMELIA, SUSANNAH BURT, ACQUILLA MILES, LEWIS MILES *W* SALLY
TO: John Moore--All interest in land of Acquilla Miles, dec'd.
75¼ acres on Horn's Creek. Deed Bk. 34-388 Edgefield
Page 390: Joshua Key -w- Martha Key and Edward Collier -w-
Louisa--their 1/6 part-1 share- of land of Acquilla Miles.
To John Moore

GOODE, PHILIP--Prev. Rev. Plats-Archives Dept.
150 A. N-s Saluda Cert. 22 Aug. 1764
50 A. Colleton 20 Jan. 1768
150 A. Craven Bd. Benj. Edwins 12 April 1768
150 Colleton 9 May 1770
50 A. Horn's Creek 24 Feb. 1771
150A. Stephens Creek 15 Mar. 1771

GOODE, PHILIP--From William Lamar -w- Penelope 19/2- May 1771--150 A.
Bd. Stephen's Creek and all vac. C. T. Deed 24-239/42
-Philip Goode--150 A. Stevens Cr. of Savannah R. 21 Feb. 1772
Bd. E. Chasteens land. Mem. 11-127
-Philip Goode--150 A. Colleton Co. Bd. Philip Goode and Geo. Mock.
Mem. 11-488 29 Oct. 1772
-Philip Goode--50 A. Granville Co. on Horn's Creek. Bd. sd Goode,
John Russell and vac.16 Sept. 1774 Mem. 13-4
-Philip Goode--8 June 1774--150 A. Granville on West side Horn's
Cree.. Orig Gr. being ½ of 300 acres to William Beale. Mem. 12-491

GOODE, PHILIP--Court Journal 25 April 1774. 38-37
   Wt. prolonged for 50 Acres in Granville-page 50. Grant sd 7 May
   1774. Page 50-John Good--200 Acres Colleton

GOODE, PHILIP--Original Will 18 Mar. 1776. Prov. 1 Sept. 1791
   Wife: Ann Goode--Plantation whereon I now live.
   Sons: Mackerness and Samuel--Land on Horn's Creek
   Dau: Martha Watkins Goode
         Ann Goode
   To: William Jones and Benjamin Jones   Pkg. 1489
   Exors: William Goode and Thomas Goode Edgefield Pro. Bx-38
   -Philip Goode, dec'd: Cit-20 Nov. 1818 Caroline M. Goode, Adm'x.
   Equity Roll shows: Widow Caroline Matilda -m- Wm. Paine, Jr.
                       3 children: Garland Goode
                                    Duke Goode
      Edgefield Pro.--12-418   Philip Goode

GOODE, POLLY--From her father, Samuel Gardner, Deed Gift 13 Jan. 1801
   Polly Goode of Hancock Co. Georgia. Negro girl-Lucy
   Edgefield Deed 20-7

GOODE, ROBERT--Provisions-1781. Also Duty. Camden Dist.
   Rev. AA-2937. Prob.-Fairfield
   -Goode, Col. Robert--Barnwell, S. C. Adm: Martha C. Goode 1841

GOODE, SAMUEL--Return 51--Duty in Militia. Indent W-488 Edgefield
   Rev. AA-2941 Archives Dept.

GOODE, SAMUEL--33 A. Colleton 1 Aug. 1769. Prev. Rev. Plats
   THOMAS--150 A. 26 July 1770 Granville on Spring Branch of
      Horn's Creek.
   WILLIAM--500 A. on Beaver Dam of Turkey Creek-Bd. Ward Taylor,
      Said Goode. Wit: 5 Mar. 1771. Cert. 15 Mar. 1771

GOODE, SAMUEL -w- Jemima. Daus: Edna and Jemima. Gr. daus. of
   Joseph Davenport-Will 5 Aug. 1788. Newberry

GOODE, SAMUEL--From John Holloway-27 Dec. 1792-150 A. in said Co.
   (formerly Colleton). Bd. Macherness Goode, James Anderson.
   Grant 2 May. 1770. Bk. EEE-302. Edgefield Deed 8-123

GOODE, SAMUEL--Of Edgefield To Garland Goode 3 June 1794--33 A. by
   original grand adj. said Garland Goode. Wit: John Goode.
   Sons of Mackerness, dec'd. 1795. Edgefield Deed 11-24
   Page 28--Mackerness Goode to Garland Goode 30 Aug. 1793
   363 A. on 96 Creek

GOODE, SAMUEL W. --Of Georgia to Edmund Pursley (or Powell) 27 Dec. 1795
   250 A. on Horns Creek. Bd. Andrew Birney, sd. Pursall(?) Mack-
   erness Goode, John Sullivan. Edgefield Deed 13-119
   (Waddell -m- Samuel Goode -m- Elizabeth Hawthorn)
   -Samuel W. Goode of Georgia to Edmund Pursell, 18 Dec. 1795. Land
   Willed to said Samuel Goode by his father on Horn's Creek of
   Stephens Creek-Bd. Andrew Burney, Mackerness Goode. Deed 13-120

GOODE, SAMUEL--Will 23 June 1800. Edgefield Prob. Bx. 38-1492
Wife: Anna Goode   Proven: 29 Aug. 1800
"4 youngest daus:" Betsy, Anna Tillitha, Lucinda-To be educated
"My 2 sons:"John, Freeman-To be educated. All land in this Dist.
Dau: Sally Martin
"   Frances Burt
Land on Six and Twenty Mile Creeks to be sold.
Exor's: Edward Burt and Reeves Martin

GOODE, SAMUEL F. and HARRIET--Children of John Goode, dec'd. 1815.
Adv's: David Williams and wife. Edgefield Eq. Roll 145

GOOD, SARAH--B/S "Bill of Sale" Maria Cooper 21 Oct. 1791. Misc. 3A-294

GOODE, SARAH--Of C. T. -- 28/9 Sept. 1792 Francis Maizere of City of
C. T. Lot in C. T. #187. Charleston Deed I-6-135

GOOD, SARAH-- Miss" Affidavit 20 April 1806 State of S. C. City of
C. T.--Amelia James, Joseph James, Mary James, Cato James--
Children of Hannah James-dau. of free Indian named Betty.
Misc. 4-C-360

GOODE, SARAH--Will 10 March 1824. Union Wills B-114
To: Simson Adams--son of Wm. Adams
    Sarah Simpson--dau. of James Goode
    Samuel Davidson--son of Wm. Davidson
    Ann Spencer
    Cinthey Gee--dau. John Gee
    Ann Glass--dau. Thomas Glass
    Pearch Corley
    Malissa Good Watson--The bed and furniture that was called
        "my daughter, Polly's"
Misses: Polly Glass, Ann Martin, Martha Fullbright
Sister: Betsy Agnes Farrel and Sarah Finley
Brother: James son and dau: Wm. and Betsy Simpson
Sister: Mary Adam's Children
        Wm. Adams, Francis Adams, Martha Byers
Sister Peggy's children:
        Polly Glass, Ann Martin, Matty Woolbright

GOODE, THEOPHILES -w- Priscilla of Putnam Co. Ga. Grant to Anthony
Cooper 22 Feb. 1802. Edgefield Deed Bk. #2-234. 1811

GOODE, THOMAS--Militia Duty. Indent I-267. Rev. AA-2988. Arch. Dept.

GOODE, THOMAS--150 A. Granville--Bd. All vac. Cert. 2 April 1771
Grant-10 April 1771 to mentioned. Mem. 10 May 1771. Del. to
Will Martin. (See Will Martin.) Mem. 10-433

GOODE, THOMAS--Gr. 10 April 1771-150 A. and Grant to Betty Martin-Gr.
mother of James Martin, Jr. 4 July 1785--Conv. by James Martin
Son of James Martin, dec'd. to Valentine White 19 July 1813. Plat.
Edgefield Deed 31-359

GOODE, THOMAS--Dec'd. Edgefield Min. Bk. Pg-254 14 July 1789. Letters
Adm. granted William Longmire, Henry Key and Jesse Scruggs, Sur.
Bond--500 pounds.

87

GOODE, THOMAS--Dec'd. Edgefield Stray paper. Adm: Wm. Longmire
Bond: 12 Oct. 1789 S: Henry Key, Jesse Scruggs
Wt. of App'r. to James Conway, John McFatrick, Wm. Tony
Inv. and Appl: Dec. 5, 1789
1 Negro man-George
12 Head Cattle
3 beds, pewter, hogs and tools

GOODE, THOMAS--Of Charlotte Co. Va. to William Price Young of City of
C. T. B/S 9 Aug. 1810--2 Negro girls-Milly and Priscilla.
Arch. Dept. Misc. 4-K 348

GOODE, THOMAS--Of Beaver Dam Creek to William Longmire 14 Dec. 1808
Dower: Elizabeth Goode. 200 A. on Beaver Dam Creek of Turkey
Creek of Savannah River. Bd. Ward Taylor, said Goode, and vac.
Ref. original Plat. Dower 3 Feb. 1809. Deed 29-313 Edgefield

GOODE, THOMAS--Dower Elizabeth to Hugh Moss 26 Jan. 1809-- 300 A.
Orig. grant Robert Shirley 15 Feb. 1769, who conv. to William
Goode, L. and Re L. 21 Sept. 1770 and conv. by William Goode to
Thomas Goode 19 March 1773--on Beaver Dam of Turkey Cr. of Stephens
Creek. Edgefield Deed 29-451

GOODE, THOMAS and DELANSON GOODE--Of Edgefield From Edmond Martin and
Lewis Colloway 11 Jan. 1809. 385 A. Bd. Wm. Pursell, Shirley
Whitley. Edgefield Mtg. Deed 29-399

GOODE, THOMAS--From Philip, William, and John Thurmond 26 Jan. 1809--
2 tracts (1) 200 A. on Beaver Dam. Orig Gr. Jesse Scruggs 3 Apl.
1772. Conv. by Jesse Scruggs 7 May 1784 to John Thurmond, Dec'd.
(2) 200 A. on Horse Pen, Br. of Beaver Dam. Pt of 966 A. Grant to
William Coursey 7 Aug. 1786 and conv. by said Wm. Coursey to said
John Thurmond, Dec'd. Edgefield Deed 29-45

GOODE, THOMAS and Elizabeth and Wm. Longmire -w- Ann to Daniel and
Joseph Brunson--150 A. orig. Gr. Abraham Martin, dec'd. on Beaver
Dam of Turkey Creek of Stephens Cr. Bd. Philip Thurmond, et al.
Edgefield Deed 22-395.
Deed Bk. 21-1--Betsy Goode ren. dower 28 April 1810

GOODE, THOMAS and JOHN--Minors--Aquilla Miles, Gdn. Bond 9 Oct. 1847.
Edgefield Prob. Bx. 58-2424

GOODE, WILLIAM--Of-Spartanburg--Served in Maryland. Rev. Pensions.

GOODE, WM.--Apt'd Dep. Surv. 6 March 1771. Old Index 00-521

GOODE, WILLIAM--Grant 22 Nov. 1771--348½ A. sold by Robert Key-dower
Martha to John Hollingsworth on Beaver Dam. Bd. Est. Wm. Terry,
Hugh Moss, Joel Rogers, except pt adj. Mrs. Terry which Wm. Terry
has enclosed. Wm. M. Burns. Plat. Edgefield Deed 33-211

GOODE, WILLIAM--A dep. Surv. 20 March 1775. Edgefield Deed 5-140

GOODE, WILLIAM--Plats-Archives Dept.
Saltcatchers 1784, 1793, and 1799
Pendleton on Toogoloo 1818

GOODWIN, BETSY--Legatee of John Gray-Will 1833. J. Gray, son in law
of Chamberlin L. Goodwin. Edgefield

GORMAN, HANNAH--Wife of John Gorman--Dower favor of Michael McKey.
Edgefield Min. Bk. Oct. 1787

GORMAN, JOHN--Apt'd. Ad'm. estate of James Carson, dec'd. Edgefield
Min. Bk. 1787

GORMAN, JOHN--Grand Juror Edgefield 1790. List 18

GORMAN, JOHN--Lic. to keep Tavern. S: William Yarborough, William
Covington. Edgefield Ct. Min. Jan. 1795

GORMAN, JOHN--See card Drury and Nancy Kirksey. Edgefield Rec. BkA-47
                                                                1831
GORMAN, JOHN--Dec'd. R. E. Sold 1831 Edgefield Sale Bk. A-52
Dist: Bud Bledsoe and wife 1/3 equal to $185.75
          Nancy Gorman-same
          Drury Kirksey and wife-same
W. L. Kemp gave Rec't. for Nancy Gorman-seems he purchased it.
Bud Bledsoe purchases at $575.00
Daniel Boone purchased share of Drury Kirksey and wife.
Receipts: 1831 and 1833

GOUGE, JOSEPH--Of N. C. Brother of Ann Marie Williams -w- John Williams
of Edgefield-Will 1794

GOULDEN, FANNY--Heir of Charity Johnson. See Johnson card. Edgefield
rec. Bk. B-161 1849

GRAHAM, JAMES -w- Polly (Mary)--Heirs of Valentine Young. Edgefield
Rec. Bk. B-19 1845

GRANT, NANCY--Dau. of Gilson Yarbrough-Will 1839. Edgefield

GRANTON, HARRIET--Heir of Ebenezer Hill. See Hill card. Edgefield
Rec. Bk. A256 1839

GRAVES, MARY--Dau. of Samuel Scott-Will 1809. George Granve-Exor.

GRAY, JAMES--Petit Juror Edgefield 1786. List 4

GRAY, JAMES -w- Mary of Chickasaw Co. Miss. P. A. to John Griffis
of Chickasaw Co. to collect from John Tomkins, Adm estate of
Reuben Carpenter, dec'd. of Edgefield Dist.--Part of Mary Gray
who was daughter of said Reuben Carpenter. 14 Oct. 1843.
Edgefield Rec. Bk. B-77

GRAY, JOHN--Grand Juror Edgefield 1786. List 5, 8, 12

GRAY, REV. JOHN H.--Of Memphis, Tenn. to James M. Caldwell-P. A. to
collect share of estate of Miss Martha Robertson--"to which I
am entitled to in right of my wife, Jane Brownlee Gray, formerly
Robertson, niece of said Martha Robertson, dec'd. Arch. Dept.
Edgefield File 12 Feb. 1850. Misc. 6-D-535
Page 536--Mrs. Mary E. Quarles, widow, of Jasper Co. Miss--Sim-
ilar P. A.
John N. Waddell-P. A. in right of wife Martha A. nee Robertson
Ann Robertson and John B. Robertson to collect from James K Robert-
son, Adm.

GRAY, JOHN I.--Heirs of Daniel Braner, dec'd.   Edgefield Rec. Bk. A-34

GRAY, JOHN J.--Will 2 March 1838.   Edgefield

GRAY, MARY ANN McGILVRAY and JOHN I. GRAY--Children of John I Gray,
     Legatees of Ulric Tobler-Will 1815. Sister-Mary Ann Gray.
     Brother in law-James Gray

GRAY, RIDLEY--Dau. of Drury Mims-Will 1817

GRAY, WILLIAM--Dec'd. R. E. Sold. Edgefield Sale Bk. A-40
     Dist: Cynthia Gray, widow 1/3 equal to $14.54
            Benjamin Johnson and wife 1/7 of 2/3 equal to $4.14.
            Thos. Ramsey -w- Durzilla   "
            Simpson, Julian, William Gray   "
            Lewis Youngblood, et ux.   "
            Sherwood Corley   "
     Rec. from widow, Cynthis Gray 1 Aug. 1829
     Land purchased by Sherwood Corley for $62.00 on Coffeetown Creek
     Quit Claim sale by Thomas Ramsey -w- Druzilla Ramsey dated 31 May
     1828 to Sherwood Corley

GREEN, ANN--Dau. John Roebuck. Edgefield Eq. Bill No. 30
     Children of Ann Green: John, Giles, William
     Ceclia Green -m- Isaac Hopkins
     Frances Green -m- Sanders Day
     -Ann Green -w- _____ Green--Heirs Robert Roebuck. See Roebuck card
     Edgefield Equity Bill 30. 1801

GREEN, BRYAN--Petit Juror Edgefield 1786. List 5,
       BRYANT "   "   "   "   " 17
       (Name possibly Greer)

GREEN, BRYANT--Dec'd. Inv. ret'd. recorded. Edgefield Min. March 1795

GREEN, FRANCES -w- Sanders Day. Equity Bill 30 Filed 1 June 1815
     See card James Day -m- Elizabeth Roebuck
     See card estate Ann Green, dau. John Roebuck. Bill #30 (Greer?)

GREEN, ISHAM--Grand Juror Edgefield 1786. List 4, 6, 16. (Greer?)

GREEN, ISHAM--Dec'd.--Let. Adm. to Mary Green, widow. Bond 600 pounds.
     S: John Moore, James McMillian. Edgefield Min. Bk. 325. April
                                                                   1790
GREEN, JACOB--Dec'd. R. E. Sold 1834. Edgefield Rec. Bk. A-171
     Dist: Keziah Green, widow   1/3 equal to $121.00
            Allen Green 1/10 of 2/3 equal to $24.00
            Joseph Bolton and wife   "
            Jno, Katherine, James, Rebecca, Mary, Thomas, Henry, and
            Manly Green each rec. 1/10 of 2/3--$24.00
     The widow, Keziah Green, in Alabama on 1 Dec. 1834

GREEN, JOHN--Petit Juror Edgefield 1789. List 15. (Greer?)

GREEN, PARTHENIA--Legatee of Lud Williams-Will 1793. Edgefield

GREEN, PHEBE--Wife of Bryan Green-Dower favor of John Barns. Oct. Ct.
Edgefield Min. Bk. 1787

GREEN, WILLIAM--Grand Juror Edgefield 1786. List 1, 4, 8, 12
    Petit " " " " 11, 20 (Greer?)

GREGORY, JONATHAN--Dec'd. R. E. Sold 1834. Edgefield Rec. Bk. A-189
  Dist: Sarah Gregory, widow 1/3 equal to $67.19
    Richard Gregory   1/7 of 2/3
    David Rankin and wife   "
    Shadrack Deas -w- Selah   "
    Nicey Gregory -m- John Hicks "
    Alexander Gregory   "
    Jno. Gregory   "
    James Rankin -w- Harriett "

GRIFFIN, FRANCES--Dau. Benjamin Bunting-Will 1823. James Griffin-
son in law of testator. Edgefield

GRIFFIN, JAMES -w- Nancy--Heirs of Mary Tillman. See Tillman card.
Edgefield Rec. Bk. B-103 1846

GRIFFIN, JESSE--Produced his account against the estate of Aaron Booth,
Amount-161 lbs. 11shillings, 3 pence--allowed by court. Jan. 1795
Edgefield Min. Bk.

GRIFFIN, JESSE and wife--Heirs of Stephen White. See White card.
Edgefield Rec. Bk. A-142. 1833

GRIFFIN, JOSEPH--Purchased a share estate of Abraham Cruise. See
Cruise card. Edgefield Rec. Bk. A-24. 1825

GRIFFIN, LARKIN--Son in law of Thomas Coleman-Will 1819. Also son in
law Joseph Griffin.

GRIFFIN, WILLIAM--Overseer of road from the Old Wells to Hightower's
Tavern. In the room of William Fudge. Edgefield Ct. Min. March
                      1795
GRIFFITHS, JOHN, SEN'R.--Grand Juror Edgefield 1794. List 19

GRIFFIS, JOHN--Will 25 Nov. 1838. Edgefield

GRIFFIS, MARY -w- John Griffis. Dau. of Christian Buckhalter-Will 1792

GRIGSBY, ENOCH--Dec'd. Edgefield Ct. Min. Jan. 1795.
Widow: Mary Grigsby, with Samuel Mays and Rhydon Grigsby--applied
for Letters Adm. with Will annexed. Bond: 1,000 pounds.
S: William Butler, and Russell Wilson.
Appr's: Wm. Butler, Jacob Smith, Russell William, Wm. Dozier
Jan. Ct. 1795--Rydon Grigsby Adm. of Peter Buffington. See B. card.
-Enoch Grigsby, dec'd.--Will proved by oath of William Butler,
William Simkins, Sampson Butler. Edgefield Ct. Min. 1795

GRIMES, WILLIAM--Will Hanover Co. Va. Edgefield Deed 8-440
  Heirs: Thomas Davis, John Colvand, William Colvand, Jonathan
      Harvey--All of Edgefield County. Conv. Arge Garner, P. A.
      29 Oct. 1792

GRISHAM, AGNESS--Dau. of Jacob Ernest-Will 1824. Edgefield

GRISAM, MARTHA--Dist. of estate Fanny Butler.   See Butler card.
    Edgefield Rec. Bk. B-37 1841

GRUBBS, SUSANNAH PRYOR--Dau. John Pryor-Will 1777. Edgefield
    Tobias Pryor Grubbs
    Elizabeth Pryor Grubbs
    William Pryor Grubbs
    "Whom I do acknowledge to be my children".

GUIGNARD, ELIZABETH--Wife of Sanders Guignard and dau. of David Rich-
    ardson-Will 1842

GULLEDGE, WILLIAM -w- Martha--Dist. estate of Joshua Bodie. See
    Bodie card. Edgefield Rec. Bk. A-308. 1839

GUN, CHARLEY--Heir of William Melton. See Melton card. Edgefield
    rec. Bk. A-118 1832

GUNNELS, ELIZABETH--Dau. of John Frazier-Will 1794. Rec'd. 1801

GUNTER, SINTHY--Dau. of Cornelias Roe-Will 1811 Edgefield

GWIN, BRYANT--Dec'd. Will proved by oaths of John Hall and James
    Parrish. Thomas Carter and Edward Green qualified as Exors.
    Appr's: John Carter, John Hall, John Tarrance, John Howard.
    Edgefield Ct. Min. March 1795.
    Morris Gwinn-Dec'd. sale estate returned by John Gwinn-Adm'r.
    March Ct. 1795

GWIN, MORRIS--Grand Juror Edgefield 1786. List 5, 10, 14, 18

HAGINS, RACHEL--Dau. John Cogburn-Will 1810

HAGINS, WILLIAM -w- Heirs of John Cogburn. Edgefield Rec. Bk. A-225
    -William Hagens--Will 28 March 1836.   1834
    -William Hagens--Father of Rebecca Bussey and Sarah Bussey--See
    Will William Robertson-1840 Edgefield.

HAGOOD, LUCRETIA--Dau. of Charles Cooper-Will 1819

HAGOOD, MARCUS (or Mark) -w- Nancy--Heirs of William Richardson-
    See Richardson card. Edgefield Rec. Bk. A-254

HAGOOD, SARAH--Dau. of Robert Mosley-Will 1796. Edgefield

HALL, FRANCIS and wife--Heirs of Littlebury Mitchell. See Mitchell
    card. Edgefield Rec. Bk. A-22 1826

HALL, JOHN--Applied for permission to keep Tavern. S: Seth Howard
    and John G. Cook. Edgefield Ct. Min. 1795. March.

HALL, JOHN W. -w- Clementine-formerly Clementine Johnson, widow of
    Joshua Johnson of Rutherford Co., Tenn. P. A. to Randolph B. Hall
    of same place to collect from estate of Joshua Johnson in South
    Carolina for themselves and as Gdns. of Virginia E. Johnson, minor
    child of said Joshua Johnson, dec'd. 8 Nov. 1842
    Edgefield Rec. Bk. B-42

HALL, JOHN, SEN!R.--Dec'd.   R. E. Sold.   Edgefield Sale Bk. A-104
Dist: James H. Walker and wife   Sampson Hall 1/7
        Frank Hall.   Richard Hall   "
        Thomas Hall   Eliza Hall   "
        Nevil Spain
        Receipt-12 March 1832 to 7 Nov. 1843.
        Frank Hall, Thos Hall, Nevil Spain sold to James H. Walker (4/7)

HALL, SAMUEL--Petit Juror Edgefield 1794. List 21

HALL, WASHINGTON--Gr. son of Josiah Langley-Will 1826

HAMILTON, ELIZABETH -w- John Hamilton--adopted dau. of Joseph Phillips-
        Will 1836.

HAMILTON, GEORGE--Heir of J. J. Still. See Still card. Edgefield
        Equity Roll 1849

HAMELTON, JAMES--Legatee of David Langley-Will 1822. Land adj. Landus
        Hamelton. Edgefield

HAMILTON, JOHN--Dec'd. Paul Abney, Adm'r. Return. Edgefield Ct. Min
                                                                    1794
HAMILTON, JOHN G. Tombstone Little Stevens Creek Baptist Church
        Born-25 Aug. 1813   Died-21 Aug. 1873

HAMELTON, MARY--Dau. of Elizabeth Miller-Will 1809. Gr.-son: John
        Hamelton. Son in law: David Hamelton

HAMILTON, RANSOM--Dec'd. R. E. Sold 1846. Edgefield Rec. Bk. B-107
        Dist: Hanah Hamilton, widow   1/3 equal to $317.10
               John B. Hamilton   1/9 of 2/3 equal to $70.46
               Joseph Cosnahan -w- Elizabeth   "
               William Johnson -w- Permelia   "
               E. W. Sego -w- Emily   "
               William Whitlock -w- Sarah Ann   "
               Eldred Posey -w- Hannah   "
               Richard Hamilton   "
               Thomas Hamilton   "
               Sampson Williamson -w- Lucinda C. V.   "

HAMILTON, WILLIAM--Of town of Hamburg-Will 8 Nov. 1836. Edgefield

HAMMOND, CATHERINE F.--Dau. of Elizabeth Clarke-Will 1827. Wife of
        E. Hammond. Edgefield

HAMMOND, CHARLES--A youth of age to choose Gdn. Chose Wm. Covington,
        Esq. Apt'd. Edgefield Ct. Min. 8 Oct. 1787
        Leroy Hammond under age to choose. Wm. Covington, Apt'd.

HAMMOND, CHARLES--Dec'd. Will proved by oath of William Covington
        Miss Catherine Hammond qualified as Ex'x. Appr's: Joshua
        Hammond, William Terrance, LeRoy Hammond, William Covington.
        Edgefield Ct. Min. Jan. 1795

HAMMOND, CHARLES--Will 7 May 1836

HAMMOND, CHRISTY--Legatee of Mary Rivers-Will 1832

HAMMOND, FRANCES -w- James Hammond and dau. of John Key-Will 1840

HAMMOND, JOHN--Grand Juror Edgefield 1786. List 1, 2,
      Petit "   "   "   " 7
John, Jr. Grand Juror "   "   " 21

HAMMOND, JOHN -w- Elizabeth--Deed of Feoffment 6 acres to Leroy
Hammond-Proved.
Deed L and Re L from Col. Leroy Hammond -w- _____? to John
Hammond for 15½ A.-Proved. Edgefield Ct. Min. Bk. 257. 15 July
                                               1789
HAMMOND, JOSHUA--Petit Juror Edgefield 1788. List 12

HAMMOND, JOSHUA--Apt'd. Overseer of road leading from Campleton to the
Pinewoods House, from the fork of the road to the first hill
above John Hall's in the room of William Terrance, excused.
Edgefield Ct. Min. Jan. 1795.
March Ct. 1795--John Hammond, Rd. Overseer, excused. Joseph
Fuller apt'd. See Fuller card.

HAMMOND, LEROY--Magistrate for 96 Dist. Aff. by Nathan iel Yongue.
Council Journal 38-13 29 Jan. 1774. Edgefield

HAMMOND, LEROY--Of Richmond Co. Ga. Edgefield File Misc. B-683
Wife: Sarah Quarles Hammond
Dau: Mary Ann Biggs Hammond
Deed gift many tracts land.
Joseph Hightower, Lewis Lee Hammond, Trustees 26 Oct. 1810

HAMMOND, LEROY--"Of New Richmond in Dist. of Edgefield--shows son of
Mary Hammond--His son: Lewis Lee Hammond "by a Cherokee Indian
Woman". Trust deed gift 19 Sept. 1802--Charles Goodwin of Silver
Bluff and Wm. Garrett of Campbelton, trustees. Various tracts.
Misc. B-183

HAMMOND, SAMUEL--Of Georgia -m- 25 May 1802 Eliza Amelia O'Keefe of
Barnwell Dist. LeRoy Hammond of Edgefield Dist., Trustee.
Charles Goodwin of Barnwell. Edgefield Misc. B-176
-Another card-same information-also mentions Plat of 612 A. with
houses-on Horse Creek. Misc. B-177

HAMMOND, SAMUEL E. -m- Ellen Lark-dau. of John Lark-Will 1822

HAMMOND, WILLIAM₮-Dec'd. Appr: 21 Dec. 1830. Abbeville Sale Bk.
Wm. Reynolds-Gdn. minor children.   Pg. 56/9

HAMMOND, WILLIAM -w- Nancy--Heirs of Philip Lightfoot. See Lightfoot
card. Edgefield Rec. Bk. B-65 1842

HANCOCK, GEORGE -w- Elizabeth--Heirs of Reuben Carpenter. See Carpenter
card. Edgefield Rec. Bk. B-77 1843

HANCOCK, JOHN--Grand Juror Edgefield 1787. List 6 and 18

HANCOCK, MARTHA -w- George Hancock. Sister of John Tarrance-Will 1824

HANCOCK, MARTHA--Dec'd. R. E. Sold 1840. Edgefield Rec. Bk. B-25
    Dist: Permelia Fulford
           Enoch Merritt -w- Sarah W.
           Siras Floyd -w- Mary Ann
           James M. Powell -w- Tyrzah
           Jane Hancock -m- Richard Odom
           Charles P. Powell -w- Martha--each 1/6 equal to $61.25
    Rec't. Jane Hancock 8 June 1845. Purch: Lewis Ellzy.

HANCOCK, THOMAS--Of Edgefield Dist. S. C.--Shot and instantly killed
    by two negro slaves. Feb. 5, 1820

HANES, EMILY -m- Joseph Tucker. See Will of Martha Tucker-Will 1834

HARDEN, WILLIAM--Dec'd. Cit: 23 Nov. 1813 Adm'x: Sally Hatcher
    Adm'r: Samuel March and Robert Lofton
    S: Abner Bl_cker and Wm. Hill, Sr.
    Deed Bk. 31-152 lists heirs as:
           William C. Hardin   John McDaniel
           Henry G. Hardin   M. Pittman
           Sarah Hardin   Rachel Harden
           Robert Lofton
    Pur: Wm. Harden, Jr. and Rachel Harden
    Robert Lofton had received gifts in property from dec'd.
    John McDaniel had rec'd. gifts from dec'd. (evidently sons in
    law of dec'd).

HARDIN, WILLIAM and Margaret--Receipt to John and Benjamin Ryan
    July Ct. 1787. Edgefield Min. Bk.

HARDY, DANIEL -w- Mary (or Polly)
       JOHN -w- Elizabeth--Heirs of Robert Roebuck. Edgefield
    Equity Bill 30 1801

HARDY, HILLARY--Gr. son of Susannah Matthews-Will 1839 Edgefield

HARDY, JAMES and wife--Heirs of estate of John Glanton, dec'd.
    Edgefield Rec. Bk. A-181 1833 Also Bk. A-162

HARDY, JOHN--Petit Juror Edgefield 1786. List 4

HARDY, JOHN and RICHARD--Appr's estate of Mary Faquar. Edgefield
    Ct. Min. 1794

HARDY, SARAH--Sister of Mary McFarland-Will 1805. Niece-Elizabeth Hardy

HARE, EDWARD--Dec'd. R. E. Sold 1848. Edgefield Rec. Bk. B-155
    Dist: Epsey Hare 1/3 equal to $216.44
           John W., Levi P., David Y., Nancy and Julia Ann B. Hare
           1/5 of 2/3 each

HARGROVE, BRITTON--Probate Records--Box 14 Pk. 493 Edgefield
          JAMES   14   512
          MARY   39   1513
          CHARLES   40   1565
          TEMPLE (Will)   60   2474
          ELIZABETH   94   3788

HARGROVE, HARRIET--Sister of Richard Lewis-Will 1838

HARGROVE, JAMES--Grand Juror Edgefield 1786. List 3 and 19

HARGROVE, JAMES--Deed Records-Direct.   13-124
     "   1799   16-529
     "   17- 39
    ANTHONY-1803   22-465
    JAMES   30- 94
    JOHN-1818   35-467
    "   37-149
    TEMPLE to Thos. Y   42-286
    "   42-399
    JOHN   45-424

HARGROVE, JAMES -w- Harriet-Heirs of Richard Lewis. See Lewis card.
    Edgefield Rec. Bk. A-215. 1835
    -JAMES HARGROVE--Edgefield Probate. (same card) Dec'd.
    Cit: 4 Nov. 1805. Pub. at Horne's Creek Meeting House and at
    Antioch. Bond 16 Dec. 1805.
    Sd: James Hargrove, L. B. Adams, James Clark.
    Pur: Lucy Hargrove, Nancy Hargrove, James Hargrove.
    (Sale shows Asbury Knight)

HARGROVE, JOHN and wife--Heirs of John McCreless. See McCreless card.
    Edgefield Rec. Bk. A-130   1836

HARGROVE, JOHN BELTON--Son of Ramsey and Francis Hargrove
    Born: 9 Nov. 1859   Died: 31 April 1917
    Ramsey Hargrove--Born 20 April 1829 Died: 17 Jan. 1888
    Mrs. Francis Hargrove--Born: 15 Nov. 1829 Died 23 Nov. 1895
    Nice Tomb. Quattlebaum Graveyard. Sleepy Creek Road, Edgefield

HARGROVE, WILLIAM--Dec'd. Edgefield Ct. Min. Bk. Pg-232. 12 Jan. 1789
    Ordered: Citation be issued to show cause why Adm. should not be
    granted to James Hargrove. Pg. 247--Letters granted.

HARGROVE, WILLIAM--Dec'd. Edgefield Ct. Min. Oct. 1794.
    Mrs. Mary Hargrove, Adm'x. authorized to sell a bay mare at the
    house of Robert Melons on 1st Mon. of Nov. next.

HARGROVE, WILLIAM--Legatee of Lewelling Goode-Will 1812. John Hargrove
    also a Legatee

HARLEY, MARY--Dau. of John Rinehart-Will 1828. Edgefield

HARLING, DAVID K.--Dec'd. R. E. Sold 1848. Edgefield Rec. Bk. B-139
    Dist: Not shown
    Receipt for total amount $135.00 by John Trapp, Adm. "To be
    applied to the payment of the debts of my intestate".

HARLING, JOHN and DAVID--Heirs of estate of Elizabeth Falkner. See
    Falkner card. Edgefield Rec. Bk. B-182. 1850

HARLING, JOHN--Dec'd. His lands. John and DavidL-bdy. Conv. lands on
    Sleepy Creek by Wm. Dorn -w- Mary to Geo. Dorn. 2 shares Harling
    Estate. See card William Dorn. Edgefield Deed Bk. 48-479

HARMAN, SARAH C--Heir of David Quattlebaum. See Quattlebaum card.

HARRID, MARK -w- Barbary--Heirs of Allen Body--Edgefield Rec. Bk. A-92
1832

HARRIL, VINOS -m- Caroline Chapman--Heir of Philip Jennings. See
Jennings card. Edgefield Rec. Bk. B-185. 1850

HARRINGTON, Y. J.--Father in law of George Pope-Will 1843

HARRIS, BENJAMIN--Grand Juror Edgefield 1786. List 5

HARRIS, BENJAMIN -w- Sophia--Edgefield Deed Bk. 1-51 1787

HARRIS, ELIZABETH *w- James Harris. Dower favor William Reynolds.
July Ct. 1787. Edgefield Min. Bk.

HARRIS, GREEN--Dec'd. R. E. Sold. 1849. Edgefield Rec. Bk. B-173
Rec't. by Wm. Worthington -w- Martha (or Weatherington)
Rec't. by Samuel Harris for Dist. share "For Wm. J. Harris, minor
by Johnson Sole, Gdn.
Rec'd. by Jared Harris for 2 shares.

HARRIS, JOHN--Dec'd. R. E. Sold 1838. Edgefield Rec. Bk. A-290
Dist: Nathaniel Saunders -w- 1/3 equal to $210.31
John Rogers and wife 1/5 of 2/3 equal to $84.12
Emely Harris -m- Elisha W. Thomson by 2 Jan. 1841-same
Sophronia Ann -m- Wesley G.Welch by 8 Jan. 1838-same
Laurian and Martha-minors 1/5 of 2/3 each. Lucy Sanders, Gdn.
Rec't's forNathaniel Sanders share from Lucy Sanders. 1839
1st tract sold John Rogers
2nd tract sold John Kirksey 1838.

HARRIS, JOSHUA -w- Elizabeth--Heirs of Bates Wrenn. See Wrenn card.
Edgefield Rec. Bk. B-95 1846.

HARRIS, LEWIS--Nephew of Lud Williams-Will 1793. Lud Harris also Nephew.

HARRIS, LUD, SEN'R.--5 Shilling Legatee of Meshack Wright-Will 1814.
Lud Harris, Jr. son of dau. Sarah. Edgefield

HARRIS, LUD, LEWIS, ELISHA WILLIS--See card Lud Williams, dec'd.
Edgefield Ct. Records Judgement 1802

HARRIS, MARY -w- John Harris--Dower favor Mrs. Rachel Chaney. April
Ct. Edgefield Min. Book.

HARRIS, MOSES--Petit Juror Edgefield 1786. List 4

HARRIS, MOSES--Of Edgefield Dist. Edgefield Wills Univ. D-2 310
Sons: David, Hezekiah, Moody, and Benjamin.
11 Aug. 1840. Rec'd. Sept. 12, 1844

HARRIS, RHODY and dau. Nancy--Distributees estate of Fanny Butler. See
Butler card. Edgefield Rec. Bk. B-37. 1841

HARRIS, SAMUEL--Gr. son of Martha Moore-Will 1822

HARRIS, SARAH--Dau. of Robert Ware-Will 1817 and wife of Lewis Harris

HARRIS, SARAH--Dau. of Margaret Ware-Will 1829

HARRIS, THOMAS--Petit Juror Edgefield 1789. List 14

HARRIS, WEST--Lic. to keep Tavern. S: Samuel Landon (?) and Joel
  Chandler. Edgefield Ct. Min. March 1795.
  Moses Harris appr. estate of Angus McDaniel. See McDaniel card.

HARRIS, WILLIAM--Dec'd. R. E. Sold. Edgefield Sale Bk. A-50
  James Shadrack--Purchaser at $250.00
  "In this case the widow, Martha, is entitled to 1/3 of 2/9
  James Shadrack, the purchaser to 3/9
  The following, each 1/9--
  Martha Harris-Dist. share--$110.14
  James Shadrack-Dist share-$50.84
  Ann Harris-Dist.share--$17.13½
  Ellen Harris "   " --   "
  James Walker and wife $17.00--Rec't. 26 Dec. 1829

HARRISON, BENJAMIN--Of Edgefield 2 Jan. 1828 Edgefield Wills
  Wife: Mary
  Sister: Sarah Harrison
  "My children": Edmund Harrison --widow: Mary Ann and 3 children
                 John Harrison--Widow, Frances and 9 children
                 Stewart Harrison -w- Susan
                 Mary -w- James Meacham
                 Ann S. -w- John H. Threlkell
                 Hartwell Harrison
                 James Harrison
                 Benjamin Harrison.
  Edmond Harrison--Widow: Mary Ann
     Children: Charles S. Harrison
               Ann N. Edwards
               Mary E. Harrison
  John Harrison--Widow: Frances A
     Children: James M.   Frances Griffin   Sarah
               Stewart   Rebecca   John
               William N.   Julia   Hugh
  Stewart Harrison, the elder--Widow: Susan -m- Wm. H. Moss
  Harrison Will in Montgomery Co. Alabama.

HARRISON, BENJAMIN, Esq: Of Berkley, Va. His 2 daus-nieces of the
  wife of Andrew Pickens-Will 1834. Edgefield

HARRISON, ELIZABETH--Dau. of Blumer White, Sen'r. -Will 1824

HARRISON, JAMES--150 A. Granville, Nobles Creek. Bd. Jacob Summers
  and vac. Cert: 1 Sept. 1772. Grant: 30 Oct. 1772. Edgefield
  File Mem. 12-72

HARRISON, JAMES--Grand Juror Edgefield 1786. List 5, 6, and 14
             Petit   "   "   "·   " 6

HARRISON, JAMES--Produced certificate of qualification as Justice of
  Peace for Edgefield Co. Said by Thomas Bacon, Esq. Edgefield
  Ct. Min. March 1795.
  March Ct. 1795--James Harrison, Esq. to adv. and sell a stray
  cow in possession of Thomas Stallworth.

HARRISON, JAMES--Will 23 July (1797?) Prov: Mar. 22, 1800
    Wife: Ann-Qual.   Record Bk. A-1800 Pg. 13
    Son: Willia, Harrison
    Dau: Ann
    Gr. son: William Rennels and Wiley Rennels
    Son: James Harrison
            Dau: Macy J.
    Son: Moses Harrison
    Dau: Mary

HARRISON, JAMES--Of Edgefield Co. 96 Dist. Edgefield Pro. Records A-10?
    Wife: Ann
    Son: William
    Gr. sons: William and Wiley Rennels
        Children: Moses, Mary and Jemima
    Gr. dau: Mary--James Harrison's dau.
    23 July ____?   Prov: 23 March 1800

HARRISON, JAMES--Orig. Will 12 May 1797. Edgefield Pro. 39-1535
    Wife: Suckey   Prov: 7 Nov. 1805
    Son: Edward--The Home Place--S-side Big Branch, adj. John Adam's
            "Flat Lick".
    Son: James--Land left to Suckey, his mother, for life.
    Suckey and Edward Qualified. Papers show wife as Susannah

HARRISON, JAMES--Legatee of James Hollingsworth-Will 1818. Dau: Polly

HARRISON, JAMES--Dec'd. Nov. 1843. Will 1841. Edgefield Bill 993
    Widow: Mary
    6 children: Laura Ann -m- 1 1828 Wm. Hollingsworth. 2 children:
            William H. Hollingsworth, and Mary Hollingsworth
            -m- 2 1835 Burrell E. Hobbs
            James S. Harrison
            Susan E. Harrison -m- Geo. C. Mayson
            Mary J. Harrison -m- Elias LaGrone
            John E. Harrison
            Robert Pickens Harrison

HARRISON, JAMES--Will 14 Feb. 1841. Edgefield.

HARRISON, JOHN--Heir estate of James Butler. Edgefield Rec. Bk. A-165
                                                                    1834
HARRISON, JOHN--Seems to be Brother in law of Wm. S. Johnson-Will 1834.

HARRISON, JOHN--Dec'd. Intestate Edgefield Filed 1849. Bill 942
    Widow: Frances-Oratrix
                Stewart Harrison   Julia Harrison
                Frances Griffin   Sarah   "
                James Harrison   John   "
                Rebecca Harrison   Hugh   "
    -Another card. Same heirs. Mentions 1090 Acres on Horn's Creek.
    Plats in file. Will filed 26 Dec. 1849.

HARRISON, MARY--Dau. Blumer White-Will 1839

HARRISON, ROBERT--Dec'd. 1833. Edgefield Eq. Roll 727 Will
     Son: Sterling Harrison
           Wiley Harrison
     Gr. dau: Mary A. M. W. Brown--testator had been apt'd. her
           Gdn. in June 1822--Her mother had -m- Shepherd Spencer, Jr.
           and they moved to Sumter Co. Alabama.

HARRISON, THOMAS--Of Granville. Will Provincial Wills Pg. 423 1752/56
     Wife: Hanah   3rd _____? 1755
     Sons: Henry, William, John, Michael, Francis
     Unborn, if any
     Son: Thomas

HART, ALFRED--Born 12 July 1844. After serving 6 months in the war,
     in the 19th S. C. Reg't.--died at (Tombstone broken off)
     Tombstone Little Stevens Creek Baptist Church Edgefield Co.
     P. A. Hart, wife of Jesse Hart--died 30 May 1870

HART, DANIEL M. -w- Mary Ann--Heirs estate of William Garrett. See
     Garrett card. Also John F. Hart -w- Jane E.. See card.
     Edgefield Rec. Bk. B-192 1850. (John F. -w- Jane E.-Another card)

HART, JAMES--Dec'd. R. E. Sold 8 Jan. 1833. Edgefield Sale Bk. A-110/12
     Dist: Derryl Hart 1/6 or $105.70
            Jesse Hart-same
            Henry Hart-same. Of Bedford Co. Tenn
            Children of Thomas Hart--Elijah and Frank Hart-same
            Daniel Leopard, et ux
            Mo. Kemp, et ux
     File contains letter from Henry Hart of Shelbyville, Bedford Co.
     Tenn--to collect his part--mentions "Jesse Burdell has lately
     returned from the Creek Country and is much pleased. He expects
     shortly to move there". Dated Shelbyville 7 May 1833--and addressed
     to Mr. Burrel Hart, Edgefield Dist. Meeting House. P. O. So. Car.

HARVELAND, JACOB--Petit Juror Edgefield Dist. 1788. List 12

HARVEY, BLASSENGAME--Of Burke Co. Georgia to William Howle, Jr. 7 Jan. 1789
     Edgefield Deed Bk. 2-132

HARVEY, ELIZABETH--Dau. of Nathaniel Evans-Will 1824. Edgefield

HARVEY, POLLY--Dau. of William Howle, Sen'r.-Will 1830. Edgefield

HARVEY, THOMAS B.--To his wife, Aquilla Harvey--Deed Gift-slave girl.
     10 Jan. 1856. Edgefield Misc. Y-599 (Age of slave-about 12 yrs.)

HARVEY, WILEY -w- Nancy--Heirs of William Pond. See Pond card.
     Edgefield Rec. Bk. A-235

HARVEY, WILLIAM and JOHN and Henry Graybill--Wit Will of Jeremiah
     Lamar of Granville. 22 March 1771. Qualified before LeRoy
     Hammone 18 May 1772.
     Heirs: Sarah Lamar, widow
             Zach Lamar, brother
             Children: John, Thomas, Rachel, and James.
     Edgefield File C. T. Wills 1771-74. Pg-250.

HARVEY, WILLIAM--Dec'd. Will. Elizabeth Harvey, Ex'x. Qual.
     Edgefield C. T. Min. 1780-90-156

100

HARVEY, WILLIAM--Dec'd. Edgefield Min. Bk. Pg-149. 14 Jan. 1788
    Will proved by oath of Hugh Middleton and Zephaniah Harvey.
    Page 156--Elizabeth Harvey apt'd. Ex'x.
    -Willia, Harvey-Will 1 Dec. 1788
        Wife: Elizabeth
        Sons: Zachariah   Thomas
              William   James
              John   Matthew
              Nehemiah
        Daus: Mary   Ann
              Eleanor   Elizabeth
              Liney

HARVEY, WILLIAM--Dec'd. R. E. Sold 1836. Edgefield Rec. Bk. A-256
    Dist: Marlin Minor -w- Elizabeth (widow) 1/3 $224.831/3
           Sarah Harvey -m- Minor Kilcrease. Rec't. 1837
           Mary   )
           William) John F. Martin, Gdn.

HARVIN, JOHN--Of Edgefield Dist. Edgefield Wills A-216
    Wife: Rebekah
    Children: Elizabeth Whitehead
              James, Rebekah, and William Harvin.
    4 April 1815. Rec'd. Feb. 21, 1806

HASTEN, ROBERT--Dec'd. R. E. Sold 1843. Edgefield Rec. Bk. B-153
    Dist: Mary Hasten, widow 1/3 - $8.16
           Rhoden, John, Susan, William, _____?, Clarissa, Patsy,
           Benjamin, Robert Hasten.

HATCH, JAMES -w- Eliza--Heirs of Henry Matthews. See Mathews card.
    Edgefield Rec. Bk. B-169 1849

HATCHER, BENJAMIN--Will 28 Jan. 1838

HATCHER, CHRISTIANA--Legatee of William Robertson-Will 1840. "In
    accordance with a promise made to my layt wife".

HATCHER, JEREMIAH, ESQ.--Produced his commission as Sheriff. Bond:
    1500 pounds. S: John Ryan, and Samuel Mays.
    Sampson Butler apt'd. Dep. Sheriff. Edgefeld Ct. Min. Jan. 1795

HATCHER, LUCY--Dec'd. R. E. Sold 1840. Edgefield Rec. Bk. B-23
    Dist: Benjamin Hatcher, husband 1/3
           Benjamin Bettis ¼ of 2/3
           Eliza Bettis-same
           Harriet Bettis-same
           John Fair -w- Mary-same
           Mary Tillman-same
    -Lucy Hatcher-Will 9 May 1834

HATFIELD, JOHN--Legatee in trust for Eliza-Dau of David Bowers-Will
    1833. Mary-Wife of John Hatfield, dau. of testator.

HAVARD, DANIEL -w- Matilda--Heirs of Shadrack Boone. See Boone card.
    Edgefield Rec. Bk. A-48 1829

HAVELY, ANN--See Will of John Clackler, Sen'r. 1790. Edgefield

HAWS, ELIZABETH--Heir of James Picket, dec'd. See Picket card.
Edgefield Rec. Bk. A-306 1839

HAYNE, WILLIAM--Petit Juror Edgefield 1786. List 5

HAYS, ELLENDER--Dau. of Jones Wills-Will 1813. Edgefield

HAZLE, HENRY--Dec'd. R. E. Sold 1833. Edgefield Rec. Bk. A-177
Dist: Mary-widow
    James and Jonathan Hazle--who as heirs and brothers of the
    whole blood, on death of Elizabeth, dau. of intestate,
    sold shares to Wm. Smith--1/3 and 3/5 of 2/3
    Sarah and William Hazle--1/5 of 2/3-$4.60

HAZEL, AMY--Dec'd. Her children; Seth, Jonathan, Henry, Rhody, Philip,
et al,--Heirs of Charity Johnson. See Johnson card. Edgefield
rec. Bk. B-161 1849

HEAD, GEORGE--Anderson Wills 8 Mar. 1817 Prov: Mar. __? 1818
Son in law: Stephen Siddal and gr. daus. Nancy and Sally and
                Gr. son, John
Gr. Dau: Elizabeth Williams
Gr. Daus: Rebecca and Mary Yancey
Son in law: William Pegg
Dau: Elizabeth -w- John Williams and the 7 children she had by
        Amos Atkinson.
Son: John Head
Son: George Head

HEAD, JAMES--Edgefield Wills C-194 Bx-8 Pk-292
Witnessed Will of Peter Dorn 29 Jan. 1826. Other witness-B. F.
Winn and Francis Dorn.
Heirs: Wife: Eve Dorn
        Sons: Peter, Abner, George-Exor.
        Dau: Lory?

HEAD, JAMES--Of Edgefield. Edgefield Deed Bk. 48-481 17 Jan. 1834
Dower Esphony Head. $150.00 To George Dorn--65 A. on Sleepy Creek
Part of an old Bounty granted Gange, and including the premises
where said Head now lives. Wit: James Permenter, Albert Dorn.

HEAD, MARGARET--Heirs of Ann McCrary. See McCrary card. Edgefield
Rec. Bk. B-160 1849

HEAD, NEWPORT -w- Margaret--Barnwell Richardson Reports Vol. 5-129
"The Complainants (who are the wife and children of one, Newport
Head) charge in their Bill that on the 28th of January 1833, Henry
Hartzog (who was the brother in law of Newport Head's wife) exec-
uted and delivered to Samuel Reed, Jr. and David Hair, a certain
deed by which the said Hartzog conveyed to the said Reed and Hair
two negro slaves, Albert and Fanny, in trust for the exclusive
use of Margaret Head (wife of Newport Head) during her life and
after her death to the use of such child or children, gr-child or
gr-children as she might have alive at the time of her death."

HEAD, SARAH--Mother of Frances N. Taylor -w- Leonart Taylor-Will 23
June 1812. Fairfield Will Bk-6-148
Thomas Head--a brother of Frances, dec'd. His estate to be div.
Henry Head--Exor. Elizabeth Head a dau. of John Gregg-Will 1817

HEAD, SARAH, James Huff, Peter Head, Stephen Head, Thomas Youngblood--
Legatees of Estate of John Head, dec'd. $1430.00 paid by Geo.
I. Strother 435 A. on Little Stephens Creek. Wit: David Richardson
Alexander McCrary. Edgefield Deed Bk-4-65. 15 July 1814
Said: J. Head, Philemon Head, James Head, Thomas Huff,(sd Henry
Huff), Thomas Huff, Thomas Youngblood

HEAD, STEPHEN--Trust Deed for wife, Margaret. Trustee-Alexander McCrary.
180 A. near Stephens Creek and horses, beds, etc.
Edgefield Deed Bk-32-295. 29 June 1815

HEARD, AMY M.--Dau. of Hillary M. Collier-Will 1841. Wife of Isaac
T. Heard. Edgefield

HEARD, CHARLES, JAMES, AND MARY A.--Loose Plats Arch. Dept. 83-160/4

HEARD, FRANCES--Dau. of Samuel McCraw-Will 33 April 1810
Sons: Edward, Stephen, and William   Abbeville Wills
Dau: Lucy Owen -w- David Owen
      Frances Heard and her infant children
      Mary Owen and her infant children
Son: Wm. McCraw
Gr. dau: Betsy McCraw
Gr. son: John Hugh's son-John

HEARD, GEORGE--Original Will 29 April 1816.   Prov: 11 Dec. 1820
Wife: Elizabeth   Edgefield Bx-14-518
Son: George Jared Heard
      Abner Heard
To: Martial Heard, minor son of Thomas Heard (living) and son of
      testator.
Son: Robert Wilson Heard
      Edman Heard-a minor
Dau: BetsyAnn Heard
Debts to be paid out of property he had before he married
Elizabeth Goode

HEARD, GEORGE--Exor. Armstrong Heard, Sr.-Wit. and Armstrong, Jr. Wit.
Will of Robert Griffin 19 Feb. 1809   Abbeville Wills
Wife: Margaret
Dec'd dau: Elizabeth McMillan
      3 children: Wiley, Leanan, and Peggy McMillan

HEARD, JOHN--Of Craven from William Allston of Craven 15 March 1734
235 A. on Waccamaw Called Heard's Island. C. T. Deed H. H. 208
Page 210-- John Heard to Joseph Prince 2 Feb. 1738-same land.

HEARD, JOHN JR.--Of Colleton from Isaac Pitchlynn -w- Jemima 4 April 1765
Part 25,000 A. grant to Wm. Livingston. Conv. to John Hamilton.
Conv. to Wm. Simpson -w- Elizabeth. Passed to Isaac Pitchlynn -w-
Jemima--562 A. on Coronaco Creek of Saluda River. Lot #10 on
Plat of Survey. Wit: John McKibbins and James Jones
Abbeville Land. C. T. Deed L-3 304

HEARD, JOHN, JR.--Of Colleton--Continued
Page 310--John Heard, Jr. of Colleton -w- LeDay(Lidea-Lidy)
to John Heard, Sr. 3 Sept. 1768. Same land. Wit: James Heard
Elisha Brooks, John Logan

HEARD, JOHN -w- Lydia of Colleton to Thomas Yates 25 Nov. 1769 200lbs.
200 A. part of 400 A. grant to Wm. Smith Feb. 1753. Died intest-
ate-eldest son, John Smith--conveyed to sd John Heard on March
8, 1768. Wit: Thomas Dillon, John Heard, Edmund Ellis C. T.
Deed G-4-11-14
Same card: John Smith -w- Mary to John Heard 8 March 1768
G-4-14-15. Wit: James Smith, Thomas Heard, Ann Heard

HEARD, JOHN AND ELIJAH--Wit. Will of George Burns of St. Paul's Par.
26 July 1770. Wm. Martin the other Wit. C. T. Wills

HEARD, JOHN--Arch. Dept. Mem 13-298
500 A. Craven on Larcooter Br. of Dutchman's Creek of Wateree
River. Bd. James Fallow and unknown person. Cert: 16 Aug. 1774
Gr. 23 Aug. 1774.

HEARD, JOHN, SR.--Of 96 Dist. Blacksmith. 6 Mi. Cr. 96 Dist.
Wife: Lydia--Land on Wilson's Creek   C. T. Wills 1774-1777-483
"All my children"   27 June 1777
All Wills were recorded in Charleston for the Provincial Period.
-Another card. Same heirs. C. T. Wills Vol. 17-640
Exor's: Francis Logan and John Edmiston.
Wit: Armstrong Heard, Charles Heard, Mat. Buchanan

HEARD, JOHN--Of Pine Grove. Dist. of Barnwell -m- set. 15 July 1809
Jane Bernard of Horse Creek, Dist. of Edgefield. Single woman.
Edgefield File. Misc. B-591

HEARD, JOHN -w- Jane--Marriage settlement between John Heard of Pine
Grove, Barnwell Dist. and Jane Heard, late Jane Bernard of
Hayes Creek Dist. of Edgefield. Single woman. 15 Sept. 1809.
Misc. B-490

HEARD, STEPHEN D.--Adm'r. of John Nix. Dec'd. Harris County, March
Term 1849. Over land sold by Nix in 1837. Cobbs Georgia Reports
Vol. 7-60. 1849
Page 380--____? Thomas J. Heard -vs- John A Heard 1850
Vol. 14-page 255--Macon Ct. 1853--Stephen T. Heard alleged that
in 1852 at Oglethorpe, Ga. while he was drunk, Daniel Higdon
induced him to play cards.

HEARD, THOMAS--House carpenter of Colleton. To: Christopher William-
Distiller. 150 pounds. 180A. Granville on NW fork of Long Cane
Originally surveyed for Jane Edminstone on 5 March 1767 and grant
sd Thomas Heard on 21 Feb. 1772. Wit: Thomas Pattison, James
E. Miller. Christopher Williams assigned this deed to Henry Hunt
of Ireland. C. T. Deed B-4-406

HEARD, THOMAS J. Of Elbert Co. Georgia marriage settlement 28 July
1864 Elizabeth Y. Arnold, Abbeville. Archives Dept. Misc. 2C-6
-Nelson Carter, Trustee. 490 A. Rabun Co. Georgia and slaves.

HEARD, WILLIAM--15 A. 96 Dist. Bd: John Sansum, John Lang?, Wm. Gogan, Joseph Davenport, Isaac Mitchell. Cert: 19 Feb. 1773. Grant: 23 June 1774. Del. to ment. 22 Nov. 1774 Archives Dept. Mem 13-115

HEARD, WILLIAM--Nephew and Legatee of Andrew Logan-Will 25 Aug. 1788 100 Acres. Abbeville Wills 1788
Wife: Lidy
Sons: John and Isaac Logan
Exor: John Wardlaw
Wit: Wm. Heard, Lon Wardlaw, and Elizabeth Wardlaw.

HEARD, DRURY--Will 4 Sept. 1840. Edgefield

HEARST, JOHN--Of Long Cane. Will 9 Sept. 1780. Prov: 25 Aug. 1782
Wife: Mary   96 Dist. Bk. *age 102
Son: Robert
Dau: Mary
Sons: John, Joseph, Thomas, George, William
Daus: Christian, Elizabeth, Mary, Margaret, and Ann

HEARST, MARY--Dau. of Sarah Perrin-Will 1828. John Hearst, Exor.

HEARST, SILAS--Dec'd. R. E. Sole 1837. Edgefield Rec. Bk. A-260
Dist: Sarah Hearst, widow 1/3 equal to $73.72
      William W. Hearst 1/4 of 2/3
      Jane Hearst-same--Moses Clark, Gdn.
      Elizabeth Hearst-same--James Clark-Gdn.
      Claresy Hearst-same--Aaron Clark, Gdn.

HEARST, JAMES--Petit Juror Edgefield 1788. List 9 and 18

HENDERSON, ELI -w- Mary--Heirs of Willis Darby, dec'd. See Darby card. Edgefield Rec. Bk. A-203 about 1828

HENDERSON, FRANCES--Dau. of Hillary M. Collins-Will 1841. Wife of Robert Henderson. Edgefield

HENDERSON, JAMES--Petit Juror Edgefield 1786. List 1, 2, 6, and 18

HENDERSON, JOHN--Petit Juror Edgefield 1789. List 13

HENDERSON, NATHANIEL--Petit Juror Edgefield 1788. List 10

HENDERSON, OBEDIAH--Dec'd. R. E. Sold 1835. Edgefield Rec. Bk. A-207
Dist: Mary Henderson, widow 1/3 equal to $141.39
      Lewis, Calvin, Elizabeth, Bennet, Thomas, Martha, Mary, Francis, Elizabeth, Obediah, and Levy Henderson 1/11 of 2/3 each, equal to $25.70. Last eight children-minors.
      Daniel Self, Gdn

HENDERSON, RICHARD--Petit Juror Edgefield 1787. List 6 and 17

HENDERSON, SHADRICK--Petit Juror Edgefield 1786. List 1, 2, and 12

HENDRICKS, DAVID--Of State of Georgia, Bullock Co. Bond to James Charter 16 Jan. 1805. Mtg. 200 A. on waters Bunky fork. Edgefield Deed Bk. 29-92

HENDRICKS, JABESH--Late of Dist. of 96. County of Edgefield. To
Edward Prince--50 A. 96 Dist. on a Br. of Savannah River. Bd.
NE John Swillivan. Pres: Hugh Middleton, Joseph Prince, and
Lilly W. Williams. Edgefield Deed Bk-2 Pg-26/7 10 Oct. 1786

HENDRICKS, JABESH--Deeds of L. and Re L from Jabesh Hendricks to
Edward Prince for 50 acres land proved by oath of Hugh Middleton,
Esq. and Joseph Prince. Edgefield Ct. Min. Bk. Pg-148. 4 Jan.
1788
HENDRICKS, JOHN--To William Barns--both of 96 Dist. 200 A. S-s Great
Saludy River on a branch thereof called Glade Lick. Grant to
Joshua Deen 3 July 1786. Edgefield Deed Bk-10 Pg-235. 29 Nov.
1790
HENDRICKS, JOHN WILLIAM --From John Sullivan -w- Sarah--224 A. on
Stephens Creek. 13 Feb. 1799. Wit: Edward Prince, Delilah Williams.
Edgefield Deed Bk. 17-89

HENDRICKS, JOHN WILLIAM From George Gizel--Dower by Sally Gizzle (sp?)
135 A. part 150 A. grant Job Red-who conv. to William Harvey at
mouth of the Ready Branch on the River. Bd. SW by Savannah River.
Edgefield Deed Bk-18-463 1800

HENDRICKS, NANCY -w- John William Hendricks--To the heirs of James
Baker, dec'd.--Dower. 28 Oct. 1806. 125½ part grant to Job Red
who conv. to William Harvey Hendricks, Sen'r. Bd. SW Savannah
River, all vac. on Ready Branch. Also 110 A. Grant to Wm. Harvey,
Sen'r. Edgefield Deed Bk. 27-239

HENDRICK, RACHEL--A witness--15 Aug. 1776 between Thomas Boatwright, Sr.
and William Boatwright. C. T. Probate. Misc. 177401779. Pg-442

HENDRICK, ROBERT -w- Mary-late relict of Wm. Howell to William Daniel
Recites: Jose Daniel died seized of sundry lands including a tract
in Edgefield. Heirs of Jesse Daniel:
        Robert Hendrick -w- Mary
        Jesse Taylor
        James Taylor (now dec'd.)
        Mary -w- Thomas Taylor
        Martha Taylor.
Edgefield Deed Bk. 29-494. Oct. 1803

HENDRICKS, SARAH, WILLIAM, AND JAMES--As Adm'rs. of David Hendricks,
dec'd. of Bullock Co. Georgia. 167 A. Edgefield Co. adj. Hugh Duffy,
Richard Teate, James Wiggins, and Wm. Moore--on Bushy fork. Part Gr.
to sd David Hendricks, dec'd. Gr. 1791. Wit: Daniel Hendricks
Luke H. Smith, Prov: in Screven Co. Ga.
Edgefield Deed Bk. 39 Pg-90 28 Dec. 1818

HENSHAW, THOMAS and wife--Heirs of William Scott. See Scott card.
Edgefield Rec. Bk. B-53 1841

HERBERT, MARGARET--Dau. of Rhydon Grigsby-Will 1826

HERNDON, JOHN--Grand Juror Edgefield 1786. List 4, 12 and 18

HERNDON, JOHN--Minor son of William Herndon-of age to choose Gdn.
Chose Thomas Adams. Edgefield Ct. Min. March 1795

HERON, FRANCES--Dau. of Samuel Savage-Will 1804

HERREN, AARON--Son of Christian Limbecker-Will 1818

HERREN, ELIZABETH--Legatee of John Purssell-Will 1794.

HESTER, JOHN--Petit Juror Edgefield 1794. List 21

HESTER, JOHN--Dec'd. R. E. Sold 1837. Edgefield Rec. Bk. A-278
    Dist: Jacob Whitehead -w- Sarah of Alabama 1/5 equal to $54.35
        Berry Franklin and wife
        Pleasant Hester
        Tapley Hester
        Heirs of Anna Don:
            (Mary--Assigned to her step mother Nancy Don 1837
    Minors(Jane--   "   " "   "   "   "   " "
         (John--Assigned to Nancy Kirkland 1838
         Rachel -m- Wm. Kirkland.
  Derrick Holsonbake gave receipt 20 Jan. 1838 for part he was
  entitled to by reason of a deed from dec'd.

HESTER, SARAH--Widow John Hester -m- Jacob Whitehead. Edgefield
    Rec. Bk. A-278. 1837

HIBLER, JACOB--To be Overseer of Road from Coffeetown Creek to
    Cyper, in room of James Sanders, excused. Edgefield Min. March
                                                   1795

HICKS, JAS. M.--Dec'd. Edgefield Sale Bk. A-136
    Distributees--Devisees--Robert Jennings purchased share of the
    widow, Jane Jennings--1/2 equal to $12.16 1/4 formerly Jane Hicks.
    Thomas E. Hicks-1/2 equal to $12.161/4

HICKS, JOHN -w- Nicey--Heirs estate of Jonathan Gregory. See Gregory
    card. Edgefield Rec. Bk. A-187/9 1834

HICKS--See Nicks, Matilda. Edgefield

HICKS, TABITHA--Dau. of Paul Abney-Will 1819

HIGHTOWER, MISS HARRIET--Marriage settlement 12 Oct. 1811 Jeremiah
[Bussey. Sd. by "John H. Bussey" Edgefield Dist. Misc. D-415

HIGHTOWER, JOSEPH--Petit Juror Edgefield 1788. List 10, 18.
                 Grand "   "   "   " 21

HIGHTOWER, JOSEPH, ESQ.--Appt'd. Coroner for Edgefield Co. Qualified
    as J. P. at Jan. Ct. 1795.
    Benjamin Hightower granted permission to keep Tavern. S: Joseph
    Hightower, and Jeremiah Hatcher. Edgefield Ct. Min. March 1795
    Joseph Hightower and Joshua Hammond--Apt'd. Commissioners to
    view and report upon a road from the Cherokee Fords to Day's Old
    Meeting House. Having returned their report, ordered that the
    said road be opened and Hightower Thorne to be Overseer of said
    road. Jan. 1795.

HIGHTOWER, JOSEPH--Marriage set. 16 Aug. 1841--Ann M. Carey. Misc. M-26

107

HIGHTOWER, MARY--Sister of Rachel Wise-Will 1842. Edgefield

HILES, SOPHIA--Dec'd. Will Proved by oath of Isaac Ardis and Qualified by William Shinholster. Edgefield Min. Bk. Pg-189
14 July 1788. Edgefield

HILEY, PRISCILLA--Dau. of Stephen Evins-Will 1827. Edgefield

HILL, ANN--Sister of Mary Foreman-Will 1790 Edgefield

HILL, BARSHEBY--Dec'd. See card of Hannah Robinson, her mother.
Edgefield Rec. Bk. A-1830

HILL, BERSHEBA--Dec'd. R. E. Sold. Edgefield Sale Bk. A-78
Dist: 1/4 each or $13.48
        Sarah Blair-widow of C. Blair, dec'd. and 8 children
        Hannah Robertson
        Gabriel Blair
        Bersheba Thomas
Purchased by Robert Jennings at $53.953/4. 1 of 8 children:
Washington Blair--Rec't. 29 Oct. 1832
1 of 8 Children: S. M. Blair--Rec't. 7 April 1840
John and Susan Kilcrease, P. A. of Mavery (sp?) Co., Tenn. P. A.
to Adam Kilcrease of Edgefield Co. to receive their part of est-
ate of Ebenezer Kilcrease formerly of Edgefield Dist. 4 July 1839
(Attached to this page)

HILL, CATHARINE--Dau. of Martha Tucker-Will 1834

HILL, EBENEZER -w- Sarah -vs- William Johnson. Slander. Referred to
Elisha Roberson and Drury Pace with Power of Umpirage to be re-
lated next court. Edgefield Min. Bk. Pg-315. Jan. 1790

HILL, EBENEZER--Dec'd. R. E. Sold 1837. Edgefield Rec. Bk. A-280
Dist: Edmond Cartledge and wife 1/2 equal to $270.04
        B̶l̶a̶k̶e̶/̶H̶i̶l̶l̶/̶o̶f̶/̶h̶i̶s̶/̶s̶u̶r̶v̶i̶v̶i̶n̶g̶/̶c̶h̶i̶l̶d̶r̶e̶n̶--struck out
        Nancy Cox 1/8 of 1/2
        Thomas Tally -w- Elizabeth-same
        John L. Kilcrease -w- Susan-same
        Millington Blalock and wife-same
        James Tomkins and wife-same
        Robert Jennings and wife-same
        Mary Lovelass and Harriet Granton--same each
"The share of Blake Hill is distributed among the other legatees
as he has not been heard of for many years". Rec't. July 9, 1839
from Martin Abney for share of his wife, Harriet.

HILL, ELIZABETH--Dec'd. R. E. Sold 1843. Edgefield Rec. Bk. B-83
Dist: Thomas Berry)1/2 each equal to $36.50
Rec'ts BythaMardaned 17 April 1844

HILL, ELIZABETH E.--Dau. of Col. James and Gracey Smyly.
Born--March 2, 1827   Died--Feb. 6, 1877
Beside above duplicate of tomb with word Grace
Tombstone Little Stevens Creek Baptist Church Edgefield Co.

HILL, FRANCES and her heirs: Mary Ann and Unity Hill--Heirs of
Reuben Carpenter. See Carpenter card. Edgefield Rec. Bk. B-77
                                                              1843

HILL, JEFFRY--Petit Juror Edgefield 1786. List 5

HILL, JOHN--Petit Juror Edgefield 1788. List 11 and 15

HILL, JOHN--Surety for John Adams. See Adams card. Edgefield Ct.
   Min. March 1795

HILL, JOHN -w- Adaline--Heirs of Martin H. Loveless. Edgefield Rec.
   Bk. B-123 1847

HILL, LODWICK--List of defaultes for not working on road from Amos
   Richardson's to Barry Travis, to wit:
   Wm. Nicholson   John Rogers
   Wm. Gains   Samuel Humphries
   Charles Partin   Wormly Bland
   John Bledsoe   John Strother
   James Buckelew   Jeseph Brown
   Josiah Howell   Absolom Wilson
   Jeremiah Strother   Joel Brown
   Presley Bland
   Joseph Lewis--who warned them to testify. Edgefield Ct. Min. 1795
                                                                March
HILL, MARTHA--Dau. Hamutal Wilson-Will 1806. See also card on Fay.

HILL, MINERVA--Legatee of William Carson-Will 1842

HILL, SARAH--Will 1822 Edgefield
   Daus: Nancy Cox   Huldy Tompkins
         Elizabeth Talley   Mary Loveless
         Susannah Kilcrease   Vinny Jennings
         Sarah Blalock   Jeannett Hill

HILL, SARAH--Dec'd. and her heir-Martin Hill--Heir estate of Joseph
   Day. See Day card. Edgefield Rec. Bk. A-242. About 1830

HILL, SUSANNAH--Dau. of Enoch Grigsby-Will 1789. Edgefield

HILL, SUSANNAH -w- Theophilus Hill and dau. of David Richardson-Will
   1842. Frances Hill also mentioned as dau. of Clarecy Bell, dec'd
   dau. of testator. Edgefield

HILL, WILLIAM--Petit Juror Edgefield 1786. List 4 and 17
   -William Hill and wife, Eliza--of Bibb County, Alabama gave a P. A.
   to Thomas J. Thompkins to collect debts due in Edgefield. 3 Jan.
                                                                  1846.
HILL, WILLIAM and wife--Heirs of Stephen Tomkins. See Tomkins card.
   Edgefield Rec. Bk. B-59 1842

HILL, WILLIAM -w- Sarah--Heirs of Abney Mays. See Mays card.
   Edgefield Rec. Bk. B-192 1850

HILL, WILLIAM -w- Sally--Heirs of Abney Mays. Edgefield Deed 31-42/3

HINDLEY, RACHEL--Dau. of John Marchant-Will 1830

HINDS, MARY--Grant 22 Aug. 1771. Edgefield Deed Bk. 32-164/5
Conv. to John Garrettby Mason Isard who married Mary Hinds.
Conv. 18 July 1789. John Garrett to Wm. Little 15 May 1793 and
Wm. Little to Wm. Jay 9 Sept. 1796. Wm. Jay to Samuel Davis -w-
Mary M. D. Davis on 10 Feb. 1813. Wm. Jay's wife--Abigail.
Samuel Davis and wife conv. to John Dolly 31 Dec. 1814. Wit:
Arthur Dillard and Owen Davis.
Page 135--Mayson Izard to Dirdath Odom 18 Jan. 1813

HINSON, DORMAN -w- Unity--Heirs of James Rushton. Edgefield Rec. Bk.
A-248 1836

HINTON, ALLEN--Petit Juror Edgefield 1789. List 14

HINTON, ALLEN--Dec'd. William Covington, Adm'r. Inv. Estate returned.
Jan. Ct. 1795--Will proved by oath of John Lin(?) and Wm. Covington
qualified as Adm'rs. with Will annexed on the resignation of High-
tower Thorne, the sole exor. Edgefield Ct. Min. March 1795
Jan. Ct. 1795--Appr's. apt'd.--LeRoy Hammond, John Hammond,
Charles Old. Joseph Fuqua

HITE, ELBERT--Marriage--7th inst. at res. of W. J. Walker by R. L.
Gentry. Mise Morgan. All of Edgefield. Edgefield Adv. Dec. 1864

HITT, SARAH--Dau. of Peter Day-Will 1789. Edgefield

HOBBS, BURREL E. And wife--Heirs of Lauchen Winn. See Winn card.
Edgefield Rec. Bk. A-64 1830

HOBBS, JESSE and wife--Heirs of estate of Jonathan Devore. See Devore
card. Edgefield Rec. Bk. A-54.

HOBBS, LAURA ANN--Dau. of James Harrison-Will 1841. Burrel E. Hobbs
seems to be the husband. Edgefield

HODGE, URIAH -w- Tabitha--Heirs of William Rodgers, Sen'r. See Rodgers
card. Edgefield Rec. Bk. B-148 1848

HOES, JOHN--Petit Juror Edgefield 1788. List 11

HOFF, CHRISTIANA--Dau. of Ulrick Ebney of C. T. -w- Sophia Elizabeth.
Ulrick Ebney's Will 3 Nov. 1763 C. T. Wills 1761-67
His dau: Anna Maria -w- John Miller
         Magdalene -w- John Spidel
Son: Christopher Eberhard Ebney.

HOFF, FREDERICK--Mem 8-249. 300 A. Berkley on Waters of Edisto,
Orangeburg township. Bd: S. E. Michael Shuler. N. E. Melchior
Smith and vac. Cert: 4 Aug. 1767. Grant 15 July 1768
Mem: 29 Sept 1768 sd Frederick Hoff
-Mem. 11-288--Frederick Hoff 1 July 1772--200 A. Berkley on Four
Hole. Bd. Michael Siegler and vac. Cert: 15 Nov. 1772
Grant: 15 May 1772   Mem: 1 July 1772. Del. to John
Timmerman (?)

HOFF, JOHN--Of C. T. to Hans Ernest Hoff of C. T. Bond and Mtg. 400
    pounds. Slave man-York. 5 May 1760. Arch. Dept. Mtg's. YY-130

HOFF, JOHN--150 A. St. Matthews Parish Bd..--All vac. Cert: 7 Jan.
    1772, Grant 15 May 1772. Mem: 1 July 1772. Mem. 11-288

HOFF, JOHN LEWIS PEGRE Im. Council Journal C. J. 38-40 25 Apl. 1774
    350 A. Granville--Grant

HOGAN, THOMAS--Dec'd. His estate in hands of Joel Abney, as Adm'r.--
    who apt'd. his wife Adm'x in his stead. By his Will 1811.

HOGANS, WILLIAM -w- Nancy--parents of Elizabeth Yarbrough -w- Gilson
    Yarbrough-Will 1839. Edgefield

HOGG, JOHN--Petit Juror Edgefield 1786. List 4

HOGG, JOHN -w- Mary -vs- Laban Odom, Adm'r. of Saunders Nobles of
    Edgefield Co. S. C.--Recites deed to the "children of Nancy Jones"
    from dec'd., Saunders Nobles. Dated 25 Dec. 1786--The children
    of Nancy Jones then being 5 in number. Mary, the complainant,
    daughter of Nancy, was born about 1794--title to pass "at death of
    Leonard Nobles". Dennis Nobles being the eldest son of said
    Nancy. Burke Co. Sup. Ct. Dudley's Rep. Sup. Ct. Ga.--1837 Pg-185

HOLDEN, JANE--Dau. of James Bones-Will 1841. Edgefield

HOLLY, JOHN W. -w- Elizabeth
    DANIEL D. -w- Rose
    P. W. -w- Mary--All heirs of George Litesy. Edgefield Rec. Bk.
    B-167. 1848

HOLLY, ALFRED--See Will of Wm. H. Cary-1836. Edgefield Wills

HOLT, POLLY--Legatee of Micajah Phillips-Will 1811 Edgefield

HOLLIDAY, LUCY--Heir of John Rhoden. See Rhoden card. Edgefield
    Rec. Bk. B-91 1844

HOLLIDAY, RANSOME, MARY ANN, et al--Heirs of Richard Lewis. See Lewis
    Card. Edgefield Rec. Bk. A-215 1835

HOLLIDAY, WILLIAM--Dec'd. R. E. Sold. Edgefield Sale Bk. A-106/8
    Dist: Samuel Bell, et ux ½ and 1/5 of ½   17 Oct. 1831
           Eli Brenson, et ux
           Bennett McMillan, et ux
           William Branson, Eli Branson--Heirs of Polly Branson
           Larkin Culbertson, et ux
           Nathan, William, Eli, James, Newton and Scott Holliday--
              Heirs of Wm. Holliday, Jr.
           Anna Holliday, dec'd. one of the original heirs--260 A. on
           Coffee Town Creek. Shows: Wm. Holliday, intestate
           Heirs: William Holliday   Peggy -m- Samuel Bell
                   Nelly -m- Eli Branson   Lidia -m- Bennett McMillan
                   Polly -m- Thomas Branson   Anna Holliday, dec'd.
    James Holliday purchased all shares except Peggy. Willed
    to following heirs: Blewford, James, William Charles Bell
                          Bell   Bell   Bell

HOLLODAY, WILLIAM--Petit Juror Edgefield 1786. List 1, 2, 8, and 16

HOLLINGSWORTH, BEERSHEBA--3rd dau. of John Oliphant-Will 1815
-Sister of William Oliphant-Will 1827. Her children:
John H. Hollingsworth   Eliza Ann A. Hollinngsworth
Diomede   "   Emeline D.   "
Mansfield   "   William H.   "

HOLLINGSWORTH, JAMES--Petit Juror Edgefield 1788. List 11

HOLLINGSWORTH, JOHN--Will 28 Sept. 1838. Edgefield

HOLLINGSWORTH, MARTHA--Dau. of Nathaniel Henderson.-Will 1801

HOLLINGSWORTH, PHEBI--Dau. of Francis Posey-Will 1787. Edgefield

HOLLISTER, J. G. -w- Catherine--Heirs of Lewis Youngblood. See
Youngblood card. Edgefield Rec. Bk. B-89 1845

HOLLOWAY, ANNE--Dau. of James Hall-Will 1794. Edgefield

HOLLOWAY, CALEB--Petit Juror Edgefield 1786. List 1, 2,
          Grand   "   "   "   "   4, 8, 16, 18
-Caleb Holloway--Will 28 March 1840. Edgefield

HOLLOWAY, DANIEL--R. E. Sold. Edgefield Rec. Bk. A-154
Dist: Henry Bloxom and wife   1/3 equal to $62.13
       Claudia Holloway, Matt E. Holloway, M. H. Holloway 1/3 of 2/3
R. E. Sold about 1833. No date on page before 1833

HOLLOWAY, DANIEL--Dec'd. R. E. Sold 1851. Edgefield Rec. Bk. B-196
Dist: Rosela Holloway, widow--eliciting to take a _____ Spt (?)
       $97.85
       Oliver G., Green, John W., Newton, Frances Ann M., --minors
       Elijah Holloway, Gdn.

HOLLOWAY, ELIJAH -w- Sophia--Heirs of William B. Rowe. See Rowe card.
Edgefield Rec. Bk. B-151 1847

HOLLOWAY, ELIZABETH--Dau. of Hezekiah Nobles-Will 1830

HOLLOWAY, JORDAN--Dec'd. R. E. Sold 1837. Edgefield Rec. Bk. A-270
Dist: Elijah, Daniel, Wiley, Martin Holloway--1/6 equal to 20 cents
       John Don -w- Matilda-same
       George Reame and wife-same

HOLLOWAY, LEWIS, SEN'R.--died intestate 1814. Married about 1787.
Of Brunswick Co. Va. Widow: Rachel
Dau: Lucy -m- James Reese--of Muscogee Co. Ga.--Moved to Han-
      cock Co. Ga. Living 1849
Son: Edward B. Holloway
Rachel was formerly widow of Thomas Williams of Brunswick Co. Va.
He died Jan. 1787. Was father of Lucy Reese.
Edgefield Bill 914-915 (or 975)
Roll 906 1850--Sarah Holloway, dec'd.
      6 children: George Washington Holloway John D. Holloway
                   David W.   "
                   Lewis E.   "
                   Sibyl Ann-widow of John Carraway Moore

HOLLOWAY, LEWIS -m- in Virginia to Rachel Williams. Widow of Thomas
Williams. Only child: Lucy -m- James Reece -vs- Rachel Holloway
Edward B. Holloway, Thomas O. Holloway, Lewis Holloway, Wyatt
Holmes, John Jones, WilliamThomas--"Sheweth": That Lewis Holloway
late of the aforesaid State and District, but ,then a resident of
the State of Virginia, there -m- a certain Rachel Williams, widow
of Thomas Williams, and mother of your orator's wife, Lucy, the
only child and heir of the said Thomas". Suit over slaves.
Alleges Rachel Holloway, the mother of Lucy had died.

HOLLOWAY, MARGARET--Dau. of William Dean-Will 1829

HOLLOWAY, MORRIS P. -m- Rebecca Moore-widow of Anderson Moore. See
Moore card. Jordan Holloway owned land adj. Edgefield Eq. #72
1819
HOLLOWAY, PERRY--Gdn. Minor children of Stephen Martin. See Martin
card. Edgefield Rec. Bk. A-36 1830

HOLLOWAY, PERRY--Heir of Peter Robertson. See Robertson card.
Edgefield Rec. Bk. B-33. 1841

HOLLOWAY, RANSOM -w- Matilda--Heirs of estate of Elizabeth Falkner.
See Falkner card. Edgefield Rec. Bk. B-182 1850

HOLLOWAY, REBECCA--Dau. of John Adams-Will 1822. Edgefield

HOLLOWAY, REUBEN--Petit Juror Edgefield 1788. List 9, 18

HOLLOWAY, THOMAS--5 Shillings--Legatee of Samuel Walker-Will 1810
States Thomas Holloway has desertrd his children who seem gr.
children of testator. Edgefield.

HOLLOWAY, WILLIAM--Adm'r. estate of Jacob Clegg. Edgefield Rec. Bk A-46
-HOLLOWAY, WILLIAM--Will 13 July 1838   1829

HOLMES, EDWARD--Petit Juror Edgefield 1787. List 7, 20

HOMES, ELIZABETH--Dau. of John Burrise-Will 1822. (Holmes?)

HOLMES, ELIZABETH--Dau. of William Howle, Sen'r.-Will 1830 (Homes?)

HOLMES, JOHN--Son: Frederick Holmes, Jr. 182 A. Grant John Walker
4 Nov. 1786. Edgefield Deed 9-68 4 June 1793

HOLMES, LEWIS and wife--Heirs of Samuel Medlock. See Medlock card.
Edgefield Rec. Bk. A-74

HOLMES, LUCY--Dau Pleasant Thurmond-Will 1830

HOLMES, MILDRED--Dau. of Charles Partin-Will 1796. Rec. 1813 (Homes)

HOMES, SHADERICK AND wife--Dist. estate of Charles Blalock. See
Blalock card. Edgefield Rec. Bk. B-69 1842. (Holmes?)

HOLMS, WILLIAM--Petit Juror Edgefield 1789. List 13
-William Helmes--Overseer of road from Cambridge to the Ridge,that
part from Barrott Travis' to Indian Creek, in room of Philip Innir
excused. Edgefield Ct. Min. March Ct. 1795

HOLMES, WYATT -m- Catherine Collier, widow of Thomas Collier. Bills
914-975

HOLSONBAKE, AHILE--Dec'd. R. E. Sold 1841. Edgefield Rec. Bk. B-35
    Dist: Ellis H. Goff -w- Nancy 1/3 equal to $42.50
           Eli, Lucy, Early, Sarah, Pickens Holsonbake-all minors ½ 2/3
                                                                   each.
HOLSONBAKE, ALFRED -w- Melissa--Heirs of Thomas Howle. See Howle card.
    Edgefield Rec. Bk. A-286. 1838

HOLSONBAKE, CATHERINE--Dau. of John Searle-Will 1820

HOLSONBAKE, DERRICK -w- Elender--Dist: estate of Hezekiah Almon, Sr.
    See Almon card. 1830. Edgefield Rec. Bk. A-62

HOLSONBAKE, HARRIET--Wife of Daniel Holsonbake and dau. of William
    King, Sen'r.-Will 1832. Edgefield

HOLSONBAKE, LETITIA--Gr. dau. of Esther Howle-Will 1840

HOLSONBAKE, MARY--Dau. of Robert Mosely-Will 1796

HOOF, FREDERICK--350 A. Craven 16 Sept. 1769. Arch. Dept. Mem. 8-499

HOOF, JAMES--from Edmund Belchen--dower, Polly C.--100 A. on waters
    of Coffee Town. Orig. Grant John Wilson. Edgefield Deed 32-317

HOOF, JOHN--Mem. 12-72 15 Jan. 1773. 250 A. Berkley-St. Georges Par.
    in Orangeburg. Bd. Samuel Parson. Cert: 10 March 1772. Grant
    30 Oct. 1772 to mentioned. Mem. 15 Jan. 1773. Del. to Margaret
    Anding.

HOPKINS, DAVID--Shown as a land owner in Edgefield Dist. in 1778.
    Charleston Deed T-5-269

HOPKINS, ISAAC--to John Ryan 4 April 1792--Edgefield Deed Bk. 6-330
    2 feather beds and farm___?
    -Isaac Hopkins -w- Cecelia-- Heirs estate Ann Green, dau. of John
    Roebuck. See card Green. Edgefield No. 30

HOPKINS, JESSE--Of Edgefield Co. Deed Gift 17 Sept. 1799 Deed Bk. 17-395
    To the daughters of Thomas Youngblood:
        Winnefred Kirksey -w- Edward Kirksey
        Elizabeth Adams -w- James Adams
        Rebecca Hargrove -w- Briton Hargrove
        Amy Williams
        Isabella Youngblood -w- Thomas Youngblood
    All lands, notes and accounts which I am possessed of. Ten head
    neat cattle; 1 horse, saddle and bridle; and all property"that I
    may hold at time of my death".
    Wit: James Youngblood and Thomas Youngblood
    -Probate Box 38 Pk-1500: Jesse Hopkins, dec'd. Cit: 22 Feb. 1800
    Read at Little Stevens Creek. Thomas Youngblood, Adm'r. "To
    cash paid Christian Hopkins--as agreed by the legatees--$20.00
    Amount paid Kelly Hopkins--?

114

HOPKINS, JOHN--His grant mentioned in Will of Joseph Griffith-1810.
Edgefield Wills Bk. A-295

HORD, GREENVILLE -w- and S. Harrison -w-. Edgefield Ct. Equity-871

HORIDE, EMMA--Dau. Eliza Hannah Simkins-Will 1837

HOUSE, ELIZABETH--Sister of Wm. Robertson-Will 1840

HOUSE, SALLY--Dau. of Hamutal Wilson-Will 1806 and wife of James House
See also card on Fay. Edgefield

HOUSTIN, JOHN A.--Gdn. Minor children of Henry Garrett. See Garrett
card. Edgefield Rec. Bk. B-31 1841

HOUSTON, JOHN A. -w- Amy--Legatees of Elizabeth Garrett-Will 1843

HOWARD, BATT and wife--Heirs of Amy Addison and of John Cogburn.
Edgefield Rec. Bk. A-225. 1834

HOWARD, CENTHEY--Dau. of John B. Bush-Will 1844. Edgefield

HOWARD, ELIZABETH--Dau. of Thomas Key-Will 1820. At time Will was
made Howard had died and she had married _____? Farrar.

HOWARD, PATSEY--Dau. of John Addison, Sen'r.-Will 1827. Edgefield

HOWARD, SALLY--Dau. of Bryant Green-Will 1794. Edgefield

HOWARD, SAM--Petit Juror Edgefield 1788. List 10

HOWARD, SAMUEL--Will proved by oath of James Howard and Joseph Wallace.
Edgefield Ct. Min. Bk. Page-304. Jan. 1790

HOWARD, SETH--Petit Juror Edgefield 1788. List 12 and 17
Grand   "   "   "   " 18
-Seth Howard--Surety on Bond John Hall-Tavern Keeper. See Hall
Card. Edgefield Ct. Min. March 1795

HOWELL, ANN--Dau. of Barbara Nail of Edgefield-Will 1795.

HOWELL, CATHERINE-m- Hon. Judge Henry Osborne. See Osborne card.
Augusta Ct. Min. 1798

HOWELL, ESTHER--"advanced age"-Will 16 Nov. 1840. Edgefield

HOWELL, HELENA--Dau. of Ann Clark, niece of Ulric Tobler-Will 1815
-Heleña Howell--Dau. of John Clarke, Sen'r.-Will 1821.
Her children: Nancy and Josiah Howell. Edgefield

HOWELL, JACKSON -w- Catherine--Heirs of Philip Jennings. See Jennings
card. Edgefield Rec. Bk. B-185. 1850

HOWELL, JOSEY -w- Sarah--Heirs estate of James Eidson. Edgefield
Rec. Bk. B-125 1847

HOWELL, JOSIAH--Default in road work. See Lodwick Hill. Edgefield
Ct. Min. March 1795

HOWELL, NATHANIEL -m- Ann--dau. of John Nail, who was son of Daniel
Nail. See Nail card. (Or Ann, dau. of Daniel Nail?)
-Nathaniel Howell--Grand Juror Edgefield 1786 List 8, 3, 16.

HOWELL, PHILIP and wife, Sarah--Of Screven CO. Georgia. David Mock
estate. Edgefield Deed Bk. 20-195. 5 May 1805

HOWLE, THOMAS H.--Dec'd. R. E. Sold 1838. Edgefield Rec. Bk. A-286
Dist: Esther Howle, widow 1/3 equal to $92.81
       Heirs of Nancy Howle-same
       Heirs of Elizabeth Howle 2/3 of 1/3 equal to $61.83
       John Chadwick 1/3 of 1/3 equal to $30.93
Rec't. by Washington Blair for his part dated Jan. 1838
  "   " Charles Dagnel, Jan. 1, 1838
  "   " John Oden for his share and share of Elias and George
           Oden, 5 Feb. 1838
  "   " Edward Shadwick in right of his wife, Stacy Anna Oden
           16 Oct. 1838
  "   " Stephen Shadwick in right of wife, Hester Oden 2 Dec. 1839
  "   " Alfred Holsenbake in right of wife, Melissa Oden.
           8 Aug. 1843
  "   " William Chadwick 25 Jan. 1844

HOWLE, THOMAS, SEN'R. Edgefield Rec. Bk. B-99
Dist: Children of Elizabeth Chadwick:- William, Elias, James
       John, Elizabeth, and Nancy Chadwick 1/6 of 1/2 each equal
       to $97.91
       Children of Nancy Odom:- John, Elias, and George Odom
       1/5 of 1/2
       Washington Blair -w- Martha 1/5 of 1/2 equal to $117.50
       James Lesure -w- Elizabeth   "   "   "   "   "
Receipt shows Elizabeth Chadwick -m- Lewis Bush
  "   " Nancy Chadwick -m- Levi Bush

HOWLE, THOMAS H.--Loose papers in Edgefield Rec. Bk.
Gr. children: John H. Oden)
               George Oden) Of Kemper County, Miss
               Elias Oden) P. A. 1844

HOWLE, WILLIAM, JR.--Petit Juror Edgefield 1788. List 11, 18, 21

HOWLE, WILLIAM, SEN!R.--Will 15 Oct. 1830 Edgefield

HOWLET, SETH--Gr. son of Wm. Jeter-Will 1793

HOWLET, PERRIN--Appr. estate of Samuel Edmunds. Edgefield Ct. Min. Jan.
                                                                   1795
HOWLET, ANCRIDGE--Dau. of Wm. Jeter-Will 1793. Gr. son: Seth Howlet.

HUCKABEE, CAROLINE A., MARYP., AND MARTHA--All nieces of Lucy Moore-
Will 1856. Friend--Rev. Green W. ___? Edgefield Pro. Bx-178/9
                                                              1856

HUFF, BENJAMIN--Orangeburg 23 April 1782. Arch. Dept. Rev. AA 3839
"Late a Sergeant in State Troops. Due a negro for his service.
Assigned claim to James McGowan"

HUFF, DANIEL--To Barkley and Mall Martin 4 March 1807--Mtg. slave-Jim.
Edgefield Deed 28-165

HUFF, DANIEL--Of Edgefield to W. Holloway Huff 26 Jan. 1808 $600.00
Negro-Jim--age 25 yrs. Edgefield Deed 29-253
Prob. 40-1557 John M. Huff, dec'd. Adm'r. Wm. H. Huff.
Bond 7 Feb. 1812. S: John Huff. Philemon Huff acknowledged
debt to estate.
John Huff-Will Proven: 1816. Date 1815
Wife: Sarah
Sons: Allen, Julius and Daniel--Land on Neuse River
Daus: Anna Edward, Mary Edward, Sally Cogburn, and Tabitha
Rainsford.

HUFF, DANIEL, SEN'R.--Edgefield Deed Bk. 36-181-182-183 30 Aug. 1819
Son: Daniel -w- Sarah W. Huff--dower. Plat and deed to Mary
McDaniel. $529.00. 823/4 A. where Daniel Huff the younger
lives. Plat made at request of both the Sen'r. and Jun'r or
younger. Part tract John Cogburn, Sr. gave to his son,
John Cogburn, Jr. 64 A. and part tract purchased from
Benjamin Pierce. Plat Cert: 21 Aug. 1818 on Cedar Creek.
Bd: John Addison, John Mims, Mrs. McDaniel, Mrs. Cogburn,
and Coody's Creek.

HUFF, DANIEL -w- Mary--Dower to Simeon Dinkins--243 A. Grant to David
Robertson and Tully Bolen. Afterwards owned by John Huff who
Willed to sd Daniel Huff, on Horn's Creek. Edgefield Deed 45-459

HUFF, DANIEL--Survey--40 A. Grant to James Douglass who also got
14 A. ____? for John Humphreys. Elapse Book

HUFF, DOUGLAS--No dower--to Joseph Hold 19 March 1816 316 A. Edgefield
Deed Bk. 33-264

HUFF, JAMES--Harris Co. Georgia Will Bk. A 1838

HUFF, JANE C. -m- set 22 Nov. 1832 James English. Mar. Bk. 12-30

HUFF, JOEL and Charles Graves--Agree to sell Joel Huff land on Goose
Creek Road. Edgefield 5E-217 1826

HUFF, JOHN, THOMAS, ANN GLASS--Joint heirs of Gabriel Stack of St.
Bartholomew. Will 1771. C. T. Wills

HUFF, JOHN -w- Sarah-Dower to Benjamin Harrison 27 Feb. 1807. 423/4
A. in Edgefield on Waters of Cedar Creek. Bd. Robert Mosely,
Col. LeRoy Hammond. Wit: Vincent Huff. Edgefield Deed 28-34
28-135--LeRoy Hammond to John Huff, Sr. 184 A. Cedar Cr. 2 Feb. 180
28-219--John Huff from Floyd Mitchel, dower, Susan, 250 A. Grant
Thomas Butler 14 Aug. 1772 who conv to Floyd Mitchel 1 Aug. 1807
28-221--John Huff from Geo. S. Cheney 200 A. Cedar Cr. Dower-Mary
Cheney.

HUFF, JOHN M.--Dec'd. Cit: 27 Dec. 1811 Adm: Wm. H. Huff 1811
  Bond: 7 Feb. 1812   S: John Robertson, Richard Christian
                              John Huff.
  Edgefield Bx-40-1557
  David Huff, the elder assessed $15.00 1817
  Philemon Huff acknowledged he owed estate 50¢
  Stephen Tillman, exor. Above belongs in file of John Huff.

HUFF, JOHN, JR. To Thos Rainford--Mtg. 26 July 1824. 94 3/4 A. where
  John Huff lately lived which he purchased. Deed 32-20 Edgefield
  Page 482--11 Oct. 1814--John Huff to Daniel Huff-Land where I now
  live, etc. Wit: William Huff

HUFF, JOHN--To son--Receipt for $1000.00 purchase price 11 Oct. 1814
  (Daniel Huff-son) 200 A. whereon I now live. Also part tract
  purchased from Col. LeRoy Hammond on W-side of School Branch.
  Wit: Richard Christmas, Philemon Huff. Edgefield Deed 32-482

HUFF, SARAH-W.--Legatee of John Gray-Will 1833 "old age"
  John Gray, Sr.--Will 20 Dec. 1823. Box 12-411
        Sons: Josiah and David Gray
        Daus: Susannah Scott and Harriet Scott
        Son: John Gray
        Dau: Mary -m- John Mims
  John Gray--Will Box 16--562   No date
        Wife: Ridley   (See next page for   )
        Sons: Matthew M. and Henry S. Gray (Wills of another   )
        Daus: Harriet S. and Lydia J. Gray (John Huff and Julias)
        Son in law: Chamberlain Goodwin
        Daus: Martha Nagey, Sarah W. Huff, Betsy Goodwin
        Wit: Wm. Frazier and M. Mims

HUFF, SUSAN--Of St. James Grove Cr. -m- Thomas Blanton. To her 3
  Brothers: Joel, Henry and William Huff. Arch. Dept. Misc. 6D-244
                                                              1849
HUFF, THOMAS--Of Rowan Co. N. C. Carpenter--from Elijah Massey of
  Kent Co. Maryland 7 Dec. 1767--purchased from John Thomas in Anson
  Co. S-side Catawba River, now Mecklenburg. Wit: Jonathan Huff,
  Samuel Thompson, and James McZachlan. Chester, S. C. Deed B-97

HUFF, WILLIAM, JACOB, ELIZABETH AND WILLIAM STEVENS--et al, Nephews
  and niece of James McLaren of Colleton, Co. died 1770. See also
  Will of Stephen Ackerman Bk. B 1786

HUGGINS, ELIZABETH--Heir of Isaac Kirkland. See Kirkland card.
  Edgefield Rec. Bk. A-302 1839

HUGGINS, MARK -w- Elizabeth-dau. of Martin Widdle of Lexington(or Witt)
  Mark Huggins an illiterate. Edgefield Equity B-34/5 1819

HUGGINS, WILL--Petit Juror Edgefield 1788. List 11

HUGHES, ELIZABETH--Dec'd. Edgefield Rec. Bk. B-103 1846
  Children: Stephen Y. Hughes
             John Clisby -w- Emily
             Alfred J. Hughes.
  Heirs of Mary Tillman. See Tillman card.

HUGHES, MARTHA--Dau. of James Bones-Will 1841. Edgefield

HUIET, DAVID -w- Mary--Heirs of John Morring. See Morring card.
    Edgefield Rec. Bk. B-21 1841

HULL, GIDEON H.--Will 30 Aug. 1840 Edgefield

HUMPHREY, EUNICE--Dau. of Samuel Satcher. Will 1813 Edgefield

HUMPHREY, AGNES--Grant 10 May 1773 sold by Joseph Eddins 7 March 1809
    Edgefield Deed Bk. 30-35,36,37

HUMPHREY, WILLIAM--Petit Juror Edgefield 1789. List 14

HUMPHRIES, SAMUEL--default on road work. See Ludwick Hill. Edgefield
    Ct. Min. March 1795.

HUNTER, ELIZABETH--Dau. of James Mathis-Will 1819 Edgefield.

HUNTER, LUCY AND CATA--Daus. of Thomas Deloach-Will 1810. Edgefield

HURST, ABRAHAM -w- Abigail--Heirs of Job Padget. See Padget card.
    Edgefield Rec. Bk. A-312 1839

HURST, JORDAN -w- Martha--Heirs of Daniel Clary. See Clary card.
    Edgefield Rec. Bk. A-288 1838

HURST, SAMUEL, ESQ.--J. P. for Granville Co. Took Probate 17 Nov. 1752
    Deed Gift Robert Wilkinson to his sister, Margaret Jones. Mtg. 22-
                                                                    480
HUTCHINSON, JOHN--Of Granville Co. Will 6 May 1767. C. T. Wills
    Wife: Sarah   Edgefield File
    Children: William, Mary, Edith, Sarah--minors
    Exers: Sam'l Green, Jonathan Thomas, Timothy Campbell

HUTCHERSON, MAXMILIAN--Brother in law of Joseph Lake-Will 1823.

HUTTON, CATHERINE C.--Legatee of James Johnson called "friend"-Will 1811
    Joseph Hutton ann exor. Edgefield

HUFF, JOHN--Orig. Will 10 April 1815. Prov: 12 Feb. 1816. Edgefield
    Wife: Sarah   Prob. Bx. 13-472
    Sons: Julias and Allen Huff in Granville Co. N. C. on Neuse
            River--200 Acres.
    To David Huff--in Edgefield
    To Daus: Anna Edwards, Mary Edwards, Sally Cogburn, and Tabitha
            Rainford.
    Paid Daniel Huss, son of Dec'd. Pd. debt due by Daniel Huff.
    John Huff a purchaser at sale.

HUFF, JULIAS--Orig. Will 15 Dec. 1849. Anderson Probate
    "my 6 children": Lamar Huff-1/3 more
                     Julian-moved to Lafayette, Indiana (letter)
                     Patsy, John and Abigail Huff
                     Samuel A. Huff--Moved to Lafayette, Ind.
                     Tippec____? Co. Prov: 1 Aug. 1850
    Received of Tabitha Huff on note. Geo. C. Elrod-Am'r.

119

INGRAM, ALEXANDER--Dau. of James Cox-Will 1798 Edgefield

INGRAM, FANNY--Step dau. of John Hardy-Will Rec'd. 1799. Also Betsy
Ingram. Edgefield

INGRAM, MARY--Seems 1st wife of or Common Law wife of Christian
Breithany. See Will. Her children: Ann Elizabeth and Sarah
Louise. Mentions deed trust made in Alabama for the benefit of
Mary and her children. (Butler County, Ala.)

JACKSON, JAOH--Petit Juror Edgefield 1788. List 9 and 18

JACKSON, REBECCA B.--Sister of Howard R. Marshal-Will 1829 Edgefield

JACOBS, JOSHUA--Petit Juror Edgefield 1786. List 4

JAMES, ZACHARIAH--Petit Juror Edgefield 1787. List 6

JARRETT, MARTHA--Dec'd. wife of Archibald Jarrett and dau. of Thomas
Key-Will 1820 Edgefield

JAY, ELIZABETH--Dau. of William Little-Will 1837

JAY, JESSE--Will 7 Aug. 1837. Edgefield

JENNINGS, DICKERSON. Edgefield Apt. 35 1815. Cit: 8 Sept. 1815
Joseph Jennings, Adm.
S: Robert Jennings, Sr. and Jr.   Bond: 2 Oct. 1814
Widow: Jane Jennings
Appr's: James Pickett, Wm. Jennings, John Searles

JENNINGS, LUCY--Dau. of Martha Tucker-Will 1834 Edgefield

JENNINGS, PATTY--Dau. of Aaron Etheredge-Will 1811. Edgefield

JENNINGS, PEGGY--Dau. of Joseph Tolbert-Will 1793

JENNINGS, PHILIP--Dec'd. R. E. Sold 1850. Edgefield Rec. Bk. B-188-190
Dist: Lucy Jennings, widow 1/2 equal to $485.75 (Total $971.50)
John Coleman   )
Anna -w- Jno Deshazier)
Thornton Coleman   )each 1/8 equal to $121.43
Children of Bartheny Chapman, a dec'd. dau.
John Chapman, Mary Chapman, and Caroline -w- Vinos Harril
Jesse Jennings 1/12 equal to $85.00
Dec'd. Brother, James Jennings, Rep:-
Enoch, John, Thomas, and William Jennings-each $20.23
Dec'd. Brother John Jennings, Rep:-
Asa, Hiram, William   )
Elizabeth -w- Benjamin Etheredge)
May -w- James Watts   ) $11.56 each
Ellen (dec'd) -w- Benjamin Partin)
Holly -w- Spear Partin   )
Sarah -w- Benjamin Partin, Sr.)

- CONTINUED -

JENNINGS, PHILIP--CONTINUED
  Children of dec'd. Brother, William Jennings:-
    Tire Jennings   )
    Elizabeth -w- Levi McDaniel   )
    Susan -w- ____? Roy (or Ray) and John Jennings.) $6.74 each
    Hasting, Lott, William, and Philip Jennings   )
    Martha -w- Helen Etheredge   )
    Ellinor Jennings   )
    Francis Jennings   )
  Children of Lucy Parten (dec'd. (wife of John Partin:-
    John and James Partin   )
    Mary -w- Allen Elliot   )
    Rebecca -w- Abner Brown   ) $11.56 each
    Catherine-wwidow of Jackson Howell)
    Lucy -w- Samuel Mitchel   )
    Nancy -w- Enoch Walton   )
  Children of dec'd. Mary Partin:-
    John J. Partin   )
    Jane--widow of Asa Evans   ) $26.98 each
    Elizabeth -w- Samuel Buchanan)

JENNINGS, ROBERT--16 Nov. 1815 35-5
  Wife: Tabitha
  Children: Clem, Mary, Boswell, Osborn, Sarah, Robert, John,
            and Elizabeth Jennings
  Wit: David Crawford, Wm. Handy, James Crawford. Prov: 25 May
  Ex: Tabitha Jennings, Joel Lockhart   1816
  Appr's: Wm. Handy, Abiah Morgan, Richard Handy, Joseph Jennings
  Debts due to: Ab. Blocker, E__? Hammond, Wm. Thomas, Wm. Robinson
  and Robert Jennings.

JENNINGS, ROBERT AND JANE--Heirs estate of James Hicks. See Hicks
  card. Edgefield Rec. Bk. A-136 About 1823

JENNINGS, ROBERT--Purchased R. E. estate of Bersheba Hill. Edgefield
  Rec. Bk. A-78 1832

JENNINGS, ROBERT and wife--Heirs of Ebenezer Hill. Edgefield Rec.
  Bk. A-220 1837

JENNINGS, THOMAS--Edgefield Will 19 March 1835 Prov: 8 April 1835
  Wife: lucy
  Children: Henry, Alticano, and Huldah--unborn if any.
  Father: Joseph Jennings
  Brother: Robert Jennings

JENNINGS, THOMAS--R. E. Sold 1852. Edgefield Rec. Bk. B-211
  Dist: Lucy Jennings, widow--1/4 equal to $234.56
        Henry L. Jennings-same
        C. L. Blair -w- Huldah-same
        Thomas Jennings-same

JENNINGS, VISAY--Dau. of Mary Hill-Will Rec'd. 1822

JENNINGS, WILLIAM--Edgefield Apt. 36. Huldah Jennings and John Key, Adm.
  Cit: 26 Dec. 1817   Bond: 14 Jan. 1818
  S: Abel and Mary Hill   Pur: Robert Jennings

JENNINGS, WILLIAM--Will 25 Dec. 1841 Edgefield

JERNIGAN, JESSE--Dec'd. Edgefield Ct. Min. March 1795
Personal estate ordered sold at his late dwelling, first Thursday
in April next.
March Ct. 1795--Inv. returned and received and part given to his
son, Henry Jernigan. Also inventoried and ruturned. Mrs.
Angelical Jernigan, Adm'x. made returns. Jan. Ct. 1795--
Angelica Jernigan, widow of Jesse Jernagen, with Wm. Bardet
applied for letters Administration. Bond: 150 pounds. S: Henry
King and Samuel Deloach. Apprs: Henry King, Thomas Dozier,
Samuel Deloach and John Smith.

JERNAGAN, JESSE--Petit Juror Edgefield 1787. List 8 and 17

JESTER, JAMES--Legatee of John Frazier-Will 1824. Edgefield

JETER, BRICELLA--Came in to Court and acknowledged her Deed of Gift
to Thomas, William, Nancy, and Elizabeth Jeter, her four children
which was ordered to be recorded. April Ct. 1787. Edgefield

JETER, ELEAZER--Dec'd.--Union Ct. Equity Bk. May Term 1826.
Minor children: James F., and William Jeter--James Jeter, Sr.
father, Gdn. L. B. Jeter, Sppt'd.
Aug. Term--Benjamin Gregory and Wm. Jeter, Adm'rs. Vincent E.
Collum and wife-widow of Eleazer Jeter.

JETER, ELIZER (sp?)--Dec'd. Noncupative Will. Died about 22 Jan. 1821
Widow: Sally--who married Vincent E. Collum.
Adm'r: Capt. Wm. Jeter and Benjamin Gregory
Bond: 8 March 1822--All to wife and children.
Union Co. Bx. 12-9 1821

JETER, FIELDING--Gr. son of Elizabeth Miller-Will 1808

JETER, JAMES--Dec'd. Original Will 4 July 1839. Union Co. Bx-25-21
Wife: Mary

Gr. son: William--son of Elizer Jeter
Gr. Dau: Mary Ann Fuller
Gr. son: Francis C. Jeter-son of John C. Jeter
Son: A___? Jeter and James Jeter
Dau: Elizabeth -w- Benjamin Gregory
Sons: L. B., Richard E., Thomas C., David S.,
Dau: Sally -w- Jesse Jeter

JETER, JAMES T.--Union Deed U-14 Pg-519
Wife: Catherine E.--dau. of John Mobley. Slaves-1849

JETER, JAMES R.--Dec'd. Will 18 May 1852 Filed 22 Jan. 1869 Union Co.
Heirs--Brothers, Sisters, Minor children   Roll 503
Thomas C. Jeter-one of Exors.
Richard C. Jeter, L. B. Jeter, James R. Jeter-D., Jesse L. Jeter-D.
Brother: A. U. Jeter and his children:-
          James B. Jeter, Orator
          Thomas R. Jeter
          Mary E. -w- James E. Douglas
          S. A. Jeter-died. Left Will
Sister: Elizabeth -w- B. F. Gregory--Her children in Will
                                                CONTINUED

JETER, JAMES--CONTINUED
    Brother: Eleazer Jeter--Only child-William Jeter-listed
    Brother: John C. Jeter--Dec'd. Children:-
                Thomas B. Jeter
                B. A. Jeter
                Adelea -w- Robert Garlington
                Arrinna -w- P. P. Butler
                Anelia -w- A. K. Thomson (Arelia?)

JETER, JOHN S.--Legatee $5.00 of John Ryan-Will 1827. Edgefield

JETER, LITTLE BERRY--Dec'd. 19 June 1874 Union Co. Bx. 61-20
    Adm'r: Dr. John P. Thomas
    Heirs listed: 3 children:-James T. Jeter, J. C. P. Jeter and
                          R. Gilliam H. Jeter

JETER, SARAH--Dec'd. dau. of John Simkins-Will 1832 (Sabra?)
    Gr. Children: Sarah Jeter and Caroline S. Jeter
    Son in law: John S. Jeter. Edgefield

JETER, R. C. and wife -vs- Daniel Thomas and H. A, Johnson--"I be-
    lieve the claim in this case was barely urged seriously--The
    Bill was to set aside a sale and assignment made of Complainants
    to Defendant Daniel Thomas who was Adm'r. of Mrs. Jeter's father,
    William Johnston, and of her distributive share of his estate.
    Dismissed. Union Co. Ct. Com. Pleas. Chancery 1831. Pg-135/6

JETER, ROSANNAH--Dau. of John Frazier-Will 1799. Rec'd. 1801

JETER, WILLIAM, SEN'R.--Grand Juror Edgefield 1786. List 3
              JUN'R.-- "   "   "   "   " 8, 14, 20

JETER, WILLIAM--Will 25 Nov. 1793 Edgefield
    Wife: Margaret
    Son: John William Jeter
    Daus: Partheny Vaughn
           Aneridge Howlet and son-Seth Howlet
           Calpharna Baker
    Sons: Hal, Joseph, Cornelius, James, Argales, and Eliezer Jeter
    Gr. Dau: Elizabeth Cruise
    Gr. Son: William Cruise
    Dau: Sarah Cross
          Nancy Mosely
    Gr. Son: George Mosely-son of Chancy Mosely (or Nancy)
    Dau: Delilah Garratt
          Priscilla Moseley-sau. Saley Mosely
    Dau: Peggy Kilcrease

JETER, CAPT. WILLIAM--Dec'd. 12 Legatees $564.49 3/4 each
    Heirs not named. Edgefield 1830-31 Box-18-8
    Dam. Bond: 3 May 1830   S: L. B. Jeter
          John C. Jeter   A. V. Jeter
          Thomas C. Jeter

JOHN, ELIZABETH--Wife Thomas John and sister of Cradock Burrell-Will
                                                                     1818

JOHNS, FRANCIS--Dau. John Clark, Sen'r.-Will 1814. Edgefield

JOHNS, OBEDIAH--Father of Jamima Collum -w- Uriah Collum-Will 1808
Obediah Johns, Jr. a witness. Edgefield

JOHNSON, BENJAMIN and wife--Heirs estate of William Gray. See Gray
card. Edgefield Rec. Bk. A-40 1829

JOHNSON, CHARITY--Dec'd. R. E. Sold 1849. Edgefield Rec. Bk. B-161
Dist: Fanny Goulden 1/4 equal to $64.87
Children of Amy Hazel, dec'd. 1/7 of 1/4 each - $9.26
Simeon Attaway -w- Frances
Seth Hazel
Hiram Abney -w- Milley
Jonathan Hazel -w- Huldah
Henny, Rhody, Philip Hazel
Children of Samuel Johnson, dec'd. 1/6 of 1/4 each $10.81
David Johnson
Charles Powell -w- Ellsey
John Moss -w- Lucinda
Morris, Bluford, and Pickens Johnson
Children of Morris Johnson, dec'd. 1/2 of 1/4 each $32.43
James Johnson
Caroline Johnson--now Davis

JOHNSON, DAVID -w- Elizabeth--Heirs of Catherine Butler, dec'd. See
Butler card. Also John Johnson -w- Alcey. Edgefield Rec. Bk. A-
298. 1838

JOHNSON, ELISHA R. and wife--Heirs of Walton Knight. See Knight card.
Edgefield Rec. Bk. B-57 1842

JOHNSON, ELIZABETH--Dau. of Daniel Butler-Will 1823. Edgefield

JOHNSON, HARLEY--Appr. Estate of James Moore. See Moore card. 1795
July Ct. 1788--Richard Johnson, Sen'r. and Richard Johnson, Jun'r.
Sureties gave bond estates Mary Watson and Patience Watson. See
both cards.

JOHNSON, HALEY--Grand Juror Edgefield 1794. List 20

JOHNSON, JAMES--Son of George Johnson and Provisional Legatee of Roger
McKinnie. Edgefield

JOHNSON, JOHN -w- Alcey--Heirs of Catherine Butler. See Butler card.
Edgefield Rec. Bk. A-298. 1838

JOHNSON, JOSHUA--Dec'd. Edgefield Rec. Bk. B-51
Dist: John W. Hall and wife--½ equal to $240.50
Virginia E. Johnson-same.
John W. Hall, Gdn. The wife: Clementine Hall. See Hall
card.
JOHNSON, JOSHUA -w- Clementine -m- 2nd John Hall. See card
Virginia E. Johnson, minor. Res. Tenn. Edgefield Rec. Bk. B-42

JOHNSON, MARTHA -w- _____? Heir of Philip Lightfoot. See Lightfoot
card. Edgefield Rec. Bk. B-65. 1842

JOHNSON, NATHAN--Edgefield Deed 2-236 To his children 1 May 1788
    Nathan, Jr.   James
    Esther   John
    Mary   Aaron
    Rachel
    Deed Bk. 3-112--Nathan Jr. -w- Shaba (sp?)1787

JOHNSON, PHILIP--Grand Juror Edgefield 1786. List 3, 8, and 14

JOHNSON, MRS. POLLY or MARY--Common law wife of William King-Will 1832
    Acknowledged as "lawful wife" in his Will.

JOHNSON, RICHARD--Grand Juror Edgefield 1786. List 1, 2, 3, 8, 18

JOHNSON, RICHARD--Uncle of James Lamar-Will 1814. Edgefield

JOHNSON, RICHARD and wife--Heirs of estate Henry Garrett. See Garrett
    card. Edgefield Rec. Bk. B-31 1841

JOHNSON, RICHARD M. -w- Elizabeth. Elizabeth legatee of Elizabeth
    Garrett-Will 1843

JOHNSON, SAMUEL and wife--Heirs of Henry Padgett. See Padgett card.
    Edgefield Rec. Bk. A-211 1835

JOHNSON, SARAH--Heir of Isaac Kirkland. See Kirkland card. (Dec'd)
    Edgefield Rec. Bk. A-302 1839

JOHNSON, SUKEY -w- John Johnson and dau. of Francis Lightfoot-Will 1803

JOHNSON, WILLIAM. Adv: Ebenezer Hill. See Hill card. Edgefield Min.
    Bk. 1790

JOHNSON, WILLIAM S.--Will 27 Dec. 1834

JOHNSON, WILLIAM -w- Permelia--Heirs estate of Ransom Hamilton. See
    Hamilton card. Edgefield Rec. Bk. B-107 1846

JONES, AMELIA -m- Henry Ware, son of Robert Ware.-Will 1817. See Will

JONES, ANDREW Of Northampton Co. N. C. to Matthias Jones of Edgefield
    P. A. 13 March 1812 to convey to Philip Rafer (Rayford?) of
    Edgefield 478 Acres purchased from John Pugh. Prov. by John
    Wheeler-J. P. and Benjamin Roberts, J. P. both of Hartford Co. N.C.
    Edgefield Deed Bk. 31-108 1812
    Page 149--Andrew Jones of Northampton Co. to Philip Rayford by
    agent, Matthias Jones.

JONES, ANDREW P. and wife--Heirs of Joseph West. Edgefield Rec. Bk.
    A-66 1833

JONES, ANNAMARIAH--Gr. dau. of Annamariah Williams-Will 1802

JONES, CHARLES--Petit Juror Edgefield 1794. List 21

JONES, CLEMENT -w- Susannah and dau. Elizabeth--Heirs of Stephen Terry
    See Terry card. Edgefield Rec. Bk. B-143. 1839

JONES, EZEKIEL -w- Elizabeth (formerly widow Allen Body)--Heirs
estate Allen Body. See Body card. Edgefield Rec. Bk. A-92 1832

JONES, GEORGE of State of Kentucky -m- set Nancy Noble of Edgefield
Dist. James Miller, Tr. Edgefield Misc. M-256. No date

JONES, HENRY -w- Sally--Heirs of Philip Lightfoot. See Lightfoot
card. Edgefield Rec. Bk. B-65. 1842

JONES, JAMES -w- Matilda--Heirs of Mary Buffington. See Buffington
card. Also Heirs Wm. H. Buffington. Edgefield Rec. Bk. A-60
1832

JONES, JEREMIAH Of Orangeburg Dist. to Joseph Cotton (or Colton) of
Columbia Co. Georgia 31 Dec. 1804. Edgefield Deed 31-378
300 Acres both sides of wagon road from Orangeburg to Cambridge.
Orig. Grant James Robertson 24 Oct. 1791--where John Jones now
lives. Dower--Elizabeth Jones.

JONES, JESSE--Dec'd. Of C. T. S. C. Will. Edgefield Deed Bk 6-87
Widow: Elizabeth Jones of Columbia Co. Ga. P. A. to Abenigo
Wright. Infant son: Jo___? (John?) Jones. 7 May 1792

JONES, JOHN--Grand Juror Edgefield 1786. List 1 and 2

JONES, JOSEPH P.--Dec'd. R. E. Sold 1846. Edgefield Rec. Bk. B-105
Dist: Patsey Jones 1/7 equal to $51.05
John Cotter -w- Mary Ann-same--Of Chambers Co. Alabama
Charles Jones -w- Roann-same
William Jones-same--OfRussell Co. Alabama
Children of B. F. Jones, dec'd:-
Stephen, Joseph, Mary, 1/3 of 2/3 of 1/7 each $11.34
Elzada Jones, widow of B. F. Jones 1/3 of 1/7
Children of a dec'd. dau. wife of B. E. Collier:-
Perrin, Mary, Georgiann and John Collier-1/4 of 2/3 of
1/7 each equal to $12.76. Martha Ann Jones, Gdn.
Mary Jones, widow of Joseph P. Jones, Jun'r. 1/7 equal $51.05
Rec't. 25 Jan 1747 (date?) by T. A. Andrews -w- Mary Ann for their
share $51.05.
Rec't. 12 Jan. 1747 by John Cotter for share his wife, Mary Ann.

JONES, LUCY--Sister of Ingram Nunn-Will 1838

JONES, LUERESIA--Dau. of John Weston-Will 1788 Edgefield

JONES, MARGARET--Dau. of John Clacker. Will 1814. Edgefield

JONES, MARGARET--Dau. of Jeptha Sharpton-Will 1838. Wife of Robert
C. Jones. An Exor. Edgefield

JONES, MARY--Gr. Dau. of Peter Day-Will 1789. Dau. Rebecca Jones.

JONES, NANCY--Her dau. Mary born 1794 -m- John Hogg. See Hogg card.
Heirs of Saunders Nobles of Edgefield. Dudley's Repts. Sup. Ct.
Ga. 1837.

JONES, QUINTING--Dau. Asa Holloway-Will 1823. Edgefield

JONES, RICHARD--Will 16 July 1838. Edgefield

126

JONES, RICHARD -w- Rebecca--Heirs estate of Joseph Day. See Day card. Edgefield Rec. Bk. A-242 1830

JONES, SARAH--Wife of Lion Jones and daughter of Isaac Parker-Will 1817

JONES, SARAH--Her heirs--Seaborn, A. P., Alexander, Simpson, Amanda, and John.--Heirs of Job Padget. See Padget card. Edgefield Rec. Bk. A-312 1839

JONES, WILLIAM AND BENJAMIN--Legatees of Philip Goode--Will 1770

JONES, WILLIAM -w- Sussiah who married ____? Cook after she had two Jones Children. See Will of her fatherJacob Fudge, Sen'r. 1789. Edgefield

JORDAN, LEVI -w- Sally--Heirs of Philip Lightfoot. See Lightfoot card. Edgefield Rec. Bk. B-65. 1842
-Levi Jordan and wife, Sally--Heirs Jesse Stone. Rec. Bk. B-45

JORDAN, RACHEL--Dau. of Solomon Bird-Will 1810. Edgefield

JOY, SARAH--Sister of Mary McFarland-Will 1805. Edgefield

JOYNER, JANE W.--Niece of Robert Watts-Will 1839. Of Wilkes Co. Ga.

JUSTICE, MARY--Dau. of Thomas Roberts-Will 1794

KAY, JOHN--Dec'd. R. E. Sold 1849. Edgefield Rec. Bk. B-
Dist: William Kay   Hiram Kay
Dicey Kay   Samuel Christian -w- Rebecca
Deborroh Spraggins Edmond Martin -w- Nancy
Wiley Kay   Wm. Thornton -w- Lianda
Eli Kay   Each 1/9 equal to $52.91

KEATING, EDWARD and SAMUEL WILLISON--as Creditors. Granted Let. Adm. estate of John Davison, dec'd. See Davison card. Edgefield Rec. Bk__ pg-233-38 1789

KELLY, JOHN--License to keep Tavern. S: Wm. Terry and Thos. Riccle Edgefield Ct. Min. Oct. 1794.

KELLY, MARY--Dec'd. R. E. Sold 1849. Edgefield Rec. Bk. B-171
Alias name--Mary Poppino. Negro connection
Mary Kelly, dec'd. 1/4 equal to $60.31
Wm. Kelly-same
John Kelly-same
Jesse Kelly-same. "A person of color" S. B. Newman, Gdn.

KEMP, CHRISTIANNA--Dau. of William Holloway-Will 1838

KEMP, HENRY J.--Dec'd. R. E. Sold 1847. Edgefield Rec. Bk. B-131
Dist: Hannah Kemp, widow 1/3 equal to $126.75
John Durst -w- Clarissa 1/7 of 2/3 Equal to $36.21
Lewis H. Kemp   Francis Kemp
Elizabeth A. Kemp John Kemp
Mary Ann Kemp   Rebecca   1/7 each $36.21
Rec't. 15 Dec. 1853 Milton Rhodes -w- Frances H.

KEMP, MARY--Widow--Heir of Richard Lewis. See Lewis card. Edgefield Rec. Bk. A-215 1835

KEMP, MARY--Mother of Richard Lewis-Will 1838. Edgefield

KEMP, MO. and wife--Heirs of James Hart. See Hart card. Edgefield
Rec. Bk. A-110 1833

KEMP, WILEY--Dec'd. R. E. Sold 1837. Edgefield Rec. Bk. A-164
Dist: Simpson Mathews and wife 1/4 $74.81
Henry I. Kemp
Sterling B. Kemp
Children of Richard Kemp, dec'd.
Wiley, James, Richard, and Mildred--1/4 of 1/4 each
$18.70

KENNEDY, JOHN--Dec'd. Citation returned and Mrs. Elizabeth Kennedy
appointed Adm'x. Edgefield Ct. Min. Bk. Page 305. Jan. 1790

KENNEDY, JOHN -m- Elizabeth Webster, widow. License--6 Aug. 1791
by Philip Clayton. Augusta, Ga. Ordinary Ct. Min. Bk.

KENNEDY, MARY, Spinster -m- Micajah Wilkerson. See Wilkerson card.
Augusta, Ga. 1791

KERNAGHAN, MARTHA B.--dau. of Charles Hammond, Sen'r.-Will 1836

KERR, GEORGE--Grand Juror Edgefield 1794. List 20

KEY, GEORGE W.--Step son of John Cheatham-Will 1840

KEY, HENRY--Will. Of 96 Dist. Edgefield Deed Bk. 1-58
Wife: Mary--Land in Amherst   Prov: 18 March 1777
Sons: Henry, William, and Tandy Clark Key--All land in S. C.
Daus: Mary, Martha, and Naomi
Millinda Letcher
William to receive, also, land bought of Wm. Holmes--Orig. Grant
John Goff.

KEY, HENRY--Grand Juror Edgefield 1786. List 3, 6, and 14

KEY, HENRY -w- Mary--Legatees of Elizabeth Garrett-Will 1843.

KEY, HENRY AND JESSE SCRUGGS--S; for Wm. Longmire--Adm. estate of
Thomas Goode. See Goode card. Edgefield Ct. 14 July 1789.

KEY, HENRY--Dec'd. "Ordered that the lost Will and Testament of Henry
Key, deceased, be admitted to the record, the same having been
legally proved before John Purves, Esquire, in the year 1777 by
the subscribing witnesses to the said Will".
Edgefield Ct. Min. April 1790. Min. Bk. Page 331

KEY, JOHN--Will 11 July 1840. Edgefield

KEY, JOHN C. G.-- m--Set. 31 Aug. 1842 Ann J. Ardis. John L. Ardis, Tr.
Edgefield Misc. M-283

KEY, MARTHA--Gr. dau. of Rachel Moss-Will 1832. Edgefield

128

KEY, PATSY -w- Joshua. Dau. Susannah Barksdale-Will 1812. Edgefield
-Was also dau. of Robert Ware. Will 1817

KEY, SARAH--Dau. of Elizabeth Bolger-Will 1836. Son in law: George
Washington Key. Edgefield

KEY, THOMAS--Grand Juror Edgefield 1786. List 4, 10, and 16

KEY, THOMAS--Commissioned to build bridge over Horn's Creek. See
Col. John Martin. Edgefield Ct. Min. Bk. Jan. 1795
Thomas Key and William Key Sureties Adm. Bond estate James Moore.
See Moore card.

KEY, THOMAS--Of Mill's Creek. Dist. of Edgefield. Deed Box 16-572
Wife: Elizabeth   Orig. Will 13 July 1820
Children: Robert   Prov: 26 Nov. 1821
           Joshua, Ex.
           Catherine Scott -w- J. M. Scott
           Polly Key
           Lucy Collier -w- Edward Collier, Ex.
           Elizabeth Farrar--formerly Elizabeth Howard and her
               children by Howard.
           Martha Key -m- Archibald Jarrett (dec'd.) and children
           Archibald Jarrett and his children 1000 acres in
               Jackson Co. Georgia.
Wit: Roger M. Williams, William Pursall, John Kerby
Large estate. Pd. Mrs. Elizabeth Wigfall

KEY, WILLIAM--Petit Juror Edgefield 1788. List 12
        Grand   "   "   "   "   20

KEY, WINNEY--Gr. Dau. of Arthur Simkins-Will 1820

KIRKLAND, BETHANY--Legatee of Aaron Allen-Will 1823. Edgefield

KIRKLAND, ISAAC--Dec'd. R. E. Sold 1839. Edgefield Rec. Bk. A-302
Dist: Mary Kirkland, widow   1/3 $19.45
       Joseph Kirkland   1/9 of 2/3 $4.32
       Heirs of Mary Kirkland-same
        "   " Sarah Johnson-same
       Philemon Kirkland-same
       Heirs of Jesse Kirkland-same
        "   " Elizabeth Huggins-same
       Isaac Kirkland-same
       Sophia Kirkland-same
       William Walker -w- Eliza-same

KIRKLAND, MOSES--Purchased R. E. from estate of Janes Don, dec'd.
See Don card. Edgefield Rec. Bk. B-113 1847

KIRKLAND, THOMAS--Dec'd. Edgefield Min. Bk. Page 335. April Ct. 1790
Will proved by oath of Arthur and Abner Watson. Mrs. Lucy Kirkland
qualified as Ex'x.

KIRKLAND, WILLIAM -m- Rachel Don, and Nancy Kirkland. See card John
Hester, dec'd. Edgefield Rec. Bk. A-278. 1837

KILCREAST, ARTHUR--Petit Juror Edgefield 1789. List 14

KILCREASE, JOHN--Heir of John Sharpton. See Sharpton card. Edgefield Rec. Bk. A-2 1827

KILCREASE, JOHN and SUSAN--Of Tennessee. Heirs of Ebenezer Kilcrease.
See back card Estate Bersheba Hill. Edgefield Rec. Bk. A-78 1832

KILCREASE, JOHN -w- Susan--Heirs of Ebenezer Hill. See Hill card.
Edgefield Rec. Bk. A-280. 1837

KILCREASE, JUDITH--Dau. of John Burress-Will 1822. Edgefield

KILCREASE, MARY--Dau. of Nathaniel Evans-Will 1824

KILCREASE, MINOR -w- Sarah--Heirs of William Harvey. See Harvey card.
Edgefield Rec. Bk. A-256

KILCREASE, OBEDIAH--Petit Juror Edgefield 1788. List 10

KILCREASE, PEGGY--Dau. of William Jeter-Will 1793. Her husband--
Elinor? Kilcrease. Edgefield

KILCREASE, ROBERT--Petit Juror Edgefield 1789. List 13

KILCREASE, SUSANNAH--Dau. of Mary Hill-Will Rec'd. 1822. Edgefield

KIMBRELL, JAMES R. -w- Martha--Heirs of Benjamin Doolittle. See card.
Edgefield Rec. Bk. A-209. 1835

KIMBRELL, WILLIAM -w- Sarah--Heirs of Morris Callihan. See Callihan.
Edgefield Rec. Bk. A-229 1835

KING, GEORGE--Petit Juror Edgefield 1789. List 14

KING, HENRY, ESQ.--Ordered to sell cattle and ___? by! James O'Harra
Benjamin Wages, and Jonathan Weaver. Edgefield Ct. Min. Oct. 1794

KING, JAMES--Petit Juror Edgefield 1786. List 5 and 21

KING, JENNET--Heir of William Sheppard. See Sheppard card. Edgefield
Rec. Bk. A-156. 1833

KING, MRS. SARAH -w- ?. Dower conveyed to Robert Spier. Acknowledged
before John Moore, Esq. Jan. Ct. 1786 Edgefield. Conv. by James
King.

KIRK, SABORN -w- Jincy--Heirs of William Pond. See Pond card.
Edgefield Rec. Bk. A-235 1835

KIRKSEY, DRURY and wife--Heirs estate of John Gorman, dec'd. See
Gorman card. Edgefield Rec. Bk. A-52. 1821

KIRKSEY, DRURY and NANCY--Letter to Mr. John Simkins Esq. Ordinary of
Edgefield Dist. "Please to collect our part of the Rale Estate of
John Gormas-dec'd. and pay Daniel Boone one hundred and seventy
five dollers-with interest thereon from the 20 Oct. 1829 till
paid. Dated Feb. 23, 1831." Wit: Isaih Martian, and Isaac Kirksey
Edgefield Sale Bk. A-47

KIRKSEY, EDWARD -w- Winney (dower) to John Kirksey $700.00--567 A. grant to John Adams on a branch of Rocky Creek. Edgefield Deed Bk. 32-491. 29 Dec. 1815

KIRKSEY, E. P. H.--Advs. Ransom Durst and another. Edgefield Eq. Bill 1385
KIRKSEY, IRVIN and wife, et al Advs. Wesley Phillips and wife, et al. Edgefield Equity Bill 1366

KIRKSEY, ISAAC--"State of North Carolina, Chatham County--Know all men by these presents that I, Isaac Kirksey of the State of Georgia, Laurens County--to Isiah Burnett of State and County above" 200 A. on Wilkerson's Creek. Orig. grant to Gideon Kirksey and reg. 11 Feb. 1788, at Chatham Ct. House. Page 336/7 Edgefield Deed Bk. 38-207 16 Aug. 1809

KNIGHT, MISS FRANCES ANNA AUGUSTA JANE -m- set 24 June 1828 Capt. John Evans of Edgefield Dist. Major James Knight, Trustee-- All of Hamburg. Mrs. Volatine, Grandmother of Frances. Edgefield File. Misc. F-411 24 June 1828

KNIGHT, WALTON--Dec'd. R. E. Sold 1842. Edgefield Rec. Bk. B-57
Dist: 1/5 share each. $6.85
    Elisha R. Johnson and wife
    Richard Roswell and wife
    William W. Knight
    Robert W. Knight
    George W. Knight

KNIGHT, WILLIAM W. --Of Richmond Co. Ga. P. A. to Elisha R. Johnson to receive share of sale of 3 lots in town of Hamburg, S. C. Sold as property of Walton Knight, dec'd. Edgefield Rec. Bk. B

KNOWLTON, JAMES E. -w- Susan--Heirs of James Rushton. See Rushton card. Edgefield Rec. Bk. A-248 1836

KOON, ADAM--A lad reared by George Reiser-Will 1816. Edgefield.

LABORDE, MRS. SARAH--Grandmother of Mary L. Danton-Will 1841.

LAEMAR, ROBERT--The elder. Son: Philip Laemar conv. to Samuel Hammond Tract gr. to Martin Campbell. Edgefield File Misc. B-177 Samuel Hammond -m- Anelia O'Keffe 25 May 1802. (Set)

LAKE, JOHN and wife--Heirs estate of John Blocker, dec'd. Edgefield Rec. Bk. A-158. 1833

LAKE, WILLIS F. -w- Lucy Ann--Heirs Nathaniel Sanders. See Sanders c   card. Edgefield Rec. Bk. B-135

LAMAR, JEREMIAH--Of Granville. Edgefield File. C. T. Wills
    Wife: Sarah   Will: 22 March 1771
    Children: John, Thomas, Rachel, and James Lamar
    Exor: Brother-Zachariah Lamar

LAMAR, JOHN--Of Granville Misc. Mtg. ZZ-350
    Son: Thomas Lamar-Mtg. 6 April 1763 to George Bussey.
    Wit: James Lamar and John Dawson

LAMAR, LIDIA--Dau. of William Marfey-Will 1794. Rec'd. 1801

LAMAR, MACK--Brother of Helen Lamkin-widow of Peter Lamkin-Will 1830

LAMAR, PHILIP--Grand Juror Edgefield 1786. List 4, 10, 18, 21.

LAMAR, ROBERT--Grand Juror Edgefield 1786. List 3, 9, 14, 18

LAMAR, THOMAS, JR.--Grand Juror Edgefield 1786. List 1, 2, 3, 8, 14, 21
         Petit   "   "   "   " 8

LAMAR, THOMAS--Son of Ann. Wife of Meliner C. Leavenworth-Will 1820
   (Thomas Gresham Lamar)
   -Son of Ann Leavenworth-Will 1836 . His daus: Ann G. Wardlaw,
   and Elizabeth Stark

LAMKIN, JAMES and wife--Heirs estate of Cad Evans. See Evans card.
   Edgefield Rec. Bk. A-100

LANDRUM, MARGARET L.--Wife of John Landrum. Dau. of James Smyly-Will
                                                       1838
LANDROM, REUBEN--Will 19 Nov. 1843. Edgefield

LANDRUM, SAMUEL--Motion to apprentice James and William Burk. See
   Burk Card. Edgefield Ct. Min. Oct. 1794

LANER, RICHARD--Petit Juror Edgefield 1786. List 3

LANG, ROBERT--Grand Juror Edgefield 1786. List 5, 10, 16, 20.

LANGFORD, EDMOND and ELIZABETH--See Will of John Jackson-Will 1787.

LANGLEY, ISHAM--Petit Juror Edgefield 1787. List 7

LANGLY, WILLIAM--Dec'd. R. E. Sold. Edgefield Sale Bk. A-128
   Dist: Lara Langley, widow 1/3 $94.42. Rec't. 10 Oct. 1831
       Stephen, Sarah Ann, Pamelia, and Francis--1/4 of 2/3
       $47.21 each. Alexander Hambleton, Adm&r.

LANKAM, LOUISA--Dau. of William Quarles-Will 1821

LAREMON, EDWARD--Dec'd. Edgefield Min. Page 138. 14 Jan. 1788
   Will proved by James and William McCarter. Martha Laremon, Qual.

LARK, JOHN--Dec'd. Will Nov. 15, 1822. Edgefield Eq. Bill 665.
   Widow: Precious Lark   Filed Nov. 1843
   Children: Elizabeth -w- Wm. Raiford
          Rachel, -w- Humphrey Boulware
          Ellen -w- Samuel E. Hammond--Out of State
          Sarah -w- James S. Stockdale " " "
          Mary -w- Stephan P. Oliver
          Catherine -w- B. McCain
          John Lark
   Land on Main Road and Mine Creek adj: Wm. Daniel, Thos. Bartel,
   Mary Watson, Mahlon Padget, George Bell, et al.

LARKE, ELIZABETH--Dau. of Samuel Savage-Will 1804

132

LASCITOR, RODAY--Dau. of Sarah Bridges-Will 1820 Edgefield

LASSETER, SAMUEL--See card Jesse Stone, dec'd. Wit. note by Elizabeth
    Clarke, dau. of dec'd. Edgefield Rec. Bk. B-65 1844

LATIMERE, AUGUSTA L.--Dau. of Elizabeth Spann (or Spain)-Will 1842
    Augusta had 4 children: Alfred, Elizabeth, Mary, and Catherine.

LAWS, ROBERT--Petit Juror Edgefield 1788. List 11 and 18

LEACH, ANTHONY--App'r. estate of Pleasant Burnett. See Burnett card.
    Edgefield Ct. Min. Oct. 1794

LEAFEVER, ISAAC--Petit Juror Edgefield 1788. List 9

LEAVENWORTH, ANN--Will 8 Feb. 1836

LEAVENSWORTH, MELINES CONKLING -m- Set 4 June 1803. Ann Lamar, widow
    of Thomas Lamar of Horse Creek, Edgefield Co. Luke Smith and
    Thomas Lamar, Jr., Trustees. Edgefield Misc. B-222

LEE, ANDREW--Grand Juror Edgefield 1786. List 1, 2, and 20

LEE, CHARLOTTE--Heir of Joseph Day. Edgefield Rec. Bk. A-242 abt. 1830

LEE, JOHN -m- dau. of Alexander Bean. See Bean card. Edgefield Deed
    31-200 1812

LEE, MARY--Dec'd. Her children legatees of Henry King-Will 1820

LEE, REUBEN--Dec'd. His widow, Ann and children heirs of estate of
    Francis Coleman. See Coleman card. Edgefield Rec. Bk. A-217
                                                            1835

LEECH, LYDIA--Above age of 14. Made choice of Thomas McGinnis and
    John Blocker as her Guardians. Edgefield Ct. April 1790. Min. Bk.
                                                                  326
LEMAR, PHILIP--One of Commissioners to build a bridge. See card
    Abram Ardis. Edgefield Ct. Min. Oct. 1794

LEOPARD, DANIEL and wife--Heirs of James Hart. See Hart card.
    Edgefield Rec. Bk. A-110 1833

LEPERD, CHARLES--Gr. son, and Sarah-a daughter of Wm. West-Will 1779.

LESURE, JAMES -w- Elizabeth--Heirs of Thomas Howle, Sen'r. Edgefield
    Rec. Bk. B-99 About 1845

LESURE, JAMES -w- Elizabeth--Heirs of Nancy Odom. See Odom card.
    Edgefield Rec. Bk. B-99 1845

LESEAR, SALLY--Dau. of William Howle, Sen'r.-Will 1830. Edgefield

LETCHER, MILLINDA--Dau. of Henry Key-Will 4 March 1776.
    Wit: James Letcher. Edgefield   Deed Bk. 1-58

LEVINGSTON, JAMES--Petit Juror Edgefield 1786. List 3

LEVINGSTON, JOHN--Legatee of John Frazier-Will 1824. Edgefield

LEWIS, EZEKIEL--Petit Juror Edgefield 1786. List 1, 2, and 4

LEWIS, ISAAC--Petit Juror Edgefield 1786. List 1, 2, 5, and 12
    Grand Juror (5 and 12)

LEWIS, MICHAEL -w- Nancy of Alabama--Heirs of Martha Mounce. See
    Mounce card. Edgefield Rec. Bk. B-47 1842

LEWIS, RICHARD--Dec'd. R. E. Sold 1835. Edgefield Rec. Bk. A-215
    Dist: Mary Kemp-widow   1/3 $157.37
        Wm. Mitchell -w- Lucy Trecy 1/7 of 2/3
        Richard Lewis
        Thomas W. Lewis
        James Hargrove -w- Harriet
        James Rowe -w- Narcessy   Each share 1/7 of 2/3
        Allen Rowe -w- Mary
        Ransom Holloway
        Mary Ann Holloway-minor
        Richard L. Holloway
        Thomas Holloway
        R. Holloway-Gdn. of minors

LEWIS, TRESSE--Dau. of Lodowick Hill-Will 1817

LIGHTFOOT, PHILIP--Dec'd. Uncle of Jesse Stone's dau. Elizabeth. See
    Stone card. Edgefield Rec. Bk. B-65 1844
  -Philip Lightfoot--Dec'd. R. E. Sold 1842. Rec. Bk. B-65
    Dist: William Lightfoot   1/7 $71.22
        Thomas   "
        Wm. Hammond -w- Nancy   1/7 each $71.22 each
        Alex'r Drambell -w- Rebecca
        Henry Jones -w- Sally
        ___? Johnson -w- Martha
        Heirs of Jesse Stone -w- Susan)
          Thomas, Henry, Patsy Stone)
        Robert Wallace -w- Nancy   )
        Elizabeth Clarke   ) 1/7 $8.90 each
        Abner Stone   )
        Jincy Rambo -w- Lawrence Rambo)
        Levi Jordan -w- Sally   )
    Page 67--same estate, same distributees, different lands.

LILLY--See Tilly Edgefield

LIMBACK, CHARLES and wife. Children of Henry Waldrun and heirs of
    James Butler. See Butler card. Edgefield Rec. Bk. A-124 1833

LIMBACKER, JESSE--Gr. child of Elles Palmer-Will 1800. Christian
    Limbacker--sole exor.

LINDSEY, BENJAMIN--Will 31 March 1841

LINDSEY, WILLIAM -w- Winney--Heirs of John Rodgers. See Rodgers card.
    Edgefield Rec. Bk. A-34. 1839

LION, ELIZABETH--Dau. of Edmund Boyd-Will 1800 Edgefield

LIPSCOMB, ____?--Dau. of John Bullock-Will 1799

134

LIPSCOMB, JOEL--Petit Juror Edgefield 1789. List 15

LIPSCOMB, NATHAN -w- Jemima--Exors. of Wiley Glover. Edgefield
    Ct. Com. Pleas 1807/10 256.

LITESEY, GEORGE--Dec'd. R. E. Sold 1848. Edgefield Rec. Bk. B-167

Dist: Margaret Litesey, widow   1/3 $65.75
    John W. Holly -w- Elizabeth 1/4 of 2/3
    Daniel D. Holly -w- Rosa-same
    P. W. Holley -w- Mary-same
    Rebecca Litesey now wife of Joseph Alawine-same.
    Page 157 shows same estate, same heirs, Rosa not married 1848

LITTLE, SUSANNA--Dau. of Rachel Mobley-Will 1826. Joel Little--
Legatee $4.00 Edgefield

LITTLE, WILLIAM--Will 11 Jan. 1837.

LIVINGSTON, PATSEY JANE--Dau. of Tolliver Bostick-Will 1813.
    Patsy Jane -w- Taliaferro Livingston.

LLOYD, ABIGAIL--Dau. of George DeLaughter, Sen'r.-Will 1830.

LOCKHART, NANCY -w- John Lockhart and legatee of Joicy Culpepper-
    Will 1837. Edgefield

LOMAN, MARY--Dau. of Stephan Evins-Will 1827

LONG, ELIZABETH--Dau. of Catherine Bates-Will 1819. "Seven children
    she had by her 1st husband, Reason Wootley".

LONG, SUSAN--Sister of William Lindsay-Will 1827
    *Susan Long-dau. Benjamin Lindsey-Will 1841

LONGMIRE, CAPT. In Edgefield Dist. Executive Journal Arch. Dept.
    1812-1310 Page 214--Reviews and Muster 1st Brigade at or near
    Capt. Longmire's in Edgefield Dist.
    Page 315: Letter--Charleston 14 Oct. 1809. "Sir: I have received
    a communication from you through your Aide de Camp, Taliaferro
    Lovington respecting the election of Lt. Col. Longmire, Lt. Col.
    the Hon. in your Brigade. I enclose you wherwith military Com-
    missions. To. Brig. Gen. Martin, Edgefield Ct. H.

LONGMIRE, GARRETT--Of Edgefield from John Stewart of Natchez Territory
    12 Feb. 1807 per agent Matthew Barrett of Edgefield. 400 A.
    Stephens Creek. Orig. Gr. Jacob Withrow 3 June 1774. Wit: John
    Wallace, Howard Longmire. Edgefield Deed 29-312
    Page 313: William Longmire from Thomas Goode -w- Elizabeth
    14 Dec. 1810

LONGMIRE, GEORGE--Dec'd. Edgefield Probate Bx. 108-2941 1785
    Bond: 8 Feb. 1785   Adm'r: Henry Ware, Jr.
    S: Wm. Livingston

LONGMIRE, HANNAH -w- John Longmire and dau. of Elizabeth Barrott-Will
    1824. Her dau: Mary -w- Caldwell Evans. Edgefield

LONGMIRE, JOHN--From John Kennedy -w- Ann. 4 Dec. 1792. Edgefield
    Deed 8-136. 1793

LONGMIRE, JOHN--Dec'd. Will 11 Sept. 1817. Prov: 6 Oct. 1817.
    Wife: Ex: John Lyon
    "My 3 children"   Wit: Edward Day, Henderson Wade
    Edgefield or Abbeville Probate Bx. 17-603 A-394

LONGMIRE, JOHN--Dec'd. Sept. 1817-Will Edgefield Eq. Roll 335
    Widow: Hannah Longmire-a defentant- has left the state and took
        part property to Alabama. John Lyon, Exor.--Sued.

LONGMIRE, WILLIAM--Survey. Arch. Dept. Plats Vol. 9-423 21 April 1785
    Cert. for Henry Gaddis, 11 July 1786. 477 A. on Gunnells Creek
    of Stephens Creek. Bd. George Lundy, Aaron Whotan.
    Page 536-Vol. 9--Baker Harvey's Survey 26 Aug. 1785 Cert. for
    Joshua Hill 5 Oct. 1786. 524 A. on Stevens Creek of Savannah
    River. Bd: Wm. Longmire, Henry Key, Janos Smith, John Sharp,
    and Ephraim Cassells-next to Wm. Longmires.
    (Plats were sometimes certified for others than originally planned
    for by order of Council).

LONGMIRE, WILLIAM--Grand Juror Edgefield 1787. List 6 and 16

LONGMIRE, WILLIAM--Granted Letters Administration Estate of Thomas
    Goode. See Goode card. Edgefield Ct. 14 July 1789. Min. Bk.
    Also estate of Ann Goode--1788. See card.

LONGMIRE, WILLIAM -w- Ann (Spinstress) to Isaac Brunson, Sen'r. 24/25
    Feb. 1790--150 A. part 500 A. grant to Wm. Coursey, 21 May 1771,
    conveyed to Wm. Longmire 24/25 Sept. 1786. Ref. Deed Rec'd. Edge -
    field County Court. Bk. A-105 in 1786. (Note--Bk. #5 was orig-
    inally Bk. G.

LONGMIRE, WILLIAM--Adm'r. of Wm. Mills-dec'd. Elizabeth Mills, Adm'x.
    Bond: 11 April 1791   S: James Coursey and Wm. Key
    Edgefield Strays

LONGMIRE, WILLIAM--Edgefield Min. Bk. Jan. 1795. License to keep
    Tavern. S: Edmond Whatley, John Sillivant

LONGMIRE, WILLIAM--Dower-Ann to Robert Key 2 March 1809 348½ A. on
    Beaver Dam Creek. Ann relinquished her inheritance to dower.
    Edgefield Deed 29-396

LOTT, JESSE--Dec'd. Cit: 3 Dec. 1782 Adm'x: Sarah Lott 96 Dist. Bk.
    Dedimus to Philemon Wall(?) to Qualify Appr's.
    Elmsly Lott--wife and heirs of Aaron Moore 1812. See Adam Moore
                                                              Card.
LOTT, JOHN -w- Charlsey, Marshall -w- Sarah and John M. Cogburn--Heirs
    of Jesse Cogburn, son of John Cogburn. Edgefield Rec. Bk. A-226
    Page 135--R. E. of Sarah Lott. Distributees:-
        Marshall   )
        Sarah -w- James Spann   ) Children of Elmsly Lott
        Lucinda, Emaline, Emily and John)

* CONTINUED *

LOTT, JOHN--Information on back of John Lott card. No other reference.
Jesse Lott-Dec'd.
   Widow: Jane   Children: Elmsly and Elbert
                              Martha -w- Herin Bush
                              Mark
                              Mary -w- Wade Barronton
                              Allen Lott
                              Luke B. Lott
Winny -w- Mathew Bettis
Mary -w- Reuben Drake
Martha Frazier
Eliza and Elisha Bettis

LOTT, SARAH--Dau. of Beheathland Mims-Will 1836. Edgefield

LOVE, WILLIAM H. -w- Rebecca--Heirs of Michael Meyer. See Meyer card.
Edgefield Rec. Bk. A-294 1838

LOVELESS, ELIZABETH--Dau. of Buckner Blalock-Will 1823. Edgefield

LOVELESS, JOHN--Of St. Mark's Parrish--Will 19 Jan. 1767. Prov: 1 Feb.
   Wife: Sarah Loveless   Marion Co. C. T. Will   1769
   Children: To be reared.
   Exor: John Hitchcock
   Wit: Gideon Gibson, Luke Whitfield, Jr. Peter Kichley.

LOVELESS, MARTIN H.--Dec'd. R. E. Sold 1847. Edgefield Rec. Bk. B-123
   Dist: Mary Loveless, the Mother 1/5 equal to $8.60
          Wilson H. Loveless-same
          John Hill -w- Adaline-same
          Benjamin F. Loveless-same
          Mary Ann Loveless.-same

LOVELESS, MARY--Dau. of Mary Hill-Will Rec'd. 1822. Edgefield
-Mary Loveless--Heir of Ebenezer Hill. See Hill card. Edgefield
Rec. Bk. A-256.

LOVELESS, THOMAS and wife--Dist. Estate of John Cockeroff, Dec'd.
Edgefield Rec. Bk. A-12 1826

LOW, JOHN--Grand Juror Edgefield 1788. List 10 and 16
John T. Lowe Grand Juror Edgefield 1788 List 20

LOW, NANCY--Dau. Arthur Simkins-Will 1820. Edgefield

LOWE, JOHN--Dec'd. R. E. Sold 1852. Edgefield Rec. Bk. B-214
   Dist: Bertha Lowe-widow 1/3
          Joshua Barton -w- Mary 1/8 of 1/3
          Kellah, Joseph, Martha, Judah, Apha, and Ellen Lowe

LOWE, NICHOLAS--Will 20 April 1843. Edgefield

LOWERY, ARMINA H. AND CONRAD--Parents of Martha Hill Outz. See Outz
card. Little Stevens Creek Church-Tombstone Record. Edgefield.

LOWERY, CONRAD MARTIN--Little Stevens Creek Baptist Church Edgefield Co.
Born: 11 March 1797-departed this life 24 March 1860
Member Baptist Church 37 years. (Wife-Graves side by side)
Mrs. Anna Hammatal Lowery
Born 16 Feb. 1797. Died 15 May 1879.
Erected by her 2 daughters: Mrs. E. E. Baxley and Mrs. A. E. Outz.

LOWERY, RICHARD--His Will proved by oath of Joseph Collier and William
Howle. Edgefield Min. Bk. Page 109. 8 Oct. 1787

LOWERY, ROBERT--Grand Juror Edgefield 1786. List 5

LOWRY, LUCY--Of Edgefield--Of Edgefield Deed Gift. Bk 12-page 58
To Henry Ware, Sen'r, of Georgia, Wilkes County--About 22 pounds
"left me by my father, John Garrett", and having no brother nor
sister left in this part of the world, but one, that is, Martha
Ware -w- Henry Ware, Sen'r.

LOWRY, LUCY--Edgefield Wills A-138 Box 41-pkg. 1653
Legacy: John Collier, son of Joseph Collier--a colt
Rev. Benjamin Harry--10 pounds
Henry Ware of Georgia)
Henry Ware of S. C.) Money they owe Testator.
Lucy Garrett, Lucy Key, Patty Thompson and Nancy Goode--
The rest.
Ex: Henry Key, Wm. Longmire, Davie Thompson--6 Jan. 1794
Wit: Joseph Collier, Amey Collier, Ann Evins.

LOWRY, POLLY--Dau. of Sarah Bridges-Will 1820. Her son: Edwin Bridges

LOWRY, RICHARD--Original Will 16 April 1787. Prov: 17 Oct. 1787
Wife: Lucy   Edgefield Box 41-1649
Brother: John and Robert
To: John Catlett Garrett-the land
Ex: John Martin and Henry Ware
Wit: Joseph Collier, Wm. Cammack, and Wm. Howle.

LOWRY, SIBLEY--Dau. of Susannah Christie-Will 1842

LOYD--See Will of John Barnes-Will 1815. Seems his dau. Nancy -m-
_____? Loyd. Edgefield.

LUCAS, JOHN--Grand Juror Edgefield 1788. List 12 and 20

LUCAS, JOHN, SEN'R.--Of Edgefield Co. Will Record A-1 Edgefield
Wife: Nary   Prov: 24 Jan. 18__?
Gr. son: Thomas Lucas-son of daughter, Jemimah
Gr. dau: Nancy Ozburn-dau. of dau. Rachel
Son: Abraham--Home plantation which was granted to James Harris.
Son: John
Notation on card --Tem away--crossed out. Prov. 24 Jan. 18__?
24 yr. Anse Ind. (?) Notation on back of card states that Will
continued for several pages further in book and lists following:
"My 9 children: Susannah M   Mary H.   Nancy H.
                Sarah F.   Jemima G.   John
                Elizabeth P. Amey W.   Abraham
John and Abraham exor's. with wife, Mary
16 Oct. 1799. Wit: Joab Wooten, Sol'm. Lucas, Wm. Griffin

LUCAS, SOLOMON--Petit Juror Edgefield 1786. List 5

LUMMERL, ROBERT -w- Sarah--Heirs of Lee Steel. See Steel card.
Edgefield Rec. Bk. B-42 1842

LUNDY, RICHARD--Petit Juror Edgefield 1787. List 6 (or Sundy)

LYLES, DAVID--Petit Juror Edgefield 1787. List 7 and 17

LYON, BENJAMIN F. AND JANE--Gr. Children of Pleasant Thurmond-Will 1830
Mem. Vol. 3 Through Pg. 11

LYON, FRANCES--Dau. of Elizabeth Thurmon-Will 1804. Edgefield

LYON, JAMES--Grand Juror Edgefield 1786. List 1, 2, 5, and 12.

LYON, JOHN--Will 14 May 1841. Edgefield

MAGRUDER, MARY A.--Niece of Lucy T. Moore-Will 1806. Edgefield
Probate Bk 178/9 1856

MALDIN, CALEB and wife--Heirs of James O'Gilvie-See O'Gilvie card.
Edgefield Rec. Bk. A-368 1839

MALLET, WILLIAM -w- Caroline--Heirs estate of John Bussey. See Bussey
card. Edgefield Rec. Bk. A-195. 1834

MANN, ELIZABETH--Dec'd. dau. of Agnes Norris-Will 1816. Her son:
Robert Mann, Legatee Edgefield

MANN, FANNY and SARAH--Legatees of Higdon Borrum-Will 1807. Edgefield

MANNING, LEVI--Dec'd. Will. Edgefield Pleadings and Judgements B-1801/2
Charles Banks and Thos. Gibson, Exors. -vs- Thomas   Pg. 80
Butler and Cullen Lark.
Page 182--Jethro Manning -vs- Jacob Bower.

MANSE, ELIZABETH--Adm'x. of John Watsman. See Watsman card. Edgefield Minutes 1788

MANTZ, STEPHEN--Appl. to keep Tavern. Appl. made for him by Capt.
A. Perin--granted. S: Abner Perrin. Edgefield Ct. Min. March
                                                              1795
MAPLES, WILLIAM--Petit Juror Edgefield 1786. List 1 and 2

MARBURY, MRS. ANN--Wife? Dower by dedimus favor of Peter Carnes and
also to John T. Lowe. Jan. Ct. 1788. Edgefield Min. Bk.

MARBERRY, THOMAS--Grand Juror Edgefield 1786. List 3 and 16

MARBEST, JOHN -w- Martha--Heirs of William B. Rowe. See Rowe card.
Edgefield Rec. Bk. B-151 1847

MARCUS, DANIEL--Petit Juror Edgefield 1787. List 6

MARCUS, DANIEL--Surety on Adm. Bond Est. George Cowan. Ct. Min. March
                                                              1795.

MARCUS, DANIEL--Edgefield Ct. Min. Oct. 1794--Daniel Marcus excused as
Overseer Road from Gunnels Creek to Horn's Creek and Timothy
Cooper appointed. See Cooper card.

MARCUS, ELLIS--Dec'd.--Will proved by oath of Barkley Martin and Peter
Chastain and ordered to be recorded. Edgefield Min. Bk. 211
13 Oct. 1788.

MARCHANT, JOHN--Dec'd. R. E. Sold. Edgefield Rec. Bk. A-90
Dist: Widow: Rachel 1/3 $42.41
        Jno. M. Davis, et ux (Rhoda) 1/8 of 2/3 $10.60½
        William White, et ux-same
        Daniel Marchant-same
        Chany Marchant-same
        Jno. Marchant-same
        Charles P. Findley, et ux-same
        William Marchant-minor-same
        James Marchant-same--also the purchaser.
Rec'ts: John M. Davis -w- Rhoda 9 Oct. 1832
         Charles F. Findley -w- Rachel 15 Feb. 1832
         Wm. Marchant 15 Feb. 1832
         Martha Marchant   )
         Wm. H. White -w- Jane)Bennett Perry, Agt. 1 Sept. 1832
         John Marchant   )18 Jan. 1832
         David Marchant 14 Nov. 1830
         Rachel, the widow, 17 April 1832

MARK, NANCY--Gr. child of David Langley-Will 1822. Elizabeth Mark
dau. of testator. Edgefield

MARLOW, WILLIAM--Will 16 May, 1838

MARS, MARIAH--Provisional Legatee of Roger McKinnie-Will 1842.

MARSH, BRYAN--Legatee of William Daniel. Will. Bryan's wife, Martha
Marsh, dau. of testator.

MARSH, JANE--Dau. of William Robinson-Will 1820 Edgefield

MARSH, MARTHA--widow, and Samuel B. Marsh and wife--Heirs of Michael
Blocker. See Blocker card. Edgefield Rec. Bk. A-14 1825

MARSH, SAMUEL--Dec'd. Will proved by oath of John Olliphant. Mrs.
Sarah Marsh, Ex. Qual. Edgefield Min. Bk. pg-263. Oct. 1789

MARSH, SAM--Petit Juror Edgefield 1787. List 7

MARSH, WILLIAM--Petit Juror Edgefield 1794. List 21

MARSHALL, JOHN--Dec'd. brother of Patty Moore, widow of Richard.
Will 1812. (Patty's Will)

MARSHALL, JOHN, SR. AND JR.--Father and brother of Patty Moore, wife
of Richard Moore. Edgefield Probate Bx. 108-28. 1812

MARSHALL, HOWELL R.--Nephew of Edward Rowell-Will 1829. Edgefield

MART, ELIZABETH--Dau. of Angelica Jernegan-Will 1796. Edgefield

MARTIN, CHARLES--Grand Juror Edgefield 1788. List 12

MARTIN, CHARLES, POLMYRE, WILLIAM, JOICY--Gr. children of Hillery
    M. Collier-Will 1841 Edgefield

MARTIN, DAVID -m- 12 March 1807 Mary--Suit for separation. Edgefield
                                                            Eq. Roll 4
MARTIN, EDMUND--Grand Juror Edgefield 1794. List 20

MARTIN, EDMOND -w- Nancy--Heirs of John Kay, dec'd. Edgefield Rec.
    Bk. B. 1849

MARTIN, ELIZABETH WARRING--Under age to choose Gdn. Mrs. Betty Martin
    appointed Gdn. S: Capt. Geo. Cowan and John Martin.
    Edgefield Ct. Min. 8 Oct. 1787.
    MARCH Ct. 1795--Application by Maj. B. Martin for permission
    for Matt Martin to keep Tavern. S: Barkley Martin and Sampson
    Butler.

MARTIN, GEORGE--Grand Juror Edgefield 1786. List 3, 12, 18, and 20

MARTIN, GEORGE -w- Harriet--Heirs of Ammy Addison and Heirs of John
    Cogburn. Edgefield Rec. Bk. A-225

MARTIN, GILES--Legatee of Edward Coleman-Will 1826. Norma Martin,
    dau. of testator. Edgefield

MARTIN, GRACEY--Dau. of Thomas Warren-Will 1815. Edgefield

MARTIN, HARRIET--Dau. of John Addison-Will 1827.

MARTIN, JAMES DONNON--Gr. son of James Jonnon. See Will. Son of
    John Martin of Georgia. Wm. Holmes also a legatee. C. T. Wills
    1771-1784-page 11

MARTIN, JAMES--Petit Juror Edgefield 1787. List 8 and 18

MARTIN, COL. JAMES--Dec'd. Edgefield Ct. Min. March 1795
    Col. John Martin and West Cook applied for Letters Administration
    S: 800 Pounds. Robert Samuel and George Key.
    Appr's: Wm. Howle, Jr. Drury Adams, George Martin and John Ealam.
    Personal estate ordered sold at house of William Newsome on Thurs.
    9th of April next.

MARTIN, COL. JOHN, Thomas Key, Aquilla Miles, Shearley Whatley, Sen'r.
    and Absolom Roberts--Commissioners to build a bridge over Harris
    Creek near where the Martinton Road crosses. Edgefield Ct. Jan.
                                                                   1795
    March Ct. 1795--John Martin app'r. Estate of George Cowan, dec'd.

MARTIN, JAMES--Dec'd. R. E. Sold. Edgefield Rec. Bk. A-72
Dist: 1/3 each equal $76.12½
    Samuel Quarles--Rec't. 21 Feb. 1831
    Cyrda Martin -w- Wm. Glascock   Rec't. 22 Feb. 1830
    Hulda Martin -w- Wm. Dunlap   "   "   "   "

MARTIN, JOHN--Grand Juror Edgefield 1786. List 1 and 2

MARTIN, JOHN--Son in law of Thomas Johnson-Will 1797.

141

MARTIN, JOHN ALLEN SCOTT--a minor and gr. son of Samuel Scott-Will 1809

MARTIN, JOHN -w- Sarah--Heirs estate of John Cockeroff. See Cockeroff
card. Edgefield Rec. Bk. A-26. 1826

MARTIN, JOHN F.--Gdn. for minor child. Wm. Harvey (or children of)
See Harvey card. Edgefield Rec. Bk. A-256 1836

MARTIN, MARSHALL--Petit Juror Edgefield 1786. List 3, 4, 17
                 Grand   "   "   "   " 21

MARTIN, NANCY--Of Alabama. Dau. of Philis Whatley-Will 1829. Edgefield

MARTIN, POLLY--Wife of Marshall Martin and Legatee Edmond Cox-Will 1793

MARTIN, POLLY--Dau. of Henry Key -w- Phebe Key-Will 1810. Edgefield
Gr. Ch: Harry Martin and Elizabeth Martin.
Other Heirs: Lucy Cabaness, Elizabeth Thurmond , Maryann Key,
             Permelia Key, John Key,Henry Key, Barzilia Key,
             James Key, and Tandy Key--children of testator.

MARTIN, PRUDENCE--Wife of Charles Martin. Adm'x. West Cook.
Ct. Com. Pleas. Pg-355. Edgefield

MARTIN, RUTH--Heir of Elizabeth Hill-See Hill Card. Edgefield Rec.
Bk. B-83

MARTIN, SALLY--Dau. of Samuel Goode-Will 1800. Reeves Martin an ex.

MARTIN, SALLY--Dau. of William Jeter-Will 1818. Edgefield

MARTIN, SARAH--Will 7 Nov. 1836.

MARTIN, SHIRLY--Dau. of Frances Posey-Will 1787. Edgefield

MARTIN, SIMON -w- Celia--Her dower acknowledged to deed favor of
William Covington. 100 A. called Poverty Hill. Edgefield Ct.
Min. Jan. 1795.
Oct. Ct. 1794--Mat. Martin rec. the Martin Rd. from Coody's Old
Mill. Rich'd Christmas, Overseer. See Christmas card.

MARTIN, STEPHEN--Dec'd. R. E. Sold 1830. Edgefield Rec. Bk. A-36
Dist: John Bracknell and wife--1/3 $98.22
      Julia Ann Martin-same
      Emeline Martin-same.
Perry Holloway--Rec't. 11 Jan. 1830 for shares of Julia Ann and
Emeline Martin-minors-as Guardian.
Rec't. by John Brackrell for share "to which myself and wife are
entitled". Land was purchased by John Brackrell.

MARTIN, THOMAS--Son in law of John Bracknell-Will 1820. Edgefield

MARTIN, WILLIAM and Grace Waring -m- Cert. See Waring card. 8 Feb. 1772
Edgefield Deed Bk. 10-150 1772

MARTIN, WILLIAM--Edgefield Ct. Min. Bk. Page 133 Oct.1787--
"Mrs. Frances Edwards, late widow of William Martin, dec'd. who
proved the Will of the dec'd in common form and produced the re-
nunciation of the other executor, Macness Goode, Ordered that she
be qualified as an Executrix."
Same page--"Mrs Wesley Martin and Rieves Martin being of full age
the guardianship of the aforesaid Wesley and Rieves was granted to
Garland Goode on his giving Bond and Security--who gave William
Matthews and Drury Matthews for the faithful discharge of the sum
of 2000 pounds. Order Apportionment of estate Wm. Martin."

MARTIN, WILLIAM--Dec'd. Edgefield Min. Bk. Page 156. 14 April 1788.
Ordered citation issue to show cause why administration of Dec'd.
estate should not be granted to Barkley Martin.

MARTIN, WILLIAM--Edgefield Wills A-3 2 Aug. 1827
Wife: Sarah
Legacies: Wm. Martin, son of James Martin, Sen'r.
James Martin, son of Andrew Moses Martin
Moses Martin, son of Andrew Moses Martin
Andrew and Jane Rosebrough Martin
William Martin, son Andrew Martin
Ginah E. (or Sinah) Martin, dau. of Andrew Martin
William Martin, son John Martin, Sen'r.
William Still, son Benjamin Still

MASON, ELIZABETH--Dau. of John Douglass-Will 1799 Edgefield

MATTHEWS, DRURY--Petit Juror Edgefield 1787. List 8
                 Grand   "   "   "   " 20

MATTHEWS, HENRY--Dec'd. R. E. Sold 1849. Edgefield Rec. Bk. B-169
Dist: Nancy Matthews, widow 1/3 $540.04
James L., William, George Matthews 1/8 of 2/3 each $135.01
James Hatch -w- Eliza-same
Lewis, Charles, and Jackson Matthews-same each.

MATTHEWS, ISAAC--Petit Juror Edgefield 1789. List 14

MATHEWS, MATILDA--Legatee of Ezekiel Perry-Will 1833

MATHEWS, MOSES--Petit Juror Edgefield 1794. List 21

MATTHEWS, SIMPSON and wife--Heirs of Wiley Kemp. See Kemp card.
Edgefield Rec. Bk. A-133 1831.

MATHEWS, SUGAR I.--Dec'd. R. E. Sold 1831. Edgefield Rec. Bk. A-38
Dist: 1/12 each equal to $82.97
     James   Willey
     Drury   Pamelia
     Blanche   Caleb
     Lewis   Luke
     Catherine   John Christian
     William   Sarah and Martha-children of Bud Matthews
                       Share jointly.
(Note on page) "It is doubtful whether one Christian is entitled
to the share hes given him.
James Matthews-Purchaser
Rec't. 24 Oct. 1831 from John Carter, Jr. for share of wife.
    "   29 April 1833 "   John Chrictie   "   "   "   "

MATTHEWS, SUSANNAH-Will 23 Sept. 1839. Edgefield

MATHEWS, WILLIAM--Grand Juror Edgefield 1786. List 5, 6, and 12

MATHIS, NANCY--Dau. of Josiah Allen. Step-dau. of Aaron Etheredge-Will
1811
MAULDON, NELLY--Dau. of Nathan Trotter-Will 1825.

MAY, BENJAMIN--Son of William C. Posey-Will 1834. (Seems middle name)
(-May-
MAY, NANCY--Dau. of Thomas Dean. Son in law of
John H. May. Dean Will 1840. Edgefield

MAY, PHILIP--Petit Juror Edgefield 1786. List 1, 2, 11.
PHILIP, JR. "   "   "   "   " 12, and 15

MAY, STAMFORD, F. and wife--Heirs estate of John Gitty. See Gitty
card. Edgefield Rec. Bk. B-119 1847

MAYBERRY, THOS. J. -w- Frances--dau. of James and susannah Boyd.
Heirs of Francis Bird. Edgefield Rec. Bk. B-137 1848

MAWBERRY, THOMAS--Grand Juror Edgefield 1787. List 8

MAYFIELD, ABRAHAM--Son in law of Joseph R. Bishop-Will 1802.
Gr. Dau: Thanac Mayfield. Edgefield

MAYNARD, JAMES -w- Mary--Heirs estate of John Clark. See Clark card.
Edgefield Rec. Bk. A-5 1827

MAYS, ABNER--Petit Juror Edgefield 1787. List 8

MAYS, ABNER7-Dec'd. R. E. Sold 1837. Edgefield Rec. Bk. A-276
Dist: Milton Perkins and wife 1/3 $101.07
John, William, and James Mays-minors 2/3 jointly $2-2.15
Wiley Culbreath, Gdn.

MAYS, ABNEY--Dec'd. Edgefield Deed Bk. 31-42/3 1812
Heirs: Stephen Whitley -w- Elizabeth
William Hill -w- Salley   (Ref. to past case)

MAYS, ABNEY--Dec'd. R. E. Sold 1850. Edgefield Rec. Bk. B-192
Dist: Wm. Hill -w- Sarah
Nancy -w- Broadway
Meady Mays (Meachy?)
John Mays, dec'd. Meady May, Adm.
Enoch Carter -w- Nancy
Wm. Carter and L. G. Carter
Simeon Wait -w- Elizabeth-Gr. Dau. of Elizabeth Whitley, formerly
Mays.
Thomas Whitley, Atty. for Elizabeth Waits and also a gr. son of
Elizabeth Whitley.

MAYS, BETSY--Dau. of George Martin-Will 1817. Wife of Matt Mays.

MAYS, JAMES--Petit Juror Edgefield 1786. List 4

MAYS, MRS. LUCINDA--Legatee of Thomas Sweny, Jr. Edgefield

144

MAYS, LUCREASY--Dau. of Daniel Rogers-Will 1843. Edgefield

MAYS, LYDIA--Dau. of Drury Mims-Will 1817.

MAYS, MATTHEW--Son of Elizabeth Whitley-Will 1819. Edgefield
     Her other children: John, Abney, Nancy (only dau.)Medy
                          Stephen Cook Whitley, son of dec'd. husband
                          John Whitley.

MAYS, SAMUEL--Petit Juror Edgefield 1787. List 8 and 18

MAYS, SAMUEL, ESQ.--Resigned as Sheriff of the County.
     Jeremiah Hatcher appointed to be Sheriff in his place. Oct. Ct.1794
     Jan. Ct. 1795--Sam'l Mays, Adm'r. of Peter Buffington. See card.

MAYS, SARAH -w- Thomas Sumter Mays. Gr. dau. of John Simkins-Will 1832

MAYSON, ELIZABETH--Sister of Henry W. Lowe-Will. Edgefield

MAYSON, JAMES ROBERT--Commissioned to build bridge. See card William
     Anderson. Edgefield Ct. Min. March 1795

MAYSON, NANCY--Sister of Washington Bostick-Will 1817. Edgefield

MAYSON, SUSANNAH E.--Dau. of James Harrison-Will 1841. Edgefield

MC CALLISTER, JANE -w- James. Sister of John Glasgow-Will 1842.
     Edgefield Probate Box 41-929

MC CAN, ROBERT--Petit Juror Edgefield 1788. List 10

MC CARTER, FRANCIS--Will 29 Oct. 1768 Edgefield File C. T. Will
     Nephew: Alexander Wylly -w- Susannah (of Colerain near Savannah.)
     Niece: Hester Wylly
     Nephews: Samuel, Richard, and William Wylly
     Niece: Helen Lawrence, et al

MC CARTNEY, WILLIAM--Petit Juror Edgefield 1789. List 14
     Will McCartie--Petit Juror 1789 List 16

MC CARTY, ELISE -w- Anna--Heirs of William Scott. See Scott card.
     Edgefield Rec. Bk. B-53 1841

MC CARTY, MARTIN -w- Cyntha--Heirs of James Rodgers -w- Sarah who were
     heirs of James Fidson. Edgefield Rec. Bk. B-125 1847

MC CARTY, PHILIP--Gdn. for Allsee Body-heir of Allen Body. See Body
     card. Edgefield Rec. Bk. A-92 1832

MC CARTY, REBECCA, PATSEY, MARY, AND WILLIAM A.--Heirs of Alexander
     Stuart. Edgefield Rec. Bk. B-197 1850. See Stuart card.

MC CARTY SUGAR M. -w- Barbary--Heirs of Cornelius Wheeler. See
     Wheeler card. Edgefield Rec. Bk. A-322 1839

MC CARTY, WILLIAM--Of New Windsor. May Term 1750 Page 249
     Charleston Ct. Records now in Archives Dept.
     Widow: Mary Ann McCarty

145

MC CHANDOL, RUKEEL--Petit Juror Edgefield 1786. List 5

MC CLENDON, JOHN--Came of age about 1822. -vs- Lewis Holmes
    Wit: Sally McClendon, Allen McClendon, Priscilla McClendon.
    Edgefield Equity #1 pg-163. 1824
    Deed Bk. 10-359--Thomas McClendon -m- Nancy Foreman, minor dau.
    of John Foreman in 1794.

MC COMB,-DAVID B.--Presiding Justice of Leon County-Mid Fla. Mary
    T. McComb a witness.- Deed from Mary Talton Blocker to John
    Bones of Augusta, Mary -w- Justice. Now of Leon Co. Fla.
    Formerly of Edgefield. Land in Edgefield on Log Creek-formerly
    property of John Blocker. Edgefield 22 Nov. 1830. Deed Bk. 45-61

MC COMB, GEORGE--Of City of Charleston, Shoemaker. Charleston Plats.
    To Henry Geddes 20 May 1790 20 Pounds current money.
    150 A. in 96 Dist. on waters of Long Cane. Bd. lands surveyed
    for Sarah Cronshure, now estate James Glasgow and vac. Bordeaus
    Township and Archibald McCleland and vac. Said George McComb.
    Wit: Alex'r Smith, Robert Manning, John Geddes. Rec'd. 20 July
    1793. Plats I-6-503

MC COMBS, ROBERT--Edgefield Ct. 14 July 1788. Min. Bk. Pg-182
    Jesse Harris Overseer of the road leading from Harlin's Ferry to
    Ninety Six returned on oath the following persons as defaulters
    Viz: James Rustin 1 day
          Francis Lightfoot, 2 days
          Timothy McKinney, 1 day.
          Robert Combs, 1 day
          Shadrack Henderson 2 days
          Thomas Johnson, 2 days
          William Huggins, 4 days
          Nelson Fields, 2 days.
    Page 191--The following persons was appointed County Constables:
        Burgess White   John Lowe,
        Thomas Howle   Samuel Garner
        Daniel Bullock   Roland Williams
        Robert Combs

MC COMBS, ROBERT--Edgefield Ct. 14 July 1789. Min. Bk. Page 252
    Ordered that Toliver Bostick be allowed Tavern License until Jan-
    uary next, he giving Bond and Security as the Law directs. Wm.
    Beal and Robert McCombs are approved of by the court as sufficient
    Security.

MC COMBS, ROBERT--Edgefield Court April 1790. Min. Bk. Pg-337
    On Motion of the County Attorney to have Robert McCombs, Constable
    removed from his office, tis ordered that the said Robert McCombs
    be removed from his said office for misbehaviour and Mal practices
    in his office accordingly.

MC COMBS, ROBERT--Edgefield Pleadings and Judgements Bk. B-1801-2
    Adv. James R. Mayson--Writ issued 6 March 1800 and served. Prom-
    issory note 16 May 1799. "Three days after date I promise to pay
    to James R. Mayson on order, the sum of 89.dollars for value re-
    ceived this 16th day of May 1799. R. McCombs. Denied but Jury
    allowed it.

MC COMBS, ROBERT--Of City of Augusta Augusta Ga. O-245 287 5 Aug. 1817
From Emanuel Wambersie, late of Savannah, by Atty, Jonathan
Battells--Lots 5 and 6 in Augusta.
Page 287--Robert McCombs from Thos Oyier of Charleston by Atty.
Isaac Herbert, Lots 1, 2, 3, and 3 in Augusta 14 Nov. 1817.

MC COMBS ROBERT -w- Mary to John M. Turner--Lot in Augusta. Augusta,
Ga. P-47 24 Dec. 1817.

MC COOMBS, ROBERT -w- Mary to Alexander Elliott--Lot in Augusta.
Augusta, Ga. 19 June 1820 R-419

MC COOMBS, ROBERT and Elizabeth Martin Appt. Gdns of Charles, Smith,
Eliza E., and Washington Martin--minor orphans of Bird Martin.
Appt. Gdns 26 Mar. 1821. Bond. S: John S. Coombs and A. R. Ralst
Augusta, Ga. Deed Bk. R-12

MC COOMBS, ROBERT--Of City of Augusta. Love and affection to Martha
McCoombs, widow of Nathaniel S. Coombs, late of Augusta, Dec'd.
House and lot where she lives. Wit: John S. Coombs, A. Bugg.
3 April 1821 Augusta,Ga. Deed Bk. T-96

MC COOMBS, ROBERT -w- Mary to Eliza Russell of Warren Co. Lot in
Augusta. Augusta, Ga. 12 July 1825. S-510

MC COOMBS, ROBERT--Augusta, Ga. 4 Feb. 1833 Slaves of his estate:

Milly	Jack	Eliza	Hannah
Samuel	Leah	William	Ann
Hetty	Jack	Nancy	William
Lavinia-old	Moses	Violet and 2 ch.	Crazy Jim

Amounts due estate of Francis H. Coombs by Sterling T. Coombs,
Adm. Geo. D. Combs, Sterling Combs.

MC CRARY, ANN--Dec'd. R. E. Sold 1849 Edgefield Rec. Bk. B-160
Dist: 1/5 each equal to $155.03
Margaret Head
Samuel McCrary, James, Thomas, and John McCrary.

MC CRARY, JNO -w- Rebecca--Heirs of Shadrack Boone. Edgefield Rec.
Bk. A-48 1829

MC CRELESS, JAMES -m- Delilah Falkner-dau. of Elizabeth Falkner, dec'd
1850. Edgefield Report Bk. B-182

MC CRELESS, JAMES -w- Delilah--Heirs estate of Elizabeth Falkner. See
Falkner. Edgefield Rec. Bk. B-182 1850

MC CRELESS, JOHN--Commissioned as Clerk and Register of Lexington
Dist. Dated 19 Dec. 1814. Also as Ordinary dated 19 Dec. 1814.
Misc. Rec. C-146

MC CRELESS, JOHN--Dec'd. R. E. Sold 1 Mar. 1836. Edgefield Rec. A-130
Dist: George, Searles, James--sons of Jas. McCreless 1/5
All 3 said to be illigitimate.
John McCreless 1/5
George McCreless--4 Legatees 1/5
John Hargrove et us--1/5
Betsy, Wilson, McCreless, Milly Corley--entitled to 1/5 as
heirs of Michael and Dicey Corley, Dec'd.

MC CULLOUGH, WILLIAM -w- Rebecca--Dist. estate of James Bradfield, Dec'd.
See Bradfield card. Edgefield Rec. Bk. A-316 1839

MC DANIEL, ABSOLEM--Petit Juror Edgefield 1789. List 17

MC DANIEL, ANGUS--Dec'd. Will. Edgefield Ct. March 1795.
Proved by oaths Richard Tutt, Lewis Youngblood, Stephen Morris.
Mrs. Ann McDaniel, Ex'x. Elias Blackburn, Exor.
Appr's: John Cogburn, Moses Harris, Lewis and John Youngblood.

MC DANIEL, LEVI -w- Elizabeth--Heirs of Philip Jennings. See Jennings
card. Edgefield Rec. Bk. B-185. 1850

MC DANIEL, STANMORE and wife--Heirs of Joseph West. See West card.
Edgefield Rec. Bk. A-66 1836

MC DONALD, ABSOLOM--Petit Juror Edgefield 1787. List 7

MC DONALD, ANGUS--Petit Juror Edgefield 1786. List 1 and 2

MC DONALD, JOHN--Petit Juror Edgefield 1794. List 21

MC DONALD, JOSEPH--Petit Juror Edgefield 1786. List 3

MC DOUGAL, ALEXANDER--Petit Juror Edgefield 1786. List 3

MC FARLAND, ARCHIBALD--Dec'd. R. E. Sold. Edgefield Rec. Bk. A-122
Dist: Mary McFarland, widow--1/3
      John   "
      Mary   "   "(the younger)
Donald M. Kellar purchased at $150.00. Mtg. holder. 1 Jan. 1827
Not dated on sale and distribution.

MC GEHEE, MRS. CHARLOTTE -w- John McGehee of Florida--Legatee of John
Fox-Will 1837. John Fox of Georgia. Sister of Albert Dozier
of S. C. Edgefield

MC GEHEE, JOHN--Legatee in trust Will of Elizabeth Clarke-Will 1827.

MC GEE, JOHN C. of Florida--Legatee of Elizabeth Spann-Will 1842
In trust for dau. of Testator--Augusta L. Latimese. Edgefield

MC GHEE, SARAH ANN--Dau. of Reuben Landrom-Will 1843. Edgefield

MC GEHEE, WILLIAM -w- Jane--Heirs of Job Padgett. See Padget card.
Edgefield Rec. Bk. A-312 1839

MC GILE, ELIZA -w- ____? McGile of Camden. Legatee of Ulric Tobler-
Will 1815. Edgefield

MC GILVRAY, MARY ANN--Niece of Ulric Tobler-Will 1815. Codicil
Full name: Mary Ann McGilvray Grey.

MC GINNIS, THOMAS and John Blocker--Apt'd. Gdn's for Lydia Leech-minor.
See Leech card. April Ct. Edgefield 1790. Min. Bk.

MC GREW, PETER--Petit Juror Edgefield 1787. List 8 and 16

MC KEE, ELIZABETH--Dau. of John Kilcrease-Will 1829.

MC KEENNA, MARTHA--Heir of Daniel Bruner-See Bruner card. Edgefield
Rec. Bk. A-34 1834

MC KENNEY, BENJAMIN--Dec'd. Inv. returned. Edgefield Ct. March 1795.
Order to sell personal property at the house of Rachel Brazil--
last Thursday in March.
Jan. Ct. 1795--Mrs. Rachel Brazil came into court and relinquished
her right of Administration on estates of her former husband, Ben-
jamin McKinney in favor of her son, John McKinney. Bond 150 pounds.
S: Frederick Swearingen, Thomas Adams
Appr's: Bibby Bush, Arthur Watson, John Salter.

MC KIE, MICHAEL--Grand Juror Edgefield 1794. List 21

MC KIE, SAWNEY--Dec'd. R. E. Sold 9 Apl. 1832. Rec. Bk. A-114
Dist: Thomas McKie
       Charles McKie
       Lively Ware   1/6 each $151.40¼
       Joseph Prince, et ux
       Daniel McKie
       Heirs of Michael McKie viz: Thomas McKie and others
       unknown.

MC KINLEY, JOHN--Of Granville Will 17 Oct. 1771. C. T. Wills
Wife: Esther   Edgefield File
Eldest son: William
Son: James
Youngest son: John
Daus: Jane, Susannah and Martha
Son in law: Robert Frimble

MC KINNEY, MORDACAI--Petit Juror Edgefield 1794. List 20

MC KINNIE, ROGER--Will 29 Mar. 1842. Edgefield

MC MANNUS, ELIZABETH--Dau. of Elisha Stevens-Will 1834. Her husband:
Goody McMannus. Edgefield

MC MASTER, REBECCA--Dau. of James Eddins-Will 1814 Edgefield

MC MILLAN, ABRAHAM--Dec'd. James McMillan, Adm. Edgefield Ct. March
Amount sale estate recorded.   1795

MC MILLAN, BENNETT -w- Lidia--Heirs of William Holliday-See Holliday
card. Edgefield Rec. Bk. A-106. 1831

MC MILLAN, JAMES--Grand Juror Edgefield 1786. List 5, 10, and 16

MC MILLIAN, JAMES and John Moore--Sureties for Mary Green, Adm'x.
estate Isham Green. See Green card. Edgefield Min. Bk. 325
April Court 1790

MC MILLAN, MATHEW--Grand Juror Edgefield 1786. List 4 and 12

MC MILLIAN, WENNY--Dau. of Joseph Bishop-Will 1802 Edgefield

MC MURPHEY, KEZIAH--Dec'd. R. E. Sold 1836/7. Edgefield Rec. Bk. A-246
   Dist: Mary McMurphey 1/3 equal to $721.00
       John M. Adams -w- Sarah S.-same (Rec. Augusta)
       Minor children of Keziah O. Malone viz:
         George Y. Malone and William R. Malone ½ of 1/3 each.
   Mary Ann McMurphey -m- Cary W. Allen and lived in Upson Co. Ga.

MC NEIL, JOHN -w- Sarah--Heirs of Lewis Youngblood. See Youngblood card.
   Edgefield Rec. Bk. B-89

MC FATNICK, ELIZABETH--Legatee of Mary Swillivant-Will 1801. Dau. of
   Testator.

MC FATNICK, JOHN--Grand Juror Edgefield 1794. List 20

MC PHATNICK, JOHN -w- Elizabeth--Heirs of Jonathan Sullivan. See
   Sullivan card. Edgefield Rec. Bk. A-1 1820

MC RATH, FREDERICK--Petit Juror Edgefield 1788. List 11

MC WHORTER, ALEXANDER -w- Ellen of Alabama and their son Eldred.Sim-
   kins McWhorter, mentioned in Will of Eliza Hannah Simkins-Will
   1837. The son is a legatee. Edgefield

MC WHORTER, ELLEN--Step daughter of Henry W. Lowe-Will 1828. Edgefield

MC WHORTER, ELINOR--Gr. dau. of Arthur Simkins-Will 1820. Edgefield

MEA, H. B. -w- Laura Ann--Heirs of Jacob Miller. See Miller card.
   Edgefield Rec. Bk. B-115 1846

MEACHAM, CHARLOTTE--Dau. of Elias Blackburn-Will 1827. Edgefield

MECARTA, MICHAEL--Petit Juror Edgefield 1788. List 12

MEDLOCK, MARY--Dau. of Beheathland Mims-Will 1836. Edgefield

MEDLOCK, SAMUEL--Dec'd. R. E. Sold . Edgefield Sale Bk. A-74
   Distributees: Widow-Nelly. 1/3 $96.25. Rec't. 17 Dec. 1829
   Stephen, Samuel, Benjamin, and Moses Medlock 1/7 of 2/3
   Phinehes Sutton -w- Nancy 1/7 of 2/3--Of Monroe Co. Ga.
   Lewis Frederick -w- Mary 1/7 of 2/3
   Leroy Singleton, Rec't. 9 Jan. 1832
   Lewis Holmes and wife, Samuel Singleton, Benjamin Singleton and
   Harriet Walker--1/7 of 2/3 jointly.
   Shows Benjamin a grandson of dec'd. P. A. 27 Dec. 1832 to Lewis
   Holmes.
   Nancy Sutton of Monroe Co. Ga. P. A. to Aaron Sutton of Monroe
   Co. Ga.

MEE, GEORGE--Dec'd. Edgefield Ct. April 1790. Min. Bk. Page 327
   Letters Administration granted Samuel Mays. Bond 200 pounds
   S: William Anderson and William Hill
   Apprs: Rowland Williams, Jacob Odom, Arthur Watson, and Hezekiah
   Watson

MEEK, BRIANT -w- Martha--Heirs of Mary Brooks and heirs of Rebecca
Ramey. Edgefield Rec. Bk. B-75. 1842

MELLON, ROBERT--Petit Juror Edgefield 1794. List 20

MELTON, _____? -m- Clementha Broadwater. See Card Scarborough.
Edgefield Rec. Bk. A-221. 1835

MELTON, MRS. HANNAH -w- Robert Melton. Dower favor of Samuel Satcher
Jan. Court. 1786. Edgefield Ct. Min.

MELTON, HANNAH--Dau. of Daniel Rogers-Will 1809. Edgefield

MELTON, LUCINDA--Dau. of John Burress-Will 1822. (Or Molton)

MELTON, NANCY--Dau. of Charles Beck, Sen'r.-Will 1823. Barnwell

MELTON, NATHAN--Petit Juror Edgefield 1789. List 13 and 20

MELTON, ROBERT--Acknowledged Deed to 1790. Wife: Hannah--relin-
quished dower 11 April 1786. Edgefield Ct. Min. 1785.

MELTON, SUSANNAH To Jacob Pope "All land claimed by my father in his
lifetime" on that side of Indian Creek. Wit: Sarah Pope, Simpson
Pope, and Miller Gentry. Edgefield Bk. 31-73

MELTON, WILLIAM--Dec'd. R. E. Sold 6 Feb. 1832. Rec. Bk. A-118
Dist: Hardy Solomon et ux (widow of intestate) 1/3 $26.80
William Melton 1/6 of 2/3 $8.93 3/4
Clem Melton-same
Heirs of Stephen Melton-same
Clem W. Melton 1/3 of 1/6
Charley Gun, et ux-same
Martha Melton-same
Sarah Williams 1/6 of 2/3
Lucinda Melton-same
Louisa Melton-same

MERRITT, ENOCH -w- Sarah--Heirs of Martha Hancock. Edgefield Rec.
Bk. B-25. 1840. See card Martha Hancock.

MERRIWETHER, MARGARET -w- Thomas Merriwether and dau. Susannah
Barksdale-Will 1812. Edgefield

MERRIWETHER, MARY ANN--Dau. of Hillary M. Collier-Will 1841. Wife
of Robert Merriwether. Edgefield

MERRIWETHER, PEGGY--Dau. of Susannah Barksdale-who was dau. of Robert
Ware-Will 1817.

MERRIWETHER, THOMAS--Dec'd. Mentioned in Will of John Key as having
devised lands to Mary Ann Key, wife of said John Key-Will 1840

MESSER, SAMUEL--Petit Juror Edgefield 1786. List 4

MESSERSMITH, JOHN JACOB--Dec'd. Edgefield Ct. Min. Jan. 1795.
John Blocker, Exor.
Appr's: Thos. McGinnis, John Stewart, Michael Shaver, Henry
Timmerman

MEYER, DAVID--Petit Juror Edgefield 1794. List 20

MEYER, DAVE and wife--Heirs of Daniel Bruner. See Bruner card.
Edgefield Rec. Bk. A-34. 1834

MEYER, JOHN--Grand Juror Edgefield 1788. List 10 and 16

MEYER, JOHN--Dec'd. Edgefield Ct. Min. March 1795.
Jesse Roundtree applied for Letters Administration. Granted.
Bond: 500 pounds. Surety: John Clark and Wm. Fudge.
Apprs: Lud Williams, George Bender, Wm. Shinholster, John Savage

MEYER, MARY--Dec'd. Will proved by oath of James Fuller. Jesse
Roundtree one of Exors. named in Will-qualified. Edgefield Ct.
Min. March 1795. Apprs: Lud Williams, George Bender, John Savage,
Wm. Shinholster. March Ct. 1795--Inv. returned and recorded.
Sale to be at house of dec'd.

MEYER, MARY--Niece, James Meyer-nephew, and Ann Meyer-niece and legatees
of Jessy Roundtree-Will 1815

MEYER, MICHAEL--Ded'd. R. E. Sold 1838. Edgefield Rec. Bk. A-294
Dist: Rebecca Meyer, widow--1/3 $158.86
       William H. Lowe -w- Rebecca)
       Elizabeth Meyer (E)   )
       James I. Meyer   )   1/6 of 2/3 each
       John M. Meyer-minor   )
       Martha I Meyer-minor   )
       A. D. Meyer   )

MIDDLETON, ELIZABETH--Dau. of Samuel Scott-Will 1809. John Middleton
an exor.

MIDDLETON, HUGH--Prov. Will of William Harvey. See Harvey card.
Edgefield Min. Bk. 1788

MIDDLETON, JOHN H. -m- set 21 March 1822 Ann Fuller. Ezekiel Evans,
Trustee. All of Edgefield. Arch. Dept. Misc. D-42

MIDDLETON, SAMUEL--Petit Juror Edgefield 1789. List 14

MILES, AQUILLA--Grand Juror Edgefield 1786. List 1 and 2

MILES, AQUILLA--Will 2 March 1797. Record Bk. A-509 Edgefield
Wife: Henrietta
Children: Catherine (Catey) -m- Francis Burt
           Susanna (Sukey) -m- Howard Burt
           Pamela -m- Daniel Holland
           Amelia -m- Martin Palmer
           Thomas   )
           Rebecca   )
           William   ) All died--no issue
           John -w- Susannah)
           Aquilla   )
                              - CONTINUED -

152

MILES, AQUILLA--CONTINUED
    CHILDREN; Continued
        Lewis -m- Sarah
            Ch: Lewis, Rebecca, Mary, Aquilla, Sarah, Harriet
        -Another Card: Edgefield Equity Bill #415 lists children in
        different order:- Catherine, Susanna, Thomas, Aquilla, John
        Amelia, Permealy (sp?)
        Also: Exors: Frances Burt, Howard Burt, Philip Burt.

MILES, ELIZABETH--Dau. of Joseph Tolbert-Will 1793.

MILES, JANE ANDERSON--Gr. dau. of Samuel Anderson-Will 1796.

MILES, RICHARD--Dec'd. R. E. Sold 1836. Edgefield Rec. Bk. A-241
    Dist: Richard Dinkins and wife 1/4 $8.37½
          Elbert Miles-same
          Aquilla Miles and Margaret Miles-minors-G. Brownlee, Gdn.

MILLEDGE, ANN--Dau. of Ann-wife of Melines C. Leavenworth-Will 1820

MILLEDGE, JOHN T.--Nephew of ?-Will 1830

MILLAN, ANN--Dau. of John Jackson-Will-no date. (Miller?)

MILLER, ELIZABETH -w- John Miller. Grand niece of Ulric Tobler-Will
                                                                  1815.
MILLER, GENCY--Grand child of James Hollingsworth-Will 1818

MILLER, GEORGE--Petit Juror Edgefield 1788. List 9 and 18

MILLER, GEORGE -m- Keziah, widow of John Nail. Son of Daniel Nail.
    Edgefield Deed Bk. 13-305 1796

MILLER, GEORGE--See Will of James Blocker-Will 1831. Also mentioned:
    Mrs. Ann B. Miller

MILLER, JACOB--Dec'd. R. E. Sold 1846. Edgefield Rec. Bk. B-115
    Dist: Jane Miller, widow 1/3 $153.91
          John H. Miller   Hugh Miller-d. before 1809
          H. B. Mead -w- Laura Ann   Mary J. Miller
          Alexander Miller   Ellen Miller
          Wiley Miller   Infant son-not named
          Each received 1/8 of 2/3 $38.48
    Rec't. 14 Jan. 1850 from Wm. Quattlebaum -w- Mary.

MILLER, JOHN--Overseer of road called Old Long Cane Road. Part from
    John Jones to Little Stephens Creek--in room of West Harris-
    excused. Edgefield Ct. Min. March 1795.
    Oct. Ct. 1788--Geo. Miller, Gdn. for Daniel Nail and Elizabeth
    Nail. See Nail card.

MILLER, JOHN--Nephew of Ann Sibell Tillman-Will 1830. Dec'd. dau.
    of testator-Francis Miller. James Miller, Exor. Edgefield

MILLER, JOHN M.--Legacy in trust for grand daughter of Casper Nail-
    Will 1833. Edgefield

MILLER, LYDIA--Legatee of Jonathan Owen-Will 1806. Edgefield

MILLIGAN, WILLIAM--Of Charleston--Edgefield Deed 30-357/8
Owned 356 A. on Turkey Creek waters of Stevens Creek. Conv. to
Daniel Bird, Sr. Now conv. by Daniel Bird 18 July 1809--Sanders
Rarden, Benjamin Tradwell, Zadock Magruder to Elijah Bird.

MILLING, DAVID--Dec'd. Sarah Milling and Hugh Milling Ex. Sarah -w-
John Buchanan. See card Lud Williams. Edgefield Judgements 1803

MILLER, CHARLOTTE L.--Dau. of John Clarke, Sen'r.-Will 1821.

MILTON, BENJAMIN--Overseer of road from Lee's Bridge to Pine House.
Part from Bibby Bush's to the Mine holes. In room of James
Brun (or Burn). Edgefield Ct. Min. March 1795.

MIMS, BEHEATHLAND--Will 25 Aug. 1836. Edgefield

MIMS, BRITTAN--Appointed Overseer Martin Road from Edgefield to Coody's
Old Mill in the room of Lewis Tillman-excused. Oct. Ct. 1794
Jan. Ct. 1795--Brittan Mims, Surety in re. Estate Miss Sally
Dalty-minor.

MIMS, DAVID--Dec'd. R. E. Sold 1852. Edgefield Rec. Bk. B-212
Dist: Elizabeth Mims, widow 1/3 $324.41
      David, Susan, Sarah, Mary, and Wm. P. Mims--All minors
      1/5 of 2/3 each. $129.76. James Blackwell, Gdn. of minors.

MIMS, DRURY--Grand Juror Edgefield 1790. List 18

MIMS, HENRY--Brother in law of John Ryan, Dec'd.-Will 1832.
Susan B. Mims-sister of Testator. Edgefield

MIMS, JOHN--Petit Juror Edgefield 1789. List 13

MIMS, LIVINGSTON--Dec'd. R. E. Sold 1839. Edgefield Rec. Bk. A-304
Dist: Mathew Mims 1/3 $10.00
      Benjamin Frazier-same
      Rep. of Livingston Mims, dec'd.-same

MIMS, MARY--Wife of John Mims. Dau. of John Gray, Sen'r.-Will 1823

MIMS, SARAH--Dau. of Samuel Scott-Will 1809. David Mims, Exor.

MINOR, MARLIN -w- Elizabeth--Heirs of William Harvey. See Harvey
card. Edgefield Rec. Bk. A-256. 1857

MINOR, NICHOLAS--Petit Juror Edgefield 1788. List 9, 14, 18.

MINOR, SARAH--Dau. of Mathew Stokes-Will 1791. Edgefield

MINOR, SPENCER--Dec'd. R. E. Sold 1846. Edgefield Rec. Bk. B-94
Dist: Nancy Minor-widow. 1/3 $193.83
      James Minor 6/8 of 2/3 $290.75
      Robert Brooks -w- Mary 1/8 of 2/3
      Martha Minor-same
(Note: James Minor must have purchased several shares)

MINTOR, JOHN--Ded. Edgefield Min. Bk. pg-191. 14 July 1788
Adm. granted to Mary Mintor. S: William Terry. Bond: 500 lbs.
                                          James Coursey

MINTER, JOSEPH--Dec'd. 1780. Copy Will Old. Will-April 18, 1784
 Joseph Minter of Granville Co. N. C. Edgefield Equity Bill 1030
 Wife: Anna Maria   Filed: 5 March 1842
 Son: John Minter-Exor.
 Dau: Mary Minter -m- John Elam-no issue
   Sally, Mary, and Anna Maria Minter
 Bro: Armstrong--Has money of Testator.
 Exor: Rowland Gooch

MINTOR, Mc ERNESS--Minor-age 15 yrs. Peter Morgan aptd. his Gdn.
 Bond: William Terry and Jesse Scruggs. Edgefield Ct. Min.
 1785-90-306. 12 Jan. 1790.
 Min. 1794--Middle Book) shows son of Wm. Minter.

MINTER, SUSAN--Dau. of Clarecy Bell who was dau. of David Richardson-
 Will 1842. Minter may be her middle name. Edgefield

MINTER, WILLIAM--Dec'd. Edgefield Min. Bk. Pg-214 13 Oct. 1788
 Ordered: Citation be issued to show cause why Adm. should not be
 granted to William Brooks.
 -Min. Bk. Pg-275 Oct. 1789--Will brought into court. Let. Adm.
 Revoked from William Brooks. Adm. with Will annexed granted to
 James Coursey. One Exor. named in Will, dead and the reason for
 appointing Lewis Tilman has ceased.

MIRE, JONATHAN--Petit Juror Edgefield 1788. List 9 and 16
     Grand "   "   " " 20

MITCHEL, AMOS--Petit Juror Edgefield 1788. List 9

MITCHEL, DANIEL--Dec'd. Let. Adm. granted to Robert Gillam with the
 consent of Amos Mitchel. Bond 500 lbs. Estate not yet adminis-
 tered. S: Hugh Middleton and John Moore. Edgefield Ct. Min.
 Bk. Pg-326. April 1790

MITCHELL, DANIEL A.--Will 27 Sept. 1841. Edgefield

MITCHEL, EDWARD--Petit Juror Edgefield 1786. List 1 and 2
     Grand "   "   " " 20

MITCHELL, GREEN B.--Will 27 Sept. 1841. Edgefield

MITCHEL, ISAAC--Appointed Guardian Lyda Michel, Beddy Michel--children
 of Daniel Michel, dec'd. (sp?)

MITCHELL, LITTLEBURY--Dec'd. R. E. Sold Sept. 1826. Rec. Bk. A-22
 Dist: Francis Hall and wife 1/3 $127.95
   Sarah A. Mitchell 1/2 of 2/3
   Eliza and Martha Mitchell 1/3 of 2/3
 Receipt headed "Courtland, Alabama, 12 Nov. 1830 from William
 Ellett for share of his wife, Sarah Ann, formerly Sarah Ann
 Mitchell--and also as Guardian Eliza Ellen Mitchell and Martha
 Amanda Mitchell. Wit: Abner Blocker.
 Laurens Co. Alabama--Certificate of appointment of William
 Elliott as Guardian on 6 June 1831 by the Orphans Court of
 Laurens Co. Alabama.
 Also shows Rec't. by William Ellett as Exor. of Francis Hall
 12 Aug. 1831.

MITCHEL, SAMUEL -w- Lucy--Heirs of Philip Jennings. See Jennings card.
Edgefield Rec. Bk. B-185 1850

MITCHEL, TRESIA--Sister of Richard Lewis-Will 1838. Wm. Mitchel, Ex.

MITCHELL, WILLIAM -w- Trecy--Heirs of Richard Lewis. See Lewis card.
Edgefield Rec. Bk. A-215 1835.

MOBLEY, JEREMIAH--Overseer of Road from John Jones to James Buckelew
in the room of Ogden Cockeroff, excused. Edgefield Ct. Min.
March 1795.

MOBLEY, JOHN--Petit Juror Edgefield 1794. List 20

MOBLEY, RACHEL--Dau. of John Douglas-Will 1799. Edgefield

MOBLEY, SUKEY--Gr. dau. of Arthur Simkins-Will 1820. Edgefield

MOCK, ANDREW--Petit Juror Edgefield 1786. List 4

MOCK, DAVID--Grandson of the wife of David Shockley. (Wife-Martha)
Deed 5 July 1790. Edgefield Deed Bk. 4-62
Page 65--Patty Stott-another gr-child.
Deed Bk. 7-89--John, George and Benjamin Mock Sd. B/S Jointly 1792

MOCK, GEORGE--Petit Juror Edgefield 1786. List 3

MOCK, NANCY--Dau. of Richard Quarles, Sen'r.-Will 1796. Edgefield

MONTGOMERY, SARAH--Dau. of Agnes Cunningham-Will 1818. Gr-son:
Robert Montgomery and Gr. dau. Molsy Montgomery.

MOORE, _____?--Dau. of John Gitty-1847. Rec. Bk. B-119
Dhildren: John R.   Eliza
           Drayton   William
           Tabitha   Henry
           Cornelia   Rec't. by D. M. Moore

MOORE, AARON--Will and CULLEN COTTON--Will Edgefield Deed 31-77
The Wills of both set aside 7 Feb. 1812 by heirs:
Simeon Perry and wife   James Barfield and wife
Jonathan Cotton   Bersheba Warenton
Arthur Cotton   Josiah Cotton
Elmsly Lot and wife

MOORE, ANDERSON--Edgefield Equity Bill M-72 Filed 8 June 1819.
Widow: Rebecca -m- Morris P. Holloway
Children: William, Right M., and Mary Ann Moore.
Owned land Edgefield Dist. Mountain Creed, adj. Jordan Holloway
John Mitchell and Spencer Smith.

MOORE, ARBEN--Edgefield Ct. Min. Jan. 1795.
Ordered: That Arben Moore be Overseer of the New Road from
Turkey Creek to where the Path from John Blocker's to Oliver's
Place crosses the road. In the room of John Blocker, excused.

MOORE, ARBIN--Edgefield Probate. Citation: 7 Dec. 1801
    Adm: Thompson Moore
    Return shows: John, Jonathan, David, Pleasant, and James
    Anderson Moore.
    Sale 1802 shows: Anne, Claracy, John, Thompson, and David Moore.
    (Relationship not shown.)Also James Blocker, Abraham Dozier,
    Michael Blocker, John Blocker, Jno. Simkins, Moses Taylor, Jordan
    Brooks, A. C. Dozier, Daniel Bough, Wm. Terry, and John Baugh.

MOORE, BEHEATHLAND FOOTE--age 7   Edgefield File Misc PP-114
    William age 5   Step father: Moses Yarborough
    George age 3   Mother: Francis Yarborough
    25 Jan. 1772 at Charleston
    Page 506--Francis Yarborough appointed Gdn. for:
        William Yarborough age 4 yrs.
        Gilson   "   " 14 months
        Elizabeth   "   " 7 yrs.
        Ann   "   " 6 yrs.   16 May 1773
    Must have been children of Moses by a 1st wife.

MOORE, BENJAMIN and Samuel--Nephews of John Crookhanks-Will 1801

MOORE, CHRESWELL--Will 1 Dec. 1838. Edgefield Wills Bx-108-23
    Wife: Mary
    Son: John C. Moore, Exor.
    Dau. (?): Eliza Ann Williams -w- Williamson Williams
    Wit: S. F. Rushton, Joseph Rushton and Turner Harris.
    Date: 4 Dec. 1838   Prov: 15 Jan. 1840

MOORE, DAVID W.--Heir estate of Luke Doby. See Doby card.
    Edgefield Rec. Bk. A-223 1836.

MOORE, ELIJAH and John Bickley, Zachry Meriwether, Tolaver Bostick,
    Surety on Bond of Joseph Bickley as Deputy Clerk of 96 Dist.
    Dated 13th May 1793.

MOORE, FRANCIS--Of Little River-Saluda. Edgefield File. C. T. Wills
    Wife: Frances--Pur. of John Box. Will 1 Nov. 1770. Qualified
        as Frances Yarborough
    Son: William Moore
    "my 3 children:" Not names.
    Exor: John Ford of Tyger River.
    Wit: John Robins, James Harvey, and Mack Goode.

MOORE, CAPT. JAMES--Of "96"--House Journal 1782 Pg-67. Edgefield File.
    Member of Committee to act -on a Petition from Officers of Lower
    Granville and Colleton Co.
    Page-89--Capt. James Moore on Committee.

MOORE, JAMES--Rev. Rec. Arch. Dept. Edgefield Co.
    State S. C. Edgefield Dist: "Know all men by these presents that
    we Richard Moore and John Moore of the State and County afore-
    said have made, ordained, constituted and appointed and by these
    presents do make, ordain, constitute and appoint Davis Moore of
    the State aforesaid and County of Abbeville, our true and lawful
    Attorney for us and in his own name to draw from the Treasury of
    this State, all Indents, Certificates, that may be due to us as
    the surviving Executors of the said Davis Moore's father's estate;
    Viz: James Moore, dec'd. 1 Feb. 1791 Rec't. 9 Feb. 1791.

MOORE, JAMES--Continued.
Rec't. by Davis Moore 9 Feb. 1791 for Indent No. 584. Bk. Z
2-584--Deputy Quarter Master General of Militia. Indents
Y-Z Page 310 at top.

MOORE, JAMES--Dec'd. Edgefield Ct. Min. March 1795.
Letters Administration granted Mrs. Mary Moore, Thomas Bacon
and Andrew Pickens. S: Thomas Key, Barkley Martin and William
Key. Apprs: Philip Lamar, Harley Johnson, Jesse Roundtree,
Fields Pardue, and Nathaniel Bacon.

MOORE, JAMES--Dec'd. Edgefield Deed 12-537. 2 March 1795
Widow: Anny -m-_____? Bostick.
Had dower in land of James Moore. Collected by ___? Deed to
part of the land to Toliver Bostick.

MOORE, JAMES -w- Betsy--Heirs of Edward Moseley--a devisee of James
Butler. See Butler card. Edgefield Rec. Bk. A-165. 1834

MOORE, JOHN AND JAMES McMILLIAN--Surety on Adm. Bond estate of Isham
Green. Mary Green, Adm'x. See Green card. Edgefield April 1790
Min. Bk. Page 325

MOORE, JOHN -w- Martha--Heirs of James Thomas. See Thomas card.
Edgefield Rec. Bk. A-6 1826

MOORE, JOHN CARRAWAY -m- Sibyl Ann Holloway, dau. of Sarah Holloway
See back card Lewis Holloway. Roll 906

MOORE, JOHN C.--Edgefield Wills 1845.
Wife: Sibby Ann   Mentions: "All my children"
Exor: Thomas Lake   Wit: Williamson Williams,
Simpson Matthias, S. H. Whatley

MOORE, JOHN M.--Edgefield File 20 May 1820 Misc. D-199 and 194
Trustee for Susanna Stott-wife of Jacob Stott of Edgefield Dist.
Page 213 of Patsy Stott wife of Abdiell Stott. Col. John
Moore, Trustee (Said John M. Moore) 300 A. on Coffee Town Creek.

MOORE, JOHN R.--Edgefield Rec. Bk. B-119 1847
Also: Cornelia, Drayton, Tabitha, Elias, William, Henry--
children of a dec'd. sister of John Gitty. See Gitty card.

MOORE, JONATHAN--Appointed Tax Collector. Bond dated 15 March 1797.
S: T. Bostick, Samuel Mays, Richard Moore. Wit: Joseph
Hightower, Arthur Simkins. Bond for faithful performance of
duties. Edgefield Misc. Rec. B-Page 18

MOORE, JONATHAN--Misc. Rec. B-451 or 690 Arch. Dept. 11 March 1811
To: Wife, Sally Moore for support of herself and his children;
James, Drayton, Davis, Mary Ann, Nancy and Bryan Washington
Moore,-any unborn children. Transfers property to Rhydon Grigsby.

MOORE, MARY ELDER--Legatee of Benjamin Ryan-Will 1808. Edgefield
Seems a dau. of Sarah Goldman-niece of Testator-who had other
children also.

158

MOORE, NICHOLSON--Gr-son of Mary Nicholson-Will 1821. Morris P.
Holloway, his trustee. Edgefield
Mariann Moore--sister of Nocholson, both children of James
A. Moore, dec'd. (Seems their mother was named Rebecca).

MOORE, NISIAH -w- Augustis Moore and dau. of George Miller-Will 1805.

MOORE, PATTY--Edgefield Probate Bx 108-28 Will 1812.
Dau: Patsy Stott--"Part of my father's, John Marshall,estate.
Son: John MarshallMoore
      Creswell Moore
Brother: John Marshall-dec'd. 1812
"That part of estate of my brother, John Marshall, dec'd. which
at his death he Willed to my husband, Richard Moore--on Choranaker
Creek-Abbeville, Dist."
Ex: Abdel Stott, Thos B. Waller, Jonathan Moore
Wit: John Hagood, Sally Moore, and Sarah Hill Prov: 7 Apl. 1814
See card Richard Moore. There were 2 Patty Moores in Edgefield.
See estate of John Moore-1806

MOORE, RICHARD--Petit Juror Edgefield 1788. List 12
          Grand   "   "   "   " 21

MOORE, RICHARD--To his children--Edgefield April 1793. 7-135-143
Son: Creswell--100 A. on Coffeetown. Bd. Wm. Davis, et al.
      John M. Moore
Dau: Tabitha   "
Son: William   "

MOORE, RICHARD--Edgefield Probate-Will 3 Dec. 1804. Bk. A
Wife: Patsey--all property
Ex: Wife qualified 12 Oct. 1807
Wit: H. M. Millan (?), Wm. Statteworth and Wm. Paine
Proven: 27 Oct. 1806.
See card of Patty Moore-1812 Will. She was Patty Marshall.

MOORE, SAMPSON--Petit Juror Edgefield 1788. List 9

MOORE, SUSANNAH--Of City of Charleston-Widow-marriage agreement with
Seth Blakely-Tailor-Of Charleston. Gr. Nephew: Peter Darr
Lincoln, son of niece, Elizabeth Ann Lincoln-widow of Charleston.
Negro Woman, Flora and her son Tom. 22 July 1819. Wit: Thomas
Ham. Charleston File Arch. Dept. Misc. 4T-412

MOORE, WILLIAM --Of 96 Dist. of Town of 96. Edgefield File. 96 Dist.
Ct. Rec. Univ. Lib. Davis Moore and Julius Nuckols, Adm's.
Sum to answer, Wm. Price. Notes said by Wm. Moore 1786.

MOORE, WILLIAM and Julius Nichols, trustees for Mary Ann Sanders--
Widow of Thos. Sanders of 96. -m- Gabriel Smithers. See Smithers
card. Edgefield File Marriage Bk #1 287. 1786

MOORE, WILLIAM -w- Isbel of Granville Co. to Thomas Butler. 300 A.
Granville Co. on both sides Stephens Creek. Gr. said Wm. Moore
14 Aug. 1772. Wit: Robert Moore, James and Agnes Moore.
17 March 1774. Edgefield File Deed Bk. 17-23

MOORE, WILLIAM--Made application by Col. Samuel Mays for permission
to keep Tavern. S: Samuel Mays and Wm. Butler. Edgefield
Ct. Min. Jan. 1795

MOORE, WILLIAM T.--Will 1820. Of St. John's Par. Berkley Co.
Brother: John Moore   Charleston Wills Bk. F
Nephew: Wm. Moore Williams   Page 411
Legacy: St. Matthew's Lodge #37
         Robert James Kirk
         James White.
Date: 7 Nov. 1820   Prov: 14 May 1822
Wit: James White, Jas. D. Mitchell and Robert J. Kirk.

MOORE, WIOTT--Dec'd   Edgefield Deed 2 Oct. 1812 Deed Bk 31-22 718
Wife, Clarecy to James A Moore and John Mitchell--agreement
to give up right in property of Wiott.

MORETON, MARY ANN--Dec'd. Edgefield Rec. Bk. A-90 Sale of land
17 May 1825. Distributees:
Lucy Clarkson 1/4 $24.06   William Moreton-same
Elizabeth Evans-same   Thomas W. Moreton-same

MORGAN, ANN S.--Dau. of Ann Sibell Tillman-Will 1830

MORGAN, CATY M.--Heir and dau. of Roger M. Williams. Edgefield Wills
D-17 1828

MORGAN, E.--Gdn. minor children of John Bussy. See Bussey card.
Edgefield Rec. Bk. A-195 1834.

MORGAN, ELAN--Petit Juror Edgefield 1787. List 6
EVAN--   "   "   "   "   "   17

MORGAN, ELBERT and wife--Heirs of Robert Samuel. See Samuel card.
Edgefield Rec. Bk. A-193. 1834

MORGAN, EVAN--Will 11 Feb. 1836. Edgefield

MORGAN, ONIAS--Dec'd. Edgefield Ct. Min. March 1795.
Abiah Morgan applied Letters Adm. S: Hugh Middleton and
William Covington. Apprs: Chas. Blackwell, James Thomas,
William Reynolds, Samuel Scott.
March Ct. 1795--Inv. returned and recorded. Order Personal prop.
be sold at house of Abiah Morgan on last Mon. in July.
March Ct. 1795--Same card: Peter Morgan, Gdn. for Mackerness
Minter. See Wm. Minter.

MORGAN, SARAH--Dau. of John Griffis-Will 1838. Edgefield

MORGAN, WILLIAM -w- Margaret--Conv. 29 April 1795. Deed 8-223

MORRELL, ROBERT--His children-legatees of Benjamin Lindsey-Will 1841.

MORRING, JOHN--Dec'd. Edgefield Rec. Bk. B-21 Dist: (1841) (1849)
    William Bush and wife 1/3
    David Huiet -w- Mary 1/5 of 2/3
    Julius Satcher -w- Martha-same
    John Morring-same
    Joel Morring-same
    Frances-same -m- Alexander Clarke

MORRIS, BARBERRY--Dau. of Christian Buckhalter-Will 1792. Also Betsy.

MORRIS, ELIZABETH--Dau. of Elizabeth Bolger-Will 1836

MORRIS, JOHN--Petit Juror Edgefield 1787. List 8

MORRIS, JOSEPH--Will 28 May 1839

MORRIS, LEMUEL -w- Martha--Heirs of Rebecca Ramey. See Ramey card.
    Edgefield Rec. Bk. B-75 1842

MORRIS, SARAH--Dau. of John B. Bush-Will 1844. Edgefield

MORROW, JOHN--Petit Juror Edgefield 1788. List 11

MORROW, REBECCA O.--Dau. of Hamatal Wilson-Will 1806. James Morrow
    an exor. See also card on Fay. Edgefield

MORROW, RUTH--Dau. of Thomas Berry-Will 1819

MORTON, WILLIAM R.--Dec'd. R. E. Sold. Edgefield Rec. Bk. A-98
    Thomas W. Morton, uncle of intestate 1/9
    Children of B. White and cousins of intestate. 1/9 $25.39 jointly.
        Joseph V. White   Abner
        Mary   Newell
        Jonathan   Margaret
        Elizabeth   1/9 Elizabeth Evans-Aunt to intestate
    Lucy Clarkson-aunt to intestate 1/9
    Newel Tullis-uncle 1/9
    Moses Tullis-uncle 1/9
    Jonathan White -w- Elizabeth-uncle and aunt 1/9
    Sarah Tullis-aunt 1/9
    Heirs of Aaron Tullis-uncle
        John, Pleasant, Martha, Tullis)
        Wm. Walker -w- Ann   ) 1/9
        Aaron, June, Thomas, Eliza Tullis)
    John B. Tullis gave Rec't. 22 Feb. 1833

MOSELY, ARTHUR--Of Abbeville Dist. Will 11 Jan. 1824.
    Dau: Rosena Mosely   Abbeville Wills Bk. 1-289
    Bro: Richard Mosely and his son, Richard
        William Mosely of Va.
    Nephew: Tarlton Mosely
    Wit: Josepy Mosely, John and William Bass.

MOSELEY, BENJAMIN--Will 18 Nov. 1794. Edgefield Wills A-75
    Wife: Priscilla-pregnant. (dau. Wm. Jeter)
    Ch'n: Penelope (Pepy), Elizabeth, Sarah, John
    Ex: Wife, George Moseley, and Thos Adams
    18 Nov. 1794.   Prov: 6 July 1795

MOSELEY, BENJAMIN--Dec'd. Edgefield Ct. Min. March 1795.
Will proven by oath of Littlebury Adams.
Priscilla Moseley, George Moseley, and Thomas Adams--Qual. as
Exors.
Apprs: Lewis Tillman, Daniel Huff, Littlebury Adams, and Butler
Williams.

MOSELEY, CHARLES--Will 25 Dec. 1808. Bk. 1-384
Wife: Charlotte
Dau: Charlotte
Son: Thomas Franklin Moseley
Exors: John N. and Philip Montague.

MOSELEY, LIEUT. DAVID--Arch. Dept. Senate Journal 9 Dec. 1799 Pg-84
Paid his pay roll for 5 men on Oconee Station in 1797 and 1798.
Journal for 1797-Dec. 4. page 109. Lieut. Moseley, Pd.

MOSELEY, COL. EDWARD, CAPT. JOHN, CAPT. HILLARY--"The following
synopsis of the contents of the Vestry Book of Lynnhaven Parish--
"Commenced 20 Nov. 1723, on which occasion were present the Rev.
James Tenant, Minister; Major Maximillian Boush, Churchwarden;
and the following named gentlemen who composed the Vestry: Col.
Edward Moseley; Capt. Henry Chapman; Mr. William Elligood; Capt.
John Moseley; Mr. Chester Sayer; and Captain Francis Land."
"At the first meeting, say Nov. 20, 1723, the Parish is made
debtor to Captain Hillary Moseley, for quit rents of glebe lands.
Old Churches, Ministers, and Families of Virginia, Lynnhaven
Parish. Vol.-1 Page-247. This is in the State Library, Columbia,
South Carolina

MOSELY, EDWARD--A devisee of James Butler. See Butler card. Edgefield Rec. Bk. A-165. 1834

MOSLEY, ELIZABETH S.--Wife of M. Mosley-gr. niece of John Ryan-Will 1827.

MOSLEY, JAMES--Of Edgefield. Edgefield Will 6 Nov. 1827. Prov: 11 June
Wife: Mary   1829
Dau: Mary
Sons: John, Middleton, Clement, and James
Daus: Frances, Harriett, and Patsey, and her dau. Eliza

MOSELEY, JUDITH -vs- William Dooley--Appeared from a Magistrate's
Judgement confirmed for 1 lb. 17sh. 8p. and cost of suit.
Oct. Ct. 1789. Min.Bk, Pg. 267. Edgefield

MOSLEY, MARY--Dau. of Joab Wooten-Will 1808. Edgefield

MOSLEY, MARY--Dau. of Isaac Van-Will 1839. Edgefield

MOSELEY, NANCY--Dau. of William Jeter-Will 1793. Gr-son-George
Mosley, son of Nancy M. Dau: Priscilla Mosley. Gr. dau: Sally,
dau. of Priscilla.

MOSELY, NANCY--Dist estate of Fanny Butler. See Butler card.
Edgefield Rec. Bk. B-37 1841

MOSLEY, PATSEY--Dau. of James Butler-Will 1811. Edgefield

MOSELEY, RICHARD--Of Abbeville. Univ. Vol. Abbeville Wills--Vol. 2-230
    Son: Henry Moseley
          Richard H. Moseley
    Gr. dau: Martha Johnson -w- Charles Johnson
          Judith Ball
          Emeline Ball-minor
    Date: 3 April 1829   Prov: 24 Oct. 1831
    Wit: A. E. Scuddy; John Baker; John English

MOSELEY, ROBERT -vs- Rainsford July Ct. 1787. Min. Bk.
    Witnesses: Ben. Moseley, and George Moseley
             Derrick Holsenback
             James Hargrove
             Edward Vann and Mary Vann
             Philip Johnson
             Henry Summerall.

MOSLEY, ROBERT--Wit. Will of Martin Cloud 22 June 1793. Wills A-218
    Deed Bk. 3-73--Robert Mosely -w- Penny conv. 12 Jan. 1787
    Deed Bk. 5-186--Robert Moseley -w- Penelope-1784

MOSELEY, ROBERT--Of Edgefield. Abbeville Wills A Dated 6 Jan. 1796
    Wife: Penelope--Land on Cedar Creek
    Daus: Rachel Davison; Anna Moseley
    Son: John
    Daus: Lydia (?); Penelope;
    Sons: Thomas; Robert; Jesse; Daniel.--Minors
    Daus: Elizabeth Vann; Sarah Hagood; Martha Stallings; Susanna
          Adams--5 Shillings
    Son: Edward Moseley--5 Shillings
          Mary Holsonbake
    Penelope and Thomas-2 youngest children.
    Exor: Lewis Tillman

MOSELEY, TARLTON--Will 20 Aug. 1826. Abbeville Wills
    Wife: Rosana--Land where his father lived to be sold with his
                 consent
    Bro: Henry and Richard Moseley--Exors.
    "My children"

MOSELEY, WILLIAM--Petit Juror Edgefield 1788. List 12
    Deed Bk. 1 Page 183 and 228--William Moseley Grant 1786 conv.
    23 Dec. 1789. Wife-Sarah
    Deed Bk. 8 Page 213--Thomas Moseley -w- Priscilla conv. 7 Aug. 1789

MOSELY, WILLIAM--Dec'd. Abbeville--96 Dist. Rec.
    17 March 1819--Citation ret. by John Archer--Let. Adm. Granted.

MOSLEY, WILLIAM--Nephew of Daniel Richardson--Will 1826. Edgefield

MOSS, JOHN -w- Lucinda--Heirs of Charity Johnson. See Johnson card.
    Edgefield Rec. Bk. B-161 1849

MOSS, RACHEL--Dau. of Elizabeth Thurmon-Will 1804. Edgefield

MOSS, RACHEL--Will 10 March 1832. Edgefield

MOTES, MATILDA--Dau. of James Goggins-Will 1843. Gr. dau. Matilda.

MOUNCE, MARTHA--Dec'd. R. E. Sold 1842. Edgefield Rec. Bk. B-47
  Dist: William Mounce
         Michael Lewis -w- Nancy of Walker Co. Ala.
         Willis D.; Mary; Robert; and Wiley D Mounce. Wiley also
         of Walker Co. Ala. Each 1/7 $17.35

MUCKLE, MARY--Dau. of Joseph Lake-Will 1823. Her son: Richard Muckle

MUCKLERATH, FRANCIS--Petit Juror Edgefield 1789. List 16

MURPHEY, ELIZABETH -w- James Murphey and dau. of Daniel A. Mitchel-
  Will 1841. Edgefield

MURPHEY, DRURY--Petit Juror Edgefield 1787. List 7

MURPHEY, WILLIAM--Petit Juror Edgefield 1786. List 5, 13, and 17

MURRAH, LEWIS -w- Sarah--Heirs of Benjamin Doolittle. See Doolittle
  card. Edgefield Rec. Bk. A-209 1835

MURRAH, SALLY--Dau. of Moses Robertson-Will 1795. Rec'd. 1800
  Mentioned Thomas Murrah. Also dau. Rachel Murrah -w- James Murrah.

MURRAH, SUSANNAH--Dec'd. See card Hezekiah Walker to Mary Williams.
  Edgefield Rec. Bk. A Loose paper. 1828

MURRAH, THOMAS--Petit Juror Edgefield 1794. List 20

MURRAY, DAVID--Dec'd. Edgefield Ct. 12 Jan. 1789. Min. Bk. Page-232
  Ordered citation be issued to show cause why Adm. should not be
  granted to Robert Stark, Jun'r.

MURRAY, JAMES H. -m- set 31 Aug. 1843. Martha Glover-dau. Jethro
  Glover, dec'd. Edgefield Dist. Misc. N-207

MURRY, JOHN--an orphan reared by Alexander Hannah-Will 1806.

MURRELL, SARAH--Sister of William Lindsey-Will 1827. Edgefield

MURRELL, VASHTI--Died 24 March 1872 age 60 years. Quattlebaum
  grave yard--Sleepy Creek, Edgefield Road

MYERS, JONATHAN--Appointed Gdn. Gracey Myers, Sally Myers and Leonard
  Myers. Children of Leonard Myers, dec'd. S: John Stirzenegger

MYERS, NANCY--Dau. of William West-Will 1779

NAGEL, MARTHA--Legatee of John Gray--Will 1833. Edgefield

NAIL, CASPER--Will 4 July 1833. Edgefield

NAIL, DANIEL AD ELIZABETH--Minor children of John Nail, dec'd. George
  Miller appointed Gdn. Edgefield Ct. Min. 13 Oct. 1788

NAIL, DANIEL--Of Beech Island, New Windsor--Edgefield Deed Bk. 13-305
  Sons: John, dec'd.--Widow-Keziah -m- George Miller
         Casper (or Gasper)
         Daniel
  Daus: Elizabeth -m- John Savage (Another card shows Ann, who marr-
         Ann -m- Nathaniel Howell   ied N. Howell to be dau. of Miller)

NAIL, CASPER, JUN'R.--Petit Juror Edgefield 1788. List 10 and 16

NAIL, GASPER, SEN'R--and his brother, Daniel Nail, Kinsmen of Ulric
    Tobler-Will 1815. (Casper and Gasper-spelled both ways.)

NAIL, JOHN--Of New Windsor. Edgefield File. C. T. Deed F-3-360 412
    Said his name "Jans Nagul" in 1766. 250 A. Grant to John Naile
    Also: Franze Nagel is shown in a probate as "Islans Neal".

NALLY, MARY--Dau. of Jacob Ernest-Will 1824

NAN, JOSEPH--Petit Juror Edgefield 1786. List 1, 2, 10, and 16.

NEAL, CASPER, SR.--Petit Juror Edgefield 1787. List 6. See Nail.

NEELY, MARY--Dau. of William Murphey-Will 1794. Rec'd. 1801

NELSON, ELIZABETH--Dau. of Daniel Regers-Will 1809

NEW, PRUDENCE--Sister of Edward Garrett-Will 1836. Edgefield

NEWBURN, DR. -w- Emily (nee Wilson)--Heirs of Mary Gillman. See
    Gillman card. Edgefield Rec. Bk. B-1103 1846

NEWMAN, ALEXANDER--Grand Juror 1787. List 6

NEWMAN, THOMAS--Grand Juror Edgefield 1786. List 3

NEWPORT, ROBERT--Petit Juror Edgefield 1787. List 7

NEWPORT, ROBERT--Of Edgefield Dist. Edgefield Wills A-181
    Son: Robert   17 Dec. 1802
    Dau: Hannah   Rec'd: 8 June 1803
    Wife: Nanny
    Daus: Nancy and Susannah

NEWTON, JAMES -w- Sarah--Heirs of Allen Body. See Body card. Edge-
    field Rec. Bk. A-92. 1832

NEWTON, ROBERT--Will 5 Sept. 1842

NEWTON, WILLIAM--License to keep Tavern. S: Butler Williams and
    Daniel Huff. Edgefield Ct. Min. March Ct. 1795

NIBLET, JOHN--Dec'd. Edgefield Min. Bk. 263. Oct. 1789
    Benjamin Mock appointed Gdn. of Caleb Niblet, an orphan under
    age to choose for himself. a son of John Niblet, dec'd.

NICHOLAS, RACHEL--Dau. Elias Blackburn-Will 1827. Her children:-
    Pabrice Nicholas, son. (sp?0
    Emily, Adaline, Mary, and Amanda, daughters.

NICHOLS, ELIZABETH--Dau. of Hezekiah Gentry-Will 1820

NICHOLS, JAMES--Appraised estate Pleasant Burnett. See Burnett card.
    Edgefield Ct. Min. Oct. 1794

NICHOLS, JOHN -w- Sarah--Heirs of John Rogers. See Rogers card.
Edgefield Rec. Bk. A-324. 1839

NICHOLS, JULIUS--C. T. Deed S5-87. 5/6 May 1785.
To: Julius Nichols, Jr. 800 pounds, amount--703 A. in Abbeville
Dist. on waters of Coronaco. Bd: George Head, Charles Head,
Elijah Moore, and James Edwards. Being part of land of James
Simpson conv. to Julius Nichols, Sr.

NICHOLS, JULIUS, JR.--Clerk of 96 Dist. Bond dated 6 May 1789.
S: Thomas Brandon, William Moore, Julius Nichols (evidently
the senior). Edgefield File. Misc. Rec. B-115

NICHOLS, JULIUS, JR.--To Garland Goode 23 May 1792--140 A. adj. said
Garland Goode. Edgefield Deed 11-21

NICHOLS, WILLIAM -w- Elizabeth--Heirs of Robert Roebuck. See Roebuck
card. Edgefield Eq. Roll. 30 1801

NICHOLSON, BEN. F. and wife--Dist. of John Blocker, dec'd. Edgefield
Rec. Bk. A-158. 1833

NICHOLSON, LIDIA--Sister of William Oliphant-Will 1827. Her children:-
John, Benjamin, Samuel, Jr. and Barsheba Nicholson.

NICHOLSON, LYDIA--2nd dau. of John Oliphant-Will 1815.

NICHOLSON, MARY--Dau. of John Douglass-Will 1799. Edgefield

NICHOLSON, NANCY--Dau. of Ann Maria Terry-Will 1823.

NICHOLSON, RIGHT--Grand Juror Edgefield 1787. List 6, 18, and 20

NICHOLSON, WILLIAM--Default in road work. See Lodwick Hill. Edgefield Ct. Min. March 1795.

NICHOLSON, WRIGHT -w- Harriet--Heirs of John Cogburn. See Cogburn card.
Edgefield Rec. Bk. A-225. 1834

NICKS, MATILDA--Dau. of Daniel Self-Will 1835. Edgefield

NIPPER, DRURY--Petit Juror Edgefield 1789. List 15

NIPPER, ELIZA--Wife of Drury Nipper. Dower favor of Jacob Fudge, Sr.
Oct. Court 1787. Edgefield Min. Bk.

NIXON, SARAH -w- Thomas H. Nixon and daughter of Jeptha Sharpton-Will
1838
NIXON, THOMAS, Dec'd. R. E. Sold 1845. Edgefield Rec. Bk. B-85
Dist: Sarah Nixon, widow 1/3 $160.87
George W. Nixon   Frances Nixon
Felix G. Parker -w- Margaret   John Nixon-minor
Hugh A. Nixon   Preston Nixon-dec'd. not M.
Jefferson T. Nixon   Susan Nixon.
Thos. H. Nixon-dec'd. not M.   Each rec. 1/9 of 2/3 $35.75

NOBLES, HEZEKIAH--Dec'd. R. E. Sold 1837. Edgefield Rec. Bk. A-274
    Dist: Alcey Nobles, widow 1/3 $56.67 (Also spelled Elcey)
    Luke Nobles   Marshall J. Bean -w- Rhoda
    John Nobles   John Bolger -w- Sarah
    Henry Blossom -w- Elizabeth Mark Nobles (Purchaser
    Each received 1/6 of 2/3

NOBLES, MARK--Petit Juror Edgefield 1787. List 8 and 20

NOBLES, REBEKAH--Dau. of Thomas Roberts-Will 1784. Rachel Nobles
    another daughter.

NOBLES, SAUNDERS AND DENNIS--Of Edgefield. See card John Hogg -vs-
    Laban Odom. Dudleys Rept's. Sup. Ct. Ga. 1837.

NOBLES, MRS. ZILPHA--wife of Lewis Nobles--Dower favor of John Lucas.
    April court 1787. Edgefield Min. Bk.

NOBLES, LEONARD--To Saunders Noble--Deed gift Negro woman. Prov.
    Oct. Ct. 1786. Edgefield Ct. Bk.

NOBLES, WILLIAM--Petit Juror Edgefield 1789. List 14 and 21

NORRELL, ISAAC--Legatee Richard Allison-Will 1787. Edgefield
    -Isaac Norrell--Petit Juror Edgefield 1789. List 13

NORRELL, WILLIAM--Grandson of Martha Moore Will 1825. Got land on
    road from Cambridge to the Ridge. Jack Norrell a witness on
    her Will. Edgefield Wills 1825
    -Norrell, William-Gr. son Martha Moore. Gr. dau. Martha Norrell

NORRIS--See Will of Josiah Langley-Will 1826.

NORRIS, N. J. -w- Mary--Heirs of Joseph West. See West card. Edge-
    field Rec. Bk. A-66. 1836

NORRIS, REBECCA--Dau. of Jacob Miller-Will 1775. Edgefield

NORRIS, THOMAS--Dec'd. Edgefield Ct. Min. Oct. 1794.
    Widow: Rebecka -m-____? White
    Son: Stephen Norris
    Other children not named.
    Appointed to divide the Property: Ruchard Tutt; John Gray;
    John Addison; and Samuel Walker

NORRIS, THOMAS -w- Martha--Heirs of Joseph West. See West card.
    Edgefield Rec. Bk. A-66 1833

NORWOOD, JOHN--Petit Juror Edgefield 1789. List 13

NORWOOD, LARKIN -w- Elizabeth--Heirs estate of James Eidson. See
    Eidson card. Edgefield Rec. Bk. B-125. 1847

NOVEL, ANN--Legatee of James Lowery-Will 1815. Edgefield

NUCKOLS, POLLY HUGHS--Sister of Anderson Watkins-Will 1828. Polly of Ky.

NUNN, INGRAM--Will 13 Nov. 1838. Edgefield

OADUM, ALEXANDER--Petit Juror Edgefield 1788. List 9
ODEN, ALEXANDER--   "   "   "   "   " 18

OADUM, MICHAEL AND JANE--Adv. Peter Hillard. Care con't. July 1788
Edgefield Ct.

ODEN, JOHN, ELIAS, GEORGE, AND STACY ANN -w- Edward Shadwick--Heirs of
Thomas Howell. See Howell card. Edgefield Red. Bk. A-286. 1838

ODEN, JOHN H.--Gr. son of Esther Howell-Will 1840. Also George and Elias

ODEN, LETISHA--Dau. of George Bussey-Will 1797. Gr. Son: Thomas Oden.

ODOM, ABRAHAM--Of Granville Co. Will 30 Jan. 1771. Edgefield File
Sons: Abraham, Jacob, David, Demsey   C. T. Wills
Dau: Mary Caroline
      Sarah Rooks--Land bought of Dennis McLendon
      Nancy Deloth
Wit: Parker Carradine

ODOM, ABRAHAM, SR. to Abraham Odom, Jr. both of Edgefield-1 grey horse.
Edgefield Deed Bk. 2-76 14 Oct. 1788. Wit: Henry Swearingen

ODOM, ABRAHAM, SR.--Dec'd. Late of Barnwell. Edgefield Pro. Bx-22-792
Cit: 29 Jan. 1821 John P. Odom applied for Let. Adm.
Bond: 12 Feb. 1821 S: Abraham Odom, Reuben Newman, Zacheus
Pursell. File does not show anything else.

ODOM, DIDATHA--From Hezekiah Walker $200.00 250 A. Edgefield Deed
Bk. 28-248. 4 Jan. 1802
-Edgefield Deed Bk. 32-135. 18 Jan. 1813--Ditdath Odom from
Ezzard Mayson $100.00 100 A. Edgefield Dist. on waters of Edisto
and road to Augusta.

ODUM, EZEKIEL--Petit Juror Edgefield 1788. List 9

ODOM, HALLASHA--From John Fortner $154.00 300 A. part of Grant to
William Donoho 5th Nov. 1792. On both sides Beech Creek.
Edgefield Deed Bk. 28-245. 3 Oct. 1801
-Hallasha Odom to Elsie Dis--Love, Good will--Deed Gift. Horse.
Edgefield Deed Bk. 29-192 9 April 1808

ODOM, HEZEKIAH--Petit Juror Edgefield 1794. List 23

ODUM, JACOB--Appointed Gdn. of Mary Watson and Peter Watson. See
Watson card. Edgefield Ct. Min. July 1788

ODOM, JACOB--Dec'd. Edgefield Pro. Rec. Bx-22-782
Martha Odom, Adm'x.   Cit: 5 March 1804
Pub. at Meeting 25 March 1804
Heirs: Martha Odom, Sr.--also mentioned part of her dec'd. dau.
        Josiah Cotton
        Martha Odom, Jr.
        Possibly others.

ODOM, JAMES--From Michael Shaver, Sr. 50 A. west side Sleepy Creek.
Edgefield Deeds 32-490

ODOM, JAMES--Of Edgefield Dist. to William Stedham--Land on Sleepy Cr.
Edgefield Deed Bk. 37-309. 19 Dec. 1817

ODOM, JAMES--Dec'd. A. Blocker, Adm.--File contains only return for
14 March 1828 covering Feb. 1824 to 1828. Shows: Paid Moses
Odom and various others. Relation not shown. Edgefield Pro.
box 22-780

ODOM, JANE--Wife of ___?Edgefield Rec. Bk. B 1839-56 Pg-25
Distributees of Martha Hancock. Rec't. 8 June 1848
Dist: 1840 show: 1/6 to each heir.
Permelia Fulford
Enoch Merritt -w- Sarah
Siras Floy -w- Mary Ann
James M. Powell -w- Tyrzah
Jane Hancock
Charles P. Powell -w- Martha

ODOM, MARTHA--Dau. of John Watson-Will 1788. Also called Mary Odom
(or 2 daus.?)

ODOM, MARTHA--To her grand daughter Patey Willis--a Stud horse named
Brutus. Edgefield Deed Bk. 26-301 18 Nov. 1805
Page 472--Martha Odom to her grand daughter, Matilda Perry-
Negro-Pegg. Wit: (to both) Elijah Watson, Ezekiel Perry,
Stamore Butler.
Bk. 27-73--To Grand son, Stanmore Watson, 125 A. land. 22 May 1806

ODOM, MARTHA--Edgefield Deed 33-32. To dau: Polly Perry and her child-
ren--slave. 15 Oct. 1811
Children: Patsey, Salley, Beckey, Matilda, Watson
Page 32/3--Mary Perry--Furniture-29 March 1812
Page 123- To son, Elijah Watson--slave
Bk. 34-75--Martha Odom to dau. Charity Cotton and children:-
Patsey Cotton, Patience, Delana, Wrothea Cotton 6 Oct. 1816
Page 77--To dau. Keziah Willis-6 Jan. 1817
Page 76 and 79--To Grand daughters: Miss Mary Perry and Martha

ODOM, MARTHA--Of Edgefield. Edgefield Wills A-397 Widow
Son: Elisha Watson   Wit: M. C. O'Neale
Dau: Charity Cotton   Charles O'Neale
     Patience Anderson   Elizabeth R. Hahnbaum
Gr. Dau: Patience Perry.-minor   4 Nov. 1817
Will 18 Jan. 1817.

ODOM, MARY--Dau. of John Watson-Will 4 April 1788. Also called
Martha Odom. Mary Odom--100 A. above McTears Creek
Edgefield Wills A-29/30

ODOM, NANCY--Heir of Thos. Howle, Sen'r. Edgefield Rec. Bk. B-99
Ch: John Odom (Rec't. shows John H. Odom)   1845
    Elias Odom
    George Odom
    Washington Blair -w- Martha
    James Lesure -w- Elizabeth

ODOM, RICHARD--Of Jones Co. Georgia to William Cates of Jones Co. or
of Edgefield? 100 A. in Edgefield Dist. on Little Saluda River.
Part grant to John Watson, Sr. and given by said Watson to Mary
Odom and Richard Odom. 3 Sept. 1809. Deed Bk. 35-440

ODOM, RICHARD -w- Jane--Heirs of Martha Hancock. See Hancock card.
Edgefield Rec. Bk. B-25. 1840

ODOM, THOMAS--Of Edgefield from John Longmire -w- Hannah $300.00
100 A. part of 200 A. grant to David Bell on 24 Dec. 1772.
Edgefield Deed Bk. 24-19 10 May 1802.
Page 232--Thos B. Odom to Samuel Hill 15½ A. part grant to David
Bell. 21 Jan. 1804-Deed

ODOM, WILLIAM--Of Berkley Co. To Edward Dempsey of C. T. 550 Pounds-Bond
Mtg: Tom and Judy 22 March 1762. Pres: Thos McCarthy.
Prov: 1 April 1762 before John Murray, J. P.
Hist. Comm. Misc. Mtg. ZZ-154

ODOM, WILLIAM -w- Mary of 96 Dist. to John Murphey of Fairfield Co.
Grant 1 Jan. 1785 to William Odom 100 A. on Ridge of Cloud's Cr.
Waters of Saluda River. 96 Dist. below the ancient boundary.
Edgefield Deed Bk. 6-92

ODOM, WILLIAM--From James Williams -w- Ruth--400 A. Edgefield Dist.
on Ephraim's Branch of Stephens Creek. Edgefield Deed Bk.
15-513/15 23/24 Sept. 1771
Page 518--From Wm. and Nancy Dean-20 Feb. 1790--146 A. on Small
Branches of Sleepy Creek, waters of Savannah R.

ODOM, WILLIAM, SR. to his Grand son--Deed Gift. Tillman Odom.
Wit: James Crabtree, David Youngblood. Mare, gun, bed, etc.
Edgefield Deed Bk. 31-431 6 Nov. 1812.

ODOM, WILLIS--Of Edgefield Dist. Edgefield Deed Bk. 34-426 Jan. 1817
To William Ellison of Edgefield . Mtg. Deed. No dower. 102 A.
on Stevens Creek.

OGILVIE, BENJAMIN--Darlington Co. Area. Arch. Dept. Mem. 11-219
7 May 1772 150 A. Craven on Jeffery's Creek. Bd. James Dozier,
Peter Pye, and vac. Cert: 9 Aug. 1771. Grant: 21 Feb. 1772
Mem: 7 May 1774 del. to Reuben White.

OGILVIE, CHARLES--Camden-Kershaw area. Fredericksburg Twp. Arch.
Dept. Mem. 11-344 13 Aug. 1772. 300 A. Wateree. N-side waters.
Bd. John Pain and vac. Cert: 7 April 1772. Grant: 21 May 1772
Mem: 13 Aug. 1772

OGILVIE, CHARLES--Mem. 2-402 5 May 1775. 400 A. Beaufort.

OGILVIE, ELIJAH--Indent X-3965-Militia duty under Col. Jacob Buxton.
Rev. AA-5616

OGILVIE, GEORGE--Mem. 2-265. 9 Dec. 1774 400 A. Craven

OGILVIE, GEORGE--Mem. . 13-536 3 July 1775. 400 A. Craven on
Branch of Cedar Creek. Bd. N. W. James Sanders and vac. John
Winn, D. S. Also 300 A. on drains of Sandy Run Bd. N.E. John
Jenkins and vac. Cert: 9 Dec. 1774. Grant 3 May 1775.
Mem. 3 July 1775 Del. to George Ogilvie.

OGILVIE, GEORGE--13 July 1795. 900 A. Santee River. Mem. 14-8

OGILVIE, JAMES--Purchased at sale of Herman Kinsler-1783. Edgefield
  Box 38-1373

OGILVIE, JAMES, JR.--From John Mauldin of Edgefield Dist. 28 March 1803
  200 A. Dist. of Edgefield on Dry Creek of Big Creek. Part Grant
  to Paul Mazyck 7 Jan. 1772. Edgefield Deed 29-403

OGILVIE, JAMES--Dec'd. Adm. Bond 4 Feb. 1828. Edgefield Pro. Bx-22-
                                                                 777
  Dist: Penelope Cotteran and Sarah Cotteran (or Cochran)
         Nancy Ogilvie   John Ogilvie
         Mary Weston   Thos. Ogilvie's children
         Judith Malden   Elizabeth Foy
         William Ogilvie   James Ogilvie
         "Penelope and Sarah died before the sale of the land,
         each leaving a husband and children."
  Original Will--4 April 1805 (Bk. A-209
         Wife: Penelope   Ex: James Ogilvie and Nathan Norwood
         Dau: Penelope Smith   Wit: John Ogilvie
               Joshua   Prov: 31 May 1805
               Ann
               Sarah

OGILVIE, JAMES--Ded'd. R. E. Sold 1839. Edgefield Rec. Bk. A-318
  Dist: William Foy and wife 1/9 of 2/shares $23.61
         William Ogilvie-same
         John Ogilvie-same
         John Coleman and wife 1/5 and 1/9 of 2/shares $129.89
         Caleb Maldin and wife- 1/0 of 2/shares
         Chesley Cocheran and wife 1/9 of 2/shares and 1/5
         C. W. Cochran and wife-same
         James and Thomas Ogilvie 1/9 of 2/shares
  Rec't. by P. S. S. Ogilvie for the share of his grand father's
  estate to his mother, Margaret Ogilvie--21 Oct. 1839.
  Rec't. by Zadock D. Cottrell for part of his wife, Eliza, dau.
  of Thos. Ogilvie, dec'd.
  Margaret Ogilvie--Mother and Gdn. of P. S. S. Ogilvie, Rebecca
  and William Ogilvie

OGILVIE, JAMES--Dec'd. Edgefield Pro. Bx. 21-771. Cit: 8 Nov. 1839
  "I do hereby relinquish my right of Adm. on my late husband's
  James Ogilvie's estate to John S. Jeter or William Foy or both of
  them this 11 day of Nov. 1839. E. W. Ogilvie.
  Paper in file addressed to "Mr. J. A. Bland, Edgefield Ct. House.
  Charleston P. O. Mark.
     "Bletcher left children
      Benjamin legt children
      Elizabeth and Chrower--alive
      Artemus
      Mrs. Vaughn left children
      Rachel Powers
      Rebecca
      John
      Eliza Temperance

171

OGILVIE, JAMES--Indent W-662. Duty Col. Winn's Regt. Rev. AA-5617

OGYLVIE, JOANNAH--Of Edgefield to her brother Gayle Hampton--P. A.
to dispose of land in Matterson Co. Va. 365 A. willed to me by
George Nevel, dec'd. of Fauqueer Co, Va. 4 Jan. 1799.
Wit: Lucy ____? andMary Pardue. Edgefield Deed 16-169

OGILVIE, JOANNA--called Hoanna Hampton from Job Glover 16 Sept. 1810
$200.00--160 A. Part grant to Samuel Glover and came to Job
Glover by heirship on Horse Creek. Dower: Mary J. Glover.
Edgefield Deed 30-270
Same Card: James Ogilvie, et al Deed 43-304 Trustees from
Wm. Foy f A. on Red Bank Creek of Little Saluda.

OGILVIE, JOHN ALEXANDER -w- Elizabeth Mary--formerly of C. T. now of
Co. of Surry. P. A. James Gardner. Misc. 5C-358

OGILVIE, JOHN--Indent Q-551. Rev. AA-5618
"Gentlemen: Please to deliver my two Indents and an Indent belonging to estate of William Person, dec'd, with the interest.
to bearer hereby, Mr. James Ogilvie, Philip Pleasant, Camden
Dist. 7 June 1785.

OGILVIE, JOHN W. -m- set 1 Dec. 1852 Mary E. Moze. Mar. Bk. 18-123

OGILVIE, MARY--Dec'd. Cit: 14 Jan. 1815 Adm: Thos J. Cook
S: Lewis Matthews, Sampson Pope. Edgefield Prob. Bx-22-790

OGILVIE, RICHARD--Prev. Rev. Plats Arch Dept.
200 A. Granville 5 Decl 1769--NE side Savannah R. on Dean's Swp.
William
400 A. Granville 4 Nov. 1772 on Rocky Br-Penny's Cr. Bd. by
Edward Thomas
Benjamin
6 Aug. 1771 on Jeffrey's Creek
James
3 Dec. 1771 200 A. Craven N/s Broad River.
Elijah
350 A. Granville 6 Sept. 1763
153 A. Fork Broad and Saluda. 7 Oct. 1755. Cert: 14 April 1756

OGILVIE, THOMAS--Will 25 Dec. 1825. Edgefield Bx-21-768
Wife: Margaret--Qual. as Ex.
Children: Philip, Rachel, Mary, Elizabeth, William

OGILVIE, THOMAS--No dower to Bartholomew Still 218 A. Waters of Turkey
Creek 8 Oct. 1823. Wit: Daniel Bullock and John Price
Edgefield Deed Bk. 40-460

OGLE, WILLIAM--Of Edgefield Dist. Edgefield Will
Son: Hercules   26 Feb ___?
Dau: Rebecca Carter   Rec'd. June 19, 1803
Gr. son: William Carter.

O'Harrow, James--Overseer 1/2 of road from Amos Richardson's to Chappell's Bridge in room of Amos Richardson. Edgefield Ct. Min. March 1795.

O'HARD (sp?) JAMES -w- Cynthia mentioned in Will of John Ryan-Will 1827 Jane Cobb and John S. Cobb-mentioned also-jointly. Edgefield

OHARA, JAMES--Dec'd. R. E. Sold 1835. Edgefield Rec. Bk. A-217
Dist: Rebecca O'Hara-widow 1/3 $8.70
Allen M. O'Hara 1/5 of 2/3 $3.48
Arthur Watson -w- Ophelia-same
William E. O'Hara-same
Frederick I O'Hara-same
Bennet M. Strozier -w- Martha

OLIPHANT, ANN_-Dau. of John Frazier-Will 1799. Rec'd. 1801

OLIVER, STEPHEN P. -m- Mary Lark-dau. of John Lark-Will 1822.

OLIVER, DYONISUS, JR.--Son of Seaborn Oliver, dec'd. and Legatee of Martha Hancock-Will 1827. Edgefield

ONEALE, CHARLOTTE--Dau. of John Abney-Will 1812. Edgefield

O'NEALL, J. B.--Brother in law of George Pope-Will 1843. Edgefield

O'NEALL, JOHN--Married Demaris Rushton--Heirs of Joseph Rushton. See Rushton card. Edgefield Rec. Bk. B-101 1846

OSBORNE, HON. JUDGE HENRY -m- Catherine Howell-spinster of Augusta. License--20 Aug. 1798. By Hon. Judge George Walton. Ordinary Ct. Minutes Bk. Augusta, Ga.

OSBORN, EDWARD -w- Nancy--Heirs of Catherine Butler. See Butler card. Edgefield Rec. Bk. A-298

OUTZ, LOUIZA--Dau. of William Holloway-Will 1838. Edgefield

OUTZ, MARTHA HILL--Wife of Daniel Outz, Sen'r. Dau. of Conrad and Amina H. Lowrey. B. April 21, 1826. D. April 5, 1865. Mother of D. A. G. Outz--only son.

OVERSTREET, JOHN -w- Heirs estate of George Carline. See Carline card. Edgefield Rec. Bk. A-42 1834

OWENS, ANN--Heir of Daniel Bruner. See Bruner card. Edgefield Rec. Bk. A-34 1834

OWENSBY, SARAH--Sister of Samuel Tomkins-Will 1826. Edgefield

OZBURN, NANCY--Gr. dau. of John Lucas-Will 1799 and dau. of Rachel Lucas Ozburn.

PACE, DRURY--Petit Juror Edgefield 1788. List 11

PACE, DRURY and Elisha Robinson. Edgefield Min. Bk. 1790.-- Umpires in suit by Ebenezer Hill. See Hill -vs- Johnson

PACE, CHARLES LEE--Edgefield
    Dread William
    Permetta Jackson
    Bartlett Barnet--Children of dec'd. Bathena Pace -w- William
    Pace of Georgia. Gr. children of Christopher Cox-Will 1813

PACKMAN, HENRY -w- Mary Ann--Heirs estate of Lewis Glanton. See
    Glanton card. Edgefield Rec. Bk. B-206 1851

PADGETT, DRYDEN--Dec'd. R. E. Sold 1849. Edgefield Rec. Bk. B-165
    Dist: Eliza Padgett-widow 1/3 $239.45
           Sarah Ann-1/3 of 2/3
           Susan Padgett-same   Manchester Padgett, Exor.
           Nancy Elvira-same

PADGETT, HENRY--Dec'd. R. E. Sold 1835. Edgefield Rec. Bk. A-211
    Dist: Penelope Padgett-widow 1/3 $477.02. Living in Bartow
           County, Alabama 1h Jan. 1837. (Widow)   Barbour?
    Samuel, Ezekiel, and Westly Padgett
    Martin Whittle and wife   1/11 of 2/3 each $86.73
    Samuel Johnson and wife
    Henry, Lucy, Chesly, Luke, Permelia, Josiah--All minors

PADGET, JOB--Dec'd. R. E. Sold 1839. Edgefield Rec. Bk. A-312
    Dist: Job and Chesly Padget
           Heirs of Sarah Jones
           Richard Yarbrough -w- Mary   Each 1/10 $67.00
           Heirs of Margaret Whittle
           Thomas Bonds -w- Malinda
           Thomas Bowers -w- Deborah
           William McGehee -w- Jane
           Abraham Hurst -w- Abigail
           William Padget
    Rec'ts by: Seaborn Jones; A. P. Jones; Alexander Jones; Simpson
                Jones; Amanda Jones; and John Jones--1843
    Rec't. 17 Feb. 1843--Joel F. Warren -w- Mary
    Rec't. by James Whittle for share of his son Sampson Whittle
    Rec't. by Mary Ann Whittle 1851 for her part Sampson's share.
    Rec't. by Nancy and Henry Rucker 1851

PADGETT, MALON -w- Polly--Heirs of James Eidson. See Eidson card.
    Edgefield Rec. Bk. B-125 1847

PALATTY, BARBERRY--Dau. of John Fleke-Will 1798.

PALMER, ELISHA--Acknowledged deed of 100 A. conv. to John Huffman-
    recorded. Edgefield Ct. Min. March 1795
    -Elisha Palmer--See Will of John Rees-1804.

PALMER, THOMAS--Petit Juror 1787. List 8

PARISH, JOHN -w- Elizabeth--Heirs of William Rodgers, Sr. See Rogers
    card. Edgefield Rec. Bk. B-148. 1848

PARKER, FELIX -w- Margaret--Heirs of Thomas Nixon. See Nixon card.
    Edgefield Rec. Bk. B-93. 1845

PARKER, JOSEPH and BENJAMIN--Legatees of William Robertson-Will 1840
"In accordance with promise made to my last wife".

PARKER, LYDIA--Gave Bond to appear in Court. Rice Swearingen, Surety.
Edgefield Ct. Min. Oct. 1794

PARKER, SALLY, JAMES H., MARK T.,--Grand children of James Smith, Sr.
Will 1823. Edgefield

PARKMAN, HENRY--Petit Juror Edgefield 1789. List 17

PARKMAN, JOSEPH -w- Peggy--Heirs estate of Elizabeth Falkner. See
Falkner card. Edgefield Rec. Bk. B-182. 1850

PARNELL, ANGELICA--Dau. of Angelica Jernagen-Will 1796. And her son:
Jacob Parnell

PART, JERUSHA--Legatee and seems dau. of Jacob Smith-Will 1805.

PARTIN, BENJAMIN -w- Ellen
       SPEAR -w- Holly
       BENJAMIN, SR. -w- Sarah
       John and James-children of Lucy Partin--Heirs of Philip
       Jennings. See Jennings card. Edgefield Rec. Bk. B-185. 1850

PARTIN, CHARLES--Petit Juror Edgefield 1786. List 4

PARTIN, CHARLES--Default in road work. See Lodwick Hill. Edgefield
Ct. Min. March 1795.

PARTLOW, SUSANNAH--Dau. of William Dozier-Will 1810

PARTRIDGE, HENRY and wife--Heirs of Joseph West. See West card.
Edgefield Rec. Bk. A-66 1836

PATRICK, HANNAH--Dau. of Andrew Lee-Will 1795. Edgefield

PATRICK, SARAH--Heir of Joseph West. See West card. Edgefield Rec.
Bk. A-66 1836

PAYNE, MARY AND ADELINE--Grand daughters of Hannah McGinnis-Will 1825
Dau: Hester Payne Son in law: Jesse Payne.

PAYNE, MARY--Dau. of David Richardson-Will 1842. Wife of David Payne.

PAYNE, REBECCAH F.--Dau. of Philip Burt-Will 1829. Son in law: James
Payne. Edgefield

PAYNE, TEMPERANCE--Dau. of Lewis Matthews-Will 1824. Edgefield

PAYNE, WILLIAM, JR.--Gr. son of William Robinson. Will 1820.

PEAK, JOSEPH and wife--Heirs of Lazarus Chadwick. See Chadwick card.
Edgefield Rec. Bk. A-86

PEARCE, ISAAC -m- Henrietta Grubber. License: 6 Aug. 1791
By: Wm. Lee, Esq. Augusta Ga. Ordinary Ct. Min. Bk-2

PEAY, HENRY C. -w- Mary--Heirs of Thomas Broom, dec'd. Edgefield
Rec. Bk. A-239 1835

PEEBLES, D. R. -w- Caroline--Heirs of Wiley Posey. See Posey card.
Edgefield Rec. Bk. B-202 1850

PEGRAM, ELIZABETH--Mother in law of Stephen Mays-Will 1813

PENNEL, CAROLINE -w- Dr. Wm. S. Pennel and dau. of John Key. Also:
ELIZABETH -w- Dr. Alec Pennel (or Seannel)

PENNINGTON, EZEKIEL--Edgefield Deed 18-454 1799. No dower.
To Morris Callihan-part grant to Sanford Urziah on Turkey and
Stephens Creeks. Plat. Sold to John Kilcrease, son-Minor
Kilcrease.
37-215--Richard Pennington to Samuel Stalmaker--Mtg-Cattle, etc.

PENNINGTON, MARTHA--Dau. of Elizabeth Bennett-Will 1820

PENNINGTON, THOMAS--Petit Juror Edgefield 1787. List 7 and 16

PENNINGTON, THOMAS--Schoolmaster--Edgefield Inventories A-1803 Pg-94
Inv. and Appr. 18 Oct. 1799. Pur: Ezekiel Pennington and a
long list.

PERKINS, ELIZABETH, CASSANDRA, MILTON--Legatees of Thomas Peterson.
Will 1827. Edgefield

PERKINS, MILTON and wife--former widow?--Heirs of Abner Mays. See
Mays card. Edgefield Rec. Bk. A-276. 1827
-Edgefield Rec. Bk. A-298 1838--Milton Perkins and wife, Catherine
Heirs of Catherine Butler. See Butler card.

PERIN, ABNER--Grand Juror Edgefield 1786. List 1, 2, 4, 10, 14, 20

PERRIN, GEORGE--Grand Juror Edgefield 1794. List 22

PERRIN, WILLIAM--Will proved by oath of Thomas Littleton. Abner Perrin
one of Exors. Qualified. Edgefield Min. Bk. Pg-111 9 Oct. 1787

PERRY, MARY--Dau. of James Rutherford-Will 1797. Mary living in
Wake County, N. C. Dau. Elizabeth Perry-living in Nash Co. N. C.

PERRY, MARY--Dau. of Benjamin Hightower-Will Rec'd. 1824

PERRY, PATIENCE--Grand daughter of Martha Odom-Will 1817.

PERRY, SIMEON and wife--Heirs of Aaron Moore 1812. Deed 31-77 Edgefield.

PETERS, JORDAN--Dist. estate of Abraham Cruise. See Cruise card.
Edgefield Rec. Bk. A-24 1825

PETERSON, MRS. CHARLOTTE--Dau. in law of Joicy Culpepper-Will 1837.
*Charlotte Peterson--Dau. of David Richardson-Will 1842

PETERSON, MARTHA--Dau. of Paul Abney-Will 1814

PEY, NANCY--Heir of Daniel Bruner. Edgefield Rec. Bk. A-34 1834

PHELPS, SETH -w- Susan--Heirs of Wiley Posey. See Posey card.
    Edgefield Rec. Bk. B-202 1850

PHELPS, SUSAN--Dau. of William C. Posey-Will 1834.

PHILLIPS, CHARLOTTE--Dec'd. Dau. of William Jeter-Will 1818.

PHILIPS, HILORY--Petit Juror Edgefield 1786. List 4 (Philps)

PHILLIPS, JOSEPH--Will 17 Mar. 1836. Edgefield

PHILLIPS, POLLEY--Dau. of John Hatcher-Will 1825. Edgefield (Polley A.)

PHOENIX, FREDERICK--Dec'd. R. E. Sold. Edgefield Rec. Bk. A-8
    Dist: Eliza, Drury, Nancy, Maria, and James--1/5 of 2/3 each
    Jacob Youngblood-Gdn. Receipts by his as Gdn. Mentions amounts
    received from John Simkins as Ordinary, and also amounts received
    from John Butler. Rec'ts: 5 Feb. 1828--1 Oct. 1828 Rec't. from
    Thomas S. Youngblood.
    PROBATE RECORDS--Frederick Phenix--Box 23 831. Only Phenix on Bk.
    Rec't. Bk. A shows sale of R. E. 7 May, 1827. Dist. same as
    above.
    Shows Elizabeth Kirksey (probably wife of Thomas Kirksey) their
    mother, and Jacob Youngblood, Gdn. of Maria and James.
    Thomas S. Youngblood was Surety on a Bond in this case.
    Deed Bk. 36-49 Shows: Elizabeth Phenis to her children--Nancy,
    Drury, Eliza, Maria, William, and James- all right of Dower in
    Estate of the late Frederick Phenix. 30 Dec. 1818.
    Widow-Elizabeth-married Thomas Kirksey as shown by Probate Rec.

PIASTER, JOHN -m- Frances Adams-dau. Marian Adams. 1842. See Adams
    card. Edgefield Rec. Bk. B-61

PICKENS, ANDREW--Appointed Adm. estate James Moore. See Moore card.
    Edgefield Ct. Min. March 1795.
    -Andrew Pickens--Will 9 Sept. 1834

PICKENS, F. W.--Son in law of Eliza Hannah Simkins-Will 1837.

PICKENS, FRANCIS W.-m- Margaret Eliza-dau. of Eldred Simkins, Sr.
    Will 1831. Edgefield

PICKET, JAMES--Dec'd. R. E. Sold 1839. Edgefield Rec. Bk. A-306
    Dist: Nancy Picket, widow 1/3 $122.90
           Mary Picket   James Picket
           Elizabeth Haws   Susan Picket
           Joicy Brown   David George -w- Milly
           Jerome Con -w- Louisa   Richard Garrett -w- Martha
           Thomas Corley -w- Lucy   Each rec. 1/9 of 2/3 $27.31

PICKET, SARAH--Dau of James. Legatee of John Searle-Will 1820

PITCHER, LEMUEL -w- Mary Jane--Heirs of Mrs. Wormley. See Wormley card.
    Edgefield Rec. Bk. B-71

177

PITTS, JOSEPH--Dec'd. (Son of Thomas, see card) Edgefield Prob. 23-835
    Mary Pitts, Adm'x. and David B. Williams, Adm'r. David Williams
    evidently married the widow.
    Cit: 31 July 1826   Bond: 21 Aug. 1826
    S: Moses Holston and Wade Holston
    Children: Eliza, Middleton, and Joseph--Clothing and boarding.
    Paid Middleton Pitts his share 1845
    Paid Thomas Youngblood for his share 1845
    Mary Pitts, Adm'x. rendered final accounts in 1845
    Mary Williams, Adm'x. return in 1828

PITTS, SARAH--Dec'd. Edgefield Prob. 23-838 Cit: 4 Sept. 1820
    Adm'rs: Jesse Pitts, sd Jane B. Pitts, and John Eidson, Jr.
    S: John Rogers, Sampson Butler
    Mentions: Jane B. Pitts, Nesly Pitts, and Jane Pitts-seems widow.

PITTS, THOMAS, Dec'd. Edgefield Prob. 22-804 Cit: 12 Sept. 1823
    Adm'r: Thomas Pitts, Jr. appointed. Joseph Pitts, Pet'd.
    S: Jesse Jay; and Boling Bishop
    Paid: Nathan Rowland   Paid Adm. Joseph Pitts his
           Daniel Pitts   dist. share
           William Whitley
           Lewis Whitley
           Janey Wheeler
           William Pitts
           Mary Pitts

PLUMMER, ASA -w- Dempsey--Heirs of John Rogers. See Rogers card.
    Edgefield Rec. Bk. A-324 1839

POLLARD, BETTY--Dau. of William White--Will 1799

POND, MARY--Grand daughter of Mary Daly-Will 1832. Men. Wm. Pond

POND, WILLIAM--Dec'd. R. E. Sold 1835. Edgefield Rec. Bk. A-235
    Dist: Lucy Pond, widow 1/3 $167.75
           William; Daniel; Henry; Richard Pond
           Seaborn Kirk -w- Jiney   1/9 of 2/3 each.
           Fielding and John Pond
           Wm. W. Day (for Wiley Harvey -w- Nancy
           Jesse Bartee and his 5 children:-
               Seaborn I., Lewis W., Thomas P., Eliza A., and Charles E.
           Sold to William W. Day.

POOL, JOHN--Road Overseer. See card Young Allen. Edgefield Ct. Oct. 1794

POPPINO, MARY--Alias Mary Kelly, dec'd. See Kelly card. Edgefield
    Rec. Bk. B-171. 1849

POPE, MRS. CHARLOTTE--Sister in law of Joel Abney-Will 1811

POPE, GEORGE--Will 5 Jan. 1843. Edgefield

POPE, JACOB--Petit Juror Edgefield 1786. List 4

POPE, MARGARET--Dau. of Frederick Williams-Will

POPE, SOLOMON--Grand Juror Edgefield 1786. List 4, 8, 18, and 19

POPE, SOLOMON--Dec'd. Will proven by oaths of Demsey Weaver and
William Cane. John Pope and Wiley Pope qualified as Exors.
Apprs: John Duglas, John Salter, Wm. Little, Lodwick Hill.
Edgefield Ct. Min. Jan. 1795

POPE, SOLOMON LEWIS--Minor. Sally Pope-Gdn. Gdnship granted 24 Sept.
1813. Edgefield Prob. Bk. A-2

POPE, WILLIAM, JOHN, SUSANNA, AND MARY ELLEN--children of Drury
Matthews-Will 1828. Brother in law-John Pope.

PORTER, RHODA--Dau. of Elles Palmer-Will 1800

PORTOR, PERMILIA--Dau. of Elizabeth M. Ray-Will 1817.

POSEY, ELDRED -w- Hannah--Heirs estate of Ransom Hamilton. See
Hamilton card. Edgefield Rec. Bk. B-107 1846

POSEY, FRANCES--Dec'd. Will proved by Elijah Walker and Benjamin
Posey. Absolum Posey qual. as Exor. Edgefield Ct. Min. Page 138
14 Jan. 1788

POSEY, WILEY--Dec'd. R. E. Sold 1850. Edgefield Rec. Bk. B-202
Dist: Elizabeth Posey, widow 1/3 $143.37
Benjamin, Mark, and Eldridge Posey
Harriet -w- William Toney $40.96 each
Susan -w- Seth Phelps
Caroline -w- D. R. Peebles
Martha Posey-a minor-Malachi Cogburn, Gdn.
Rec't. by Malachi Cogburn for share of his wife Louiza 18 March 185?

POSEY, WILLIAM--Dec'd. R. E. Sold 1838. Edgefield Rec. Bk. A-284
Dist: Mark, Eldredge, Benjamin and Wiley Posey 1/4 each $256.73
William Toney, Gdn. of minors.

POUND, JOHN--Petit Juror Edgefield 1789. List 14

POVERY, CATHERINE--Dau. of Elizabeth Zinn-Will 1793

POW (E), ROBERT--Petit Juror Edgefield 1786. List 4

POWELL, CHARLES P. -w- Martha--Heirs of Martha Hancock. See card Jane
Odom. Also James M. Powell -w- Tyrzah. Edgefield Rec. Bk. B-25
                                                                      1839
POWELL, CHARLES -w- Ellsey--Heirs of Charity Johnson. Edgefield Rec.
Bk. B-161. 1849

POWELL, EDMOND--Petit Juror Edgefield 1787. List 6

POWELL, JAMES M. -w- Tyrzah--Heirs of Martha Hancock. Also Charles
P. Powell -w- Martha. Edgefield Rec. Bk. B-25. 1840

POWELL, MILLY--Dec'd. R. E. Sold. Edgefield Rec. Bk. A-20 May 1825
Dist: Roland, Reison, Elizabeth, and Mary Powell-1/4 each. $50.51
D. A. Mitchell, Atty. in fact for heirs gave receipt 5 Feb. 1808

POWER, JANE--Widow of John Power, and heir of. Edgefield Prob. 178-9
  Mary, Charlotte,Jane, and Georgianna--Nieces of.   1856
  Lucy T. Moore-Will 1856.

POWERS, WILLIAM -w- Elizabeth--Heirs of William Chapman. See Chapman.
  Edgefield Rec. Bk. A-160 1833

PRATER, EDWARD--Dec'd. Appl. for Let. by Sarah Prater. 16 July 1791
  Augusta, Ga. Ordinary Ct. Min. Bk. Pg-1

PRATOR, MARY ANN--Dau. of Joseph Griffith-Will 1810

PRESSLY, MARY--Dau. of Sarah Wise-Will 1837. Son in law-Enoch Pressly.

PRICE, MARTHA--Legatee of Henry Clark-Will 1840. Seems his niece.

PRICE, PHEREBY--Widow of Daniel Price. Dau. Christopher Cox, Sr.
  Will 1817.

PRICE, SUSANNAH--Legatees of Thomas Anderson-Will 1795

PRICE, THOMAS--Son in law of William Robertson-Will 1812.

PRICE, WILLIAM -w- Jane--Heirs of John Bracknell, Dec'd. Edgefield
  Rec. Bk. B-176. 1849

PRINCE, EDWARD--Petit Juror Edgefield 1787. List 8

PRINCE, DANIEL--Will 16 July, 1843.

PRINCE, JOHN--Gr. son of John E. Turner-Will 1843.

PRINCE, JOSEPH--Legatee of George Mock, Sen'r. Will 1790

PRINCE, JOSEPH and wife--Heirs of Sawney McKie. See McKie card.
  Edgefield Rec. Bk. A-114 1832

PRINT, DUDLY--Petit Juror Edgefield 1787. List 7

PRIOR, TOBIAS and wife--Heirs of Daniel Bruner. Edgefield Rec. Bk. A-34
                                                                      1834
PROSSER, ELIZABETH--Heir of Robert Starke. See Starke card. Edgefield
  Rec. Bk. B-71 1842

PUCKET, DANIEL--Son of Elizabeth Mackquarter -w- Moses Mackquarter-
  Will 1797.

PULLY, THOMAS--Petit Juror Edgefield 1789. List 14

PURSEL, EDWARD--Petit Juror Edgefield 1790. List 17

PURSEL, JOHN--Petit Juror Edgefield 1788. List 10

PURCEL, JOHN--Dec'd. Edgefield Ct. Min. March 1795. Inv. Returned.
  Jan. Ct. 1795--Will "further approved" by oath of Ebenezer Hill.

PURSLEY, DORCAS--See Will of Benjamin Harry, Sr. 1810. He names his wife: Dorcas Pursley-he also names his wife Hannah Harry.

PURSLEY, JOHN, WILLIAM, MOSES, ANDREW--See Will of John Clackler, Sr. 1790. Edgefield

PURSSELL, MARTHA--Dau. of Micajah Phillips-Will 1811. Zacheus Pursell an Exor.

PURSELL, WILLIAM--Dec'd. R. E. Sold 1839. Edgefield Rec. Bk. A-320
Dist: Rolon A. Duck -w- Mary 1/3 $60.83
Edmond Purcell)
Alexander ") Minors--2/3 equal to $40.56 each. R. A. Duck, Gdn.
Tappenus ")

PURVIS, MARY SARAH--See card William Anderson. Edgefield Rec. Bk. A-15

QUARLES, LUCY--Dau. of John Sullivan-Will 1836

QUARLES, MARTHA--Dau. of Robert Harrison-Will 1827

QUARLES, MARY AND SUSANNAH--Grand daughters Allen Anderson, Sr. Will 1828
QUARLES, NANCY--Dau. Samuel Gardner-Will 1801. Wife of Wm. Quarles.

QUARLES, RICHARD--Petit Juror Edgefield 1789. List 15
-Richard Quarles--Surety for Alexander Cowan as Tavern Keeper.
Edgefield Ct. Min. March 1795.

QUARLES, SAMUEL--Heir of James Jamrtin. See Martin card. Edgefield Rec. Bk. A-72. 1831

QUARLES, SARAH--Dau. of Mary L. Yeldell-Will 1835.

QUARLES, WILLIAM G. -w- Elizabeth of Loundes Co. Alabama, and Wm. O. Quarles-minor--Heirs of Ellen Sullivan, dec'd. Edgefield Rec. Bk. B-111 1847

QUATTLEBAUM, DAVID--Dec'd. Partition Suit in Equity. Cit. to Appear
Rose Ann Quattlebaum, widow 1/3   10 Aug. 1846
Children: John,P.; Joseph; William; Henry M.;)(1/10 of 2/3 and
          Sarah C. Harmon   )(1/6 of 1/10 each
          George; James and Nancy C. Quattlebaum. 1.10 of 2/3
Land on Coffeetown Creek. Bd. by John Anderson, E. B. Belcher,
S. H. Mundy, and john Rush

QUATTLEBAUM, JAMES A. B. 30 Jan. 1840 D. 6 May 1864. Entered Confederate Service. Was killed Wilderness fight.--Quattlebaum Grave Yard--Sleepy Creek Road, Edgefield

QUATTLEBAUM, JOHN--Petit Juror Edgefield 1787. List 8

QUATTLEBAUM, COL. JOHN--B. 27 Aug. 1807 D. 13 Dec. 1865
Age: 58 yrs. 3 mos. 16 days. Quattlebaum Grave yard, Edgefield

QUATTLEBAUM, PHILIP--Heir of J. J. Still. See Still card. Equity Roll 1849

QUATTLEBAUM, WM. -w- Mary--Heirs of Jacob Miller. See Miller card. Edgefield Rec. Bk. A-115 1846.

181

RABURN, HANNAH--Dau. of Charles Partin-Will 1796. Rec'd. 1813

RAGSDALE, JANE--Sister of Dionisious Oliver-Will 1816

RAIDFORD, ELIZABETH--Dau. of John Lark-Will 1824. Wm. Raidford, Exor.

RAINSFORD, JAMES--Heir of Lucy T. Moore-Will 1856. Edgefield Wills
    Bx-178-9 1856

RAINSFORD, TABITHA--Dau. of John Huff-Will 1815

RAINSFORD, THOMAS--Will 5 April 1834

RAMAGE, JAMES--Will 28 March 1837

RAMBO, ALBERT--Grand son of Mary Daly-Will. Augusta Rambo, also.
    Matilda Rambo, Gdn.

RAMBO, DANIEL-vs- Henry Dana Artemus Word--Richland Co. Ga. Bills-163
    Alleges: Lawrence Rambo, father of Plaintiff, deceased was joint
    owner of lands with Henry Dana. File contains plat showing
    division among--"Daniel Rambo, the only living child and heir at
    law of Lawrence Rambo, dec'd. and Henry Dana Artimus Word, only
    legal heir of Henry Dana Word, dec'd. Lands on N-Edisto River.
    Shows: Henry Dana Word of Columbia, Lawrence Rambo of Black Cr.
    Lands in Orangeburg. Henry Dana Artemus Word-a minor-filed ans.
    by Gdn. alleging his father died in 1817. File contains many
    Plats, Receipts, letters, etc.

RAMBOW, JOSEPH B. -w- Jincy--Heirs of Jesse Stone. See Stone card.
    Edgefield Rec. Bk. B-45. 1842

RAMBO, LAWRENCE--Of Granville Co. 96 Dist. Will 11 June 1775. 96 Dist.
    Eldest son: Reuben
                Lawrence, Benega, Joseph
        Daus: Ellender, Elizabeth, Rebecca, Margueretta
                Ruth Herndon

RAMBO, LAWRENCE--Petit Juror Edgefield 1786. List 5

RAMBO, LAWRENCE -w- Jancy--Heirs of Philip Lightfoot. See Lightfoot
    card. Edgefield Rec. Bk. B-65. 1842

RAMBO, MARY--Widow of Lawrence and Benajah Rambo -w- Rachel--Edgefield
    Deed Bk. 2-14. 1787.
    Bk. 15-511-2 June 1798--Rachel Rambo to her children: James;
    Lawrence; Polly; Sarah; Rachel.
    -Mrs. Mary Rambo -w- Lawrence Rambo--Dower favor Stephen Tilman.
    April Ct. 1787. Edgefield Min. Bk.

RAMBO, RACHEL -w- Benaja Rambo relinquished dower. Edgefield Min. 1785-7
    Page 131--Reuben Rambo -vs- Lewis Nobles--1787
    -Oct. Ct. 1786 Edgefield Min. Rachel Rambo-dower favor Samuel Doolittle
    -Jan. Ct. 1786--Rachel Rambo-dower favor Wm. Dobey.
    -July Ct. 1787--Rachel Rambo--Dower favor Fielding Renolds.

RANEY
RAMEY, REBECCA--Dec'd. R. E. Sold 1842. Edgefield Rec. Bk. B-75
    Dist: Newel Tullis and wife 1/5 $74.00
           Thos. Garrett -w- Nancy of Cherokee Co. Ala. 1/5
           Hezekiah Edwards and wife 1/5
           Andey Reynolds and wife 1/5
           Heirs of Mary Brooks--each 1/4 of 1/5 $18.50
               Briant Meek -w- Martha
               William Brooks, John Brooks, Francis Brooks
    Receipt received of O. Towles, Esq. Ordinary for Edgefield Dist.
    S. C. Eighteen Dollars 50 cents in full of my Distributive share
    in the Real Estate of my grandmother, Rebecca Raney, dec'd.
    Said: Lemuel Morriss, Martha Morriss

RAMPEY, JAMES -w- Martha--Heirs estate of Robert Etheredge. See
    Etheredge card. Edgefield Rec. Bk. A-173. 1834

RAMPY, PETER--Petit Juror Edgefield 1786. List 1, 2, 6, 17. Name
    also spelled (on card) Rappy, and Rambey

RAMPY, PETER, SEN'R.--Will 16 Oct. 1843

RAMSEY, EPHRAIM--On motion of Charles Goodwin, Esq., Ephraim Ramsey,
    Esq. was introduced to this Bar and enrolled as an attorney, he
    having promised to produce his credentials to the next court.
    Edgefield Min. Bk. Pg-259. 15 July 1780

RAMSEY, JAMES--Petit Juror Edgefield 1787. List 6

RAMSEY, MARY--Dau. of Nathaniel Henderson-Will 1801

RAMSEY, SAMUEL--Grand Juror Edgefield 1786. List 1, 2, 5, and 10

RAMSEY, SAMUEL--Dec'd. Edgefield Min. Bk. Page 231. 12 Jan. 1789.
    Adm. granted to Elinor Ramsey, widow of deceased.
    S: Thomas Anders and John Harkins

RAMSEY, THOMAS -w- Druzilla--Heirs estate of William Gray. See Gray
    card. Edgefield Rec. Bk. A-40 1829

RANDALL, GEORGE -w- Phoebe--Heirs of Robert Roebuck. See Roebuck card.
    Edgefield Equity Roll 30 1821

RANDOL, JOHN -w- Mary of 96 Dist to Jacob Wooten 1787 Deed Bk. 2-36
    Deed Bk. 5-20--John Randal of Winton Co. to Wm. Day 1787
    Bk. 3 193/223--John Randol -w- Mary to John Hammond 1758
    Bk. 6 167/173--George Randol -w- Phebe 1792
    Bk. 8 193/9   "   "   Grant 4 March 1793

RANDOLPH, GEORGE -w- Phoebe--Heirs of Robert Roebuck. See Roebuck
    card. Edgefield Equity Roll 30 1801 (Name possibly Randall)

RANDOLPH, JAMES and Eliza Ann--Heirs of Richard Tutt. See Tutt card.
    Edgefield Rec. Bk. A-126 about 1820

RANEY, ELENOR--Dau. of Henry King-Will 1820

RANKIN, DAVID -w- _____?
    JAMES -w- Harriet--Heirs estate of Jonathan Gregory. See
Gregory card. Edgefield Rec. Bk. A-187/9 1834

RASTOW, JAMES--Petit Juror Edgefield 1787. List 6

RATLIFF, RICHARD--From Joseph Ashton Pr. Shff. dec'd. 5 Oct. 1812.
    700 A. Waters Horn's Creek. Edgefield Deed 31-178/9
    Page 185--Richard Ratliff -w- Anna to Lewis Cantelou. Land
formerly conv. by John Martin and Joseph Ashton. 1812

RAWDON, TIMOTHY--Petit Juror Edgefield 1789. List 13

RAY, _____? -w- Susan--Heirs of Philip Jennings. See Jennings card.
Edgefield Rec. Bk. B-185 1850

RAY, ELIZABETH MARABLE--Dau. of Francis Jones-Will 1800

RAY, HENRY -w- Elizabeth -- To Masten Smith 22 Aug. 1797. Edgefield
    Deed Vol. 15-3

RAY, LUCY--Dau. John Bailey-Will 1842. Gr. dau. Nancy Ray.

REAMS, GEORGE and wife--Heirs of Jordan Holloway. See Holloway card.
    Edgefield Rec. Bk. A-270 1837

REARDON, TIMOTHY -w- Harsey--Heirs estate of Francis Bird. Also Benj.
    Reardon -w- Abbey heirs same estate. Edgefield Rec. Bk. B-131
                                     1848
REAVES, ANNA and children--Heirs of William Ferguson. See Ferguson
    card. Edgefield Rec. Bk. B-208.. 1851

REDDICK, MARGARET--Dau. of Ann Clark-Niece of Ulric Tobler-Will 1815
    Wife of Peter Reddick.
    -Margaret Reddick--Dau. of John Clark, Sr. Will 1821. Her children;
    Ulrick, Sarah, and James Reddick.

REDICK, ULRIC--Legacy in trust for Sarah, dau. of Casper Nail-Will 1833

REDFIELD, ISZZA--Brother in law of Thomas G. Lamar-Will 1830

REED, SUSANNAH--Dau. Daniel Rogers-Will 1809

REID, JOHN RYAN--Son of Doctor R. Reid and legatee of John Ryan-Will 1827
    Legatee: Lacon Ryan-son Benj. Ryan.

REESE, JAMES -w- Lucy--dau. of Lewis Holloway-died 1814. Edgefield
    Bills 914 975

REESE, JUDAH--Dau. Ellen Palmer-Will 1800. Gr-child-Thomas Reese

REESE, SARAH--Dau. of John Clacker-Will 1814

REYNOLDS, ANDEY and wife--Heirs of Rebecca Ramey. See Ramey.
    Edgefield Rec. Bk. B-75 1842

REYNOLDS, ELIZABETH -w- Fielding Reynolds--Dower favor of John Herndon.
    Jan. Ct. Edgefield Min. Bk. 1788

REYNOLDS, GEORGE -w- Elizabeth--Heirs of William Chapman. See
    Chapman card. Edgefield Rec. Bk. A-160 1833

REYNOLDS, JOHN--Gave Bond to appear in Court. Fielding Reynolds,
    Surety. Fielding Runnels-Overseer of road. See card Benj. Adams.
    Edgefield Ct. Min. Oct. 1794.

REYNOLDS, LEWIS (or Runnels)--Gdn. minor children of Jacob Goleman.
    Edgefield Rec. Bk. B-39 1841

REYNOLDS, MARY ANN--Dau. of Ann Maria Terry-Will 1823

REYNOLDS, PRISCILLA--Dau. of Joab Wooten-Will 1803

REYNOLDS, THOMAS, Sen'r.--Will 30 Aug. 1841

REYNOLDS, WESTLEY -w- Elizabeth--Heirs of Elizabeth Clark. See Clark
    card. Edgefield Rec. Bk. B-191 1849

REYNOLDS, WILLIAM--Petit Juror Edgefield 1787. List 7 and 16

REYNOLDS, WILLIAM AND WILEY--Heirs of James Harrison. See Harrison
    card. Edgefield Probate 1800. (Or Runnels)

REYNOLDS, WILLIAM AND WILEY--Gr-children of James Harrison-Will 1806

RHODES, COLEMAN -w- Harriet--Heirs of Jesse Swearingen. See Swearingen
    card. Edgefield Rec. Bk. B-87. 1845

RHODEN, JOHN (Rhodes?)--Dec'd. R. E. Sold 1844. Edgefield Rec. Bk.
    Dist: Susan Rhoden, widow 1/2 $38.04   B-91
            Patsy, Charles, George, Elijah, Nancy, William Rhoden--
            Lucy Holliday formerly Rhoden
            Dorcas Rhoden
            Patsy and Elisha Rhoden--1/10 of 1/2 share each-$3.80
            (First Patsy referred to as "the elder").

RODES, MRS. FRANCIS--Wife of Wm. Rodes. Dower favor Ulyses Rogers
    Oct. 1786. Edgefield Ct. Min.

RHODES, JAMES--Dec'd. R. E. Sold. Edgefield Rec. Bk. A-56
    Dist: Rice Golman -w- Druscilla
           Roland Rhodes-Rec't. 3 Oct. 1831
           Collen   "   7 Jan. 1833   Each rec. $37.22½
           Roy Ford   "   3 Mar. 1834
           Jacob Smith -w- Sally--Rec't. 11 June 1831. Formerly Sally
           Coleman Rhodes--Rec't. 3 July 1839   Rhodes
           Melton Rhodes
           Rice Golman Purchases at $282.00

RHODES, MARY--Dec'd. and her heirs--Heirs of Joseph Day. Edgefield
    Rec. Bk. A-242 about 1830

RHODES, MILTON -w- Francis H.--Heirs of Henry J. Kemp. See Kemp card.
    Edgefield Rec. Bk. B-131 1847

RHOADS, PATIENCE--Dau. of Sarah Bridges-Will 1820

RICE, ELLEN -w- Simon Rice and dau. of David A. Mitchell-Will 1841

RICHARDSON, ABRAHAM--Petit Juror Edgefield 1787. List 8 and 14

RICHARDSON, AMOS--Petit Juror Edgefield 1789. List 14
           Grand   "   "   "   "   21

RICHARDSON, DAVID--Petit Juror Edgefield 1788. List 12

RICHARDSON, DAVID--Applied for permission to keep Tavern. S: David
    Williams, and William Moore. March Ct. Amos Richardson res.
    rd. to Barry Travis. 1795

RICHARDSON, DAVID--Will 31 May 1842.

RICHARDSON, ELIZABETH--Dau. of Charles Powell.

RICHARDSON, JEFFERSON*Will 23 Dec. 1835

RICHARDSON, WILLIAM--Dec'd. R. E. Sold 1836. Edgefield Rec. Bk. A-254
    Dist: Thomas Gilliard -w- Dione 1/5 $95.65
          Randal Robinson -w- Elizabeth-same
          David W. Richardson-same
          John W. Tinsley -w- Clarissa-same
          Marcus Hagood -w- Nancy-same. Marcus Hagood formerly of
            Greenville Dist. S. C. Now res. of Alabama, St. Clair
            County. P. A. to David Richardson 17 Nov. 1836.

RIDDLE, JOHN G. -m- set. 5 May 1842 Susannah Hill. Edgefield File
    Arch. Dept. Misc. M-180

RIDDLE, THOMAS--Surety for John Kelly, Tavern Keeper. Edgefield Ct.
    Min. Oct. 1794.

RILEY, FRANCIS--Niece of Caleb Holloway-Will 1840

RILEY, MARY--Dau. of William Little-Will 1837

RINGLAND, GEORGE--One of Commissioners to build bridge. See card
    Abram Ardis. Edgefield Ct. Min. Oct. 1794.

RIPLEY, AMBROSE--From Wm. Hill -w- Ann 27 Dec. 1793--Deed Bk. 9-50

RISH, CATHERINE--Dau. of John and Barbary Rish, and Gr-dau. of Catherine
    Long-Will 1852

RISH, WILLIAM -w- Martha Ann-Heirs of Wm. H. Cannon. Rec. Bk. B-215
    Edgefield 1851

RIVERS, MRS _____?--Grandmother of Peter Farrow, Jr. See card Stephen
    Garret -vs- Jeremiah Wilborn. Edgefield Equity Bills No. 14
    Filed 19 April 1817

RIVERS, JOHN--Of Mecklenburge Co. Original Will 20 May 1779.
    Wife: Not named--may be pregnant   Prov: July 1790
    "My children: 1.
               2.   Ex: Friend-Robert Thomson
               3.   Wit: David Thomson
    Sister: Lucy Rivers   Elizabeth Thomson
    Brother: Jones Rivers

RIVERS, JOHN--Petit Juror Edgefield 1788. List 12 and 16

RIVERS, JONES--Grand Juror Edgefield 1786. List 3, 12, 16.

RIVERS, JONES -w- Mary--Exor's: estate Robert Garrett, dec'd. See
    Garrett card. Edgefield April Ct. 1790. Min. Bk. Pg. 332

RIVERS, JONES--Dec'd. Inv. estate returned. Edgefield Ct. Min. March
                                                              1795
RIVERS, MARY--Original Will 26 Nov. 1802. Edgefield Pro. Bx. 44-1861
    Dau: Lucy Garrett
    Sons: John Rivers and Thomas Garrett
    To: William, Stephen, Thomas Garrett
        Abraham M. Wade   Lucy Garrett
        Charles Hammond   John Rice
    Cit: 7 Nov. 1811. Ad'm. granted to Wm. Garrett. Will Annexed.
    Purchasers 1802: Stephen, William, John C., Thomas, S., and T.
                    Garrett, Martin Wade, Lucy Garrett, Lucy Wright
                    George Palmer.

ROACH, MARY ANN D.--Dau. of Charles Hammond Sen'r. -"ill 1836.

ROBERTS, ABSOLEM--Petit Juror Edgefield 1787. List 6 and 17

ROBERTS, ELIZABETH--Dau. of John Griffis-Will 1838. Son in law-
    Absolem Roberts.

ROBERTS, JOHN--Petit Juror Edgefield 1787. List 7 and 16

ROBERTS, JOHN--Dec'd. R. E. Sold. Edgefield Rec. Bk. A-120
    Dist: Avary Roberts   )
          John Roberts   ) Shares sold to Sterling Powell-who
          Ephraim Salmons, et us) re-sold to James Clark 5/8
          Mary Floy   )
    William Stubblefield, et us--1/8
    Nimrod Dickens and children, viz: Mary and Serena
    Heirs of Dudly Roberts, viz: Allen, Wilson and Harriet

ROBERTS, JOHN and wife--Heirs of Jonathan Sullivan. Edgefield Rec.
    Bk. A-1 about 1820

ROBERTS, LEROY--Personal Property sale of Geo. Cowan, dec'd, at his
              house. Edgefield March Ct. 1795.
    Absolem Roberts appr. same estate.
    Jan. Ct. 1795--Absolem Roberts commissioned to build bridge. See
    card Col. John Martin.

ROBERTS, MARY--Of Chatham Co. Ga.--Legatee of Robert Watts-Will 1839

ROBERTS, MRS. NANCY -w- Absolem Roberts--Dower favor of Thomas Carter.
    April Ct. 1787. Edgefield Min. Bk.
    -Nancy Roberts--dau. of Mary Swillivant-Will 1801

ROBERTS, POLLY--Dau. of John Clarke, Sen'r.-Will 1814

ROBERTS, REUBEN--Dec'd. Let. Adm. to Mrs. Elizabeth Roberts-Qual.
Bond given   S: Rolan Williams, James Cox, John Carter
Edgefield Ct. Min. Bk. pg-113 Oct. 9, 1787
Same page: Deeds L and Re L from Robert Bas__? proved by oath of
Reuben Roberts. John Roberts, Grantee

ROBERAS (OR ROBERTS) S. J. -w- Eliza--Heirs of Francis Bird. Edgefield
Rec. Bk. B-137 1848

ROBERTS, THOMAS--Dec'd. Edgefield Min. Bk. Page 138. 14 Jan. 1788
Will proved by Sherwood Whatley and Edmond Whatley. and Absolem
Roberts qualified as Exor.

ROBERTS, THOMAS--Dec'd. Edgefield Min. Bk. Pg-232 12 Jan. 1789
Will proved by oath of John Martin, Jeremiah Roberts. Mary
Roberts qualified as Ex'x.

ROBERTSON, ANN -w- James. Dau. of Pleasant Thurmond-Will 1830.
Mary M. Robertson another daughter
Elizabeth Rebertson   "   "
Her children: Caroline Cheatham
               Benjamin F. Lyon
               Jane Lyon

ROBERTSON, BETSY--Dec'd. wife George. Heir of Wm. Cunningham. See
Cunningham card. Edgefield Rec. Bk. A-140

ROBERTSON, ELISHA--Petit Juror Edgefield 1789. List 13

ROBERTSON, ELISHA and Drury Pace--Umpire case Ebenezer Hill. See Hill
card. -vs- Wm. Johnson-Slander

ROBERTSON, ELISHA--Of Edgefield Co. Edgefield Wills A-108 2 Oct. 1792
Dau: Lydia Garner
Gr-son: William Eliot
Wife: Salley or Sarah (both ways used in Will)
Y-son: Elisha Gill Robertson
Ex: Wife and Wm. Robertson. Rec'd. Oct. 1795

ROBERTSON, GEORGE C.--Grand son Sarah Cunningham-Will 1841. Listed
with Mary Tompkins, a grand daughter.

ROBERTSON, HANNAH--Heir of Bersheba Hill. See Hill card. Edgefield
Rec. Bk. A-78. 1831

ROBERTSON, MARY AND GEORGE--Grand children of Joseph Cunningham-Will
1825.
ROBERTSON, JAMES -w- Mary (formerly widow Jas. Beall)--Heirs of estate
of Joshua Beall. See Beall card. Edgefield Rec. Bk. A-80. 1838

ROBERTSON, JOHN--Of Madison County, Miss. Edgefield Wills A-370
Brother: William Robertson of S. C. to take charge of Estate
          and children. Raise the children and divide the remainder.
Exors: James Childress, Washington Eddins, James Scrugg, and
        Daniel Tilman--to take charge until brother could come.
12 March 1816

ROBERTSON, MARY AND GEORGE--Gr-children of Joseph Cunningham-Will

188

ROBERTSON, MARY--Dau. Samuel Cook. Will 1813. Edgefield

ROBERSON, MOSES--Petit Juror Edgefield 1789. List 14

ROBERTSON, PETER--Dec'd. R. E. Sold 1841. Edgefield Rec. Bk. B-33
    Dist: Mary Robertson, widow 1/3 $118.02
          John Robertson
          Perry Holloway   Each of children 1/4 of 2/3
          Elizabeth Coleman
          Edmond Atcherson and wife

ROBERTSON, WILL--Petit Juror Edgefield 1788. List 11.

ROBERTSON, WILLIAM--Edgefield Wills 23 July 1812 Prov: 9 Oct. 1812
    Wife: Nancy--300 A. home place
    Daus: Sarah and Nancy
    Sons: Joseph--Land on Long Cane Creek
          William--Land where he lives
          Sandford--Land where he lives.
    Friend: Ambrose Min (or Mam)--Land where he lives
    Niece: Polly Robertson
    Son in law: Thomas Price

ROBERTSON, WILLIAM and wife--Heirs of Stephen Tomkins. See Tomkins
    card. Rec. Bk. A-282. 1828. Edgefield

ROBERTSON, WILLIAM SEN'R.--Will 9 Aug. 1838

ROBERTSON, WILLIAM--Will 17 Sept. 1840

ROBINSON, HANNAH--Of Augusta, Ga. to Henry Robinson of Augusta--P. A.
    to collect from Rep's. of Christopher Blair of S. C. and all
    money entitled to from estate of my mother, Barsheby Hill, dec'd.
    Edgefield Rec. Bk. A. Loose paper.

ROBINSON, RANDOL -w- Elizabeth--Heirs of William Richardson. See
    Richardson card. Edgefield Rec. Bk. A-254. 1836

ROBINSON, WILLIAM--Grand son: Wm. Payne, Jr. Edgefield Wills C-216
                 Dau: Margaret Conner and son Wm. R. Conner
                     Jane Marsh and son: Wm. R. Marsh
    1 March 1820 Prov: 10 Nov. 1826

ROCHELL, JOHN, SEN'R. -m- set. 9 April 1843 Charlotte Cochran. Little-
    bury Cochran, Trustee. Edgefield Dist. Misv. N or M-56

RODGERS, JAMES -w- Sarah--Heirs estate of James Eidson. See Eidson
    card. Also William Rodgers -w- Sarah. See same card. Edgefield
    Rec. Bk. B-125 1847

RODGERS, JOHN--Dec'd. R. E. Sold 1839. Edgefield Rec. Bk. A-324
    Dist: Simen J. Salter -w- Nancy 1/2 $434.62
          Mary, Richard, Robert, and Jonathan Rodgers 1/9 of 1/2
          Dempsey Rodgers -m- Asa Plummer by 1840 $46.29
          Edward White -w- Susan of Walton Co. Ga.   "
          Jno. Nicholas -w- Sarah   "
          William Dozier -w- Elizabeth   "
          William Lindsey -w- Winney   "

RODGERS, THOMAS -w- Caroline--Heirs of Nathaniel Sanders--See Sanders
card. Edgefield Rec. Bk. B-135 1848

RODGERS, WILLIAM, SEN'R.--Dec'd. R. E. Sold 1848. Edgefield Rec. Bk.
Dist: Elizabeth Rodgers, widow 1/3 $435. 52   B-148
       William and Luke Rodgers--1/11 of 2/3 $79.38
       James Rodgers
       Uriah Hodge -w- Tabitha
       Chesley Rodgers   All received 1/11 of 2/3
       Rebecca Ann Rodgers
       John Parrish -w- Elizabeth
       Catherine Rodgers-minor-Seaborn Temples, Gdn.
       Sophia, Druscilla, and Allen Rodgers
Rec't. by Seaborn Temples -w- Rebecca Ann 26 Nov. 1849
   "   " John Parish -w- Elizabeth 17 Oct. 1850

ROEBUCK, ELIZABETH (or Clara?) -m- James Day. Edgefield Equity Bill
Filed 1 June 1815. No. 30 See Day card.

ROEBUCK, JOHN--Petit Juror Edgefield 1786. List 5

ROEBUCK, MRS. MARY-w- John Roebuck--Dower favor Benj. Cook.
April Ct. 1787. Edgefield Min. Bk.

ROEBUCK, ROBERT--Appointed Overseer of Road from Hatcher's Pond to the
Old Wells in the room of Thos. Moseley, excused. Edgefield Ct.
Min. Jan. 1795

ROEBUCK, ROBERT--Dec'd. 1801 Edgefield Eq. Bills 30 1815
Children: Winnefred Roebuck -m- Wm. Cannon
           Elizabeth -m- John Hardy
           Mary (or Polly) -m- Daniel Hardy
           Clara -m- _____? Day
           Benjamin
John Roebuck--7 children-Said Robert Roebuck
                         Phoebe -m- Geo. Randall or Randolph
                         Ann -m- ____? Green
                         Rolly
                         Elizabeth -m- William Nichols
                         Ezekiel
                         James

ROEBUCK, ROLLEY--Petit Juror Edgefield 1788. List 12

ROGERS, ALEXANDER--Son of William Rogers. Legatee of Alexander
Downer-Will 1818. Res. of Georgia.

ROGERS, CHARLOTTE--Gr. dau. of Peter Day.-Will 1789.

ROGERS, DANIEL**Will 7 April 1843

ROGERS, JOHN and wife--Heirs of John Harris-See Harris card.
Edgefield Rec. Bk. A-290
-John Rogers--default in road work. See Lodwick Hill. Edgefield
Ct. Min. March 1795.

ROGERS, JOHN -w- Mary Ann-Heirs of William Chapman. See Chapman card.
Edgefield Rec. Bk. A-160 1833

ROGERS, MARY--Dau. of Elizabeth Weaver-Will 1830. Edgefield
    Her dau: Dimpley (?) Rogers. Her son: John Rogers

ROGERS, SARAH'S heirs--Tempy; Levi; and Sophronia--Heirs of William
    Sheppard. See Sheppard card. Edgefield Rec. Bk. A-152 1833

ROLIN, WILLIAM--Petit Juror Edgefield 1789. List 13

ROOTES, PETER--Pitit Juror Edgefield 1787. List 8

ROPER, BENJAMIN -w- Emily--Heirs of John Cogburn. See Cogburn card.
    Edgefield Rec. Bk. A-225 1834

ROPER, BENJAMIN--Will 2 Nov. 1841

ROPER, ELIZABETH--Dau. of Drury Adams-Will 1814. Step child of Testator:
    Benjamin Roper and Polly Roper.
    Daniel Roper--Exor.

ROPER, MARY--Dau. of Edward Holmes-Will 1822. Edgefield

ROPER, SOPHIA--Dau. of John Clackler-Will 1814

ROSE, CAROLINE--Dau. of William C. Posey-Will 1834. (Rose may be
    middle name). Edgefield

ROSEDON, RHODA T.--Dau. of Asa Holloway-Will 1823. Edgefield

ROSEMAN, JANE--Dau. of Daniel Rogers-Will 1843.

ROSS, DOROTHY--Sister of Mary McFarland-Will 1805.

ROSS, THOMAS--Petit Juror Edgefield 1788. List 9

ROTEN, BETSY--Gr. dau. of Annamariah Williams-Will 1832.

ROTTEN, WILLIAM--Petit Juror Edgefield 1789. List 1 and 2

ROTTEN, WILLIAM -w- Catherine--Heirs estate of John Cockeroff. See
    Cockeroff card. Edgefield Rec. Bk. A-26.

ROUNDTREE, JESSE--Petit Juror Edgefield 1789. List 13
    -Jesse Roundtree-Appr. estate of James Moore, dec'd. Also appointed
    Adm. estate John Meyer. See Meyer card. Edgefield Ct. Min. March
                                                                    1795.
ROUNDTREE, MARY--Dau. of Benjamin Hightower-Will Rec'd. 1824

ROUNDTREE, MARY--Niece of Rachel Wise-Will 1842

ROWAN, JAMES--Petit Juror Edgefield 1789. List 15

ROWE, ALLEN -w- Mary--Heirs of Richard Lewis. See Lewis card.
    Edgefield Rec. Bk. A-215. 1835

ROWE, DAVID--Petit Juror Edgefield 1794. List 21

ROWE, JAMES -w- Narcessy--Heirs of Richard Lewis. See Lewis card.
    Also Allen Rowe -w- Mary. Edgefield Rec. Bk. A-215 1835.

ROWE, NARCISSA AND MARY--Sisters of Richard Lewis-Will 1838.

ROWE, WILLIAM B.--Dec'd. R. E. Sold 1847. Edgefield Rec. Bk. B-151
    Dist: Mary Rowe, Sen'r. Mother of dec'd. $4.40
           Pinckney Rowe   1/8   "
           Andrew J. Rowe   "   "
           Elijah Holloway -w- Sophia   "   "
           John Marbert -w- Martha   "   "
           David M. Smith -w- Eliza   "   "
           Marty, Malinda, Austin Rowe   "   "   Each

ROWELL, EDWARD--Dec'd uncle of Howard R. Marshall-Will 1829

ROWELL, RICHARD and wife--Heirs of Walton Knight. See Knight card.
    Edgefield Rec. Bk. B-57 1842

ROWLAND, NATHAN--Paid legacy in estate of Thomas Pitts 1823/4. Also
    purchased much at the sale. Edgefield Probate 22-804

ROZAR, SHADRACK--Petit Juror Edgefield 1788. List 12 and 15
ROZIER, CATHERINE--Dau. of Michael Vessells-Will 1805

ROZIER, JOHN -w- Elizabeth--Heirs of Van Swearingen and Rice Swearingen.
    See both cards. Edgefield Rec. Bk. A-237 1836

RUBARD, WILLIAM--Dec'd. Joel Abney, Exor. Abney Will 1814--apts Walter
    Abney in his stead. Edgefield

RUCKER, HENRY -w- Nancy--Heirs of Job Padgett. See Padgett card.
    Edgefield Rec. Bk. A-312 1839

RUNNELS, JULIA S.--Legatee of Caleb Holloway-Will 1840. His niece.
    Lewis Runnels an exor.

RUSH, BARBARA--Dau. of George Long-Will 1818

RUSH, DAVID and wife--Heirs estate of Edmond Flinn. See Flinn card.
    Edgefield Rec. Bk. B-121 1846

RUSHTON, BENJAMIN -w- Harriet--Heirs estate of James Eidson. See
    Eidson card. Edgefield Rec. Bk. B-125. 1847

RUSHTON, GAINES F.--Will 23 March 1842. Edgfield

RUSHTON, JAMES--Dec'd. R. E. Sold 1836. Edgefield Rec. Bk. A-248/9
    Dist: Samuel Deen -w- Amey   1/8 $31.46¼ $66.46½
           James E. Knowlton -w- Susan   "   "
           John Rushton, David Rushton   "   "   Each
           Derman Hinson -w- Unity   "   "
           James, William and Benj. Rushton   "   "   Each

RUSHTON, JOSEPH--Dec'd. R. E. Sold Jan. 1846. Edgefield Rec. Bk. B-101
    Dist: Eliza Rushton, widow   1/3 $324.41
           Elizabeth " , minor-W. N. Moore, Gdn. 1/3
           Demaris   "   "   "   "   "   "
    Rec't. shows Demaris married John L'Neall. Rec't. dated 29 May
                                                                1846.
RUSHTON, NANCY--Dau. of James Ross-Will 1822. Wm. Rushton, Exor.
    Joseph Rushton, a witness. Edgefield

RUSSEL, ROBERT--Petit Juror Edgefield 1786. List 4 and 17

RUSTIN, ABIGAIL--Dau. of John Douglass-Will 1799

RUTHERFORD, MICHAEL--Dau. of Joseph Griffith-Will 1810

RUTLAND, PATSEY--Dau. of Ezekiel Posey-Will 1833

RYAN, BENJAMIN, JR.--Being of age to choose. Came into court and
    made choice of Benjamin Ryan, sen'r. as Gdn. Edgefield Ct. Min.
    9 Oct. 1787. Min. Bk. Page 110

RYAN, BENJAMIN--Grand Juror Edgefield 1794. List 22

RYAN, JOHN--Grand Juror Edgefield 1786. List 1 and 2

RYAN, MRS. MARTHA -w- John Ryan--Dower favor John Lucas. Oct. 1786.
    Edgefield Ct. Min.

RYAN, JOHN--From Isaac Hopkins. See Hopkins card. 2 Feather beds,
    furniture, etc. Edgefield Deed Bk. 6-330 4 April 1792

RYAN, JOHN--Produced certificate of qualifications as J. P. for this
    County--Said: by Hon. Arthur Simkins. Edgefield Ct. Min. Jan. 1795

RYAN, JOHN--Dec'd. R. E. Sold 1843. Edgefield Rec. Bk. B-81
    Dist: Benjamin Gallman -w-   1/2 $184.94
    Heirs of Benjamin Ryan, dec'd.   1/2
    Viz: Benjamin I. Ryan
          Stanmore B. Ryan (shows 1 place Pickens B. E. Ryan)
          Pickens B. Ryan
          Benjamin G. Ryan-child of Jno. E. F. Ryan
          John, Stanmore, and Eliza L. Ryan--Children of L. Ryan
          Mary Smith-child of Peggy Smith formerly Ryan

SADLER, MARTIN -w- Jemima Ann--Heirs of Matthew Thornton. See Thornton
    card. Edgefield Rec. Bk. A-244 1826

SAFFORD, HENRY and Eliza--Uncle and Aunt of John Ryan-Will 1832.

SALE, JOHNSON--Gdn. for Wm. F. Harris-Minor. See Green Harris (dec'd)
    card. Edgefield Rec. Bk. B-173 1849

SALMONS, EPHRAIM and wife--Heirs of John Roberts. See Roberts card.
    Edgefield Rec. Bk. A-120 about 1830

SALTER, ANN--Dau. of Charles Partin-Will 1796. Rec'd. 1813.

SALTER, JACKSON, SAMUEL, GIDEON, WILLIAM--Heirs of James Eidson. See
    Eidson card. Edgefield Rec. Bk. B-125. 1847

SALTER, SIMON J. -w- Nancy--Heirs of John Rodgers. See Rodgers card.
    Edgefield Rec. Bk. A-324.

SAMPLE, LEWIS and wife--Distributees of John R. Abney-1835/6. See
    Abney card. Edgefield Rec. Bk. A-233

SAMUEL, ROBERT--Grand Juror Edgefield 1786. List 3, 12, 18, 21.

SAMUEL, ROBERT--Dec'd. R. E. Sold 1834. Edgefield Rec. Bk. A-193
    Dist: Elizabeth Samuel, widow   1/3 $423.83
          Elbert Morgan and wife   1/7 of 2/3 $121.09
          Robert, George, Lucy, Susan, Elizabeth--All minors. John
    P. Mays, Guardian. Each 1/7 of 2/3

SAMUEL, SALLY--Gr-dau. of Ann Conner-Will 1824.

SAMUEL, SARAH--Dau. of Nicholas Ware, Sen'r.-Will 1799. Rec'd.-1801

SANDERS, JAMES--Road Overseer. Excused and Jacob Hibler appointed.
    Edgefield Ct. Min. March 1795

SANDERS, JOHN -w- Ruth--Stepson of James Robertson-Will 1802

SANDERS, LUCY--Sister of Burgess White-Will 1830
SANDERS, NATHANIEL--Dec'd. R. E. Sold 1848. Edgefield Rec. Bk. B-135
    Dist: Lucy Sanders, widow 1/3 $26.32
    Roger Thomas -w- Caroline 1/4 of 2/3 $13.16
    Mary Ann Welch-a minor-same
    Willis F. Lake -w- Lucy Ann-same
    John Sanders--a minor-same.

SANDERS, WILLIAM--Edgefield Wills A-362 28 March 1816
    Wife: Joanna-and child (seems unborn) Rec'd. 25 Aug. 1816
    Sister: Martha Williams-also mentions Stephen Williams

SANDRIDGE, DAVID--Appointed Overseer of the road from Campbell to the
    Augusta Road. In the room of Barkley Martin-excused. Edgefield
    Ct. Min. Oct. 1794.

SATCHER, FANNY--Dau. of Arthur Watson-Will 1806

SATCHER, JULIUS -w- Martha--Heirs of John Morring. See Morring card.
    Edgefield Rec. Bk. B-21. 1841

SATCHEL, SAMUEL--Petit Juror Edgefield 1789. List 15

SATERWHITE--See Will of Wiley Glover-1804. Edgefield

SAUNDERS, NATHANIEL -w- Lucy--Heirs of John Harris. See Harris card.
    Edgefield Rec. Bk. A-290. 1838

SAVAGE, ELIZABETH--Dau. of Barbara Nail-Will 1795. Edgefield

SAVAGE, JOHN -m- Elizabeth, daughter of John Nail who was son of
    Daniel Nail. See Daniel Nail card. (Or Elizabeth-dau. of
    Daniel Nail?) Edgefield Deed Bk. 13-305

SAVAGE, JOHN--Petit Juror Edgefield 1786. List 4 and 18
           Grand   "   "   "   " 20

SAVAGE, SAMUEL--Grand Juror Edgefield 1794. List 20

SAWYER, ELIZABETH--Dau. of Thomas Warren-Will 1815. Edgefield

194

SAWYER, ELKENAH--Petit Juror Edgefield 1789. List 15
-Elkanah Sawyer--Qualified as a Justice of Peace for Edgefield Co.
Edgefield Ct. Min. March 1795.

SAWYER, GEORGE--Petit Juror Edgefield 1787. List 6

SAWYER, SIBBEY -w- John Sawyer-dau. of Hardy Matthews-Will 1829

SAXON, MARY--Dau. of Thomas Wilson-Will 1795. Edgefield

SCOTT, _____? and wife--Heirs of William Holliday. See Holliday card.
Edgefield Rec. Bk. A-106 1831

SCOTT, CATHERINE--Dau. of Thomas Key-Will 1820. Wife of J. M. Scott.

SCOTT, SUSANNAH AND HARRIETT--Daus. of John Gray, Sen'r. - Will 1823

SCOTT, MARTHA--Dau. of Hillary M. Collier-Will 1841. Wife of Samuel
C. Scott. Edgefield

SCOTT, PATSY--Dau. of John Gorman-Will 1798. Edgefield

SCOTT, SAMUEL--Appr. Estate of Featherstone Cross. See Cross card.
Edgefield Ct. Min. 1795.

SCOTT, THOMAS--Petit Juror Edgefield 1794. List 20

SCOTT, WALTER--"Late Indian Trader"--Dec'd. Misc. B-575. Edgefield File
Daus: Betty, Peggy, Polly, Sally Scott--All of Cherokee Nation
P. A. to Charles Goodwin of Edgefield to collect for land on
Savannah River.

SCOTT, WILLIAM--Dec'd. R. E. Sold 1841/2 Edgefield Rec. Bk. B-53
Dist: Thomas Hanshaw and wife 1/3 $62.62
       Elias McCarty -w- Anna
       Allen Creed -w- Sally
       Hammond Cumbo -w- Polly   1/8 of 2/3 each
       Elisha Barker -w- Susan $15.65
       Henry, John and Rebecca Scott
       Alpha Scott -m- Bartlett Franklin before 4 Jan. 1847
Page 55--Shows another tract--same heirs.

SCRUGGS, JESSE and Henry Key--S: Wm. Longmire, Adm. estate of Thomas
Goode. See Goode card. Edgefield Ct. 14 July 1789. Min. Bk.

SCRUGGS, JESSE--Petit Juror Edgefield 1789. List 15

SCURRY, THOMAS, SEN'R.--Will 14 March 1837. Edgefield

SCURRY, THOMAS, JUN'R.--Will 13 Sept. 1842. Edgefield

SEANNEL, ELIZABETH -w- Dr. Abel Seannel and dau. of John Key-Will 1840

SEARLES, JOHN--Grand Juror Edgefield 1794. List 21

SEARLES, SALLY--Dau. of Zadoc Bussey-Will 1822

SEAWRIGHT, MARY--Dau. of John Gibson-Will 1821. Edgefield

195

SEGO, E. W. -w- Emily--Heirs estate of Ransom Hamilton. See Hamilton
card. Edgefield Rec. Bk. B-107. 1846

SEIBLES, CORNELIA AND BETSY--Nieces of Helen Lamkin-widow of Peter
Lamkin. Will (Helen's) 1830. Martha Seibles-sister of Testator.
William Seibles-husband of Martha

SELF, DANIEL--Gdn. for minor children of Obediah Henderson. See Henderson card. Edgefield Rec. Bk. A-207. 1835

SELF, DANIEL--Will 16 Nov. 1835.
Wife: Mary
Son: John
Daus: Dicey Fulmer, Martha Hicks, Lucy Sturkie
Son: Daniel Pressley Self.

SELLERS, THOMAS--Petit Juror Edgefield 1788. List 10

SESSION, FREDERICK--Petit Juror Edgefield 1786. List 4
-Edgefield Ct. Min. March 1795. Frederick Sesson, dec'd. Amount
sale estate returned by Wm. Humphries, exor.

SEYBERT, EDLAINE -w- George Seybert. Dau. of Isaac Lasseter-Will 1834

SHADRACK, JAMES--Heir of William Harris. See Harris card. Edgefield
Rec. Bk. A-50 1827

SHADWICK, AARON, JOHN, ABEL, SARAH AND WILLIAM--Heirs of John Sharpton.
Edgefield Rec. Bk. A-2 1827. (Name possibly Chadwick)

SHADWICK, DAVID--Petit Juror Edgefield 1789. List 13

SHADWICK, EDWARD -w- Stacy Adda Oden
"   STEPHEN -w- Hester Oden--Heirs of estate of Thomas Howle.
See Howle card. Edgefield Rec. Bk. A-286. 1838

SHANKLING, HARRIET--Niece of William Moore-Will 1818. Edgefield.
Received $3000.00

SHARPTON, JEPTHA--Will 20 Dec. 1838

SHARPTON, JOHN--Dec'd. Edgefield Rec. Bk. A-2 1827/28
Dist: John Kilcrease 1/2 and 1/4 of 1/2
Abel Sharpton
John, Aaron, Sarah, and William Shadwick--children of D.
Shadwick entitled to 1/4 of 1/2
William Shelton and wife 1/4 of 1/2 John Goff, Adm.

SHAVER, MICHAEL--Petit Juror Edgefield 1788. List 10 and 16

SHAVER, MICHAEL--Dec'd. Edgefield Sale Bk. A-7 1829 7 May, 1832 Rec'd.
Dist: William Shaver 1/2
Francis Shaver, widow 1/3
Polly and Nancy Shaver 1/3 of 1/2--Richard Berry, Gdn.

SHAW, POLLY--Dau. of James Butler-Will 1811

SHAW, THOMAS and wife--Heirs of Rebecca Ballantine who was heir of
James Butler. See Butler card. Edgefield Rec. Bk. A-124. 1833

SHELLEY, JAMES--Gdn. of minor children of Mary Buffington. See
     Buffington card. Edgefield Rec. Bk. A-60. 1832

SHELTON, WILLIAM--Heir of John Sharpton. Edgefield Rec. Bk. A-2 1827

SHEPPARD, GEORGE I AND FRANCES--Children of James Sheppard. Gr-children
     of Joicy Culpepper. Edgefield Wills D-126   1837

SHEPPARD, JAMES--Son in law of Joicy Culpepper-Will 1837

SHEPPARD, LEVI--Died intestate. Newberry 3-59
     Widow: Polly -m- David Thomas
     Children: Nancy -m- Washington Floyd
                John T. Sheppard
                Sally -m- Thomas Rainey
                Levi Sheppard-minor

SHEPPARD, MARY--Dau. of Agnes Cunningham-Will 1818

SHEPPARD, WILLIAM, SEN'R.--Dec'd. Edgefield Rec. Bk. A-156 1833-43
     Dist: Joicy Smith 1/3 $27.26
            Thomas T. Sheppard
            Henry Boozer and wife
            Honories, Jain, Stanmore, Jenetta, and David R. Sheppard--
            Each of above received 1/14 of 2/3
     Representatives of Wm. T. Sheppard, dec'd. Viz:
            James G.; Ben F.; Temperance; and Elizabeth-1/14 of 2/3
     Representatives of Levi Sheppard. Viz:
            John T.; Nancy and Levi-1/14 of 2/3
     Representatives of Sarah Rogers. Viz:
            Temp; Levi; and Sophronia Rogers-1/14 of 2/3
     Real Estate of William Sheppard. Distributees continued:
     John; Lewis and George Sheppard-1/14 of 2/3 each
     Fred Boozer 1/2 of 1/14 of 2/3
            George, Honorea, Sheppard,
            Henry Boozer and wife--brothers and sisters of the whole blood
            Henry Boozer in right of wife. Sd. dec'd. 1/2 of 1/14 of 2/3
     Rec't. Joice Smith and Jennet King 1843 in Newberry

SHERIFF, THOMAS--Petit Juror Edgefield 1787. List 7

SHERIFF, SUSIE--Dau. of Francis Posey-Will 1787

SHINHOLSTER, WILLIAM--Grand Juror Edgefield 1787. List 8, 12, and 20

SHINHOLSTER, WILLIAM--Son of Sophia Hiles-Will 1788

SHINHOLSTER, WILLIAM AND ISAAC ARDIS--Prov. Will of Sophia Hiles.
     Edgefield Min. Bk. 1788

SHINHOLSTER, WILLIAM--Guardianship made at July Court resigned and
     Abraham Ardis appointed Gdn. for William Shinholster, Jr.
     Edgefield Min. Bk. Pages 324/5 April 1790

SHINHOLSTER, WILLIAM--Appr. estate of John Mays. See Mays card.
     Edgefield Ct. Min. March 1795.

SHIPS, PHIL--Petit Juror Edgefield 1786. List 5 and 17

SHIVELEY, JOHN--Petit Juror Edgefield 1794. List 20

SHOCKLEY, DAVID--See David Mock card.

SIBLEY, ELIZABETH--Sister of Howard R. Marshall-Will 1829

SIEBLES, BETSY--Gr. dau. of Lydia Lamar-Will Rec'd. 1835. Dau. of
        Testator--Martha I Siebles.

SIGLER, GEORGE--Will 17 June 1837

SIMKINS, ELIZA HANNAH--Will 2 Nov. 1837

SIMKINS, JESSE--Dec'd. Edgefield Sale Bk. A-32. Bond for sale 1 Feb.
        R. E. sold at private sale to widow. Distributees not   1834
        shown. Proceeds not accounted for on 15 Mar. 1833.

SIMKINS, JOHN--Petit Juror Edgefield 1788. List 10

SIMKINS, MARY -w- Arthur Simkins, Jr. Legatee and seems dau. of Abram
        Ardis-Will 1816.

SIMKINS, WILLIAM--Petit Juror Edgefield 1789. List 13
                Grand   "   "   "   "   20

SIMKINS, WILLIAM--Appointed Overseer of road from where Blocker's
        Path crosses to the Court House, in the room of Elias Blackburn,
        excused. Edgefield Ct. Min. Jan. 1795.

SIMONS, CHARLES--Petit Juror Edgefield 1789. List 13

SIMMONS, ELIZABETH--Dau. of William Hudson-Will 1809.

SIMINS, JOHN--Applied for permission to keep Tavern. S: David
        Thompson and Sampson Butler. Edgefield Ct. Min. March 1795.

SIMS, JULY--Dau. of William White-Will 1806.

SINGLETON, LEROU, SAMUEL, BENJAMIN--Heirs of Samuel Medlock. See Medlock
        card. Edgefield Rec. Bk. A-74 1829

SIVERINGHAM, JOHN--Petit Juror Edgefield 1789. List 14

SKANNAL, MARGARET--Dau. of Elias Blackburn-Will 1827.

SKILLEN, SUSAN--Heir of John Gitty. Edgefield Rec. Bk. B-119 1847

SLATON, ISAAC -w- Sarah--Heirs of Isaac Bush. Edgefield Rec. Bk. A
        264. 1836.

SLATON, ISAAC -w- Sarah--Grand children of Isaac Bush-Will 1836

SLEIGH, ANDREW J. -m- Mary N. Adams--dau. of Mariam Adams. See Adams
        card. 1842. Edgefield Rec. Bk. B-61

SMEDLEY, NEOMY--Legatee of Nathan Melton-Will 1805.

SMITH, ALLEN -w- Eliza--Dist. of estate Joshua Bodie. See Bodie card.
Also James Smith -w- Mary, dist. same estate. Edgefield Rec. Bk.
A-308. 1839

SMITH, CATHERINE--Dau. of Thomas Gentry-Will 1820.

SMITH, DAVID M. -w- Eliza--Heirs of William B. Rowe. See Rowe card.
Edgefield Rec. Bk. B-151 1847

SMITH, DEMPSEY--Gr-dau. of Daniel Rogers-Will 1843. Also Eliza Smith-
another Grand daughter. Edgefield

SMITH, EASTHER--Dau. of Solomon Bird-Will 1810

SMITH, ELIZA--Dau. of Benjamin Bunting-Will 1823.

SMITH, EZEKIEL--Petit Juror Edgefield 1788. List 11

SMITH, HELEN--Wife of Archibald Smith and Kinswoman of Ulric Tobler-
Will 1815. And her dau. Eliza Smith

SMITH, JACOB--Grand Juror Edgefield 1786. List 3, 10, and 16.

SMITH, JACOB B.--Nephew of Thomas G. Lamar--Will 1820

SMITH, JACOB -w- Salley--Heirs of James Rhodes. See Rhodes card.
Edgefield Rec. Bk. A-56. 1831

SMITH, JACOB--Grand son of Ann Leavenworth-Will 1836. Edgefield

SMITH, JACOB--Dec'd. Left land to James Ball-which was original grant
to Simeon Smith. Now conv. by Sarah Smith to James Ball. 4 April
Edgefield Deed 31-409/10   1812

SMITH, JAMES M.--Will 30 Nov. 1830. Edgefield

SMITH, JAMES -w- Mary--Dist. estate of Joshua Bodie. See Bodie card.
Also Allen Smith and wife, Eliza.

SMITH, JOHN--Petit Juror Edgefield 1789. List 14

SMITH, JOICY--Heir of William Sheppard. See Sheppard card. Edgefield
Rec. Bk. A-156 1833

SMITH, KELAND--Petit Juror Edgefield 1768. List 9
             Grand   "   "   "   "   20

SMITH, NORTEN AND WYLY--Step sons of Frederick Sisson-Will about 1792.

SMITH, MARTHA--Dau. of Susannah Christie-Will 1842

SMITH, MARY--Dau. of Peggy Smith--Heir of John Ryan. See Ryan card.
Edgefield Rec. Bk. B-81 1843

SMITH, MATILDA--Step daughter of Henry W. Lowe-Will 1820.

SMITH, MESSER--Petit Juror Edgefield 1789. List 15

SMITH, NANCY--Dau. of Francis Posey-Will 1787.

SMITH, PEGGY G. -w- ____? Smith--Grand niece of John Ryan-Will 1827

SMITH, ROBERT M.--Grand son of William Dean-Will 1829

SMITH, SARAH--Dau. of Stephen Teer-Will 1810

SMYLY, DAN C.--Little Stevens Creek Baptist Church
    Sacred to the memory of Dan C. Smyly who departed this life on
    the 31st July 1851. Aged 28 years and 26 days.
    -Gracey J. Smyly--Sacred to the memory of Gracey J. Smyly consort of
    James Smyly who departed this life on the 31st Aug. 1835. Aged
    41 years and 21 days. Also her infant daughter.

SMYLY, JAMES -w- Gracey-dau. of James Coates-Will Rec'd. 1817.
    -James Smyly-Will 31 Oct. 1838
    -Smyly, Col. James -w- Gracey J.--Their dau. Virginia -m- Dr. D. G.
    Tompkins. See Tompkins card. Little Stevens Cr. Church Tomb.
    -Sacred to the Memory of Col. James Smyly who departed this life
    the 27th Dec. 1838. Aged 49 years, 3 mos, 20 days. Little
    Stevens Creek Baptist Church Tomb.
    -In Memory of John S. Smyly who was born October 17th 1819 and
    died March 16, 1867.
    -In Memory of M. A. Smyly who was born February 24th 1825 and died
    November 27, 1865.
    -Wm. Scott Smyly born 4 January 1822. Died 30 January 1856

SOLOMON, HARDY -w- (formerly widow)--Heirs of William Melton. See
    Melton card. Edgefield Rec. Bk. A-118 1832

SPAIN, NEVIL and wife--Heirs of John Hall. See Hall card. Edgefield
    Rec. Bk. A-104 1832

SPANN, ELIZABETH--Will 4 Jan. 1842. Edgefield

SPANN, JAMES--Son of Elizabeth Clarke of Augusta-Will 1827

SPANN, JAMES -w- Sarah--Heirs of Sarah Lott. See Lott card. Edgefield
    Rec. Bk. A-138 1833

SPEERS, ROBERT--Petit Juror Edgefield 1787. List 8 and 16

SPENCER, ELIZABETH--Dau. of Robert Harrison-Will 1827.

SPIKER, MRS KETTY--Dau. of the wife of Nathaniel Bacon-Will 1805.

SPIKER, PATSEY and ANNA -w- Wm. Spiker of Alabama--Sisters and heirs
    of John Gitty. See Gitty card. Edgefield Rec. Bk. B-119 1847

SPIRES, WILLIAM -w- Harriet--Heirs of Mary Tillman. Edgefield Rec.
    Bk. B-103 1846. See Tillman card.

SPRAGGINS, DEBORAH--Heir of John Kay, dec'd. Edgefield Rec. Bk. B-
    1849
SPRAGINS, ISABELLA, NANCY, AND SALLY--Grand children of Nathaniel
    Abney-Will 1806. Edgefield

SPRAGINS, PATTY WILLS--Dau. of Francis Jones-Will 1800. Son in law--
Thomas Spragins.

SPRAGGINS, THOMAS--Petit Juror Edgefield 1788. List 12 and 15

SPRAGINS, THOMAS--Commissioned to view ground for road. See card
Wm. Moore. Edgefield Ct. Min. Jan. 1795.

SPRAGGINS, WILLIAM--Grand Juror Edgefield List 4, 8, and 16. No date.

SPRAT, JOHN--Petit Juror Edgefield 1788. List 12

SPRINGER, LIDIA--Dau. of Joseph Bishop-Will 1802.

SQUIRES, ANNE--Sister of Samuel Tomkins-Will 1826.

STAGS, RICHARD--Dec'd. Edgefield Min. Bk. Pg-155 14 Jan. 1788.
Ordered citation be issued--kin to appear at next court-otherwise
Adm. to be granted George Cowan.

STALLINGS, MARTHA--Dau. of Robert Moseley-Will 1796.

STALLWORTH, THOMAS--In charge of estate of James Harrison. See Harrison
card. Edgefield Ct. Min. March 1795.

STALNAKER, ADAM--Excused as Road Overseer-Ct. House to the Ridge-and
Wm. Bush appointed. See card Bibby Bush. Edgefield Dt. Min.
March 1795.

STALNAKER, SAMUEL--Petit Juror Edgefield 1788. List 9

STALNAKER, SAMUEL -w- Abigail--Heirs of Reuben Carpenter, dec'd. See
card. Edgefield Rec. Bk. B-77

STARK, ROBERT--Clerk of Court of Edgefield Indicted by Grand Jury for
Extortion. Absconded. Min. Bk. Page 249. 13 April 1789.
-Accused of taking illegal fees from widow Suckey Body. See Body
card. Min. Bk. 1790

STARK, ROBERT--Grantee 23 June 1774. Conv. to Benj. Bell. Bell to
Samuel Walker. He to William Daniel on 17 June 1799 conv. to
Philip Raiford. Edgefield Deed Bk. 20-220 1779

STARK, ROBERT, JR.--See card of David Murray, dec'd. Edgefield Eq. 72
1819
STARK, ROBERT--Dec'd. R. E. Sold 1842. Edgefield Rec. Bk. B-71
Dist: Elizabeth Prosser 1/7 $167.72
Robert Starke-same
Theodore Starke-same--Died and left Will
Bolling Starke-same
Mrs. Willison-same
Mrs. Wormely-same
Horatio Starke-same. See card Mrs. Wormley

STARK, SARAH--Dau. of Ann Leavenworth-Will 1836. Grand daughter of
Eliza Stark, son: Thos. G. Lamar. Edgefield

STARR, ELIZA--Widow of George Starr. Heir of Thomas Broom. See
Broom card. Edgefield Rec. Bk. A-239

STARR, SUSANNA -w- Henry Starr. Dau. of David Bowers-Will 1833.

STATSWORTH, MARY--Dau. of John? Adams-Will 1822

STEEL, LEE--Dec'd. R. E. Sold 1842. Edgefield Rec. Bk. B-42
    Dist: Cynthia/Taylor)   (
          Joel Burnham   )All struck out (1/3 $75.79
          Daniel Pardue)   (Each
    The rightful distributee is Robert Summeral(sp) -w- Sarah
    David Steel.

STEFFIL, JOHN JAMES--Petit Juror Edgefield 1788. List 11

STEIFLE, PHILIP H.--Dec'd. R. E. Sold 1839. Edgefield Rec. Bk. A-300
    Dist: Mary Steifle, widow 1/3 $58.66
          Philip H. Steifle 1/4 of 2/3 $29.33
          Mary H   "   -same
          William M.   "   "
          George F.   "   " (minor)

STEPHENS, EVENATES--Petit Juror Edgefield 1789. List 16

STEPHENS, IGNATIUS--Petit Juror Edgefield 1787. List 8

STEPHENS, JOSIAH--Petit Juror Edgefield 1788. List 10 and 18

STEVENS, ELIZABETH--Dau. of John Fleke-Will 1798

STEVENS, JOSIAH--Of Little Stevens Creek. Edgefield Co. to Elisha
    Stevens of said Creek "Love and affection" 200 A. Wit: Alexander
    Bean, Frederick Williams, Josiah Thomas. Edgefield Deed Bk. 6-144
    28 Feb. 1791

STEVENS, MOURNING M.--Legatee of Henry Clark-Will 1840.

STEVENS, SARAH--Wife of Josiah Stevens. Edgefield Wills A-53. 3 Aug.
    Son: Robert Bryant   Rec'd. Sept. 1793   1795
         William Bryant
    Son in law: William Dean
    Dau: Nancy Dean
    Gr-son: Frederick Williams.
    Wit: John Coursey and Jas. Scott.

STEWART, ALEXANDER--Dec'd. R. E. Sold 1850. Edgefield Rec. Bk. B-197
    Dist: Thos. Stewart $124.64   Patsy McCarty-same
          Polly Stewart-same   Mary M. McCarty $62.32
          Desdemonia Stewart-same   Wm. A. McCarty-same
          Rebecca Stewart-same
          Children of Elizabeth Stewart, dec'd. Viz: (Now Thompson)
          William, Thomas, Alexander, Narcilla, Nella, Polly, and
          Tabitha Thompson--Each $17.80

STIDHAM, NANCY--See Will of John Hill-1804. Edgefield

STILL, DAVID -w- Catherine of Madison Co. Miss. To Shemel Nicholson
of Edgefield 134 Acres on Sleepy Creek of Savannah River.
Edgefield Deed Bk. 34-411   28 Feb. 1817

STILL, ELIZABETH--Applicant for Part. Former widow dec'd. John Still
-vs- Minors Francis Ann, Nancy, and William Still-Joseph Still, Gdn.
Cit. to appear 4 Nov. 1839. Order 4 Nov. 1839 for App'r. to divide. 1/3 to be alloted to Elizabeth, the widow. and 2/3 to minors
names. Land on Sleepy Creek. Bd: Alfred May, Sarah Deen, Wiley
Adams, and others.

STILL, MARTHA--Dau. of Martha Hancock-Will 1827.

STILL, ISABELLA, et al -vs- James Still. Edgefield Equity Bill 824/5

STILL, J. J.--Edgefield Equity Roll 60-2477. James Still, Sdm'r.
Bond: 3 Dec. 1849 S: James Dorn and John Quattlebaum
Dist: Abner Still, dec'd. J. J. Still, Adm'r. $1272.06
       Philip Quattlebaum   "
       George Hamilton   "
       Benjamin Still   "
       Wiley Adams   "
       William Still   "
       Children of P. A. Whatley   "
       Widow's share   "

STILL, JAMES--Quattlebaum Graveyard, Sleepy Creek Rd. Edgefield.
Born-- April 1822. Died 22 July 1902.
Mrs. Vary Still?
Infant son of E. G. and Mary Cogburn-Oct. 18, 1905

STILL, JOHN--Edgefield Prob. Ct. Rec. Box 45-1932/3 Prov: 1799
Jane Still, et al, Exors. Son in law--Jacob Youngblood.
Nothing in package but Will.

STILL, JOHN -w- Elizabeth -vs- Fanny Bartlett, by her trustee, Sarah
Adams, now Sarah Dean.
William, Wiley, Mary Ann, and Sarah Adams--minors under 21
Devisees of Charles Adams. Decree 21 Sept. 1827. Bk. A--
Summons in Partition. Lands on Sleepy Creek adj. William
Youngblood, Simeon Deen, Sarah Deen.
John Still -w- Elizabeth 1/6   Wiley, Mary, and Sarah Adams
Fanny Bartlet-1/6   1/6 each.
William Adams 1/6

STILL, JOHN--Dec'd. R. E. Sold 1841. Edgefield Rec. Bk. B-29
Dist: Elizabeth Still, widow 1/3 $195.16
       Francis Ann; Nancy; and William Still--Minors.
       William Deen, Atty for heirs.

STILL, JOSEPH AND JAMES I.--Heirs of Alexander Bean. See Bean card.
Edgefield Deed Bk. 31-200 1812

STILL, JOSEPH--Edgefield Ct. Records 52-2178. Elijah Still, Adm'r.
Bond: 9 Oct. 1843. S: John Cogburn, and John Quattlebaum

STILL, MARY L.--Quattlebaum Graveyard-Sleepy Creek Road.   Edgefield
Died: 24 July 1872 (or 32) age 62.
Benjamin Still--Died 29 Dec. 1875--age 26 yrs.

STILL, THOMAS--Edgefield Equity Bills 27-982. Martha Still, Adm'x.
Bond: 1 March 1824. S: Lewis Curry, Benj. Curry, Eli Morgan

STILL, WILLIAM--Son of Benjamin. Legatee of William Martin-Will 1827

STIRON, THOMAS A.--Son in law of Jonathan Glanton-Will 1823

STOCKDALE, JAMES S. -m- Sarah Lark-dau. of John Lark-Will 1822

STOCKES, ELIZABETH--(or Stokes)--Gr-dau. of Charles Hammond, sen'r.-
Will 1836. And her daughter: Lucy May Stokes

STOKES, RICHARD--Of Lunenburg Co. Edgefield Deed 8-355 1 May 1789
To his Grand children:
Evans, Ludwell, Batt, Wilmuth, Greenbury, and Robert Stokes.
To receive Plantation and personal property.
Wit: George Barnes, Woodson Knight, James Barnes, Wm. Blakley
and Wm. Cain.

STONE, JESSE -w- Susan and their children-Thomas, Henry and Patsy
and also Abner Stone--Heirs of Philip Lightfoot. Edgefield
Rec. Bk. B-65. 1842

STONE, JESSE--Dec'd. R. E. Sold 1842. Edgefield Rec. Bk. B-45
Dist: Thomas Stone   1/10 $6.51
Elizabeth Clark
Patsey Stone
David Stone's children viz: Susannah and David
Jincey Rambow -w- Joseph B. Rambow
Abner Stone
Levi Jordan -w- Sally
Robert Wallace -w- Nancy
Children of Jesse Stone, dec'd. Viz: Eliza (or Susannah
Henry Stone
1/10 to each child and to the 2 children of David 1/10
Rec't. Martha Stone for share R. E. of my father, Jesse Stone.
7 April, 1847

STONE, JESSE--Dec'd. Edgefield Pasted in Rec. Bk. B-65.
"Sir: Please to send the amount that is in your hands that is
coming to me from my father, Jesse Stone, Real Estate. Also
the amount that is due me from oncl Philip Lightfoot, Decst.
Rear Estate and C. by Atticus Tucker, and this shall be your
Receipt in full for the same this August 30th, 1844. Samuel
Lassater, Elizabeth Clarke."

STOTT, HENRY--Nephew and heir of John Gitty. See Gitty card.
Edgefield Rec. Bk. B-119 1847

STOTT, PATTY--Edgefield Probate Bx 108-28 1812
Dau. of Richard (Will 1804) and Patty (Will 1812) Moore.
She seems wife of Abdel Stott who was ex. of Will of Patty Moore.

STRAWDER, TEMPERANCE--Dau. of Solomon Pope-Will 1794

STRINGER, JONATHAN AND WILLIS--Gr. sons of Michael Burkhalter-Will 1804.

STROOP, JAMES--Petit Juror Edgefield 1789. List 15

STROTHER, WILLIAM--Dec'd. Will--Edgefield Ct. Min. Oct. 1794.
Proved by oaths of David Pits and Henry King.
Joyce Strother, John Strother, and Solomon Pope all qualified
as Exors. Appr's: Amos Richardson, Wright Nicholson, sen'r.
Wick Hill, Bartlet Bledsoe
Jan. Ct. 1795. Inv. Est. Wm. Strother returned and received.
March Ct. 1795: Jeremiah Strother--default on road work.

STROTHER, WILLIA? A.--Grand son of Joicy Culpepper-Will 1837.
David R. Strother, and George Strother-other gr. sons.

STROZIER, BENNET M. -w- Martha--Heirs of James O'Hara. See O'Hara
card. Edgefield Rec. Bk. A-217 1835

STUART, JOHN--Petit Juror Edgefield 1787. List 6 and 17.

STUBBLEFIELD, WILLIAM and wife--Heirs of John Roberts. See Roberts
card. Edgefield Rec. Bk. A-120. about 1820

STURGES, OLIVER--His wife a kinswoman of Ulric Tobler-Will 1815.

STURGIS, ANDREW W. -w- Susan--Heirs of John Quarles. See Quarles card.
Edgefield Rec. Bk. B-73 1842

STURGINAKER, JOHN--Grand Juror Edgefield 1786. List 1, 4, and 6

STURZENEGGER, JOHN -w- Charlotte Ulrica--She was cousin of Ulric
Tobler-Will 1815.

STURKIS, LUCY--Dau. of Daniel Self-Will 1835.

SULLIVAN, BETSEY--Dau. of Samuel Doolittle-Will 1799. Prov. 1800

SULLIVAN, ELIZA--Dau. of Ann Conner-Will 1824.

SULLIVAN, ELLEN--Dec'd. R. E. Sold 1847. Edgefield Rec. Bk. B-111
Dist: Samuel P. Getsen -w- Mary A. 1/6 $112.16
William G. Quarles -w- Elizabeth-same
Seaborn O. Sullivan-same
Thomas L. Sullivan-same
Dawson B. Sullivan-same
William B. Quarles-a minor-same. Wm. Gardner, Gdn.
Elizabeth Quarles a sister of dec'd.
Middle initials shown by receipts.

SULLIVAN, JOHN--Will 17 Oct. 1836.

SULLIVAN, JONATHAN--Dec'd. Edgefield Sale. Bk. A-Pg. 1
    Dist: John McPhatuck -w- Elizabeth
            John Roberts -w-
            Pressley Sullivan
            Gabriel Blair -w- Rebecca
            Robertson Dagnal -w-
            David Sullivan's heirs.
            Elisha Sullivan's sole heir
            Orion Sullivan--Jonathan Taylor, Gdn.
    PAGE 4--Elisha Sullivan estate--
            Jonathan Taylor and wife 1/3 Gdn. of-
            Orion Sullivan-minor 2/3

SULLIVAN, PRESLEY--Dec'd. R. E. Sold 1835. Edgefield Rec. Bk. A-213
    Dist: Elizabeth Sullivan, widow relinquished her part.
            Sampson Sullivan
            Butler Williams -w- Mary
            John Adams -w- Catherine   Each 1/5 $55.81
            Presley G. Sullivan
            John Sullivan-minor

SULLIVAN, PRESLEY G.--Will 5 July 1836. Edgefield

SULLIVANT, PATRICK--Petit Juror Edgefield 1789. List 14

SUMMERALL, JOSEPH--Petit Juror Edgefield 1789. List 13 and 23

SUMMERALL, JOSEPH--Permission to keep Tavern. Edgefield Ct. Min.
    March 1795. S: Ebenezer Hill and Jiles Letcher.

SUMARAL, MARY--Legatee of John Tarrance-Will 1824.

SUMMERLIN, JOSEPH -w- Mary--Heirs of Morris Callihan. Edgefield Rec.
    Bk. A-229 1835. See Callihan card.

SUNDA, MARY--Widow--Heir of Shadrack Boone. See Boone card. (his widow)
    Edgefield Rec. Bk. A-48.

SUTTON, CHARLES -w- Mary--Dist. estate of Hezekiah Almon, sen'r..See
    Almon card. 1830. Edgefield Rec. Bk. A-62

SUTTON, PHINEHAS -w- Nancy of Georgia--Heirs of Samuel Medlock. See
    Medlock card. Edgefield Rec. Bk. A-74. 1829

SWEARINGEN, JAMES--Brother in law of Guardian of Susan Ann-minor
    dau. of George Delaughter. Edgefield Eq. Roll 976.

SWEARINGEN, JESSE--Dec'd. R. E. Sold 1845. Edgefield Rec. Bk. B-87
    Dist: Eliza Swearingen 1/10 $47.21
            Lucinda; Abner; Larken G.; James H.; William R.; John;
            Coleman Rhodes -w- Harriet
            May A. Swearingen
            James Swearingen-seignor (His name first on list in book
            listed last thru error. He received same amt. as others.)
            Each received 1/10 $47.21

SWEARINGEN, MARTHA--Dau. of Beheathland Mims-Will 1836.

SWEARINGEN, MARY--Dau. of Noah Cloud-Will 1834. Gr. son: Henry
   Swearingen. Edgefield

SWEARINGEN, MARY--Heir of Isaac Bush. See Bush card. Edgefield
   Rec. Bk. A-264 1836

SWEARINGEN, RICE--Dec'd. Edgefield Rec. Bk. A-237
   Widow: Keziah
   Children: Louisa Ann; Maranda; Martha;
            Elizabeth -m- John Rozier
            Susan and Francis.

SWEARINGEN, RUE--Appointed Overseer of road from the County line to
   head of Horse Creek in the room of William Day-excused. Edgefield Ct. Min. Jan. 1795.
   Van Swearingen, Esq. qual. as J. P. for this county.
   Frederick Swearingen Surety for Bibby Bush. See Bush card.
       "   "   "   " Benj. McKenney. See McKenny card.

SWEARINGEN, THOMAS--Petit Juror Edgefield 1789. List 13

SWEARINGEN, VAN, SEN'R--Petit Juror Edgefield 1786. List 5 and 9

SWEARINGEN, VAN--Will 30 Dec. 1835. Edgefield

SWEARINGEN, VAN--Dec'd. R. E. Sold 1836. Edgefield Rec. Bk. A-237
   Dist: Lark Swearingen 1/3 $26.50
         James   "   "   "
         Heirs of Wrice Swearingen, dec'd.
         Keziah, widow 1/3 of 1/3
         Rick; Louisa Ann; Maranda; Martha; Elizabeth;
         Susan and Francis--1/7 of 2/3 each $2.50

SWILLIVAN, JONATHAN--Dec'd. Let. Adm granted John Swillivan.
   S: Littleberry Adams and John Curry
   Apprs: Absolom Roberts, Sheally Whatley, Sr., Edmand Whatley,
          Aaron Herrin. Edgefield Ct. Min. March 1795.
   March Ct. 1795--John Swilliven, Overseer of Road from Horn's
          Creek to Mill Creek on the Martinton road--in room of
          Aaron Harris, excused.
   March Ct. 1795--John Swilliven-Surety on Adm. Bond estate of
          George Cowan, dec'd.

SWILLIVAN, MARTHA ANN and SOPHIA ANN--Gr-daughters of Martha Hancock.
   Will 1827. Dec'd. dau. Frances Swillivan

SWITZER, LEONARD--Of Granville Co. Will 6 Nov. 1766. C. T. Wills
   Wife: Ann
   Son: Leonard Switzer--Land on Beach Island where I now live.
   "My 3 daus" Katharine; Elizabeth and Ann.
   Exor: John Stwizennager and Casper Nail. Edgefield File.
   Son-Leonard-minor.

TAIKET, DELILAH--Dau. of Hezekiah Gentry-Will 1820

TALBERT, ELISHA (or Ezra) -w- Emmeline D. Talbert-dau. of John
   Hollingsworth, and Legatee of same. Will 1838. (Name seems to
   be Ezra).

TALBERT, MARY--Gr-daughter of William Elzm-Will 1805

TALBERT, MARY R.--Dau. of John Burress-Will 1822. Her husband Ansel
Talbert.

TALBERT, NANCY--Dau. of Joseph Collier-Will 1818. Wife of John Talbert

TALBERT, WILLIAM--Petit Juror Edgefield 1786. List 4

TALBERT, WILLIAM--Edgefield Wills A-10 Bx-46 Pkg-1961-Will 13 Aug. 1788
    Wife: Martha (?) and her dau. Pamela
    Ex: Wife and Henry Key and Tanda Key. Rec'd. Oct. 1789.
    -Oct. Ct. 1789. Min. Bk. Pg-263--William Talbert, dec'd. Will
    proved by oath of Wm. Key. Mrs. Martha Talbert, Ex'x. Qual.
    Appr: James Talbert, Marshal Martin, Wm. Longmire, and John
    McFatrick.

TALLICE, JUDITY--Dau. of Pleasant Thurmond-Will 1830

TALLY, ANN--Dau. of Elizabeth Thurman-Will 1804

TALLY, BETSY--Legatee of John Thurmond-Will 1773 (or 1793)

TALLY, CHARLES -w- Martha--Heirs of Scarborough Broadwater. See
    Broadwater card. Edgefield Rec. Bk. A-221 1835

TALLY, ELIZABETH--Dau. of Mary Hill-Will Rec'd. 1822.

TALLY, ELIZABETH--Dau. of Zadoc Bussey-Will 1822

TALLY, JOHN -w- Mary, and Anna--Heirs of Edward Moseley-a devisee of
    James Butler. See Butler card. Edgefield Rec. Bk. A-165. 1834

TALLY, MACEY--Legatee William Robertson-Will 1840. Formerly Macey
    Barnes. Edgefield

TALLY, THOMAS -w- Elizabeth--Heirs of estate Ebenezer Hill. See Hill
    card. Edgefield Rec. Bk. A-280. 1837

TALLY, THOMAS -m- Eliza Collier, dau. Edward Collier. Edgefield Ct.
    Bills 914 975.

TAMEHILL, PATSEY--Dau. of Pleasant Thurmond-Will 1830

TARRANCE, WILLIAM--Dec'd. Edgefield Ct. Min. March 1795.
    Son: John Tarrance applied Let. Adm.
    Bond: 300 pounds.
    S: Joseph Hightower and Charles Hightower Thorne
    Appr's: Joshua Hammond, C. Hightower Thorne, John Carter, and
    John Hall. March Ct. 1795. Inv. returned and recorded.

TATE, HENRY--Will 14 May 1836.

TATE, JESSE To John Arnold--300 A. part 800 A. grant to Wm. Downs in
    1775, who conv. to George Blanton, and from Blanton to sd Jesse
    Tate. Spartanburg Deed Bk. A-120 1782

TATE, RICHARD--Petit Juror Edgefield 1794. List 21

TATE, MATTHEW--Eldest son and heir of Rev. Joseph Tate, late of Lancaster County, State of Pennsylvania--To: James Lark of Thickety Creek. 432 A. Plantation on Fairforest Creek. Bd: Moses Foster, John Thomas, Henry White and Handcock Smith and Peter Smith. (This Conveyance struck out) Spartanburg Deed A-21 1779

TAYLOR, HENRIETTA--Dau. of John Fleke-Will 1798.

TAYLOR, JOHN--Will 2 Feb. 1841.

TAYLOR, JONATHAN and wife--Heirs of Jonathan Sullivan. Edgefield Rec. Bk. A-1 About 1820. See Sullivan card.

TAYLOR, NANCY--Dau. of John Clark, Sen'r.-Will 1814.

TAYLOR, POLLY--Dau. of Nathan Trotter-Will 1825.

TAYLOR, REBECCA--Dau. of George DeLaughter, Sen'r.-Will 1830

TAYLOR, SARAH--Dau. of John Gibson-Will 1821

TAYLOR, THOMAS--Permission to keep Tavern. S: Mosey Taylor and Jesse Cox. Edgefield Ct. Min. March 1795.

TAYLOR, WALLER (?)--Grand Juror Edgefield 1794. List 20

TEDAR, DAVID--His children provisional legatees of Roger McKinnie-Will 1842. Edgefield

TEER, ANNA--Dau. of Hezekiah Gentry-Will 1820

TEMPLES, SEABORN -w- Rebecca Ann--Heirs of William Rodgers, Sen'r.. See Rodgers card. Edgefield Rec. Bk. B-148 1848

TEMPLETON, E. B. and wife--Heirs of Richard Hampton. See Hampton card. Edgefield Rec. Bk. B-109 1846

TERRY, ANNA MARIA--Widow of John Terry. See card William Holmes, Sr. -Ann Maria Terry--Will 26 Aug. 1823. Edgefield

TERRY, JANE--Grand daughter of John Elam-Will 1824. Also Gr. dau: Hans

TERRY, JOHN--Lic. to keep Tavern. S: James Coursey and John Spratt. Edgefield Ct. Min. March 1795.
Oct. Ct. 1794--Wm. Terry Surety for John Kelly as Tavern keeper.

TERRY, SALLEY--Dau. of Annamariah Williams-Will 1802, and wife of Wm. Terry. Also: Dau. Annamariah Terry
Gr-dau: Elizabeth Terry, dau. of John Terry. Edgefield

TERRY, STEPHEN--Dec'd. R. E. Sold 1839. Edgefield Rec. Bk. B-143
Dist: John Terry and Stephen C. Terry--1/4 each $254.87
Elizabeth, dau. of Clement Jones -w- Susannah-same
Children of James Terry, Viz: Thomas; James; Hilliard J;
Samuel C.; James Meggs -w- Ann; Richard; Susan; Frances A.
Moses P.; and William. Last 2-minors. R. E. Terry, Gdn.
R. E. Terry of Bibb Co. Alabama.

TERRY, STEPHEN--Dec'd. R. E. Sold 1039. Edgefield Rec. Bk. A-314
    Dist: Heirs of James Terry, dec'd. 1/4 $254.87
        John Terry-same
        A. G. Banthall -w- Elizabeth-same
        Stephen C. Terry-same

TERRY, WILLIAM--Petit Juror Edgefield 1788. List 10

THIRSTON, STREET--Son in law of John Gowan-Will 1809

THOMAS, BERSHEBA--Heir of Bersheba Hill. See Hill card. Edgefield
    Rec. Bk. A-78. 1832

THOMAS, JAMES--Petit Juror Edgefield 1786. List 5

THOMAS, JAMES--Appr. estate of Featherstone Cross. Edgefield Ct. Min.
    March 1795.
    Oct. Ct. 1787--John Thomas, Gdn. of Samuel Eskridge. See Eskridge
                                                                card.
THOMAS, JAMES--Dec'd. R. E. Sold 5 June 1826. Edgefield Rec. Bk. A-6
    Dist: John L. (or T.) Moore -w- Martha 1/3
        Thomas Bradbury -w- Nancy 1/3 of 2/3
        Mary Ann Thomas 1/3 of 2/3
        Clarissa Thomas 1/3 of 2/3

THOMAS, CAPT. JOHN of Green Co. Georgia From Josiah Thomas of Edgefield
    Negro woman-Jenny. Edgefield Deed Bk. 8-97 9 May 1793

THOMAS, JUDAH--Sister of Martha Foreman and Mary Foreman-Will 1790
    Ann Hill another sister. Isaac Foreman a brother. Edgefield

THOMAS, LUCY--Dec'd. dau. of John Hatcher-Will 1825.

THOMAS, MARY--Heir of Daniel Bruner. See Bruner card. Edgefield
    rec. Bk. A-34. 1834

THOMAS, PATRICK--Grant 4 May 1755 on Little Saluda to Robert Davis,
    Sen'r. To James Davis, to Jacob Smith to Stephen Crenshaw.
    On 19 March 1812 conv. to Isaac Hudson and also 500 A. adjoining.
    Part of 1000 A. grant to Jacob Smith 1 April 1793. Edgefield
    Deed Bk. 31-413/14 1812

THOMAS, ROBERT--Of Co. Edgefield. Edgefield Wills A-109. BX-46 Pkg-
    Wife: Sarah-pregnant   Robert Thomas   1957
    Dau: Mary Thomas   Francis Thomas
        William Thomas   Josiah Thomas,cousin-4 yrs. school
        Micajah Thomas   William Thomas, Brother
    2 Aug. 1795   Rec'd. Oct. 1795

THOMAS, SARAH--Gr. dau. of Sarah Stevens-Will 1793.

THOMAS, WILLIAM--Dec'd. R. E. Sold June 1826. Edgefield Sale Bk. A-18
    Dist: Mary Thomas, widow 1/3 $212.98
        Elizabeth Thomas -m- Joel Curry
        Mary Thomas
        Sarah C. Thomas
    6 April 1829 Rec't. from Daniel Prescott for share of wife
    2 Feb. 1835   "   "   Joel Curry   "   "   "   "
    10 May 1835   "   "   Daniel Prescott as Gdn. of Sarah and
                            Mary-minors. Seems Prescott -m- widow.

210

THOMAS, WILLIAM--His children provisional legatees of Roger McKinnis-
Will 1842.

THOMASON, ELIZABETH--(Widow of George of Laurens. See his card)
   Dau: Hariet Thomason   Spartanburg Bk-D-444
         Minerva   "   -in trust "unfortunate"
   "my 2 sons": G. C. Thomason)
                 A. L. Thomason) Land entitled to uncer act of Congress
   Dau: Cynthia Cooper
   "My 9 children, to wit:"--Rebecca Tuck; Nancy Prince; Wm. T.
   Thomason; A. B. Thomason; Cynthia Cooper; G. C. Thomason; Minerva
   Thomason; A. L. Thomason; Harriet Thomason; "late Husband, George
   Thomason. 1 Nov. 1855. Rec'd. 14 Dec. 1855

THOMASON, WILLIAM--"Son of John Thomason, dec'd.--a poor boy of Spartanburg County. Apprenticeship to William Poole 20 Sept. 1787.

THOMASON, WILLIAM TURNER--To his son, John Thomason, land on Taylor's
   Creek. Grant to Henry Walker. See John Thomason card. Spartanburg
   Deed M-132

THOMASON, WILLIAM T.--Dec'd. Spartanburg Division of Per. and R. E.
   Widow: Phebe Thomason
           George; John; and Stephen Thomason
           Betsy -w- Blake Massingale
           Sinthia -w- Zachariah Wyatt
           William; Sally; Polly; Mark; Delilah; and Arnold Thomason.
   Land grant to William Thomason 1785 on both sides of Taylor's
   Branch of Lawson's Fork of Pacolet River. Part. Oct. Term 1804.

THOMPSON, DAVID--Petit Juror Edgefield 1788. List 12 and 18

THOMPSON, ELIZABETH--Dau. of Angus McDaniel-Will 1795.

THOMPSON, EMILY--Sister of Frank Butler-Will 1827.

THOMPSON, EMILY--Dec'd. Grandmother of Emily Jones, dec'd. Mother.
   Waddy Thompson, grandfather. John Jones-father. 2 Jones children.

THOMPSON, ROBERT--Petit Juror Edgefield 1786. List 1, and 2.

THOMPSON, SARAH--Niece of Sally Stewart-Will 1821.

THOMPSON, WILLIAM, THOMAS, ALEXANDER, NARCILLA, NELLA, POLLY, TABITHA--
   Heirs of Alexander Stewart. See Stewart card. Edgefield Rec. Bk.
                                                              B-197
THORN, ANNY--Dau. of Allen Hinton-Will 1794. Margaret Thorn another
   dau. March Ct. Min. Bk. 1795--Charles Hightower Thorne-surety
   Adm. Bond estate of Wm. Tarrance. See Tarrance card.

THORNTON, ABNER--Petit Juror Edgefield 1789. List 13

THORNTON, JOB--Dec'd. R. E. Sold 1843. Edgefield Rec. Bk. B-63
   Dist: Newton Thornton   Hematral Thornton 1/4 each
          Martha Thornton   Abigail Thornton $119.00
   John Dorn, Gdn. Rec't. by Elbert Bledsoe 14 Mar. 1845 for my
   dist. share and by Henry Bledsoe, Marshal J. Bean, Gdn. for
   Martha Thornton.

THORNTON, MATTHEW--Dec'd. R. E. Sold 1836/7 Edgefield Rec. Bk. A-244

    Dist: Martin Saddler -w- Jemima Ann 1/2 $438.00
         William S. Thornton-minor   "   "
    Martin Saddler, Gdn. of minor.

THORNTON, WILLIAM--Gr. son of Wm. Stalworth, sen'r.-Will 1806. (Minor)

THOWER, SALLY--Dau. of Aaron Etheredge-Will 1811. Legacy--Land whereon
    Lewis Thower lives.

THREEWITS, CATHERINE -m- set 17 Sept. 1738 Joseph Griffin. Edgefield
    Misc. K-246. Hist. Com.

THURMOND, ELENOR--Dau. of George DeLaughter, Sen'r.-Will 1830.
    Her dau: Drusilla Thurmond

THURMOND, ELIZABETH--Dau. of Henry Key-Will 1810

THURMAN, JOHN--Grand Juror Edgefield 1787. List 8 and 14

THERMOND, PHILL--(Philip?) Grand father of Eliza Addison - Dau. of
    Joseph R. Addison by his 1st wife-Will 1832.

THURMOND, PLEASANT -m- set. 15 Dec. 1818. Sarah Quarles(Seems widow
    of Richard Quarles-owned his land) Wm. Lomax, Tr. Edgefield
    Misc. D-97

THURMOND, WILLIAM -w- Henrietta--Heirs of Benjamin Doolittle. See
    Doolittle card. Edgefield Rec. Bk. A-209

TILMAN, FREDERICK--Petit Juror Edgefield 1786. List 3 and 10

TILLMAN, GEORGE--Dec'd. Adm. granted to Lewis Tilman and Francis
    Tilman. Edgefield Ct. Min. Bk. Pg-245. 13 April 1789.

TILLMAN, JONATHAN -w- Tabitha--Heirs of John Cogburn. Edgefield Rec.
    Bk. A-225. 1834. See Cogburn card.

TILLMAN, JONATHAN--Will 25 May 1840. Edgefield

TILMAN, LEWIS AND FRANCIS--Qualified as Exor. and Ex'x. estate of
    George Tilman, dec'd.

TILMAN, LEWIS--Grand Juror Edgefield 1794. List 20

TILLMAN, LEWIS--Appr. estate of Benjamin Moseley. See Moseley card.
    Edgefield Ct. Min. March 1795.

TILLMAN, MARY--Heir of Lucy Hatcher. See Hatcher card. Edgefield
    Rec. Bk. B-23

TILLMAN, MARY E. -w- Benjamin Tillman. Great niece of John Ryan-
    Will 1827. Edgefield

TILLMAN, MARY--Dec'd. R. E. Sold 1846. Edgefield Rec. Bk. B-103
   Dist: James Griffin -w- Nancy 1/8 $185.66
          Lucy Bettis   "
          Benjamin Tillman   "
          Paschal Tillman   "
          Elsey Bland -w- Demaris Bland "
          Grand children-children of Mary -w- Joab Wilson. (Dec'd. dau.
            Emily Wilson, now -w- Dr. Newburn
            Mary E.   "
            James G. "   1/5 of 1/8 each $37.13
            Martha J."
            Permelia "
          Children of Elizabeth Hughs-a dec'd. dau.
            Stephen Y. Hughes
            John Clisby -w- Emily D.   1/3 of 1/8 each
            Alfred J. Hughs
          Children of Jonathan Tillman-a dec'd. son
            William Spires -w- Harriet 1/4 of 1/8
            Benjamin P.; Eliza H.; John V.; and John U. Tillman--
            Tabitha Tillman, Gdn.
   Rec't. by John Clisby -w- Emily D. of Coosee Co. Alabama

TILLMAN, POLLY--Dau. of Lucy Hatcher-Will 1834.

TILLMAN, SOPHIA ANN--Dau. of Martha Hancock-Will 1827. Wife of
   Benjamin Ryan Tillman

TILMAN, STEPHEN--Petit Juror Edgefield 1787. List 7 and 16

TILLORY, AGNES--Dau. of Elizabeth Thurman-Will 1804.

TILLERY, JOHN--Petit Juror Edgefield 1788. List 12 and 15

TILLERY, MARY--Dau. of William White-Will 1799. And her 2 children
   Robin and Mary. Son in law: David Tillery.

TIMMERMAN, DAVID--Dec'd. R. E. Sold 1850. Edgefield Rec. Bk. B-180
   Dist: Charlotte, Timmerman, widow--1/3 $259.41
          Elizabeth; Martha; Jacob B.; Malachi; Francis E.; and
          Simeon Timmerman--1/6 of 2/3
   Rec't. shows Elizabeth -m- David Timmerman

TIMMERMAN, HENRY--Petit Juror Edgefield 1787. List 8, 13, 17.

TIMMERMAN, PETER--Petit Juror Edgefield 1788. List 10

TIMMONS, HANNAH--Will 9 May, 1817. Spartanburg.

TIMMONS, JOHN to Abner Timmons 150 A. N-side Brown's Branch--Part
   1000 A. where sd John Timmons now lives. Spartanburg Deed A-71
                                                               1785.
TINSLEY, CATY--Grand daughter of John Cunningham-Will 1818

TINSLEY, JOHN W. -w- Clarissa--Heirs of William Richardson. See
   Richardson card. Edgefield Rec. Bk. A-254.

TINSLEY, MARY--Dau. of Anthony Foster-Will 1804 Spartanburg.

TINSLEY, POLLY--Eldest dau. of John Red-Will 1825. Spartanburg 2-48

TOBLER, ANN--Dau. of Elizabeth Sturzenegger-Will 1802

TOBLER, JOHN--Petit Juror Edgefield 1789. List 14

TOBLER, JOHN--Will 8 June 1789. Edgefield Deed Bk. 2-29
    Wife: Christian
    Son: John
    Daus: Christian; Elizabeth; Ann.
    Sons: Frederick; Ulric; and John Joakim
-Edgefield Min. Bk. Pg-234. Edgefield 14 July 1789.
John Tobler, dec'd--Will proved by the oath of John Myers and
ordered to be recorded.
-Edgefield Min. Bk. Pg-302. Edgefield Ct. Jan. 1790
John Tobler, dec'd--Christian Tobler qualified as Ex'x.

TOBLER, ULRIC--Of Savannah, a trustee in Will of John Clark, sen'r.
Will 1821. His Will in Edgefield. Ulric Bender Clark-a son of
Testator. Edgefield

TOBLER, ULRIC--Dec'd uncle of John J. Gray-Will 1838.

TOD, THOMAS -w- Ann to Edward Musgrove--Plantation in Spartanburg
County N-side Enoree River. Bd. said River. 100 A. part of
property of Wm. Cox, dec'd. which he sold to John Briggs, now
dec'd., whose heirs sold to said Thomas Tod. Spartanburg Deed
Bk. A-69 1785

TOD, THOMAS -w- Ann to Tilman Bobo--500 A. Grant to Thos. Tod 15 June
1775. By William Bull, Gov. on Cedar Shoal Creek of Enoree River.
Spartanburg Deed Bk A-58 1786.

TOD, THOMAS -w- to John Thomas, Sen'r. of Spartanburg Co. 440 A. on
S-side of Tyger River above ancient boundary. Being part 640 A.
grant to Major Parsons, 21 Jan. 1785. The other part being land
where said Maj. Parsons now lives. Spartanburg Deed Bk. A-79 1786

TOLBERT, JOSEPH--Edgefield Wills
    Wife: Sarah
    Dau: Mary Cason (Eldest and Elizabeth Miles
    Gr-dau: Permelia Tolbert
    Dau: Nancy Ware and her dau., Sarah Ware

Son: John Tolbert	Will 29 Dec. 1793
Dau: Peggy Ginnis (or Jennings)	Prov: March 1794
Son: Jeremiah Tolbert	Wit: Allen Robinson
Dau: Phebe Tolbert	Thos. Jennings
Son: Stephen Tolbert	Jeremiah Tolbert
Daus: Agnes and Fanny Tolbert	

TOLLESON, JOHN--Will 24 July 1820. Spartanburg Bx-6 Bills

Widow: Anny (Amy?)	Dau: Levicy -w- Richard Kirby
Sons: Muse and Stephen Tolleson	Anna -w- Maj. Gossett
Dec'd. dau: Nancy Bryant	Son: Eli Tolleson
Dau: Lidia -w- Josiah Sparks	Dau: Ity -w- James Quin
Son: "Dumb" John Tolleson	Her son: Barriman Quin

CHILDREN OF DEC'D. DAU. NANCY BRYANT:

Elizabeth -w- John Harvey	Sally -w- Wright Kirby
Charlotte Bryant	Eli Bryant
William T. Bryant	Mise Briant Both sp.
John Briant	James Briant used.
Polly -w- Wm. Harvey	Alfred Briant

TOLLESON, MUSE -w- Sarah--Spartanburg 1825 Box 6 Bill 6

TOMKINS, AUGUSTUS M.--Will 4 March 1843. Edgefield

TOMPKINS, DR. D. G.--Little Stevens Creek Baptist Church, Edgefield
    Born: 5 May, 1830   Died: 4 Sept. 1895
    -In memory of Mrs. H. Virginia, wife of Dr. D. C. Tompkins and
    daughter of Col. James and Gracey J. Smyly
    Born: 10 Sept. 1831   Died: 27 Dec. 1867
    -Tompkins, D. G. and E. A.--Tombs of their children
    Langdon-age 3 died 19 Sept. 1873
    Nathalia-died May 12, 1879
    -Clifford Tompkins-Born 14 May 1874 Died 23 Nov. 1898

TOMPKINS, ELIZABETH--Dau. of John Adams-Will 1822. Susannah Tompkins
    another daughter?.

TOMPKINS, HILDY--Dau. of Mary Hill-Will Rec'd. 1822. Edgefield

TOMKINS, JAMES and wife--Heirs of Ebenezer Hill. Edgefield Rec. Bk.
    A-280 1837

TOMKINS, JOHN -w- Polly--Heirs of Wm. Cunningham. See Cunningham card.
    Edgefield Rec. Bk. A-140

TOMKINS, MARY--Dau. of William Robertson, Sen'r.-Will 1838

TOMKINS, MARY--Grand daughter of Sarah Cunningham-Will 1841. Listed
    with George C. Robertson, a grand son.

TOMKINS, STEPHEN--Dec'd. R. E. Sold 1838. Edgefield Rec. Bk. A-282
    Dist: James Tomkins 1/3 $376.96
           Robert Jennings 1/3
           Elizabeth Tomkins, widow 1/3 of 1/3
           Wm. Robertson and wife 1/5 of 2/3
           Brantley; Richard F.; Lucinda; and Stephen Tomkins-same
           Thos. Gerguson, Gdn of four minors.
           Rec't. Wm. C. Robertson 7 May 1838

TOMKINS, STEPHEN P.--Dec'd. R. E. Sold 1842. Edgefield Rec. Bk. B-59
    Dist: Mary Tomkins, widow 1/3 - $187.66
           William Hill and wife   Elizabeth Tomkins
           Thomas Tomkins   Caroline   "
           Francis   "   Samuel   "
           Nancy   "   Amanda   "
    1/8 of 2/3 each $47.41. James Green, Gdn.

TOMSEY, SAMUEL--Son in law of Matthew McMillan-Will 1797. Prov.

TONEY, WILLIAM -w- Harriet--Heirs of Wiley Posey. See Posey card.
    Edgefield Rec. Bk. B-202 1850

TOWLES, TOLIVER -w- Ellen--Heirs estate of John Clark, dec'd. See
    Clark card. Edgefield Rec. Bk. A-5 1827

TRAPP, JOHN--Adm. estate of David K. Harling. See Harling card.
    Edgefield Rec. Bk. B-189

TRAVIS, BARET--Petit Juror Edgefield 1789. List 13
-Travis Barrett--Permission to keep Tavern. Edgefield Ct. Min.
March 1795. S: John Bledsoe and Abso'm Wilson

TRAYLOR, JOEL--Will 10 Oct. 1839. Spartanburg.

TRAYLOR, POLLY--Legatee and seems daughter of Isham Foster-Will 1816
Spartanburg.

TROOP, GEORGE--Dec'd. Edgefield Min. Bk. Pg-260 15 July 1789.
Will proved by oath of George Miller and ordered to be recorded.

TROTTER, JOSEPH--Petit Juror Edgefield 1787. List 7 and 16

TUBLEY, DAVID--Grand Juror Edgefield 1786. List 1, 2, 6, and 12

TUCKER, ANN--Dau. of Joseph Wofford-Will 1825 Spartanburg 2-109

TUCKER, EMILY A.--Dau. of Andrew Berry--Will 1854. Spartanburg 16

TUCKER, LANDON--Dec'd. Mentioned in Will of Thomas Jennings-Will 1835.
To wife: Lucy Jennings "All my distributive share of the
personal and real estate of Landon Tucker, dec'd. which I have
heretofore received. Edgefield

TUCKER, MARTHA--Dau. of Leana Jones, widow Thos. Jones. Will 1822.
Edgefield

TUCKER, MARTHA--Will 16 June 1834. Widow of Landon Tucker.

TULLIS, NEWEL, MOSES, SARAH and others--Heirs of Wm. R. Morton. See
Morton card. Edgefield Rec. Bk. A-98 1831
-Newel Tullis and wife--Heirs Rebecca Ramsey. Edgefield Rec. Bk.
B-75 1842

TURNER, ABRAHAM -w- Judith--Dist. of John Bodie. See Bodie card.
Edgefield Rec. Bk. A-308. 1839

TURNER, CHRISTIA--Sister of Benjamin Hatcher-Will 1838. Wife of
Wm. Turner. Edgefield

TURNER, FRANCIS--Sister of William Stewart-Will 1826. Edgefield

TURNER, GEORGE--Gr. son of John Fleke-Will 1798. Edgefield

TURNER, JOHN--Will 9 May 1813. Edgefield

TURNER, JOHN E.--Will 12 June 1843. Edgefield

TURNER, MATHIAS--Will 27 May 1818. Edgefield

TURNER, ROBERT--Will 17 Jan. 1843. Edgefield

TURNER, SUSANNAH--Dau. of John Gorman-Will 1799. Edgefield

TURNER, THOMAS E. and wife--Heirs of estate of Lazarus Chadwick. See
Chadwick card. Edgefield Rec. Bk. A-86. 1831

TURNER, WILLIAM: SARAH: ELIZABETH--Children of Susannah Christie-Will 1842.

TURPIN, MATHEW--Petit Juror Edgefield 1788. List 12

TUTT, ELIZABETH of Alabama--Grand daughter of Elizabeth Barrott-Will 1827. Edgefield

TUTT, JAMES--Petit Juror Edgefield 1786. List 3

TUTT, RICHARD--Dec'd. R. E. Sold. Edgefield Rec. Bk. A-126
    Dist: Mat. Minor -w- Elizabeth 1/5
          Elizabeth Tutt, widow of Jno. Tutt and their children:
              Frances, Hannah, and Mary Tutt
          Farma Tutt-widow of Henry Tutt and their children:
              James Randolph and child-Elizabeth Ann Randolph
          Mary P. Tutt

TUTT, RUTH--Sister of Samuel Howard-Will 1789. Edgefield

URNION, SARAH--Dau. James King-Will 1833. May be part of given name or middle name-Urnion.

UPTON, ELIZABETH--Dau. Thomas Roberts-Will 1784.

UTZE--See Will of Jacob Timmerman-1826.

VANN, EDWARD--Petit Juror Edgefield 1787. List 7 and 17

VANN, ELIZABETH--Dau. of Robert Moseley-Will 1796. Edgefield

VAN, ISAAC--Will 10 April 1839. Edgefield

VARDELL, JOHN--Petit Juror Edgefield 1794. List 20

VAUGHN, PARTHENY--Dau. Wm. Jeter-Will 1793.

VERNON, JAMES JORDAN--Legatee of Margaret Jourdan-Will 1825. James Vernon, Sen'r. an Exor. Spartanburg 2-64

VESSELS, JAMES--Petit Juror Edgefield 1788. List 12

VICE, DORCAS--Dau. William Meaders-Will 1814--Spartanburg. 2-18

VISE, LETTY--Dau. Elsworth Moore-1854. Spartanburg Wills Bx 45-1

VIMBAL, FRANCES--Dau. Moses Robertson-Will 1795. Rec'd. 1800 Mentions John Vimbal. Edgefield

VOINSET, JOHN--Will 16 April 1820--Spartanburg. 144

WADE, ABRAHAM--Legatee of Mary Rivers-Will 1802. Edgefield

WADE, ABRAHAM W.--Wit. Will of John Wright. 1801.

WADE, ASA--A minor of age to choose Gdn. Chose David Boswell. Appointed. Bond 50 pounds. S: R. Johnson and Jeremiah Hatcher. Edgefield Ct. Min. Oct. 1794.

WADE, DOLLY--Sister of James Lamar-Will 1814

WADE, HENDERSON--Wit. Will of John Longmire 1817-Sept. 11th. Edgefield Wills A-394

WAGSTER, RICHARD--Legatee of John Blalock-Will 1814

WAIT, AARON--See Will of Anna Teer-Will 1827.

WAITES, MARY--Heir of Catherine Butler. See Butler card. Edgefield Rec. Bk. A-298. 1838

WAIT, SIMEON -w- Elizabeth--Heirs of Abney Mays. Edgefield Rec. Bk. B-192 1850

WALDO, ELIZABETH--Dau. of Ann Leavenworth-Will 1836.

WALDRAM, ANN--Dau. of James Butler-Will 1811

WALDREN, HENRY and children--James, Charles, William, Nancy, John, et al-Heirs of Roland Williams, Jr. Edgefield Rec. Bk. A-124. 1833

WALKER, ALEXANDER -w- Elizabeth Ann--Legatees of John Hollingsworth-Will 1838. Eliza Ann dau. of John Hollingsworth. Edgefield

WALKER, CAROLINE--Dau. of Capt. John Allen and Legatee of Wilson Wooroof-Will 1809. Edgefield

WALKER, ELIZABETH -w-John Walker--Legatee of Francis McElworth-Will 1801. Their daughter: Margaret Walker. Legacy-Wm. Walker, Sen'r.

WALKER, HARRIET--Heir of Samuel Medlock. See Medlock card. Edgefield Rec. Bk. A-74 1829

WALKER, HEZEKIAH--Dec'd. Edgefield Ct. Min. March 1795. Amount of sale returned on oath of Samuel Walker. Recorded. Jan. Ct. 1795--Inv. estate returned. Order to sell personal property at house of Samuel Walker, Friday 13th Jan.

WALKER, HEZEKIAH--Of Winn County, Miss. Conv. to Mary Williams of Edgefield Dist. All the estate of Sampson Williams and Roland Williams in the R. E. of Susannah Murrah, dec'd. in Edgefield Dist. on the Ridge Road. 4 April 1828. Wit: Lewis Holmes, John Carter, Jonathan Williams. Edgefield Rec. Bk. A-Loose paper.

WALKER, HEZEKIAH--Mentioned in Will of Bibby Bush-Will 1812. Seems to be son or dau.

WALKER, JACKSON AND HARRIET--Orphans of John H. Walker--Thomas Johnston appointed Gdn. by Ordinary of Putnam County, Georgia on 24 Mar. 1 Edgefield Rec. Bk. A-308--Loose paper 1826

WALKER, JAMES--Applied for Let. Adm. on estate Joseph Walker. Bond: 5 pounds. S: William Hardin and John Day Apprs: Robert Samuel, Phill May, sen'r. and Jun'r. and William Griffin. March 1795--Return made by Jos. Walker, Adm.--Order to sell personal property at house of James Walker 1st Mon. in April next. March Ct. 1795--Amount sale returned by James Walker. March Ct. 1795: Joseph Walker wit. Will Lewis Clark, dec'd.

WALKER, JAMES and wife--Heirs of William Harris. See Harris card. Edgefield Rec. Bk. A-50

-James Walker and wife--Heirs of John Hall, dec'd. See Hall card. Edgefield Rec. Bk. A-104 1832

WALKER, JOHN--Petit Juror Edgefield 1788. List 10

WALKER, MARTIN--Son in law of Hendley Webb-Will 1826. Edgefield

WALKER, NANCY--Heir of Roland Williams, Jr. Edgefield Rec. Bk. A-70. See Roland Williams card. 1830

WALKER, ROBERT and wife--Heirs estate of James Butler. See Butler card. Edgefield Rec. Bk. A-165. 1834

WALKER, SAMUEL--Grand Juror Edgefield 1788. List 10 and 18

WALKER, WILLIAM--Petit Juror Edgefield 1786. List 1, 2, and 15

WALKER, WILLIAM -w- Eliza--Heirs of Isaac Kirkland, dec'd. Edgefield Rec. Bk. A-302 1839

WALL, AMEY--Dau. of James Hall-Will 1794.

WALL, BENJAMIN--Of Chatham Co. Georgia--Legatee of Robert Watts-Will 1839. Edgefield

WALL, SAMPSON--His children provisional legatees of Roger McKinnie.

WALLACE, BEAUFORT A.--Will 19 May 1841

WALLACE, JESSE -w- Frances--Heirs of Elizabeth Clarke. Edgefield Rec. Bk. B-191 1849

WALLACE, JOHN--Petit Juror Edgefield 1788. List 11 and 18

WALLACE, JOSEPH--Prov. Will of Samuel Howard. See Howard card. Edgefield Min. Bk. 1790.

WALLACE, LUCY--Dau. of Elias Morgan-Will 1804. Gr. son: Elias Wallace. Edgefield

WALLACE, NORMAN--See Will of John Fox-1837.

WALLACE, ROBERT -w- Nancy--Heirs of Jesse Stone. See Stone card. Edgefield Rec. Bk. B-45

WALLACE, ROBERT -w- Nancy--Heirs of Philip Lightfoot. See Lightfoot card. Edgefield Rec. Bk. B-65 1842

WALLACE, WILLIAM--Petit Juror Edgefield 1786. List 3

WALLICON, DANIEL--Dec'd. Ordered cit. be issued to show cause why Adm. should not be granted to Francis Little. Edgefield Min. Bk. Pg-233 12 Jan. 1789.

WALTER, LEONARD--Legatee of Henry Chiles-Will 1791

WALTON, CALEB and wife--Heirs estate of John Clark, dec'd. See
Clark card. Edgefield Rec. Bk. A-5

WALTON, E.--Heir estate of Wm. Bladon. See Bladon card. Edgefield
rec. Bk. A-258. 1837.

WALTON, JOHN--Son of Enoch Walton. Gr. child of James Hollingsworth-
Will 1818. Dec'd. dau: Lilly Walton. Edgefield

WALTON, EVELINE L.--Niece of Anderson Watkins-Will 1828.

WALTON, JOHN--Dec'd. R. E. Sold. Edgefield Sale Bk. A-84
Dist: Arthur Watson and wife 1/3   Total Amt. $201.50
James Walton-minor--Geo. Stockman, Gdn.   2/3
Rec't. from Arthur H. Watson for share of his wife from estate
of her former husband, John Walton-5 Dec. 1830

WALTON, LUCINDA--Gr. dau. of Elisha Stevens-Will 1834

WALTON, NANCY--Dau. of William Little-Will 1837. Sarah Walton
another dau.

WALTON, SUSANNAH--Dau. of Martha Tucker-Will 1834.

WARD, CHRISTOPHER--Petit Juror Edgefield 1788. List 12

WARD, FRANCES,--Dau. of William Elam-Will 1805

WARD, FREDERICK--Petit Juror Edgefield 1786. List 4

WARD, RICHARD and wife--Dist. estate of Isaac Bush. See Bush card.
Edgefield Rec. Bk. A-264. 1836

WARDLAW, ANN G.--Dau. of Thos. G. Lamar-son of Ann Leavenworth-Will
1836.
WARE, NANCY AND SARAH--Daus. of Joseph Tolbert-Will 1793.

WARE, NICHOLAS--Dec'd. Will 11 June 1799.
Children: Reuben Ware, Henry Ware, Sarah Samuel, Robert Samuel.
Edgefield Record Bk. A-1860 Pg-401

WARE, LIVELY--Heir of Sawney McKie. See McKie card. Edgefield Rec.
Bk. A-114 1832

WARE, WINEY--Dec'd. dau. of Drury Mims-Will 1819.

WARING, GRACE and Wm. Martin--"Formerly Merchant on the Congaree"
Marriage Cert. 8 Feb. 1772 by Christian Thews.
Edgefield Deed Bk. 10-150

WARREN, CHARLES--Will 30 March 1837. Edgefield

WARREN, JOEL -w- Mary--Heirs of Job Padgett. See Padgett card.
Edgefield Rec. Bk. A-312 1839

WARREN, JOHN--Dec'd.   R. E. Sold 1834.   Edgefield Rec. Bk. A-169
    Dist: Nathan Bodie and wife 1/3 $140.031/3
            Nancy A. Warren 1/3
            Arthur M. Warren 1/3

WARREN, LYDIA--Dau. of Arthur Watson, Will 1806.

WARRIN, THOMAS--Petit Juror Edgefield 1794. List 20

WARREN, THOMAS--Overseer on Road from Anderson's Ferry to the Watering
    Place. Part from Cloud's Creek to the District line. Edgefield
    Ct. Min. March 1795.

WASH, AMELIA--Dau. of Leana Jones-widow Thos. Jones-Will 1822. "Son"
    William Wash-husband of Amelia. Edgefield

WATERS--See Will Reuben Blalock-1829. His dau: Shady Ann Lydia
    Waters Blalock. Son: Patillo Reuben Blalock. Edgefield

WATERS, MARY--Dau. of James Cox-Will 1798.

WATERS, MARY ANN--Dau. of Rhydon Grigsby-Will 1826.

WATERS, PETER-Age 38   Rachell-age 8
    Mary   "   30   David-age 6
    Elizabeth-age 14   Sarah-age 3
    Misc. 3M-162--Will of Mary Waters of Abbeville County--96 Dist.
    dated 4 July 1792. Prov: 14 Sept. 1798.
    Data on Peter Waters from Immigrant List--C. J. 34-60 13 Feb. 1768
    Legatees: Dau. Elizabeth Sombes and her children:
                        Mary Steil
                        Sarah Steil
                        Her 2 sons
                        Her 2 daus. Jennet and ____?
                Dau: Rachell Beel
                Son: David Waters
                Dau: Sarah Partter
                Dau: Martha Burns
                Dau: Gennet Waters
                Gr. son: William Steel--Born after arrival.
    Affidavit by Samuel Armstrong that he was personally and intimately
    acquainted with Peter Waters and his wife, Mary, formerly Mary
    Smyth of Ballineana County of Antrim, Ireland, that Peter died
    about 15 years ago.

WATERS, THOMAS--Orator -m- Mary Ann Grigsby-one of daus. of Rhydon
    Grigsby-who made Will 24 Mar. 1826. Mary Ann died shortly after.
    Edgefield Equity Bill No. 387. Filed 21 Jan. 1829.

WATKINS, FREDERICK -w- Jane--Heirs estate of William Ferguson. See
    Ferguson card. Edgefield Rec. Bk. B-208. 1851

WATKINS, MARTHA--Dau. of Philip Goode-Will 1776.

WATKINS, RICHARD--Will 29 May 1835.

WATSMAN, JOHN-Dec'd. Edgefield Min. Bk. Pg-139 14 Jan. 1788
    Adm. Granted to Elizabeth Manse. She gave Bond 300 Pounds.
    S: John Frederick and James Frederick.

WATSON, ANN--Legatee of Isabella Gottier. Aff. by John Heatly
    17 Dec. 1798. Arch. Dept. Misc. 3M-82

WATSON, ARTHUR and wife--Heirs of John Walton. Edgefield Rec. Bk. A-84
    -Arthur Watson--150 A. on Cloud Creek. Cert. 20 Sept. 1765. Grant
    10 July 1766. Edgefield Mem. 9-102
    -Mem. N-272--250 A. Bd. Michael Watson, Heirs of John Pierson.
    Del. to John Douglas.
    -Arthur Watson--Grand Juror Edgefield 1788. List 10, 18, 21
    -Arthur Watson-Will 7 Feb. 1806. Prov: 12 Sept. 1806.Will Bk. A-239
        Sons: Richmond; Hezekiah; and Abner
        Dau: Fanny Satcher
             Patience Eidson
             Lydia Warren
        Sons: Arthur Rice; and Absolom.
    -Deed Bk. 3-154--Arthur Watson 16 Jan. 1788 to John Watson, Sen'r.
        land on Cloud's Creek. Grant to sd Arthur Watson 5 Jan. 1787.
    Wit: Abner Watson and Hezekiah Watson
    -Arthur Watson -w- Ophelia--Heirs of James O'Hara. See O'Hara
    card. Edgefield Rec. Bk. A-217 1835

WATSON, BENJAMIN--Grant of 1st Oct. 1787-Wife-Polly-dower-conv. to
    John Grice (or Grist) about 420 A. 24 April 1810. Edgefield
    Deed Bk. 30-159
    -Benjamin Watson--on Long Cane 174 Mem. 13-16

WATSON, DORCAS -m- Archibald Breazeal 1809.) Moses Waddel's
    Marga ret Watson -m- James Wilson 1819) Marriages

WATSON, ELIJAH, SEN'R.--Will 23 Mar. 1841

WATSON, ELISHA--Son of Martha Odom-Will 1817.

WATSON, JAMES--Of Granville-Will 26 Nov. 1770. C. T. Wills. Orig1771/4
    Wife: Sarah Qual. Ex'x.   23
    Dau: Elizabeth -w- James Gray
         Sarah -w- John Gray
    Sons: Samuel and James--Exors.

WATSONE, JOHN -w- Ann. Late Ann Blair. Sale-store account. Ct. Com.
    Pleas. Arch. Dept. Feb. 1746. Pg-125.

WATSON, JOHN--Dec'd. Will. Aug. Term 1750. Pg-381. C. T. Records
    Widow: Anne Watson, Ex'x.
            Note to John Maltby & Son made in London March 1, 1746.
    Watsons, res. of S. C.   John Watson, Jr.

WATSON, JOHN--100 A. Long Cane Settlement. Cert: 10 Dec. 1767.
    Grant 13 May 1768. Mem. 8-232
    Mem-240--100 A. on Rocky Creek Cert: 12 Sept. 1771. 500 A. on
    Gunnels Creek. Cert 6 April 1772.

WATSON, JOHN -w- Elizabeth--To George Underwood. Greenville Deed Bk.
A-45. 1787

WATSON, JOHN--Orig. Will 4 April 1788. Edgefield Prob. Bx. 47-2030
Wife: Ann Watson
Sons: Arthur; Jacob; William
Daus: Charity Anderson
       Cale(sp?) Watson
       Martha Odom
       Lucretia Jones
Part Michael Watson's estate on which John Watson, Jr. lives.
To son John Watson.
To son Willis Murphey Watson--Plantation.
Dau: Mary Odom

WATSON, LEWIS--Of Edgefield--Deed 2-111 20 Oct. 1787 To Brother Samuel
Watson, P. A. to collect from estate of Capt. Michael Watson.
Arthur Watson, Adm'r.

WATSON, LEWIS -w- Matilda--Heirs estate James Eidson. See Eidson
card. Edgefield Rec. Bk. B-125 1847

WATSON, MARTHA--Grant on Edisto River and land on Horse Creek of Cloud's
Creek. Grant-Jacob Odom. Sold by her as Martha Odom to Josiah
Colton 21 May 1806. Edgefield Deed Bk. 31-132.

WATSON, MARY--Of C. T., Widow to Rev. Robert Smith of C. T. P. A.
23 Sept. 1776. Arch. Dept. SS-115

WATSON, MARY AND PATIENCE--both of age to choose Gdn. Chose LeRoy
Hammond and Jacob Odom--who gave Bond with Richard Johnson, Sr.
and Richard Johnson, Jr. as Sureties. Edgefield Ct. Min. 14 July
12 Jan. 1789--Jacob Odum allowed 90 pounds out of   1788
estate of Michael Watson, dec'd. for the board of the children
of said Watson.

WATSON, MICHAEL--50 A. on Cloud's Creek. Bd: John Dooly. Cert. 21 Dec.
1769. Grant 5 March 1770.
100 A. on Cherokee Ponds--Cert. 11 Feb. 1771 Mem. 136-137
150 A. Near Cloud's Creek. Cert. 1 Oct. 1771

WATSON, MICHAEL--Will 26 May 1782 Prov: 22 July 1782.
96 Dist. Book.
Same card: Burditt Eskridge--Will 23 March 1779
                                Prov: 20 Aug. 1782

WATSON, MICHAEL--200 A. 96 Dist. Cloud's Cr. of Little Saluda.
Wm. Holdston mentioned -vs Wm. Daniel, D. S. 1773. Mem. 13-169

WATSON, CAPT. MICHAEL--Edgefield Deed Bk. 31-60
Recites: Grant to Frederick Strother 2 Aug. 1757 conv. to Elias
Daniel. Conv. to Joseph Howel. Conv. to Capt. Michael Watson.
No dower--Fell to heirs-Elijah Watson who conv. to Richard
Duncan 29 June 1797. 50 A. Cloud's Creek
Same card: Martha Odum to Josiah Cotton 21 May 1806. Bk. 31-132
3 grants of 928 A. Wit: Elijah Watson and Jeremiah Williams

WATSON, REBECCA--To Daniel Bullock 18 June 1796--Receipt for a slave-
Phillis-as all demands of "my father, Artimas Watson's Estate".
Wit: Benj. Watson. Edgefield Deed 16-339

WATSON, SUSEY--Dau. of Isaac Bush-Will 1836. See Bush card.

WATSON, STANMORE--Dec'd. Died 24 Mar. 1849. Left Will. Bill 994

WATSON, WILLIAM--Dec'd. of S. C. Will. Arch. Dept. Mtg. KK-464
Dau: Elizabeth Watson-her Gdn-Richard Buckley of Boston, New
England. Richard Buckley gave P. A. to Joseph Moody of C. T.
18 Aug. 1737

WATSON, CAPT. WILLIAM--Appointed Commander of a Scout Boat 1 May 1749.
Arch. Dept. Misc. HH-10

WATSON, WILLIAM--Mem. 7-231. 300 A. on Little Saluda-Cloud's Cr. Gr.
22 Feb. 1759 to mentioned. Mem. 3 April 1759.

WATSON, WILLIAM--"Of Baton Rouge-in the Province of West Florida" Will
Father: James Watson-if not in Britain
Mother: Jane Watson
Brother: John Watson of Charleston, S. C.
Uncle: Mark Valentine, dec'd. "my share of his estate"
Brother: Adam Watson   )
Sisters: Mary and Isabella) Residents of New Britain.
Codicil 3 July 1781 Misc. 40-434

WATSON, WILLIAM--Mem. 13-373
Heir: Michael Watson conv. to Henry Key in 1772. Land on
Stephens Creek.

WATSON, WILLIAM--Petit Juror Edgefield 1786. List 5

WATTS, JAMES -w- Mary--Heirs of Philip Jennings. See Jennings card.
Edgefield Rec. Bk. B-185. 1850

WATTS, ROBERT--Will 12 Feb. 1839. Edgefield

WEATHERINGTON, ELIJAH--Appr. in re estate of Pleasant Burnett, dec'd.
See Burnett card. Edgefield Ct. Min. Oct. 1794
See also card Green Harris, dec'd. Bk. B-175 1849

WEAVER, FREDERICK--Petit Juror Edgefield 1789. List 14

WEAVER, JEAN--Dau. of John Douglas-Will 1799

WEVER, JONATHAN--Will 1 May 1841

WEAVER, LYDIA--Dau. of Nathan Trotter-Will 1828

WEVER, SARAH E.--Sister of Mary L. Danton-Will 1841.

WEBB, HENLY--Petit Juror Edgefield 1786. List 1, 2, 11,16, 21
HENRY

WEBB, POLLY--Dau. of Angus McDaniel-Will 1795.

WEBB, SELAH--Dau. of John Douglas-Will 1799

WEBB, SARAH--Dec'd. dau. of Agnes Norris-Will 1816.

WBB, TURNER--Edgefield Ct. Min. 1832. Bk 178. Loose paper.
Widow: Mary Webb--"This is to certify that I, being the widow
of Turner Webb, late dec'd. have given up the Adm. to G. B.
Mitchell. 3 March 1832. Mary Webb"

WEBSTER, ELIZABETH--Widow. -m- John Kennedy. Lic. 6 Aug. 1791 by
Philip Clayton. See Kennedy card. Edgefield Ord. Ct. Min. Bk.

WEEMS, WILLIAM--Proved Will of Mary Fauqua as witness. See Fauqua
card. Edgefield Ct. Min. Oct. 1794.

WELBORN, AMY--Gr. daughter of Joseph Collier-Will 1818

WELCH, EDWARD W.--Grand son of John McFatrich-Will 1817.
Grand daughter: Betsy and Maryan Welch. Absolom Welch, Exor.

WELCH, MARY ANN--Minor. Heir of Nathaniel Sanders. See Sanders
card. Edgefield Rec. Bk. B-135. 1848

WELCH, WESLEY G. -w-Sophronia Ann--Heirs of John Harris.
Edgefield Rec. Bk. A-290. 1838. See Harris card.

WEST, JOSEPH--Dec'd. R. E. Sold. Edgefield Sale Bk. A-66
Dist. 1.8 each $21.78
Arthur West   Henry Partridge and wife
William West, dec'd.   Joseph West
Andrew P. Jones and wife   Mary -w- H. J. Norris
Thomas E, Norris -w- Marthy   Stanmore McDaniel and wife.
Rec't--Thos E. Norris 5 Nov. 1836
Rec't. Sarah Patrick 16 Nov. 1833

WEST, REBECCA--Legatee Ezekiel Perry-Will 1833

WEST, WILLIAM--Will 14 July 1779. Prov. by Dedimus to Wm. Melton of
Green County, Georgia 23 Aug. 1792
Wife: Mary
Son: William
       Thomas--Part tract belonging to Matthew Melton
       James--Land on Edisto where formerly lived
To: Martha Cox
Dau: Sarah Lepard
Gr. son: Charles Leperd
Daus: Nancy Myers; Elizabeth Allen; Betty; Priscilla and Patience
To: John; Joseph; and Jacob West

WESTBROOK, ANN--Sister of Howard R. Marshall-Will 1829

WESTEN, SARAH--Dau. of Hicks Jones-Will 1826

WHATLEY, FEREBY--Will 28 Oct. 1840

WHATLEY, EDMUND LAMKIN--Nephew of Peter Lamkin-Will 1826

WHATLEY, EDWARD--Appointed Adm'r. estate of George Cowan, dec'd.
Shearley Whatley, sen'r. Appr. same estate. Jan. Ct. 1795--
Shearley Whatley commissioned to build bridge.. See card Col
John Martin. Edgefield Ct. Min. March 1795

WHATLEY, HELLEN ANN--Dau. of Col. Abner Whatley and Legatee of Helen
Lamkin, widow of Peter Lamkin-Will 1830

WHATLEY, P. A.--His children--Heirs of J. J. Still. Edgefield Eq.
Roll 1849. See Still card.

WHATLEY, SHERWOOD AND EDMOND--Prov. Will of Thomas Roberts. See
Roberts card. Edgefield Min. Bk. Pg-138. 14 Jan. 1788

WHATLEY, SHIRLY--Petit Juror Edgefield 1786. List 4
    SHERWOOD--"   "   "   "   " 7

WHEELER, CORNELIUS--Dec'd. R. E. Sold 1839. Edgefield Rec. Bk. A-322
    Dist: Barbary Wheeler -m- Sugar McCarty 16 Feb. 1841
           Cullin or Cornelius Wheeler
           Ellen   Each received 1/6 $20.83
           John
           Catherine -m- Caleb White before 17 Mar. 1843
           William.
    Rec't. by Cornelius Wheeler of Covington Co. Ala. 7 Nov. 1844.
    P. A. to Giles Bryant and David Dewey.

WHEELER, DANIEL, SR.--Will 23 Dec. 1843.

WHEELER, JOHN--Petit Juror Edgefield 1788. List 12

WHIG, JANE--Dau. of John Marchant-Will 1830

WHITE, ABNER V.--Dec'd. R. E. Sold 1851. Edgefield Rec. Bk. B-200
    Dist: Edward W. White 1/2 $427.50
           Susan White, widow--1/3 of 1/2
           Margaret C. White-minor--2/3 of 1/2

WHITE, BLUMER--Will 30 Oct. 1839.

WHITE, BURGESS--Petit Juror Edgefield 1786. List 3

WHITE, BURGESS--Made motion to apprentice James and William Burk.
See Burk card. Edgefield Ct. Min. Oct. 1794.

WHITE, DANIEL -w- Sarah--Heirs of Bates Wrenn. See Wrenn card.
Edgefield Rec. Bk. B-95 1846

WHITE, EDWARD -w- Susan--of Walton Co. Ga.--Heirs of John Rodgers.
See Rodgers card. Edgefield Rec. Bk. A-324 1839

WHITE, HARDY--Legatee of Henry Clark-Will 1840. Edgefield
    -Hardy White--Gdn. of Tabitha Bladon-heir of William Bladon. See
    Bladon card. Edgefield

WHITE, JOHN T. -w- Civel--Heirs estate of Willie Darby. See Darby card.
Also Wiley White -w- Francis. Edgefield Rec. Bk. A-203 about 1828

WHITE, JOHN V. and Mary et al,--Heirs of Wm. R. Morton. See Morton
card. Edgefield Rec. Bk. A-98 1831

WHITE, MARGARET--Dau. of Thomas Berry-Will 1819. Rebeckah White another daughter. Edgefield

WHITE, PEGGY--Dau. of John McFatrick-Will 1817.

WHITE, STEPHEN--Dec'd. R. E. Sold 1833. Edgefield Rec. Bk. A-142
Dist: Blumes White 1/4 $120.13 1/8
      James Yeldel -w- Sarah
      John White
      Jane S. White.
Rec't. 12 Feb. 1833 from Jesse Griffis in right of wife.

WHITE, WILLIAM--Commissioned to build bridge. See card Wm. Anderson.
Edgefield Ct. Min. March 1795.

WHITE, WILEY -w- Francis--Heirs estate of Willis Darby. See Darby
card. Also John T. White. Edgefield Rec. Bk. A-203. 1828

WHITE, WILLIAM -w- Jane--Heirs of John Marchant. See Marchant card.
Edgefield Rec. Bk. A-70 1832

WHITEHEAD, ELIZABETH--Dau. of John Harvin-Will 1805

WHITEHEAD, JACOB -w- Sarah of Ala.--Heirs of John Hester. See Hester
card. Edgefield Rec. Bk. A-278. 1837

WHITEHEAD, JAMES--Petit Juror Edgefield 1794. List 20

WHITEHEAD, WILLIAM -w- Rachel--Heirs of James Don. See Don card.
Edgefield Rec. Bk. B-113

WHITLEY, ELIZABETH--Dau. of Abney Mays-Will 1804

WHITLEY, STEPHEN -w- Elizabeth--Heirs of Abney Mays-Will 1812 (?)

WHITLEY, THOMAS and Elizabeth--Heirs of Abney Mays. Edgefield Rec. Bk.
B-192 1850

WHITLEY, ELIZABETH--Dau. of Isaac Bush-Will 1836.

WHITLOC, JOHN--Petit Juror Edgefield 1788. List 11

WHITLOCK, JOHN and wife--Heirs of Isaac Bush. See Bush Card. Edgefield Rec. Bk. A-264. 1836

WHITLOCK, WINFREY--Will 12 Sept. 1833

WHITLOCK, WILLIAM -w- Sarah Ann--Heirs estate of Ransom Hamilton.
Edgefield Rec. Bk. B-107 1846

227

WHITNER, ELIZA AMANDA--Grand daughter of Elizabeth Clark-Will 1827.
Also legatees: Eliza Ann Whitner, dau. Her children: Benj.
F. Whitner and Joseph N. Whitner, trustees.

WHITNEY, FRANCIS--Petit Juror Edgefield 1788. List 11

WHITTLE, ELISHA and wife--Heirs of Allen Body. See Body card.
Edgefield Rec. Bk. A-92

WHITTLE, MARGARET--Her heirs: husband-James and son: Sampson.
Heirs of Job Padgett. Edgefield Rec. Bk. A-312 1829

WHITTLE, MARTIN and wife--Heirs of Henry Padgett. See Padgett card.

WIDEMAN, LEONARD--Dec'd. Summons 1832 to: (83-84)
Savile Wideman, widow
Leonard; Frances; Henry; Samuel; Edward Wideman
Meredith Wideman -w- Catherine
Joseph Duval -w- Lucy
Sarah Moseley

WILBORN, JEREMIAH--Adm. estate of Peter Farrow, Jr. See card Stephen
Garrett -vs- Jeremiah Wilborn. Edgefield Eq. Bills No. 14
Filed 19 April 1817.

WILLIAMS, ABSOLOM--Youth, a son of Charles Williams, chose Capt.
Drury Pace as his Gdn. Appointed. Edgefield Ct. Min. 14 Jan. 1788
14 July 1788--Drury Pace appointed Gdn. of Charles Williams-son
of Charles Williams, dec'd. Not old enough to choose.

WILLIAMS, ANNAMARIAH--Will 1802. Her daughter-Mary Elam
Also Massy (Marcy or Mercy) Pa rtman -w- Henry Partman
William and Joseph Minter, grand sons of Annamariah Williams
Ezebell and Stephen Clement--Grand children of Annamarih Williams.

WILLIAMS, BUTLER--Petit Juror Edgefield 1786. List 5
-Butler Williams applied for license to keep Tavern. S: Britton
Mims and Littlebury Adams. Edgefiela Ct. Min. March 1795.

WILLIAMS, CHARLES--Grant 12 Dec. 1763 sold by Absolom Williams 25
Sept. 1794. Edgefield Deed 12-75

WILLIAMS, FREDERICK--Petit Juror Edgefiela 1788. List 12 and 17

WILLIAMS, FREDERICK--Grand son of Sarah Stevens-Will 1793.

WILLIAMS, FREDERICK -w- Amy to John Dorn, Sen'r. 115 A. land on waters
Sleepy Creek, Little Stevens Creek, Turkey Creek, Stevens Creek
Savannah River? Wit: Robert Conolly and Amy Williams
Edgefield Deed Bk. 44-321 30 March 1830

WILLIAMS, JINCEY -m- Wm. Parker and she is mentioned in Will of Isaac
Parker 1817 as widow of dec'd. son.

WILLIAMS, JOHN--Grand Juror Edgefield 1786. List 1 and 2

228

WILLIAMS, JOHN--Dec'd. Will Prov. by John Hamilton. Oct. 1794.
William Caldwell and Joseph Williams Qual. as Exors.
Appr's: John Bullock, Wm. Robinson, Leonard Waller and
Nathan Lipscomb.
Jan. Ct. 1795--John Williams a Surety for Bibby Bush as Tavern
Keeper.
March Ct. 1795--John Williams, Gdn. of James Coody-minor.

WILLIAMS, JOHN--Of Edgefield.   Edgefield Wills A-89
Wife: Ann Maria--Land adj. Joseph Collier
Son: Joseph Williams
Bro. in law: Joseph Gouge--In N. C.
Dau: Mary Williams
Son: James Atwood Williams
Dau: Elizabeth Caldwell and Wm. Caldwell
Son: Duke Williams
Dau: Rebecca Williams. 24 Sept. 1794. Rec'd. 4 Oct. 1794

WILLIAMS, JOHN--Heir of Daniel Bruner. See Bruner card. Edgefield
Rec. Bk. A-34. 1834

WILLIAMS, JOHN HENRY--Nephew Henry K. Boyd-Will 1825.
Winney Williams a witness with Ann Collier and Snoden Griffin

WILLIAMS, LUCRETIA--Dau. of William Bush-Will 1837.

WILLIAMS, LUD--Grand Juror Edgefield 1786. List 4, 10, and 16

WILLIAMS, LUD.--Dec'd. Edgefield Judgements and Pleadings, Mar. 1803
Summons to Lud Harris; Lewis Harris; and Elisha Willis
John Buchanan -w- Sarah late Sarah Milling, Exor. of David
Milling, dec'd.

WILLIAMS, MARTHA--Wife of Roland Williams. Dower favor of Rachell
Quinsey and also to Thomas Rowe. 2 Deeds. Oct. Ct. 1787.

WILLIAMS, MARTHA--Sister of William Sanders-Will 1816. Mentions
Stephen Williams.

WILLIAMS, PATSEY M.--Dau. of William Jeter-Will 1818. Also called
Folley.

WILLIAMS, PETER -w- Nancy--Heirs of Scarborough Broadwater. See
card. Edgefield Rec. Bk. A-221 1835

WILLIAMS, POLLY--Sister of Pressly G. Sullivan-Will 1836.

WILLIAMS, THOMAS--His widow, Rachel -m- Lewis Holloway. See Holloway
card. Edgefield

WILLIAM, ROBERT--Gdn. to Olinda Williams. Came into court and gave
Bond. S: John Swillivan and Robert Long. March Ct. 1795.
March Ct. 1795--Lud Williams-Appr. estate of John Meyer. See
Meyer card.

WILLIAMS, ROGER M.--Appointed Mgr. of Election held in Edgefield at
house of John Longmire. Acts, etc. 1809-95
Page 108--Roger M. Williams-Justice of Peace for Edgefield

WILLIAMS, ROGER M.--Edgefield Wills Bk. D-17
Wife: Mary   14 Nov. 1828
Children: Sterling Q.; Mackerness G.; Butler; Betsy Gardner;
          Polly Doolittle; and Caty M. Morgan.

WILLIAMS, ROLAND: SAMPSON: MARY--Purchasers estate of Susannah Murrah.
See card Hezekiah Walker. Jonathan Williams-wit. Edgefield
Rec. Bk. A. Loose Paper. 1828

WILLIAMS, ROLAND, JR.--Dec'd. R. E. Sold. Edgefield Sale Bk. A-76
Dist: 1/8 each
Mary Williams--Rec't. 29 June 1830 $37.50 Full share
Nancy Walker   " 24 Jan. 1830
Jonathan Williams" 2 July 1830 $12.37½
William Williams " 25 June 1831
Joel Deas and wife
James Deas and wife
Sampson Williams
Roland Williams

WILLIAMS, SAMUEL--Son in law of Nicholas Lowe-Will 1843.

WILLIAMS, SARAH--Heir of William Melton. See Melton card.
Edgefield Rec. Bk. A-118 1832

WILLIAMS, SARAH--Dau. of William Flin, Sen'r.-Will 1837.

WILLIAMS, STEPHEN FRANCIS SAMUEL--"Illegitamite son" of Samuel
Tomkins-Will 1826.

WILLIAMS, THOMAS--Minor son of William Williams of age to choose Gdn.
Chose John Swilling. Appointed. Edgefield Ct. Min. March 1795.

WILLIAMS, WILLIAM--Dec'd. Robert Owen, Adm. Inv. returned by Adm.
Edgefield Ct. Min. Oct. 1794.
Oct. 1794--Williams, Owen--of age to choose Gdn. Chose Robert
Owen Williams. Bond 500 pounds. S: James Baker and Robert
Speer. The Court appointed said Robert Owen Williams as Gdn.
for Miss Volinda Williams.

WILLIAMS, WM. -w- Ruth--Heirs of Shadrack Boone. See Boone card.
Edgefield Rec. Bk. A-48. 1829

WILLIAMS, WILLIAM -w- Eliza Ann--Legatees of Creswell Moore-Will 1839.

WILLIAMS, WILLIAMSON--Nephew of Lewelling Goode-Will 1812

WILLIAMS, WINYFRED--Sister of Wade Bussey-Will 1817.

WILLIAMS, WINEFRED--Cousin of John Boyd-Will 1825. Sister of Testator;
Mariah Williams. Nephew: John Henry Williams and mentions Legacy
of Henry K. Boyd, brother of John Boyd, Testator. Mentions ch. of
Winefred: Osburn, Patsy, and Elizabeth. Dr. John W. Williams,
an Exor.

230

WILLIAMSON, SAMPSON -w- Lucinds--Heirs estate of Ransom Hamilton.
See Hamilton card. Edgefield Rec. Bk. B-104 1846

WILLIAMSON, DR. VINCENT P. Arch. Dept. Misc. D-401
Widow: Eliza--Of Edgefield

WILLIS, CALEB -w- Catherine--Heirs of Cornelius Wheeler. See Wheeler
card. Edgefield Rec. Bk. A-322 1839

WILLIS, ELIHU--See card Lud Williams. Edgefield Judgements. 1802

WILLIS, RHODA--2nd dau. of George Smith-Will 1824.

WILLISON, MRS.--Heir of Robert Starke. Edgefield Rec. Bk. B-71 1842

WILLISON, SAMUEL AND EDWARD KEATING--As creditors, granted Let. Adm.
on estate of John Davison, dec'd. See Davison card. Edgefield
Min. Bk. Pg-233. 1789

WILLS, MARY--Dau. of Edward Coleman-Will 1826.

WILSON, ALEXANDER--Dec'd. Edgefield Ct. Min. Jan. 1795.
Elijah Rogers applied for Let. Adm. Bond: 200 Pounds
S: John Hill and John Anderson.
March Ct. 1795.--Thomas Wilson--Commissioned to vuild bridge.
See card Wm. Anderson.
March Ct. 1795--Absolom Wilson--Default in road work.

WILSON, GEORGE--Grand son of James Scott--Will 1804.

WILSON, JOAB -w- Mary, dec'd. Edgefield Rec. Bk. B-103 1846
Children: Emily -m- Dr. Newburn
Mary E.
James Y.
Martha J.
Permelia F.--Heirs of Mary Tillman. See Tillman card.

WILSON, KEZIAH--Dau. of Wright Nicholson.-Will 1807.

WILSON, MARGARET--Dau. of Elizabeth Zinn-Will 1793

WILSON, MARY--Dau. of Martha Moore-Will 1822. Gr-daus: Martha and
Mary Ann Wilson.

WILSON, POLLY--Dau. of William White-Will 1799

WILSON, ROBERT--Petit Juror Edgefield 1788. List 13

WILSON, RUSSELL--Surety for Wm. Dozier--License to keep Tavern.
Edgefield Ct. Min. 1795

WILSON, RUSSELL--Qual. as J. P. for this County. Edgefield Ct. Min.
Jan. 1795.

WILSON, SAMUEL--Petit Juror Edgefield 1794. List 21

WILSON, THOMAS--Grand Juror Edgefield 1786. List 1, 2, 4, and 12
Petit   "   "   "   " 21

WILSON, WILLIAM--Petit Juror Edgefield 1789. List 14

WILSON, WILLIAM -m- Rebecca Youngblood-dau. Peter Youngblood. See
    Youngblood card. Of Augusta, Ga. Edgefield File.

WINFREY, THOMAS LEMAR--Son of Judith Winfrey, dec'd. and Legatee of
    Robert Lamar, Sen'r.-Will 1806

WINN, H. -w- Susan--Heirs of Isaac Bush. See Bush Card. Edgefield
    Rec. Bk. A-264. 1836

WINN, LEUCHEN--Dec'd. R. E. Sold. Edgefield Sale Bk. A-64
    Dist: 1/6 each $17.65
    Burrel E. Hobbs and wife.
    Stephen F. Blackwell -w- Mariah W. of Virginia. Order 19 Apl. 1830
    Elizabeth F. Winn -m- Arthur Freeman-Rec't. 26 July 1830
    Warren F. Winn-minor) B. E. Hobbs, Gdn.
    Sarah Winn-minor   )   Rec't. 10 April 1832
    Susan Winn -m- George F. Penn--Rec't. 10 April 1832
    James Jones Purchaser-Pd. $112.17 5 Dec. 1831

WINN, PRUDENCE--Sister of Jeremiah Lamare-Will 1806

WINN, SARAH--Dau. of James Hall-Will 1794

WINN, WILLIAM, JOHN, EZEKIEL--Children of Elizabeth Wimberly -w- of
    William Wimberly-Will 1802

WISE, RACHEL--Legatee of Jessy Roundtree-Will 1815
    -Rachel Wise-Will 3 March 1842.

WISE, SARAH--Will 7 Nov. 1837.

WISE, WASHINGTON -w- Teresa--Heirs of John Cogburn. See Cogburn card.
    Edgefield Rec. Bk. A-225 1834

WISEMAN, DANIEL--Legatee of Mathew Coleman-Will 1840

WITZEL, MRS. ELEANOR -w- John Witzel--Dower favor Wm. Shaw. Jan. Ct.
    1786. Edgefield Ct. Min.
    -Edgefield Ct. Min. 1785-90 Page-20--Eleanor Witzel relinquished
    Dower 12 April 1786.

WOOD, JANE--Heir estate of William Ferguson. See Ferguson card.
    Edgefield Rec. Bk. A-208. 1851

WOOD, JEREMIAH--Son: Joseph Wood. Dau: Mariah Wood--Legatees of
    Nathaniel Bacon-Will 1805. Edmond Wood also Legatee.

WOOD, JOSEPH--A minor of 18 yrs age--Came into Court and chose Samuel
    Scott as Gdn. Jan. Ct. 1790. Min. Bk. Pg-307

WOOD, MABEL--Legatee of Lewelling Goode-Will 1812

WOOD, THOMAS -w- Sarah--Heirs of Francis Coleman. See Coleman card.
    Edgefield Rec. Bk. A-219 1835.

WOOTLEY, REASON--1st husband of Elizabeth Long-dau. of Catherine Bates-
Will 1819. Edgefield

WOOTEN, THOMAS--Petit Juror Edgefield 1786. List 5

WORD, FRANCES--Dau. Charles Cooper-Will 1819.

WORD, PHEREBY--Dau. of Isaac Bush-Will 1836.

WORENTON, BERSHEBA--Heir of Aaron Moore. See Moore card. 1812.
Edgefield Deed 31-77

WORMELY, MRS.--Heir of Robert Starke. See Starke card. Edgefield
Rec. Bk. B-71. 1842
-Estate Robert Stark of Edgefield. Rec. Bk. B-71 Loose Paper
Mrs. Wormley dec'd.--3 children: John C.; Hugh W.; and
Mrs. Mary B. Carter.
Sophia Gildart-dec'd. 5 children: John W.; Sophia -m- John B. Fox;
Mary Jane -m- Lemuel Pitcher; Elizabeth Egliston and Francis
Gildert.
Horatio Stark, dec'd. 4 children: Mary Wilkinson; Theodore;
Josephine and Horatio Stark.

WORTHINGTON, WILLIAM -w- Martha--Heirs of Green Harris, dec'd. See
Harris card. Edgefield Rec. Bk. B-173 1849

WRENN, BATES--Dec'd. R. E. Sold 1846. Edgefield Rec. Bk. B-95
Dist: William Wrenn 1/8 $32.37
         Mack   "
         Jackson   "
         Bates   " Jr.   Each 1/8 $32.37
         Joshua Harris -w- Elizabeth
         Daniel White -w- Sarah
         Silvester Dunston-formerly Wrenn
         Daniel Evans -w- Nancy.
Edgefield Stray Paper:
"State of Alabama, Coosa County--Know all men by these presents
that I, Mack Wrenn, a citizen of the State of Alabama". Power of
Atty. to Bates Wrenn of Edgefield to collect share of father's
estate. 11 Oct. 1847.

WREN, PRESLEY--Grant 31 Aug. 1774. 200 A. on Stephens Creek-Colleton.
Arch. Dept. Grant Book--Royal 33-125

WRIGHT, JOHN--Dec'd. Will 8 Jan. 1801. Prov: 23 March 1802.
Wife: Mary   Edgefield Record Bk. A-1800-539
Dau: Richardson Wright
     Mary Ann Richardson Wright
     Frances Wright
     Susannah Richardson Wright
     Patsy Moss Wright
     Betsy Brown
Exor: Matt Martin
Wit: John C. Garrett, Elisha Palmore, Abraham M. Wade.

WRIGHT, JONATHAN and Benjamin Darby--Surety for Jacob Foreman, Gdn.
his children. Edgefield Min. Bk. Page 310   Jan. Ct. 1790

WRIGHT, MESHOCK--Grand Juror Edgefield 1794.   List 21

WROTEN--See Roten. Edgefield

YARBOROUGH, AMBROSE--Elapsed 877A--Grant to Stephen Layton, Exor. of
Ambrose Yarborough for Jeremiah Yarborough, heir of Ambrose
Yarborough.

YARBOROUGH, GILSON--Half brother of William Moore-Will 1818

YARBOROUGH, FRANCES--Appointed Gdn. "Her 4 children" Misc. PP-506
William age 4 yrs.   Elizabeth age 7 yrs.
Gilson age 14 mos.   Ann age 6 yrs.

YARBOROUGH, GILSON--Half Brother of Wm. Moore-Will 1818. Got land on
Big Creek where he now lives.
-Gilson Yarborough--Will 24 Jan. 1839

YARBOROUGH, MARY and ANN. C. T. Wills
Son: James Armstrong Yarborough
Dau. and Gr. son of James Armstrong of Camden Dist.--Will 1780
Wit. Wm. Yarborough.   13 Nov.

YARBOROUGH, MOSES--Late of St. Mark's Par. Craven Co. C. T. Wills
Wife: Frances   2 Oct. 1772
Oldest child: Elizabeth Yarborough-minor)
                Ann   )These 3 by 1st wife
                William   )
                Neilson by Frances
Step sons: William and George Moore.
Had land on Saluda River.

YARBROUGH, RICHARD -w- Mary--Heirs of Job Padgett. See Padgett card.
Edgefield Rec. Bk. A-312 1839

YARBOROUGH, THOS GRIFYS (or Griggs) Fairfield Wills 1850 Bk. 1-23
Wife: Rachel--sole heir
Exor: John Irviner (or Turner) and Jesse Kirchland
Wit: Martha Irviner (or Turner) and Elizabeth Irviner or Turner
Rec't: 9 Oct. 1800

YARBOROUGH, WILLIAM--License to keep Tavern. S: John Gorman and J
Jesse Griffin. Edgefield Ct. Min. Jan. 1795.

YATES, ABRAHAM--Son of Thomas Yates, dec'd. Too young to choose Gdn.
Court appointed Thomas Anderson, Gdn. Edgefield Ct. Min.
14 Jan. 1788.

YELDEL, JAMES -w- Sarah--Heirs of Stephen White. See White card.
Edgefield Rec. Bk. A-142. 1833

YOUNG, JOHN--Son of Col. Wm. Young of Ala. Legatee of John Fox-Will
1837. Also to Caroline Patterson, formerly Caroline Young.

YOUNG, WILLIAM--"Late of Dist of 96 but at present of City of C. T.
Brothers: Thomas and Richard Young. Edgefield File. C. T. Will B-
    Land in Bahama Islands to William and John, sons of Ann   868
    Alexander, now wife of Jacob Ernest on Brushy Creek, Saluda in
    96 Dist. and "Caroline, the daughter of Olive____, dau. of
    Frederick Glover of Cambridge Town, 96 Dist.

YOUNG, WILLIAM--Son in law of Martha Fox-Will 1803

YOUNG, VALENTINE, SR.--Dec'd. Edgefield Rec. Bk. B-19 (Of Abbeville)
    Heirs: Valentine Young, Jr.
           Thomas Young   )Of Lowndes Co.
           Washington J. Young   )Miss. P. A.
           Elizabeth Young now -w- Abraham Burden)to Valentine
           Polly Young now -w- James Graham   )Young, Jr.
    Real Estate sold. Distributees:
           Mary Young, widow 1/3
           Thomas; William; W. J.; Isaac; Valentine Young
           Abraham Burden -w- Elizabeth
           William Franklin -w- Nancy
           James Franklin -w- Margaret
           James Graham -w- Mary
           Each 1/9 of 2/3 $12.71. Settlement date: 1 Jan. 1841

YOUNGBLOOD, ABNER--Wit. Edgefield Deed Bk. 34-461 2 Dec. 1816
    Deed from James Cleveland, Daniel Moseley and John Cleveland
    to William Hagens-2 Dec. 1816. Other Wit. William Robertson
    Edna Christian

YOUNGBLOOD, ANDREW AND WILLIAM WRENN--From Mary Cary; Jonathan Young
    and Abram Young. Plantation Grant to Jacob Young 16 Feb. 1785.
    Edgefield Deed Bk. 31-66/7 12 Nov. 1802

YOUNGBLOOD, ANDREW--Witnessed Will of John Walker 7 Sept. 1805.
    Edgefield Wills A-214

YOUNGBLOOD, ANDREW--478 A. Edgefield 1 Aug. 1814. Land Grant Books
    in Archives Dept. Charleston 59-191

YOUNGBLOOD, BENJAMIN--Of Richmond Co. from John Mears 14 Dec. 1796.
    Part of 300 A. on waters of Spirel Creek. Augusta, Ga.
    Deed Bk. L-320

YOUNGBLOOD, CATHERINE--Archives Dept. Mem. 10-101
    300 A. on Saluda R. Berkley Co. Bd. Wm. Lowe, Maurice Gwinn,
    James Chapells. Surv. Cert: 7 Mar. 1770. Grant 2 May 1770.
    Mem. 27 May 1770. Benj. Durbrow.
    -Arch. Dept. Land Grant Bks. Royal 19-398
    300 A. Berkley 2 May 1770
    78 A. Craven 23 June 1774
    -Arch. Dept. Edgefield File Mem. 13-388
    Mem. by Richard Dean. 50 A. on Saluda R. 96 Dist. Also 50 A.
    on Savannah R. Cert. 8 July 1774. Grant 9 Sept. 1774
    -Edgefield Deeds 13-402 10 May 1796
    Catherine Youngblood-her grant for 300 A. Recites Will of Francis
    Sinquefild dated 4 Dec. 1780. Devised inter alia 400 A. to be
    divided between his 2 daughters, Rachel and Jane Sinquefild. Part
    of which was part of Grant of 300 A. to Catherine Youngblood which
    said Francis and his brother Samuel Sinqufild purchased at a
    Sheriff's sale.

YOUNGBLOOD, CATHERINE--Of Spartanburg Dist. Edgefield Deed Bk. 32-439
To Allen Marshall 23 Jan. 1816--P. Atty. to collect from Estate
of George Youngblood, the money due her from the Estate of her
father, Abraham Youngblood. Also to see to a parcel of land on
Turkey Creek. Prov. in Greenville Dist. before Thos. Edwards.

YOUNGBLOOD, CHARLES--Edgefield Council Journal 36 Pg-52 5 Feb. 1772
Petition to Certify Plats for 78 A. in Craven and 72 A. in Craven.

YOUNGBLOOD, DAVID--Land Grant Books in Archives. State 15-145
156 A. Charleston 1 Jan. 1786.
88 A. Charleston Round 0]17-380?] 5 March 1787

YOUNGBLOOD, DAVID--Edgefield Deed Bk..31 Pg-431--Witnessed Deed from
Wm. Odom, Sr. to his grand son, Tillman Odom. Dated 6 Nov. 1812.
Sd: David Youngblood.

YOUNGBLOOD DAVID--Edgefield Will 1816. Prov: 1822. Bequest of
Thomas Youngblood to son David Youngblood for life-then to his
son-Simeon. Parcel of land on Sleepy Creek beginning on an Ash
corner, and on Ephraim's Branch, thence down said branch to a
maple corner on Harkin's old line; thence on Harkin's old line
to a Sweet gum corner on Sleepy Creek; thence to a Pine on
William Youngblood's land.

YOUNGBLOOD, DAVID--Of Edgefield. Deed Bk. 40-37 19 Oct. 1822
To: Wiley Berry--B/S, beds, furniture, plantation tools, etc.
Sd: David Youngblood

YOUNGBLOOD, DAVID--Edgefield Deed Bk 40-177 7 Oct. 1823
To: Wiley Berry 100 dollars-lease for 4 years 200 A. on Sleepy
Creek. Ephraim's Branch. Bd. by Thomas Youngblood, William
and James Youngblood.

YOUNGBLOOD, DAVID--Edgefield Deed Bk. 40-73 14 March 1823
To: William Kirksey $200.00 Lease for 4 years. 200 A. on Sleepy
Creek--Bd. by John Davis; Moses Odom; Thos Youngblood; William
and James Youngblood.

YOUNGBLOOD, DAVID--Edgefield Deed Bk. 45-117 20 Dec. 1830
To: James Keith, Jr. of Pickens Dist. $500.00 Land on waters of
Sleepy Creek. Bd. on Harkin's Old line; William Youngblood.
Wit: Simeon Youngblood 8 Jan. 1831. and Lemuel Keith.

YOUNGBLOOD, DAVIS -m- Lucretia Munro, widow of Daniel Munro. See
card Daniel Munro--Desaussure's Rep.

YOUNGBLOOD, ERASMUS--Witnessed Deed dated 28 June 1819. Emanciation (sp?)
of slave by Eldred Simkins, et al. Edgefield Deed Bk. 35-158

YOUNGBLOOD, ERASMUS J. -w- Eliza--Edgefield Deed Bk. 45-138 25 Feb. 1831
To: Arthur T. Wigfall--Recites -m- settlement of Levi Durand
Wigfall and wife Eliza T. Wigfall and Lewis Wigfall partion of R.
E. between Erasmus J. and wife Eliza and Arthur T. Wigfall--case
heard in Charleston.

YOUNGBLOOD, ERASMUS J. (OR I)--Dower-Eliza Youngblood To: U. L. Griffin, Esq. in trust for Jno. Covar -w- Elizabeth. Parcel of land in Village of Edgefield. Formerly property of Arthur Simkins and by him conveyed to his grand son, the said Erasmus I. Youngblood. Edgefield Deed Bk. 47-44 Oct. 1834

YOUNGBLOOD, ERASMUS J. -w- Elizabeth-(Children of Erasmus I. and Eliza) Arthur Wigfall, Trustee. Deed from Nancy Lowe in trust for life then to Arthur W. Youngblood; Lewis; Erasmus H.; and Eliza-also children of Erasmus I and Eliza. Edgefield Deed Bk. 47-297/8 16 July 1835.

YOUNGBLOOD, ERASMUS J.--Edgefield Deed Bk. 44-121 22 Dec. 1839. To: Abner Whatley-Mtg. 300 A. 2 miles south of Edgefield on Waters of Cedar Creek, waters of Horn's Creek.

YOUNGBLOOD, GEORGE--Augusta Chronicle and Gazette Vol. XI-500 1 July 1767 For himself and the heirs of Abraham Youngblood -vs- Heirs and Creditors of P. Youngblood--Shows George and Abraham, sons of Peter, dec'd. Had deed gift from their father dated 27 Nov. 1777 for 200 A. on White Oak Creek, Co. of Columbia. In Sup. Court. These papers are in the Hogsden Library in Savannah, Ga.

YOUNGBLOOD, GEORGE--Edgefield Deed Bk. 18-351 3 Dec. 1799 From: "Daniel Mazyeke--eldest Captain in the late second Reg't. of foot in the State aforesaid on Continental establishment. Commanded by Lieut. Col. Francis Marion". 150 A. surveyed for Robert Larry on 26 Jan. 1773 and 4 April 1775 Conv. sd. Daniel Mazyeke 1/2 Jan. 1776-in 96 Dist. on Mine Creek of Little Saluda.

YOUNGBLOOD, GEORGE--Edgefield Deed Bk. 17-215--Wit. Deed from Margaret Harlem to Samuel Jenkins 24 Jan. 1799.

YOUNGBLOOD, GEORGE and Thomas McDaniel--Wit. deed from Jno. Logan of Colleton to Major Moody Burt of Edgefield on 12 Sept. 1802. Land on Stevens Creek, in Edgefield Dist. Edgefield Deed Bk22- -Deed 23-290-George Youngblood and John Terry--Wit Deed 327 from Sampson Butler and wife to Jesse Pain, 1st Mar. 1802.

YOUNGBLOOD, GEORGE -vs- Samuel Key--Edgefield Bk. marked "Clerk of Ct. 1807-1815--Bk #3" #13-1807--Decree for Plaintiff-$46.69. Rec't. by Nancy Youngblood 7 Mar. 1809. Her signature.

YOUNGBLOOD, GEORGE--Dec'd. Cit. 30 Jan. 1808. Edgefield Prob. records Adm'x: Nancy-widow -m- 2nd H. W. Lowe Ira Youngblood (died 1829) and Eleanor Youngblood-minors--Had interest in Estate of Emalie Youngblood. Summons in Part: Henry W. Lowe appointed Gdn. of: Ira; Eleanor; Erasmus J; Emaline; Matilda Youngblood--Surety- Nicholas Lowe. Bond: 10 June 1811. -Erasmus J. -m- Eliza Wigfall, dau. of Levi Durand Wigfall -w- Eliza T. Wigfall. Eliza died, left 5 children: Erasmus H.; Arthur; Lewis; Eliza; and Jacob.

YOUNGBLOOD, GEORGE--Dec'd. Edgefield Probate Box 32-1161
    Widow: Nancy   Cit: 30 Jan. 1808
    Children: Ira and Eleanor--minors
    1790 Census--George Youngblood 1 man, no boys, 3 females.

YOUNGBLOOD, HENRY--Land Grant Bks. Arch. Dept. Royal 15-15
    200 A. Branch Coffeetown Creek. 28 Aug. 1767
    -Mem. Vol-9-348--Henry Youngblood-200 A. on Branch of Coffeetown
    Creek of Sav. River. Bd.--All vac. Cert: 4 Feb. 1767.
    Grant 28 Aug. 1767.

YOUNGBLOOD, HENRY--Charleston Prov. Inv.Y-1767-71-301. Of Colleton.
    Dec'd. Inv. and Appr--Large estate--16 Jan. 1770. Many horses.
    Accts and notes due by: John Sutton; John Youngblood; Wm.
    Robinson; James Williams; Henry Smith; Thos. ___?; Robert Wallace;
    and Charles Bird. Apprs: James Lockridge, Robert Bryan, and
    Robert Wallace

YOUNGBLOOD, ISAAC--Land Grant Bks in Arch. Dept. State 5N-476/7
    54. A. Charleston. 5 Dec. 1785.
    57 A. Charleston. 5 Dec. 1785.
    289 A. Charleston 5 Mar. 1789
    339 A. Charleston 5 Mar. 1787
    180 A. Charleston 7 May 1787
    75 A. Charleston 3 Sept. 1787

YOUNGBLOOD, ISABEL--Dau. of William Dean-Will-1829

YOUNGBLOOD, JACOB--Arch. Dept. State Grants 10-79
    370 A. 96 Dist. on 5 June 1780. South side of Turkey Cr. waters
    of Stephens Cr. Wm. Moultrie. Surv. Cert. 21 Oct. 1784.
    -206 A. 7 May 1787 in Orangeburg. "Situate in the Dist. of
    Orangeburg--waters of South Edisto. S/s. Bd. Ne. on land run
    for Joseph Youngblood, all other sides vac.
    -Edgefield Deed Bk. 7-252 21/22 March 1792 Jacob Youngblood to
    John Aldridge--185 A. on Turkey Cr. of Stephens Cr. of Savannah
    R. on S-s said Creek--being part of 370 A. grant said Jacob
    Youngblood 5 June 1786. Pres: Isaac and Patience Aldridge and
    Jas. Scott.
    -Edgefield Deed Bk. 23-212 16 June 1795--Jacob Youngblood Wit.
    Deed from John Still, Sen'r. to John Still, Jr.--his son. All
    of Edgefield. 25 pounds sterling. 175 A. on Little Stephens Cr.
    Wit: James Holt, Jacob Youngblood, Wm. Coursey.
    -Edgefield Deed Bk. 20-417 1796--Jacob Youngblood from John Crab-
    tree -w- Margaret--all of Edgefield--314 A. on branches of Stephens
    Cr. Grant to Abraham Crews on 5 Aug. 1793 and by him conv. to said
    John Crabtree 17 April 1796. Wit: Frederick Williams; James
    Youngblood; Thomas Youngblood.
    -Jacob Youngblood and James Adams witnessed Deed from Jonathan
    Esery to Edward Kirksey 20 Feb. 1805. Page 422 same book
    -Edgefield Deed Bk. 31-45 19 Jan. 1797.--Jacob Youngblood of
    Edgefield to Catherine and Seaborn Youngblood--70 A. on Turkey Cr.
    of Stephens Cr. Edgefield Co. Bd. by lands of Thomas McGinnis;
    Nathaniel Russel and John Stewart. Wit: Caleb Burton, Benj.
    Weaver.

YOUNGBLOOD, JACOB--Edgefield Deed Bk 39-245 30 Aug. 1822 Bd. land
   conv. by Wm. Odom to Moses Odom. On Sleepy Cr. of Turkey Cr.
   By: John Dorn and John Falkner.
   -Jacob Youngblood-Will 1816. Prov: 1822 Edgefield--Bequests
   by Youngblood to son: Thomas Youngblood-Will 1816--Did not
   devise anything specific to his son Jacob Youngblood, but did
   appoint him an Exor. as follows. "Appoint my sons, jacob;
   and Thomas Youngblood; and my son in law, James Adams Exors."

YOUNGBLOOD, JACOB--Edgefield Deed Bk. 40-366 10 March 1823.
   Jacob Youngblood from James Falkner 100 A. on waters Sleepy Cr.
   of Turkey Cr. of Sav. R. Part grant to John Crabtree. Wit: Amos
   Falkner, Nathan Sharpton, and Terry Corley.

YOUNGBLOOD, JACOB--Edgefield Deed Bk. 43-13 15 Sept. 1826. Jacob
   Youngblood and J. Dabbs Wit. deed from Jno. C. Allen to Wilson
   Kemp. Dated 15 Sept. 1826. Jacob Youngblood to Probate 15 Sept.
                                                                1826
YOUNGBLOOD, JACOB, JR.--Name on Jury list Fall Term 1st Jan. 1829.
   Also Spring Term 1822. Edgefield Ct. Com. Pleas. 1829-34

YOUNGBLOOD, JACOB--Of Edgefield Dist. Deed Bk. 45-157 18 Dec. 1830
   To: "my 3 sons": Thomas S; James; and David Youngblood--re-
   serving life interest 100 A. land on Sleepy Cr. Said: Jacob B.
   Youngblood. Wit: James Smyly, Henry W. Mitchell.

YOUNGBLOOD, JACOB, SEN'R.--Edgefield Probate. Cit: 14 March 1831
   Rec'ts. for shares by: Jacob and Thomas S. Youngblood.
   Rec't. in file from dec'd. dated 5 Nov. 1827-as Gdn. of Phenix
   Minor.
   Receipt Bk. A-8--Shows: Jacob Youngblood as Gdn. of Heirs of
   Frederick Phenix: Eliza; Drury; Nancy; and James Phenix

YOUNGBLOOD, JACOB--Mentioned in Will of Robert Dunn 28 Oct. 1844.
   Will directs to be sold "The small tract of land where Jacob
   Youngblood now lives"--about 50 A. Abbeville Wills

YOUNGBLOOD, JAMES From Sylvanus Stevens--200 A. waters Turkey Cr.
   Orig. Gr. Wm. Blackley 13 April 1769. Edgefield Deed Bk. 2-69

YOUNGBLOOD, JAMES -w- Jemima to Zachariah Speers--150 A. on Kiowee
   Cr.--Flat Branch. Augusta Ga. Deed Bk. F-1-155 20 June 1787
   -James Youngblood of Richmond Co. 21 Oct. 1789. Deeds IG-90
   From Isaac Fuller -w- Mary 150 A. on Kiokee Cr. Orig. Gr. to
   Isaac Fuller 28 May 1788. Wit: Nathan Youngblood and John
   Fuller, Sen'r.

YOUNGBLOOD, JAMES--Of Rocky Creek. Edgefield Wills A-32 3 Aug. 1791
   Oldest son: Jeremiah   Wife: Mary
                Eli   Ex: Thomas Youngblood and
                Thomas   Abraham Youngblood
      Son in law: James Baker   Wit: Mary Usry and Jas. Scott
                       Prov: March 1792.

YOUNGBLOOD, JAMES--Edgefield Will 1816. Prov: 1822. Bequest of
   Thomas Youngblood to son James for life and then to his son
   Thomas. "All the rest and residue of my lands not heretofore
   devised.

239

YOUNGBLOOD, JAMES--Edgefield Deed Bk. 37-129. Manumission to slave.
Thomas Youngblood; Frederick Williams; Charles Adams; James
Bean; and James Adams; J. P. "We the underwritten Justices of
the Quorum and freeholders of the said District, the latter
having been duly summoned by said Alexander Bean--do hereby
respectfully certify upon the examination of a certain slave by
the name of Jesse, described as in the above deed. Satisfactory
proof has been given to us that the said slave is not of bad
character and is capable of gaining a livlihood by honest means.
Given under our hands this 11th day of April anno domi 1820.

YOUNGBLOOD, JAMES--Dec'd. Edgefield Prob. Bx. 32-1145. Cit: 9 April 1827
Adm'x: Nancy Youngblood   Adm'r: Thomas S. Youngblood
S: Jacob Youngblood and Frederick Williams
Elizabeth and Lucretia Youngblood-minors. Wilson Kemp, Gdn.
Paid: Wm. R. Youngblood, Gdn. 4 or 5 shares
"   Jacob Youngblood
"   Mary Richardson full share.
-Estate of Nancy Youngblood. Cit: 9 July 1832
Adm'r: Thomas S. Youngblood
Surety: James Youngblood and John Falkner.

YOUNGBLOOD, JAMES--Edgefield Deed Bk. 47-314. Witnessed a Deed dated
8 Dec. 1834 from William Culclazar to James Smyly. Dower--
Elizabeth Culclazar.

YOUNGBLOOD, JEREMIAH--Wit. Deed from Azariah Lewis to William Buckhalter.
Edgefield Deeds Bk. 14-279 13 May 1793

YOUNGBLOOD, JEREMIAH -w- Susannah (spinster)To: John Palattey--50
A. Edgefield Co. Rocky Creek of Little Stephens Creek, a branch
of Turkey Creek, a prong of Big Stephens Creek of Savannah River.
Part of 200 A. grant to Wm. Blakely 13 April 1769 who conv. to
Peter Mehl who conv. to Silvanus Stephens who conv. to James
Youngblood on 18/19 Oct. 1788 who, by Will, bequeathed it to
Jeremiah Youngblood. Edgefield Deed Bk. 16-464 25 Nov. 1794

YOUNGBLOOD, JEREMIAH AND MARY--Wit. deed from James Barker, sen'r. to
James Barker, Jr. Edgefield Deed Bk. 12-199 21 May 1795.

YOUNGBLOOD, JESSE--Of East Florida--Dower-Mary Youngblood. To: Thomas
Youngblood of Edgefield Dist. Tract of land shown by Plat-viz:
Andrew Youngblood Plat 193 A. Rec'd. in Bk and page 184-this
15 Dec. 1813. On Coffeetown Creek. A branch of Stephens Creek
of Savannah River. Edgefield Deeds 33-378
-Andrew Youngblood and Thomas Youngblood, both of Edgefield--
to Asa Holloway-land on Coffeetown Creek-200 A. being grant to
Henry Youngblood 28 Aug. 1767. Resurveyed for Andrew Young-
blood 3 Dec. 1813. Dower by Martha -w- Andrew Youngblood. Wit:
Henry Youngblood.

YOUNGBLOOD, JOHN, JR.--Augusta Ga. Deed F-1 Pg-92 2 Nov. 1770 To:
Geo. Rosbrough-300 A. in Richmond Co,
-John Youngblood of state of Georgia to Ignatious Few--200 A. land
on waters of Kegg Creek-Richmond Co. Ga. Orig. grand said John
Youngblood 1st Nov. 1774. Wit: Isaac Fuller, Charles Stewart.
Augusta Ga. Deed Bk. A2 115 10 Sept. 1782

YOUNGBLOOD, JOHN AND PETER--Augusta, Ga. Deed Bk. IG 37 23 April 1784
    Dower: Martha. To: Joshua Grinnage. Shows Peter and John
    heirs of Benjamin Youngblood. 100 A. grant Benjamin Youngblood.
    Between Uchee and Little Kiokee Creek, Richmond Co. Ga.

YOUNGBLOOD, JOHN--Land grants in Arch. Dept. State 12-218. 200 A.
    96 Dist. 15 June 1784

YOUNGBLOOD, JOHN -w- Mary of Richmond Co. Ga. to Jacob Gore. 100 A.
    land on waters of Little Kiokee Cr. Grant 5 Oct. 1784. Adj.
    other lands of John Youngblood. Wit: Sam'l Robison, Daniel
    McNeil, Abraham Youngblood. Augusta Deed Bk. A-1-81 7 Jan. 1788
    Min. of Sup. Ct. show John Y. Petit Juror 1783, James and Isaac
    Mar. 30, 1787.

YOUNGBLOOD, JOHN of Edgefield to Conrad Gallman--220 A. Grant sd.
    Youngblood on 5 June 1786. Dower Catherine Youngblood 18 Sept. 1797
    Edgefield Deed Bk. 13-254. 9 May 1797

YOUNGBLOOD, JOHN Y--Dec'd. Abbeville Probate Bx. 110-3259
    David Thomas Adm'r. Warrant of Appr-10 April 1826.
    Appr: John Marshall; John Burnett; Benj. Johnston; John Thomas
    and William Thomas.

YOUNGBLOOD, JOHN and Aaron Hill and Bryan Deen--Wit Will of Thomas
    Deen dated 10 Jan. 1840. Wife: ____? Children: Benjamin Deen
    Nancy -w- John N. May, and William Deen.

YOUNGBLOOD, JOSEPH and MARGARET--Augusta, Ga. Deed IG-58 21 Oct. 1788
    To: Lewis Barnes. Shows: Peter Youngblood, dec'd.
        Widow: Susannah Youngblood
                Samuel; Joseph; Rebecca -w- Wm. Wilson;
                Liddy -w- Cain Gentry; Lewis; Sarah; Margaret; and
                Susannah. Now all of state of S. C.

YOUNGBLOOD, LEWIS--Land Grant Bks. Arch. Dept. State-9-196
    150 A. Ninety Six. 3 April 1786
    -99 A.   "   "   6 Jan. 1800 Charleston 46-239

YOUNGBLOOD, LEWIS--Abbeville County Prob. Bx. 104-2553.Bond: 5 Sept 1808
    Larkin Reynolds, Adm'r. S: Thomas Wilson and Joseph Motes
    Sale purchasers: Rachel Youngblood-nearly all
                      Peter   "   1 saddle
                      Bird Martin
                      Wm. Douglas and John Turner
                      John Walter-stack of foder(sp)
    Adm. Bond Rachel Youngblood 20 Mar. 1810
    S: John Merriweather and Jackson Tyner. Bx. 110-3260

YOUNGBLOOD, LEWIS--Edgefield Wills C-86 Bx-32 Pk-1148
    Wife: Mary
    Sons: Abner; Gideon; Thomas; Basil; William Youngblood
    Daus: Catherine and Sarah Youngblood
    11 Feb. 1822 Rec'd. 27 Mar. 1822
    Div. of estate in 1846 shows: Whitfield Brooks share of widow 1/3
    Basil Youngbloods Widow 1/3 of 1/7 of 2/3. Ch: Thos and Martha
    Sarah -w- John McNeil
    Catherine -w- J. S. Hollister
    Martha-dau. of Gideon -m- W. J. Bickers

241

YOUNGBLOOD, LEWIS--Edgefield Judgements and Summons Spring Term 1821
Let. Adm. to Mary Youngblood 23 Feb. 1822.
-Youngblood, Nancy, dec'd.   Let. Adm. to Thomas S. Youngblood
30 July 1832.

YOUNGBLOOD, LEWIS -w---Heirs estate of William Gray.   See Gray card.
Edgefield Rec. Bk. A-40 1829

YOUNGBLOOD, LEWIS--Dec'd.   R. E. Sold 1845. Edgefield Rec. Bk. B-89
Dist: SAME HEIRS as ref. Edgefield Wills.

YOUNGBLOOD, LUCY--Dau. of William Nance-Will 11 Jan. 1841.
Dau: Rebecca Nance
      Lucy Youngblood and Samuel Youngblood
      Thomas Nance
      Alexander Nance
Gr. son: William Crosly
Wife: Mentioned-not named.   York Co. Bx. 3-109 Probate

YOUNGBLOOD, MARTHA--Of Richmond Co. from James Jenkins of Columbia Co.
$50.00 5A. in Richmond Co. Augusta, Ga. Deed H-372. 24 Feb. 1802

YOUNGBLOOD, MARY--Will Feb. 4 1836. Son: William Youngblood-only
legatee. Edgefield

YOUNGBLOOD, MARY--139 A. Colleton Co. 1 July 1811. Land Grants Arch.
Dept. State K4 262

YOUNGBLOOD, MARY--Edgefield Deed Bk. 43-86 20 Aug. 1827. To H. & R.
Drake--All of the Clay on her land in a pond which lands are
contiguous to lands now belonging to Dr. Abner Landrum and Sarah
Burns. Sd. Mary Youngblood. Test: William Youngblood and
Eldred Riddle.

YOUNGBLOOD, NANCY--Deed Gift to "my 3 daus" (Nancy-widow of George Y)
Eleanor; Emeline and Matilda Youngblood--$250.00 out of "my part
or portion of sd estate" Should they all die, then to be divided
between "my other 3 children". Edgefield Deed Bk. 31-141 15 Jan.
1812
YOUNGBLOOD, NANCY--Dau. of Ira Youngblood from Benjamin Darby, her
grandfather-Deed gift-Slave, Louisa. Edgefield Deed Bk. 33-149
13 May 1816.

YOUNGBLOOD, NANCY--Dec'd. Edgefield Prob. Bx. 32-1147
Cit: 9 July 1832--Pub. at Mountain Creek
Bond: 30 July 1832
Adm: Thomas S. Youngblood,
S: James Youngblood and John Falkner

YOUNGBLOOD, PATIENCE--Her first husband, Stanmore Butler. Dau of
Nancy who was dau. of Arthur Simkins. Buried about 1½ Mi. from
Edgefield in Simkins Burial Ground a Cedar Field.

YOUNGBLOOD, PETER--Charleston Book Prob. Rec. 1758-63 Pg 618
And James Johnston Wit. Deed Gift from Bushrod Thomas and Elizabeth
his wife to their grand daughter Gresilla Hawkins. 100 A. adj.
Thos. Odall's survey on 96 Creek. Also cattle, etc. 28 May 1763.
Prov. before James Mayson, J. P. by Peter Youngblood, Jr.
May 25, 1763. Rec'd. 10 June 1763

YOUNGBLOOD, PETER -w- Martha--To Joshua Grinnage 100 A. land between Uche
and Little Kiokee. Grant to 19 Jan. 1773. Augusta, Ga. 23 April
1784. Deed B2-194

YOUNGBLOOD, PETER--Royal Grant 28-366--350 A. Colleton Co. 11 Feb. 1773
Peter Jr.--200 A. on Chavious Creek 2 May 1770. 19-397

YOUNGBLOOD, PETER -w- Mary of Granville Co. S. C. to John Frazier
100 A. in Granville Co. on Beaver Dam Creek, branch of Savannah
River on S. and lower side of sd creek--in the S. and upper
course of a tract of land granted to John Lamar, sen'r. 1 Aug.
1756. Who conv. to sd Peter Youngblood. Wit: ___? Ray;
Jenkins Harris; Moses Harris. Edgefield Deeds 6-130 27 Jan. 1774

YOUNGBLOOD, PETER--Minutes Sup. Ct. Augusta, Ga. Page 24.
Court 25 March 1783. The State -vs- Peter Youngblood--Larceny
Gave Bond himself 100 pounds. John Gibson and Thos Grier, Sr.
50 Pounds.

YOUNGBLOOD, PETER -w- Susannah--Augusta, Ga. Deed IG-58 1783
Children: Samuel; Joseph; Lewis; Rebecca -w- Wm. Wilson; Liddy
-w- Cain Gentry; Sarah; Susannah; Margaret Youngblood
All of S. C.

YOUNGBLOOD, PETER--Rev. War Box in Arch. Dept. Waste Book. Page 5
"Special Indents to General Tax 1788. Rec'd. from Peter Youngblood on accounts collected by him in St. Bartholomew's parish.
518.6.4

YOUNGBLOOD, PETER--Land Grants Bk. Charleston 36-216.
20 A. Charleston 5 May 1794.

YOUNGBLOOD, PETER--Edgefield Wills C-114--Mentioned in Will of Arthur
Simkins, sen'r. 17 Oct. 1820. Bequeath to son John Simkins
"Tract or parcel of land lying eastwardly of village of Edgefield
and of lands now occupied and claimed by Mrs. Tutt and bounding
on lands of Benjamin Frazier which tract I purchased of Peter
Youngblood."

YOUNGBLOOD--Will of Rebecca D'Oyley Pinckney. Walterboro Wills 1-89
Dec'd. dau: Rebecca Gay Youngblood
           Her dau: Elizabeth Singleton Youngblood
                    Sarah Youngblood
Dec'd. son: Cotesworth Pinckney
Gr. son: Edward Edmond Bellinger 23 May 186. (Not abstracted in
                                                 full)
YOUNGBLOOD, SARAH--Dau. of John Still-Will 26 Sept. 1797. Wife of
Jacob Youngblood. Edgefield

YOUNGBLOOD, SARAH--Legatee of Elizabeth McCoy-Will 22 Aug. 1817.
Other heirs: Susannah Cockcroft, Letty Cogburn, Elizabeth
             Cogburn, dau. of John Cogburn, and Mary Cockcroft.
Edgefield Wills C-25 Box 42 Pkg-1734

YOUNGBLOOD, SEABORN I.--Of Cock Co. East Tennessee. Edgefield Deed Bk.
35-179 11 Aug. 1818. To: Allen Marshall, Esq. of Greenville
Dist. S. C. P. A. to collect my money, part of my father's estate,
or whatever property is coming to me by my father's estate."

YOUNGBLOOD, SIMON--Land Grant Bks. In Archives. Charleston 41-256
1½ A. Orangeburg 1 June 1795

YOUNGBLOOD, SIMEON and James Keith to James I Still-Land on Sleepy Cr.
Edgefield Deed Bk. 45-155 7 March 1831

YOUNGBLOOD, THOMAS--Edgefield Mem. Vol. 10-321
200 A. on Sleepy Creek of Savannah River. Bd. John Harkins and
vac. Cert: 6 Dec. 1769. Grant: 3 Nov. 1770
-Thomas Youngblood--Royal Grant 21-262 Archives Dept.
200 A. Colleton 3 Nov. 1770
-Edgefield Deeds 21-289 29 April 1794--Thomas Youngblood from
James Johnston -w- Sarah 20 Pounds Sterling--150 A. orig. grant
to said James Johnston on 31 Aug. 1774.

YOUNGBLOOD, THOMAS--Archives Dept. Rev. Record 4475
"State of South Carolina-Ninety Sis District--Thomas Youngblood
appeared before me, one of the Justices of the Peace for said
District and made oath that he was one of the Drovers under Thomas
Leak and was sent by him to drive beef Cattel from Myron Smith;
John Fleek; Peter Dorst; and the widow Dorn, and drove the said
cattel to General Green's Army--but saith on his oath that the
number of cattel that was drove from each place he has forgot.
Sworn to before me 17th June 1783. John Moore, J. P.

YOUNGBLOOD, THOMAS--Petit Juror Edgefield 1786. List 1, 2, 7, and 15
          HENRY   "   "   "   1787   " 8

YOUNGBLOOD, THOMAS--Edgefield Deed Bk. 17-515(The elder-of Edgefield)
From Minor Winn of Winnsborough 29 Aug. 1799--300 A. on waters
of Mountain Creek a branch of Stephens Creek. Orig. gr. to John
Hope on 28 July 1775. Who conv. to Joseph Kirkland nov. 25. 1777.
Who conv. to sd Minor Winn 12/13 Feb. 1789.

YOUNGBLOOD, THOMAS--Grant Bk. Archives Dept. Charleston 64-6
49 A. Edgefield Stevens Cr. 7 Feb. 1820
80 A. Edgefield 6 July 1801 47-39
31 A. Edgefield 6 July 1801 47-390
378 A. Edgefield, Sleepy Cr. 6 July 1801 32-63
208 A. Edgefield, Sleepy Cr. 4 Feb. 1793

YOUNGBLOOD, THOMAS--Son of Jacob -m- dau. of Alexander Bean. See Bean
card. Edgefield Deed 31-200 1812

YOUNGBLOOD, THOMAS -w- Levisey, dau. of Alexander Bean, and heir.
Heirs and Rep's: Christiana Bean;
                  James -w- Mary-dower
                  Alexander -w- Isabella-dower
                  John -w- Janie-dower
Edgefield Deed Bk. Joseph Still -w- Elizabeth
32-196   James I Still -w- Isabella
14 Feb. 1815   John Lee -w- Sarah
                  Thomas Youngblood -w- Levicy-to-Abraham Eddins

YOUNGBLOOD, THOMAS--Of Sleepy Creek. Edgefield Wills C-87. 28 Mar.
    Wife: 1816
    Son: William; Thomas; David Youngblood
    Gr. son: Simeon-son of David
    Son: James and his son; Thomas
          Jacob
    Son in law: James Adams. Rec'd. 28 Mar. 1822
    Edgefield Probate Box 32-1149. Will 28 Mar. 1816. Prov. 1822
    Heirs: Wife-Amy
            Children: Thomas -m- Jane Head
                       Jacob -m- Sarah Still
                       David and son, Simeon
                       James and son, Thomas
                       Elizabeth -m- James Adams
                       Amey -m- Frederick Williams
                       Winnefred -m- Edward Kirksey
                       Rebecca -m- Briton Hargrove
                       William--All living in 1822

YOUNGBLOOD, THOMAS and Asa Holloway--Wit Will of Benjamin Hagood
    5 Jan. 1817. Edgefield Wills A-380

YOUNGBLOOD, THOMAS--Edgefield Deed Bk. 34-215 1817. Affidavit that
    in a fight with Samuel Rowe, 7 May last, (1817) he, Thomas
    Youngblood got his "right ear bit and considerably cropped by
    the sd Rowe being also sworn deposeth and saith that the above
    facts are fast and true". Said Thomas Youngblood, Samuel Rowe.

YOUNGBLOOD, THOMAS and Levicy--Deed from James Bean--Alexander Bean;
    Elizabeth and Joseph Still; Isabella and James I Still; Levicy
    and Thomas Youngblood; John Lee -w- Tabitha; John Bean and William
    Bean. Conv. 438 A. to Wm. Colclazier.
    Dower: 30 Aug. 1821
        James Bean -w- Polly
        Alexander Bean -w- Isabella
        Joseph Still -w- Elizabeth
        James Still -w- Isabella
        Thomas Youngblood -w- Lovicy
        John Bean -w- Jane
        William Bean -w- Susannah

YOUNGBLOOD, WILLIAM--Of Colleton Co. S. C. To John Dawson and William
    Dawson 18 Jan. 1805. Mtg. Slaves. Arch. Dept. Misc. Mtg. #M-24

YOUNGBLOOD, WILLIAM--State Grants Arch. Dept. 15-42
    200 A. Colleton 6 May 1805
    400 A. Colleton 24 Jan. 1814 L4-275
    755 A. Colleton 15 Jan. 1818 L4-474

YOUNGBLOOS, WILLIAM--Bequest by Thomas Youngblood to son William at
    death of wife. 200 A. on Sleepy Creek-beginning at Ephraim's
    branch on an Ash Corner, thence running as the cross fence now
    stands to a black oak station, near a west course to the original
    old line; thence on the said old line to a pine corner; thence
    near a SE course to a white oak corner, thence nearly northeast
    to a Stake; thence nearly SE to a persimmon corner; thence on
    Adamses line to a Post Oak corner; thence to the east fork of
    Ephraim's br. thence down said branch to the fork; thence up the
    main branch to the beginning corner.

YOUNGBLOOD, WILLIAM -vs- Fed. Williams. Wit: Thomas Youngblood and
Jane Youngblood. Edgefield Case # 434 Decree 25 Oct. 1822
439 -vs- Jacob Youngblood
440 -vs- James   "
441 -vs- Alexander Bean

YOUNGBLOOD, WILLIAM--Dec'd. York 1845.
Heirs: Jane -w- W. S. Wood
        Emily Thomason
        J. H. Suggs
        Jesse Williams
        William Morton-son in law, Dec'd.
        J. C. Thomason
        J. W. Youngblood
        Samuel C. "
        Mrs. Wildes.

YOUNGBLOOD, WILLIAM R.--Edgefield Record Bk-P
Alabama, Pike Ct.--To the Sheriff of Edgefield Dist. Sir: You
Will be good enough to pay the bearer, W. T. Hubbard, the money
collected from Simeon Dean for me and this shall be your receipt,
for same. Yours Oc. William R. Youngblood. 29 Aug. 1831

YOUNGBLOOD, WILLIAM of Abbeville -m- set. 22 Dec. 1847. Brunetta
Lightfoot of Edgefield. Hist. Com. Misc. T-71. Edgefield.

ZEGLER, DAVID--Petit Juror Edgefield 1787. List 6

ZIMMERMAN, PETER--Petit Juror Edgefield 1786. List 1 and 2

ZINN--See Will of Meshack Wright-Will 1814

ZIN, CRONOMUS--26 Aug. 1774 100 A. in room of another. Wt. now out
of date. C-J-38 153

ZIN, JACOB--Surety for Joseph Dick--License to keep Tavern. See Dick
card. Edgefield Ct. Min. March 1795.

ZIN, VALENTINE--Petit Juror Edgefield 1788. List 10

ZUBLY, ANN--Dec'd. Est. sold 1796. Edgefield Eq. Rep. #1-37
5 children: Eleanor -m- John Clarke
             Ann -m- Walter Taylor
             Sarah -m- _____ Ardis
             Mary -m- _____ Burney
             Charlotte -m- John Sturgeneggar

ZUBLEY, POLLY AND CHARLOTTE--Legatees of Casper Nail, Sen'r.-Will 1793.
Sister: Ann Zubley

ZUBLEY, DAVID--Deed Gift 18 Dec. 1787. Edgefield Deed Bk. 1-186
Dau: Ann -w- Walter Taylor. Land

ZUBLEY, DAVID--Dec'd. Edgefield Min. Bk. Pg-335. April 1790
Will proved by oaths of John Sturzenegger and Ann Zubley.
Mrs. Ann Zubley qual. as Ex'x.

ZUBLEY, JOHN JOACHIM--Of Savannah. Will 8 July 1780. C. T. Wills Pg 190

    Wife: Anne
    Son: David
          John --Died 1790. See letter. (Who did he marry?)
    Dau: Ann
          Ann Bard -w- Peter Bard of New York
    Sister: Helena Bell
    Brother in law: Conrad Nail and Niece Ann Nail
    Sister: Mary Evans
    Brother: David Zubley.
    Grand child: Helena Zubley.

HAVARD, Daniel - 21
    Matilda - 21
HAWKINS, Gresilla - 241
HAWS, Elizabeth - 176
HAWTHORN, Elizabeth - 85
HAZEL, Amey - 1
    Amy - 123
    Henry - 123
    Huldah - 123
    Jonathan - 123
    Philip - 123
    Rhody - 123
    Seth - 123
HAZEN, Amy - 8
HEAD, Alexander Spencer - 8
    Benjamin - 65
    Charles - 165
    George - 165
    Jane - 244
    Margaret - 146
HEARN, Drury - 10
    Martha - 10
HEARST, Claresy - 40
    Elizabeth - 40
    Jane - 40
    Joseph - 28
    Silas - 40
HEATLY, John - 221
HEMPHILL, Jane - 82
HENDERSON, Eli - 53
    Martha - 111
    Mary - 53,182
    Nathaniel - 111,182
    Obediah - 75,195
    Shadrack - 145
HENDREN, Ephraim - 66
HENDRICKS, William Harvey-105
HENNING, James - 14
HERBERT, Isaac - 146
HERNDON, John - 2,183
    Ruth - 181
HERRIN, Aaron - 206
HESTER, John - 60,71,128,226
HEUSTON, Oswell - 79
HIBLER, Jacob - 193
HICKS, James - 120
    John - 90
    Martha - 195
    Nicey G. - 90
HIGDON, Daniel - 103
HIGGINS, Robert - 13
HIGHTOWER, Benjamin - 175,190
    Joseph - 93,157,207
    Mary - 175,190
HILER, Sophia - 7
HILES, Sophia - 196
HILL, Aaron - 240
    Abel - 120
    Adaline - 136
    Ann - 185,209
    Barsheby - 188
    Benjamin - 79
    Bersheba - 18,120,129,187,
        209
    Ebenezer - 1,18,37,49,88,
        120,124,129,136,
        172,179,187,205,
        207,214
    Elizabeth - 16,77,141
    Frances - 13,35
    Jesse - 48,76,77
    John - 2,136,201,230
    Joshua - 135
    Lodowick - 133
    Lodwick - 19,27,73,115,165,
        174,178,189
    Ludwick - 118
    Martin - 55
    Mary - 19,49,120,129,136,
        207,214
    Mary Ann - 35
    Salley - 76,143
    Samuel - 169

HILL, Sarah - 55,58,77,143,158
    Susannah - 48,185
    Tresse - 133
    Unity - 35
    William (Wm.) - 65,94,143,
        149,185,214
HILLARD, Peter - 167
HINSON, Dorman - 191
    Unity - 191
HINTON, Allen - 48,210
HITCHCOCK, John - 136
HITT, John - 55
    Sarah - 55
HOBBS, Burrel E. - 231
    Burrell E. - 98
    Jesse - 58
    Mary -98
HODGE, Tabitha - 189
    Uriah - 189
HOFF, William - 5
HOGANS, William - 59
HOGG, John - 125,166
    Mary - 125
HOLD, Joseph - 116
HOLDSTON, Wm. - 222
HOLLADAY, James - 13
    Peggy - 13
HOLLAND, Daniel - 151
    Pamela - 151
HOLLEY, Mary - 134
    P.W. - 134
HOLLIDAY, Lucy - 184
    William - 14,24,51,148,194
HOLLINGSWORTH
    Eliza Ann - 217
    Emmeline D. - 206
    James - 35,98,152,219
    John - 87,206,217
    Laura Ann - 98
    Mary - 98
    Wm. - 98
    William H. - 98
HOLLISTER, Catherine - 240
    J.S. - 240
HOLLOWAY, Asa - 3,125,190,
        239,244
    Caleb - 21,80,185,191
    Christianna - 126
    Daniel - 20
    Douglas - 84
    Elijah - 191
    Jesse - 22
    Jordan - 16,60,155,183
    John - 85
    Lewis - 157,183,228
    Louiza -172
    Lucy - 183
    Margaret - 56
    Mary Ann - 133
    Matilou - 67
    Morris P. - 155,158
    Paul - 83
    Quinting - 125
    R. - 133
    Rachel - 228
    Ransom - 67,133
    Rebecca - 155
    Rhoda T. - 190
    Richard L. - 133
    Sarah - 157
    Sibyl Ann - 157
    Sophia - 191
    Perry - 141,188
    Thomas - 133
    William (Wm.) - 40,41,126,
        172
HOLLY, Daniel D. - 134
    Elizabeth - 134
    John W. - 134
    Rosa - 134
HOLMES, Catherine - 45
    Edward - 190
    Gabriel - 57

HOLMES, Lewis - 57,145,149,217
    Mary - 190
    William (Wm.) - 127,140,208
    Wyatt - 112
    Wyett - 45
HOLSONBACK(HOLSENBAKE)
    Ahile - 80
    Alfred - 115
    Derrick - 5,106,162
    Elender - 5
    Mary - 162
HOLSTON, Moses - 177
    Wade - 177
HOLT, James - 237
HOMES, Shadrick - 18
HOPE, John - 243
HOPKINS, Christian - 113
    Coclia G. - 89
    Isaac - 89,192
    Jesse - 113
    Kelly - 113
HOUSTIN (HOUSTON)
    John A. - 74
    O. - 79
HOWARD, Adrah - 36
    Batt - 43
    E. - 68
    Elizabeth - 128
    John - 91
    Samuel - 216,218
    Seth - 4,91
    Ruth - 216
HOWE, Esther - 18
HOWEL, Joseph - 222
    Nath'l - 40
HOWELL, Ann - 163
    Catherine - 120,172
    Esther - 167
    Helena - 40,114
    J.H. - 65
    John - 81
    Jackson - 120
    Joseph - 114
    Josey - 65
    Josiah - 108
    Mary - 105
    N. - 163
    Nathaniel - 163
    Nancy - 114
    Thomas - 167
    William - 105
    Sarah - 65
HOWLE, Agnes - 60
    Elizabeth - 112
    Esther - 18,38,52,113
    Milley - 9
    Polly - 99
    Sally - 132
    Thomas - 18,31,37,38,52,113,
        132,145,168,195
    William - 9,60,99,112,132,
        137,140
HOWLET, Aneridge - 122
    Seth - 122
HUBBARD, W.T. - 245
HUDSON, Elizabeth - 197
    Isaac - 209
    Susannah -,77
    William - 77,197
HUFF, Anna - 64
    Daniel - 73,161,164
    Henry - 102
    James - 102
    John - 44,64,181
    Mary - 64
    Salley - 44
    Tabitha - 181
    Thomas - 102
HUFFMAN, John - 173
HUGGINS, Elizabeth - 128
    William - 145
HUGH, John - 102
HUGHES, Emily D. - 41

MERRIWEATHER (MERIWEATHER)
    John - 240
    Mary - 49
    Peggy - 10
    Thomas - 49
    Zachry - 156
MESSERSMITH
    John Jacob - 19,63
MEYER, Dave - 26
    John - 190,228
    Mary - 72
    Michael - 136
MICHAEL, West - 20
MICHEL, Beddy - 154
    Daniel - 154
    Lyda - 154
MIDDLETON, Agatha - 74
    Caroline - 74
    Hugh - 43,74,100,105,154,159
    John - 74
MILES, Acquilla - 84
    Aquila - 30,87
    Aquilla - 140
    Elizabeth - 213
    Lewis - 84
    Margaret - 59
    Richard - 59
    Sally - 84
MILLAN (?), H.M. - 158
MILLER, Anna Maria - 109
    Elizabeth - 42,92,121
    George - 4,158,163,215
    Jacob - 31,149,166,180
    James - 63,125
    James E. - 103
    John - 109
    Keziah - 163
    Mary - 31
    Rebecca - 166
    Wm. - 61
MILLING, David - 228
    Sarah - 27,228
MILLS, Elizabeth - 135
    Wm. (William) - 135
MILN, Alexr. - 13
MIMS, Beheathland - 27,136,149,
        205
    Britton - 52,227
    Burton - 76
    Drury - 29,88,144,219
    John - 116,117
    Livingston - 71
    Lydia - 145
    M. - 117
    Martha - 205
    Mary - 117,149
    Ridley - 89
    Winey - 219
MIN, Ambrose - 188
MINOR, Elizabeth - 100,216
    Marlin - 100
    Mat. - 216
    Phenix - 238
    Spencer - 25
MINTER, Joseph - 66,227
    Mary - 66
    Mackerness - 159
    Susan - 13
    Wm. - 159,227
MITCHEL, Daniel A. - 163
    Elizabeth - 163
    Floyd - 116
    Lucy - 120
    Robt. - 61
    Samuel - 120
MITCHELL, D.A. - 178
    David A. - 185
    Ellen - 185
    G.B. - 224
    Henry W. - 238
    Isaac - 104
    Jas. D. - 159
    John - 159
    Lucy - 133

MITCHELL, Littlebury - 66,91
    Wm. - 133
MOBLEY, Catherine E. - 121
    John - 121
    Rachel - 134
MOCK, Benjamin - 164
    David - 115,197
    George (Geo.) - 84,179
MONTAGUE, John N. - 161
    Philip - 161
MOODY, Joseph - 223
MOORE, Aaron - 9,48,135,175,
        232
    Anderson - 112
    Betsey - 33
    Cornelia - 78
    Creswell - 229
    David W. - 59
    Drayton - 78
    Elijah - 165
    Eliza - 78
    Elsworth - 216
    George - 233
    Henry - 78
    James - 8,123,128,176,190
    James W. - 33
    John - 81,84,89,129,148,154,
        243
    John Carraway - 111
    John L. - 209
    John R. - 78
    John T. - 209
    Letty - 216
    Lucy - 115
    Lucy T. - 20,40,138,179,181
    Martha - 51,96,166,209,230
    Oliver - 61
    Patty - 139,203
    Rebecca - 112
    Richard - 139,203
    Sibyl Ann - 111
    Tabitha - 78
    W.N. - 191
    William - 32,78,105,165,185,
        195,200,233
MORETON, Mary Ann - 40,67
    Wm. R. - 40
MORGAN, Abiah - 120
    Caty M. - 229
    E. - 32
    Elbert - 193
    Eli - 203
    Elias - 218
    Franklin E. - 50
    Mise - 109
    Peter - 83,154
MORRING, John - 31,40,118,193
MORRIS (MORRISS)
    Joseph - 33
    Lemuel - 182
    Martha - 182
    Sarah - 33
    Stephen - 147
    Thomas - 82
MORROW, James - 79
MORTON, William - 245
    Wm. R. - 67,215,226
MOSELEY, Benjamin - 211
    Daniel - 234
    Edward - 33,157,207
    Elizabeth - 216
    John - 28
    Joseph - 28
    Martha - 200
    Priscilla - 122
    Robert - 3,200,216
    Sarah - 227
    Thos. (Thomas) - 189
MOSELY, Chancy - 122
    Edward - 70
    George - 122
    Mary - 113
    Nancy - 32,122
    Robert - 113,116

MOSELY, Saley - 133
MOSLEY, Rachel - 54
    Robert - 54,91
    Sarah - 91
MOSS, Hugh - 87
    John - 123
    Lucinda - 123
    Rachel - 127
    Susan - 97
    Wm. H. - 97
MOTES, Joseph - 240
MOTTE, Wm. - 60
MOULTRIE, Wm. - 237
MOUNCE, Martha - 133
MOZE, Mary E. - 171
MUHLIN, Arthur - 36
MUIRHEAD, James - 57
MULLIN, Dance - 79
    Elizabeth - 79
MUNDAY (MUNDY)
    Jno. W. - 11
    S.H. - 180
MUNRO, Daniel - 235
    Lucretia - 235
MURFEY, William - 60
MURPHEY, John - 169
    Mary - 164
    William - 164
MURRAH, Lewis - 60
    Sarah - 60
    Susannah - 217,229
MURRAY, Anne E. - 65
    David - 200
    John - 169
MUSGROVE, Edward - 213
MYERS, John - 213
    Nancy - 224
NAGEL, Franze - 164
NAGEY, Martha - 117
NAGUL, Jans - 164
NAIL, Ann - 115,246
    Barbara - 114,193
    Casper - 22,73,152,183,
        206,245
    Conrad - 246
    Daniel - 115,152,193
    Elizabeth - 152,193
    Keziah - 152
    John - 115,152,193
    Maria - 22
    Rebecca - 73
    Sarah - 183
NANCE, Alexander - 241
    Lucy - 241
    Rebecca - 241
    Thomas - 241
    William - 241
NAPPER, Elizabeth - 54
NEAL, Islans - 164
NEALL, John L. - 191
NEIL, Casper - 7
    Louisa - 7
NELSON, Wm. - 83
NEVEL, George - 171
NEWBURN, Dr. - 212,230
    Emily - 212,230
NEWMAN, Reuben - 167
    Richard - 61
    S.B. - 126
NEWSOME, William - 140
NEWTON, James - 21
    Sarah - 21
NICHOLAS, Jno. - 188
    Sarah - 188
NICHOLS, Elizabeth - 189
    James - 30
    Julius - 158
    William - 189
NICHOLSON, Ben F. - 20
    Harriet - 43
    Keziah - 230
    Mary - 3,158
    Repsy - 54
    Samuel - 17

POWELL, Edmund - 85
  Elizabeth - 185
  Ellsey - 123
  Feroby - 31
  James M. - 94,168
  Martha - 94,168
  Sterling - 186
  Tyrzah - 94,168
POWERS, Elizabeth - 38
  Rachel - 170
  Wm. - 38
PRESCOTT, Daniel - 209
PRICE, Jane - 23
  John - 171
  Thomas - 188
  Wm. - 23,158
PRINCE, Edward - 105
  Joseph - 102,105,148
  Nancy - 210
PRIOR, Mary - 24
  Tobias - 24,26
PROSSER, Elizabeth - 200
PRYOR, John - 91
  Susannah - 91
PUCKETT, Jesse - 61
PUGH, John - 124
PURSALL, William - 128
PURSELL, Edmund - 85
  John - 106
  Wm. - 87
  Zacheus - 167
PURSLEY, Edmund - 85
PURVIS (PURVES)
  John - 75,127
  Mary Sarah - 6
PUSSELL, William - 62
PYE, Peter - 169
QUARLES, Elizabeth - 204
  Francis - 45
  John - 31,204
  Mary - 29
  Mary E. - 88
  Mary Ann - 22
  Nancy - 155
  Richard - 29,48,155,211
  Samuel - 140
  Sarah - 211
  William - 22,45,73,131
  William B. - 204
  William G. - 204
QUATTLEBAUM, David - 96
  Elizabeth - 2
  Geo. - 61
  John - 2,202
  Mary - 152
  Philip - 202
  Wm. - 152
QUIN, Barriman - 213
  Ity - 213
  James - 213
QUINSEY, Rachell - 228
RAFER, Philip - 124
RAIFORD, Elizabeth - 131
  Philip - 52,53,200
  Wm. - 131
RAINEY, Sally - 196
  Thomas - 196
RAINFORD, Tabitha - 118
  Thos. - 117
RAINSFORD, Tabitha - 116
RALSTON, A.R. - 146
RAMBO (RAMBOU)
  Jincey - 203
  Jincy - 133
  Joseph B. - 203
  Lawrence - 133
RAMEY, Rebecca - 25,64,77,150,
      160,183
RAMPEY, James - 66
  Martha - 66
RAMSAY (RAMSEY), Druzilla -89
  John - 11,81,84
  Rebecca - 215

RAMSAY (RAMSEY), Sarah - 56
  Thos. - 89
RANDAL (RANDALL), Geo. - 189
  John - 56
  Phoebe - 189
RANDOLPH, Geo. - 189
  Phoebe - 189
RANKIN, David - 90
  Harriett - 90
  James - 90
RAY, Elizabeth M. - 22,31,178
  George W. - 41
RAYFORD, Philip - 124
EADFORD, Anne - 57
  William - 57
REAME, George - 111
REARDEN, Abbey - 17
  Benj. - 17
REARDON, Harsey - 17
  Timothy - 17
REAVES, Anna - 69
RED, Job - 105
  John - 212
  Polly - 212
REDDICK, Margaret - 40
REDFORD, Absolum - 57
REED, Samuel - 101
REES, John - 173
REESE (REECE)
  James - 111,112
  Lucy - 111,112
REGERS, Daniel - 164
  Elizabeth - 164
REID, Nathan - 75
REISER, George - 130
RENNELS, Wiley - 98
  William - 98
RENOLDS, Fielding - 181
REYNOLDS, Andey - 182
  Elizabeth - 38,40
  Geo. W. - 38
  Larkin - 240
  Westby - 40
  William (Wm.) - 93,96,159
RHODEN, John - 110
RHODES, Coleman - 205
  Frances H. - 126
  Harriet - 205
  James - 81,198
  Mary - 55
  Milton - 126
RICCLE, Thos. - 126
RICE, John - 186
RICHARDSON, Abraham - 9
  Amos - 5,29,108,172,204
  Charlotte - 175
  Clarecy - 13,154
  Daniel - 162
  David - 5,13,91,102,108,
      154,174,175
  Elizabeth - 91
  James - 7
  Mary - 7,174,239
  Ruth - 29
  Susannah - 5,108
  William - 78,91,188,212
RIDDLE, Eldred - 241
RINEHART, John - 62,95
  Mary - 95
  Rebecca - 62
RISH, Martha Ann - 34
  William - 34
RIVERS, Jones - 75,76
  Mary - 75,76,93,216
  Mr. - 75
  Mrs. - 76
ROBERAS, Eliza - 17
  S.J. - 17
ROBERSON, Elisha - 107
ROBERTS, Absolem - 206
  Absolom - 140
  Absolum - 48
  Benjamin - 124

ROBERTS, Elizabeth - 216
  John - 59,69,83,192,204,205
  LeRoy - 48
  Mary - 126
  Thomas - 126,166,216,225
  Rebekah - 166
ROBERTSON, Alexander - 26
  Ann - 88
  Betsy - 51
  David - 116
  Elisha - 66,74
  Elizabeth - 9,114
  Frances - 216
  George - 45,51
  George C. - 214
  Hannah - 107
  James - 11,45,125,193
  Jane - 26
  Jane B. - 88
  James K. - 88
  John - 117
  Lydia - 74
  Martha - 88
  Martha A. - 88
  Mary - 214
  Moses - 9,163,216
  Peter - 8,44,112
  Sally - 163
  William - 10,32,39,82,91,100,
      114,174,179,207,
      214,234
  Wm. C. - 214
ROBINS, John - 156
ROBINSON, Allen - 213
  Elisha - 172
  Elizabeth - 185
  Hannah - 18,107
  Jane - 139
  John - 14
  Margaret - 46
  Martha - 62
  Randal - 185
  William - 46,120,139,174,
      228,237
ROBISON, Allen - 52
  Sam'l - 240
ROBUCK (ROEBUCK), Clara - 54
  Elizabeth - 54,89
  James - 89
  John - 89,113
  Robert - 34,54,89,94,165,182
ROCHE, Matthew - 82
RODGERS, Charlotte - 55
  Cyntha - 65
  James - 55,65,144
  John - 133,192,235
  Sarah - 65,144
  William - 65,109,173,208
ROE, Corneliua - 91
  Sinthy - 91
ROGERS, Charlotte - 55
  Daniel - 8,144,150,183,190,
      198
  Elijah - 230
  Hannah - 150
  Joel - 87
  John - 62,96,108,165
  Jno - 38,177
  Levi - 196
  Lucreasy - 144
  Mary Ann - 38
  Nancy - 8
  Sarah - 196
  Sophronia - 196
  Susannah - 183
  Temp - 196
  Ulysses - 184
ROOKS, Sarah - 167
ROPER, Benjamin - 3,43
  Emily - 43
ROSBROUGH, Geo. - 239
ROSS, James - 191
  Nancy - 191